Interest Groups Unleashed

Paul S. Herrnson
University of Maryland

Christopher J. Deering
George Washington University

Clyde Wilcox
Georgetown University

Los Angeles | London | New Delhi
Singapore | Washington DC

Los Angeles | London | New Delhi
Singapore | Washington DC

FOR INFORMATION:

SAGE Publications, Inc.

2455 Teller Road

Thousand Oaks, California 91320

E-mail: order@sagepub.com

SAGE Publications Ltd.

1 Oliver's Yard

55 City Road

London EC1Y 1SP

United Kingdom

SAGE Publications India Pvt. Ltd.

B 1/I 1 Mohan Cooperative Industrial Area

Mathura Road, New Delhi 110 044

India

SAGE Publications Asia-Pacific Pte. Ltd.

3 Church Street

#10-04 Samsung Hub

Singapore 049483

Printed in the United States of America

Library of Congress Cataloging-in-Publication Data

Interest groups unleashed / editors, Paul S. Herrnson, Christopher J. Deering,

Clyde Wilcox.

p. cm.

Includes bibliographical references and index.

ISBN 978-1-4522-0378-2 (pbk.)

1. Pressure groups—United States—History—21st century. 2. Elections—United States—History—21st century. I. Herrnson, Paul S., 1958– II.

Deering, Christopher J., 1951– III. Wilcox, Clyde, 1953–

JK1118.I59 2013

322.4'30973—dc23   2012017420

This book is printed on acid-free paper.

Acquisitions Editor: Charisse Kiino

Editorial Assistant: Nancy Loh

Production Editor: Brittany Bauhaus

Copy Editor: Gretchen Treadwell

Typesetter: C&M Digitals (P) Ltd.

Proofreader: Jennifer Gritt

Indexer: Diggs Publication Services, Inc.

Cover Designer: Myself Included Design

Marketing Manager: Jonathan Mason

Permissions Editor: Adele Hutchinson

Certified Chain of Custody
Promoting Sustainable Forestry
www.sfiprogram.org
SFI-01268

SFI label applies to text stock

12 13 14 15 16 10 9 8 7 6 5 4 3 2 1

Interest Groups Unleashed

Contents

About the Editors

Paul S. Herrnson is the Director of the Center for American Politics and Citizenship, Professor of Government and Politics, and Distinguished Scholar-Teacher at the University of Maryland. He has published several books, including *Congressional Elections: Campaigning at Home and in Washington* (2012), *The Financiers of Congressional Elections* (2003), and *Voting Technology: The Not-so-Simple Act of Casting a Ballot* (2008). He has received several teaching awards and has served as an American Political Science Association congressional fellow and president of the Southern Political Science Association.

Christopher J. Deering is a Professor of Political Science at George Washington University. He is coauthor of *Committees in Congress* (3rd ed., 1997), and has written on committees, leadership, Congress's role in foreign and national security policymaking, federalism, and executive-legislative relations. He is a former American Political Science Association congressional fellow and Brookings research fellow.

Clyde Wilcox is Professor of Government at Georgetown University. He has published a number of books and articles on campaign finance, interest groups, religion and politics, gender politics, public opinion, and science fiction and politics. He is coauthor of *The Interest Group Society* (2008) and *Interest Groups in American Campaigns: The New Face of Electioneering* (2005). He has served as an expert witness in federal cases about campaign finance and has lectured about American elections throughout the U.S. and abroad.

About the Contributors

Robert G. Boatright is an Associate Professor of Political Science at Clark University. He is the author of *Interest Groups and Campaign Finance Reform in the United States and Canada* (2011) and *Expressive Politics: Issues Strategies of Congressional Challengers* (2004), and the editor of *Campaign Finance: The Problems and Consequences of Reform* (2011). He has written several articles and book chapters on campaign finance, congressional elections, and interest groups. He is currently completing a book on congressional primary challenges.

Peter L. Francia is an Associate Professor of Political Science at East Carolina University. He has authored numerous publications on U.S. elections, campaign finance, and the political and electoral activities of labor unions and business groups, including the book, *The Future of Organized Labor in American Politics* (2006). Most recently, Francia served as an associate editor on the reference volume, *Guide to Interest Groups and Lobbying in the United States* (2011).

Michael Franz is an Associate Professor of Government and Legal Studies at Bowdoin College. His research interests include campaign finance and political advertising. He is the author or coauthor of four books, including *Choices and Changes: Interest Groups in the Electoral Process* (2008) and *The Persuasive Power of Campaign Advertising* (2011). He is currently the codirector of the Wesleyan Media Project, which tracks and codes political ads on television.

Jake Haselswerdt is a PhD candidate in the Political Science Department at George Washington University. He is currently working on a dissertation on the political causes and consequences of tax breaks. His research interests include Congress, public policy, and American political economy. He has presented his work at the annual meetings of the American Political Science Association, the Midwest Political Science Association, and the Social Science History Association.

David Karpf is an Assistant Professor of Media and Public Affairs at George Washington University. He previously served as a postdoctoral research associate at the Taubman Center for Public Policy at Brown University. His research, which has appeared in the *Journal of Information Technology and Politics* focuses on the Internet's effects on political competition and political organizations, how changes to the media and technological environment affect the political economy of interest group mobilization, and how these changes give rise to new types of political institutions and processes.

Jonathan Mummolo is a doctoral student in Georgetown University's Department of Government. He has written on various facets of the Tea Party, including the movement's impact on elections and policy. His research interests include social movements, race and ethnicity, intergroup relations and elections. Prior to beginning graduate study, Mummolo worked as a newspaper reporter, and has written for *The Washington Post*, *Newsweek* and *Newsday*.

John J. Pitney Jr. is the Roy P. Crocker Professor of American Politics at Claremont McKenna College in Claremont, California. A former American Political Science Association congressional fellow, he has written extensively on congressional politics, presidential campaigns, interest groups, political parties, and public policy. He is author of *The Art of Political Warfare* (2001) and coauthor of *American Government and Politics: Deliberation, Democracy, and Citizenship* (2010) as well as *Epic Journey: the 2008 Elections and American Politics* (2011). His current research interests include the 2012 election and the politics of autism.

Suzanne M. Robbins is an Assistant Professor of Government at George Mason University. Her research investigates how institutional rules structure the behavior of political organizations throughout the political process. In addition, she studies the role of information, the creation of campaign finance networks, and the structure of group networks. Of particular interest are how context and information effect behavior and political and policy outcomes. Her research has appeared in *Policy Studies Journal* and *Political Research Quarterly* as well as chapters in edited volumes.

Ronald G. Shaiko is a Senior Fellow and the Associate Director for Curricular and Research Programs at The Nelson A. Rockefeller Center for Public Policy and the Social Sciences at Dartmouth College. He served as the Fulbright Distinguished Chair in American Politics at the University of Warsaw in 2000–2001. From 1990 to 2000, he taught at American University, where he founded and served as the academic director of the Lobbying Institute. He served as an APSA congressional fellow in 1993–94 and as a democracy fellow at USAID in 1998–99. He has authored and edited three books, published more than thirty journal articles and chapters, and more than a dozen U.S. government reports.

Preface

Money, information, nationally recognizable leaders, dues paying members or followers, economic clout, and the capacity to mobilize supporters or help shape the public agenda are among the major resources interest groups marshal to influence public policy. A group's goals and the specific mix of assets it possesses go a long way toward explaining the strategies and tactics it uses. These factors also help explain the balance of power among groups associated with different sides of policy issues. The political, legal, and technological environments in which groups operate also structure interest group strategies, tactics, and political clout. These have been subject to substantial change in recent years, creating new opportunities and challenges for interest groups seeking to influence the policy making process. How various groups have responded to these changes is the major focus of this book.

The rights of citizens to organize and petition government are enshrined in the First Amendment to the Constitution. Groups of farmers, workers, bankers, religious activists, environmentalists and others long have used their money, personal energy, and political connections to influence national government. The executive branch and the courts have been the targets of some interest group efforts, but most lobbying is directed toward Congress.

Interest groups also have used elections to influence federal policymaking. Many have capitalized on the fact that politicians are highly attuned to things that are relevant to their tenure in office by making campaign contributions, expenditures, and endorsements, and by recruiting volunteers. Because the Constitution does not explicitly mention the rights of interest groups to participate in elections, groups have had to operate under changing regulations, particularly in the area of campaign finance.

In the 1970s and 1980s, for example, most interest groups first made decisions about whether they would be involved in elections, and then they decided what form their participation would take and the level of resources they would commit to it. Many groups formed political action committees (PACs) to raise money from individuals that they could contribute directly to candidates or spend independently (without a candidate's knowledge or consent) to influence electoral outcomes. Others communicated endorsements directly to group members. And still others sent volunteers into the field to help candidates and parties.

In the 1994 elections, conservative interest groups helped Republicans gain fifty-four seats in the U.S. House of Representatives and eight Senate seats to end a generation of Democratic control of Congress. That election did more than bring a new partisan regime to Congress; it also fundamentally altered the relationship between interest groups and lawmakers. GOP leaders sought to deny access to labor unions and other groups that had supported Democratic candidates, and worked closely with conservative groups to enact legislation inspired by the party's Contract with America. More fundamentally, the House Republican leadership hatched a plan—dubbed the *K Street Project*—to build a network between corporations, trade associations, and lawmakers. The leaders encouraged interest groups to hire former GOP lawmakers and staff as lobbyists, who could then work closely with Congress.

For the next five election cycles, labor unions, environmental groups, and other liberal organizations sought to develop new strategies and to increase their efforts to help the Democrats regain control of Congress, including working throughout the election cycle to increase the number of competitive seats. In 2006 their efforts bore fruit and in 2008 Democrats expanded their majority in Congress and won control of the White House.

The heightened competition for control of Congress and the White House combined with the polarization of the parties to raise the stakes for groups affected by the federal government. This new reality led many groups to increase their electoral involvement, in part, by searching for new methods of participation and challenging campaign finance laws. Recent Supreme Court decisions, most notably *Citizens United v. Federal Election Commission,* freed many interest groups from the legal constraints that had previously limited their revenue sources and political activities. These rulings have enabled groups to raise unlimited funds from the general treasuries of corporations, trade associations, labor unions, and other groups and to spend these funds to explicitly attack federal candidates. The rise of social media provided groups (and candidates and political parties) with new means for electioneering. We selected *Interest Groups Unleashed* as the title for this book to highlight the fact that so many aspects of the strategic environment that served to regulate group activity in the past have been weakened recently or eliminated altogether.

As a result of this confluence of forces, interest groups no longer channel their electoral activity solely through PACs. Some groups use at least one other type of organizational entity, such as a 527 committee, a super PAC, or one or more 501(c) organizations. Moreover, some interests have organized into entities that are not groups in the traditional sense. That is, they are neither a set of professionals and volunteers who work together in an office, nor are they a cadre of leaders that farms out its fundraising and advertising efforts to direct mail and communications experts. Rather, they consist of a website that enables individuals to make campaign contributions, disseminate political information, or organize events without consulting a hierarchy of organizational leaders.

The groups that participate in contemporary federal elections are more diverse, and they can choose to raise their funds from a wider array of sources and participate in a broader range of activities than in the past. The complexity of the entities groups can currently use for electoral action, and the limited reporting requirements associated with some of these entities, has made group activity in federal elections less transparent. But all groups are not created equal; nor do all groups, regardless of resources, choose to participate in the same way. Indeed, as the chapters in this volume demonstrate, the emergence of new opportunities for fundraising, spending, and organizing have had a significant effect on how many interest groups participate in federal elections and little effect on others.

It is not too much of a stretch to say that no recent Supreme Court decision has become so widely covered in the media as *Citizens United v. FEC*—perhaps with the obvious exception *Bush v. Gore.* Indeed, a Lexis-Nexus search for the case name in U.S. newspapers and the wire services for a two-year period from January 2010 to December 2011 results in nearly 1,700 hits. "Since the Supreme Court's *Citizens United* decision" or "most notably in *Citizens United,*" and variants thereof, have become virtual catchphrases in American campaign journalism. Such phrases also appear frequently in the pages that follow. For that reason, we have provided two somewhat extended excerpts of the Court's majority opinion, written by Justice Anthony Kennedy, and the dissenting opinion, written by Justice John Paul Stevens, for students and instructors who might want to place the chapters that follow in their legal context. The full opinions (along with two other separate opinions) are, of course, readily available online. But they are both lengthy and densely packed with internal legal citations. So much so, that they are difficult to read. Our edited versions retain the essential structures of the two opinions but without some unnecessary legal analysis and the disruptive citations. We hope readers will find them useful.

This project could not have come to fruition without the participation of numerous individuals. First, and foremost, we owe a debt of gratitude to our chapter authors. They were good natured about our badgering them to uncover what, if any, innovations the groups they were researching employed in the 2010 election, responsive to our suggestions for revision, and never complained about what they probably perceived to be a never-ending stream of reminders about deadlines. We wish to thank the interest group leaders who consented to be interviewed, provide documents, and participate in other ways in the project. Acknowledgments also are due to the Federal Election Commission and Center for Responsive Politics, which for many years have provided scholars, journalists, and others interested in money and politics with information about the financing of federal election campaigns. Many thanks to Charisse Kiino at Sage/CQ Press for supporting the project from start to finish, to Brittany Bauhaus who ably managed the book through the production process, and to Gretchen Treadwell for her helpful copyediting. Finally, we wish to thank Mike Charlebois of the Center for American Politics and Citizenship at the University of Maryland for helping to manage the project.

—Paul S. Herrnson
—Christopher J. Deering
—Clyde Wilcox

Introduction

Paul S. Herrnson, Christopher J. Deering, and Clyde Wilcox

On January 21, 2010 the Supreme Court handed down a landmark decision in a case called *Citizens United v. Federal Election Commission.* The 5-4 decision (with the conservative wing of the Court prevailing) determined that labor unions, nonprofit organizations, and corporations could use funds from their own treasuries to mount media campaigns in direct support for or opposition to candidates for federal office. So far as the majority was concerned, this was largely a matter of free speech. As Justice Anthony Kennedy, writing for the majority, opined,

> When government seeks to use its full power, including the criminal law, to command where a person may get his or her information or what distrusted source he or she may not hear, it uses censorship to control thought. This is unlawful. The First Amendment confirms the freedom to think for ourselves.[1]

Not surprisingly, this decision brought a firestorm of commentary that ranged from "the end is nigh" type horror to polite, but smug, shrugs suggesting, "it's about time." The former came largely from Democrats. In his 2010 State of the Union Address, and with the Court itself sitting immediately in front of him, President Barrack Obama suggested that the decision would "open the floodgates for special interests" and urged Congress "to pass a bill that rights this wrong."[2] The latter came largely from Republicans. Alabama senator Jeff Sessions, the ranking Republican on the Judiciary Committee, characterized comments by Obama and others as "alarmist rhetoric" and urged his colleagues not to "impugn the integrity of the justices."[3]

Throughout American history, interest groups have sought to influence public policy. The right of citizens to organize and petition government is enshrined in the First Amendment to the Constitution, and groups of farmers, workers, bankers, religious activists, environmentalists, and others long have used their money, manpower, and ability to lobby national government. Interest groups lobby government officials, the media, and the general public in an effort to influence laws and regulations.

Interest group activity in elections also dates back to the earliest days of the republic. In some ways electoral activity is an extension of lobbying. It is very frequently the case that to change policy, you have to change the politicians who make policy. The Constitution does not explicitly mention the rights of groups to be active in elections. Thus, groups have operated under a constantly evolving set of legal restrictions. For much of the twentieth century, corporations and labor unions could not use their treasury funds to support federal candidates directly—with corporate contributions first restricted by the Tillman Act of 1904 and both corporate and labor restrictions further restricted via the Taft-Hartley Act of 1947.

In the 1970s and 1980s, most interest groups had standing decisions about first whether they would be involved in elections, and then to what extent and using what resources. Many groups formed *political action committees (PACs)* to give money to candidates, others communicated endorsements directly to their members, and still others sent volunteers into the field to help candidates and parties. But the polarization of politics, combined with heightened competition for control of Congress and the White House, have led many groups to increase their electoral involvement, and to be involved in new ways. In addition, activists have begun to form ad hoc groups that operate in one election cycle, channeling resources from donors to advance particular candidates or causes. Recent Supreme Court rulings have freed interest groups from many restraints. A careful examination of group strategies in the 2010 midterm elections is important both in and of itself and because it foreshadows the activities of interest groups in future elections.

In 2010, interest groups engaged in record-breaking levels of activity in congressional elections, in an election that returned the House Republicans to majority power. In the 1994 elections, conservative interest groups helped Republicans gain fifty-four seats in the U.S. House of Representatives and eight Senate seats to sweep away a generation of Democratic control. That election did more than bring a new partisan regime to Congress; it also fundamentally altered the relationship between interest groups and lawmakers. GOP lawmakers sought to deny access to the policy process to labor unions and other groups that had supported Democratic candidates. The Republicans also worked closely with conservative groups to draft implementing legislation for the *Contract with America*—a ten-point "detailed agenda for national renewal" announced six weeks before the 1994 midterm elections. More fundamentally, then House Republican majority whip Tom Delay (R-Texas), and Republican strategist Grover Norquist launched the *K Street Project*, which sought to build a network between corporations, trade associations, and lawmakers by encouraging these interest groups to hire former GOP lawmakers and staff as lobbyists, who could then work closely with Congress.[4]

Playing catch-up for the next five election cycles, labor unions, environmental groups, and other liberal organizations sought to develop new strategies and to increase their efforts to help the Democrats regain control of Congress. In 2006 their efforts bore fruit, and in 2008 Democrats expanded their majority in Congress and won control of the White House.

In the fall of 2010, myriad interest groups engaged in full combat with an unusually large number of competitive House and Senate seats being contested. With a flagging economy and the usual midterm presidential losses, the election brought a tidal wave of GOP victories—gaining sixty-three House and six Senate seats. Superficially, the role of interest groups in the 2010 campaigns resembled that of 1994. The Chamber of Commerce worked closely with a coalition of business interests, and in many races cooperating with the National Rifle Association. Labor unions used their members to mobilize voters in an attempt to overcome the hangover from the 2008 postelection euphoria. They teamed with the Sierra Club and the National Organization for Women to prop up shaky incumbents—targeting their resources to those who were still competitive while abandoning those who were seen as no longer electable in a truly bad year for the incumbent party.

But the role of interest groups in the 2010 elections was far greater, and more complicated, than in 1994. Since the 2010 election, interest groups have been unleashed. In the earlier election, most interest group activity was channeled through PACs, which raised money in relatively small contributions from their members and mostly gave that money directly to candidates. In 2010 interest groups had access to a far wider array of resources, and were engaged in a far wider array of activities. As explained in Chapter 1, groups no longer channel their electoral activity solely through PACs; many also use at least one other type of organizational entity such as a 527 committee, a super PAC, or a 501(c)(4), (c)(5), or (c)(6) committee—not infrequently in concert with 501(c)(3) foundations feeding "research" findings to them. Still others help found and fund new organizations that sprout up and disappear after a single election cycle. Most of these alternative organizational forms are far less transparent than PACs, increasing substantially the difficulty of tracing interest group activities in elections.

Consider, for example, two headlines from *The Washington Post* and *The New York Times*: "DeFazio Tries to Find Out Who Is Behind Mysterious Attack Ad" and "Hidden Under Tax Exempt Cloak, Political Dollars Flow."[5] The first, from the *Post,* detailed an $86,000 ad buy by a group called Concerned Taxpayers of America supporting an underdog Republican House candidate in Oregon who said, "I'm delighted to have their support, but the truth is, I have no idea who is doing this." The buy, arranged by a Washington, DC–based organization, exceeded total ad expenditures by the candidate himself. The second, from the *Times,* outlines a $1.6 million campaign by Americans for Job Security in support of an Alaska referendum to restrict a gold and copper mine in Bristol Bay, Alaska. According to records, Americans for Job Security has a single employee, but spent $6 million during the 2010 primary season and another $4 million in late September attacking ten Democratic candidates for House seats. In both cases, the sources of the funding remained murky. Although still on the FEC's books, Concerned Taxpayers was effectively dormant through the end of 2011, reporting disbursements of $85, no receipts, and $474 cash on hand. Americans for Job Security seems to have disappeared entirely.

The sheer volume of interest group activity in elections has exploded. In the past three election cycles, groups have dramatically expanded their electoral efforts. But in 2010, Dave Levinthal of the nonpartisan Center for Responsive Politics predicted that interest group spending in the 2010 elections would "obliterate all previous records." Indeed, the Center estimates something approaching $4 billion was spent on these contests. The Chamber of Commerce announced plans to spend up to $75 million, and some suggested that the AFL-CIO would spend up to $100 million. Republican operative Karl Rove created two affiliated organizations, American Crossroads and Crossroads GPS (see Chapter 8), which raised tens of millions of dollars.

This increased activity is possible because Court rulings have removed most source limitations on the funding of group efforts (see *Citizens United v. Federal Election Commission*). In 1994, PACs, which were the dominant players in the campaigns, could accept no more than $5,000 from an individual and could use treasury funds only to pay for the overhead of the committee. Currently, there is no limit on the amounts that individuals and corporations can give in support of interest group electoral campaigns, so that a single donor can underwrite a massive media campaign. And, 2010 was the first campaign since the lifting of the ban on corporate campaign contributions.

Furthermore, the explosive power of new technology also unleashes interest groups. The Internet has made it easier for groups to create and spread video advertising, and groups like MoveOn.org, examined in Chapter 10, now sponsor contests for the best student ads, which are virally distributed through social network sites. The Chamber of Commerce (Chapter 2), Unions (Chapter 6), the National Rifle Association, and many other groups distribute advertisements over the Internet, and in some cases have volunteers show them to potential voters on iPads and other handheld devices. Advances in microtargeting make it easier for groups to mail very narrowly targeted messages to critical segments of the electorate. Tea Party groups (Chapter 9) are engaged in old-fashioned rallies, but also have created effective Internet fundraising networks to help candidates in one state raise money from donors located across the country.

The 2010 campaign was, therefore, ideal for this collection of essays focusing on interest group electoral activities. First, the election proved pivotal in contemporary politics with the Republican takeover of the House, the advent of so-called super PACs (introduced in more detail in Chapter 1), and record-breaking sums spent on a midterm election. Second, interest groups were able to mobilize new resources and new technologies in a campaign that was not focused primarily on a single presidential race but rather on a shifting set of House and Senate races that were more than unusually competitive. Third, the complex new forms of interest group organization and disclosure mean that earlier studies of group involvement in elections are quite dated.

Thus, this collection of studies provides an overview and offers a series of studies focusing on groups, communities of interest, and networks of groups in the 2010 election cycle. To be sure, no given collection of essays can perfectly represent the interest group community present in the 2010 elections or in any other. But this cross-section well illustrates the sorts of responses that organized interests had to *Citizens United* and the other court cases and events that unleashed the unprecedented participation of interest groups in the electoral process.

In Chapter 1, Paul Herrnson lays the foundation for comprehending the case studies that follow. The chapter provides an overview of the shifting regulatory environment that governs the participation of organized interests in federal elections. Once defined almost exclusively by PAC spending, interest group expenditures in federal elections are currently made by a variety of interest group entities including corporations, trade associations, labor unions, super PACs, so-called 501(c) organizations, and 527 committees, and traditional PACs. Given that each type of entity offers different advantages to its sponsors, it is not surprising that some wealthy interests have created clusters of different entities to pursue their objectives. What is surprising is the rapidity with which members of the interest group community have adapted to the weakened regulatory environment. Previously active groups that had not spent large sums to directly influence elections—corporations, trade associations, and unions, along with the 527s committees, 501(c) organizations, and super PACs they fund—accounted for a substantial portion of all interest group spending in the 2010 midterm election. Herrnson demonstrates that in the post–*Citizens United* era a great deal of interest group spending is financed using monies raised from sources and in amounts that were once prohibited under federal law. And unlike the previous era, the sources of many of those funds are hidden from public view.

With this legal and regulatory foundation set, we then turn to four chapters that focus on traditional groups—corporations and other business-oriented groups. By traditional, we mean that the organizations are long-standing participants in the electoral process. But in two cases—the health groups Suzanne Robbins examines in Chapter 3 and the defense contractors Jake Haselswerdt and Christopher Deering discuss in Chapter 4—they also employ a traditional *access strategy* that emphasizes rewarding incumbents and the incumbent party rather than a more ideologically driven approach. As Robert Boatright demonstrates in Chapter 2 on the Chamber of Commerce, however, this is hardly a strategy etched in stone. The Chamber was among the most aggressive exploiters of the decision in *Citizens United*. It continued to donate (lopsidedly) to Republican candidates through its PAC—a replacement strategy, so-called because it emphasized shaping governing coalitions rather than simply assuring access by focusing on incumbents. But it also spent more than $40 million on its "voter education campaign" in a successful attempt to alter Congress's partisan makeup. In Chapter 5, Michael Franz then looks more broadly at the important and growing corporate role in elections. Franz's argument is that barriers to corporate participation diminished substantially in the 2010 cycle and, on more normative grounds, that that level of participation might well be worrisome.

Having considered the role of corporate interests, we then turn to another perennial of the American electoral environment, Peter Francia's assessment of labor's role in the 2010 elections in Chapter 6. Francia shows how evolution in the labor union movement, from manufacturing dominance to service industry dominance in the context of an increasingly global economy, has reshaped the labor movement politically. Most important, it has pushed the American Federation of State, County, and Municipal Employees; the National Education Association; and the Service Employees International Union to the fore. But even with expansion on these less traditional fronts, overall union membership has declined and with it the capacity of labor to influence electoral outcomes. This circumstance is, of course, exacerbated by the *Citizens* decision inasmuch as the constraints on business have been simultaneously loosened.

While labor and business represent "old" interests, Chapter 7, on the League of Conservation Voters by Ronald Shaiko, represents a relative newcomer to the panoply of organizations engaged in lobbying and electioneering—a fellow traveler among groups that emerged as part of the political ferment of the 1960s and 1970s. As Shaiko notes, the League is interesting, in part, because it has a fully elaborated structure—with a PAC, a 501(c)(3) organization, two (c)(4)s, and a 527 group. They spend large sums, $5.7 million in the 2010 cycle, and give directly to federal candidates while spending independently at the same time. But as with other liberal leaning groups in the 2010 election, Shaiko shows that the outcomes were sorely disappointing for the biggest spending environmental organization.

The last three case studies illustrate interest group responses that were influenced by the emergence of opportunities to tap into the passions of an angry electorate, new technologies, and changes in the regulations governing campaign finance. John Pitney's analysis in Chapter 8 of American Crossroads and Crossroads GPS demonstrates just how consequential the *Citizens United* decision can be if fully exploited. Jointly, the two groups masterminded by Karl Rove laid out a whopping $70 million during the 2010 election cycle. And, consistent with the challenge-and-response nature of electoral politics, Pitney shows how the Rove effort was spurred by Obama's 2008 success with a legal assist from the Supreme Court, leaving Democrats to wonder how they might create their own Crossroads.

In Chapter 9, Jonathan Mummolo's assessment of the Tea Party demonstrates that what might appear to the casual observer to have been numerous locally based grassroots movements was actually a national phenomenon nurtured and coordinated by several well-established conservative-leaning interest groups. Through some sophisticated horse trading with local Tea Party activists, FreedomWorks, the Tea Party Express, and other Republican-allied groups were able to harness the activists' energy in pursuit of their own political agenda.

Finally, in Chapter 10, David Karpf's analyses the emergence of netroots associations in the electoral arena. These online entities combine the energy of traditional grassroots activists with the technological savvy and reach of political bloggers and others who organize using social media and the Internet. Karpf notes that netroots associations, including MoveOn.org and the DailyKos, are by definition on the left. After discussing their election efforts in 2010, Karpf anticipates that upcoming elections will feature just as many online groups and activities by online entities on the right.

These cases are followed by a brief conclusion in Chapter 11 that draws together some of the observations made in the preceding chapters in order to provide some generalizations about interest group responses to political change. Shifting regulations, increased competition, and technological innovation characterize the environment in which contemporary interests must organize to influence elections and the larger political process. This chapter seeks to explain why and how some groups responded to some aspects of change and others did not. It also speculates about the future of interest group politics in the United States. A string of federal court rulings combined with a highly partisan and competitive atmosphere and a new suite of tools for organizing to create what could be considered a perfect storm in the interest group universe. These forces combined to unleash the efforts of a select group of interests in the 2010 election but they are sure to be even more consequential during upcoming election cycles.

Endnotes

1 Opinion of the Court (Kennedy), *Citizens United v. Federal Election Commission* (558 U.S. 08-205): 40.

2 Obama's comments elicited a rare public retort from Chief Justice John Roberts who did not appreciate being publicly chastised while obliged to sit silently through the occasion. By tradition the justices attend but do not react to a president's remarks. Roberts found this "troubling": "The image of having the members of one branch of government standing up, literally surrounding the Supreme Court, cheering and hollering while the court—according to protocol—has to sit there expressionless, I think is

very troubling." Quoted in Jay Reeves, "John Roberts: Scene at Obama's State of the Union Was 'Very Troubling.'" *The Huffington Post*, March 9, 2010.

3 Quoted in Robert Barnes and Anne E. Kornblut, 'It's Obama vs. the Supreme Court, Round 2, Over Campaign Finance Ruling," *The Washington Post*, March 11, 2010.

4 See Jim Vandehei, "GOP Monitoring Lobbyists' Politics," *The Washington Post*, June 10, 2002.

5 Karen Tumulty, "DeFazio Tries to Find Out Who is Behind Mysterious Attack Ads," *Washington Post*, September 25, 2010; and Mike McIntire, "Hidden Under Tax-Exempt Cloak, Political Dollars Flow," *The New York Times*, September 23, 2010.

CHAPTER 1

A New Era of Interest Group Participation in Federal Elections

Paul S. Herrnson

The 2010 midterm congressional election will be remembered for many things: an electorate angry over the worst economic recession since the 1930s, the Tea Party movement channeling that anger against moderate Republicans and many Democrats, the defeat of numerous senior Democratic members of the House and Senate, and the Republicans' capitalizing on the volatile political environment to achieve a net gain of sixty-three House and six Senate seats. All of these occurrences are important, but they are associated with an unusual election cycle that occurred in a unique political environment. Two developments associated with 2010 that will prove more enduring concern the participation of a new array of organizations in federal elections and a corresponding increase in interest group spending.

Throughout American history interest groups have recruited candidates, made endorsements, rounded up campaign volunteers, provided financial and other assistance to candidates and political parties, and carried out their own independent campaign efforts on behalf of their preferred politicians. Interest group spending in elections, and the role of money in politics in general, has aroused the suspicions of Americans and periodically created pressure for reform. Nevertheless, the impact of much reform legislation fades fairly quickly. Among the most recent challenges to laws governing money in elections are a string of Federal Election Commission (FEC) decisions and Supreme Court rulings, culminating with the verdict in *Citizens United v. FEC*.[1] The combined effect of these resolutions was to free interest groups from many legal constraints. As a result, the 2010 congressional elections ushered in a new era of interest group participation in federal elections.

This chapter provides an analysis of the contours of interest group activity in contemporary elections. First, it provides a brief analysis of changes in the regulatory environment governing interest group activities in federal elections. Next, it discusses the legal entities that contemporary interests use to carry out election activities. Then, the final section analyzes the roles of interest groups in the 2010 elections.

A Shifting Regulatory Environment

The history of campaign finance reform in the United States is characterized by a pattern that fits most regulatory politics: public outcry in response to a scandal or some other crisis results in the enactment of legislation intended to address a salient problem; individuals and organizations whose activities are constrained by the new law find ways to maneuver around it or challenge it in the courts; and, eventually, a much weakened regulatory regime remains in place. Then, a crisis leads to a new call for reform and the cycle begins all over.[2]

The Bipartisan Campaign Reform Act of 2002 (BCRA), the last federal campaign finance law enacted prior to the 2010 election, is no exception to the rule. Long in the making, it sought to plug some of the loopholes that had opened under its predecessor, the Federal Election Campaign Act of 1974 and its amendments (collectively referred to as FECA). These loopholes were created by wily politicians, party officials, interest group leaders, and others who brought lawsuits in the federal courts, sought to influence Federal Election Commission regulations, circumvented the law, or just plain ignored it. Their efforts resulted in the emergence of so-called soft money and issue advocacy advertising in federal campaigns.

Soft money has been defined as funds parties and other organizations raise outside of the FECA's regulatory framework and from sources and in amounts otherwise prohibited by the FECA. *Hard money*, by contrast, includes all funds raised within that framework. More specifically, hard money originates as contributions that individuals voluntarily give to federal candidates, party committees, and political action committees (PACs) or as independent expenditures they use to influence federal elections. Hard money is subject to a variety of expenditure limits and disclosure requirements.[3] Most soft money is collected from corporations, trade associations, labor unions, and other wealthy groups and individuals. Soft money was originally used to strengthen party organizations and finance partisan voter registration and mobilization drives.

Issue advocacy advertisements refer to party and interest group broadcast ads intended to influence the outcomes of federal elections but do not *expressly* advocate the election or defeat of a federal candidate. Most of these ads are negative in content and end with a statement, such as "Call Congressman X and tell him not to raise your taxes." Because these ads avoid the few select words the Supreme Court defined as *express advocacy*, including *vote for, elect, support, cast your ballot for, vote against, defeat,* or *reject,* they are considered outside the FECA's regulatory framework.[4] As a result, prior to the enactment of the BCRA, interest groups and political parties were able to fund issue advocacy ads with soft money.

By the start of the twenty-first century, voter mobilization efforts and issue advocacy advertising funded by interest group or party soft money became central elements of what have been sometimes referred to as *outside campaigns.*[5] Some of these campaigns involved hundreds of millions of dollars. One feature of party issue ads was that voters could easily identify the party as their organizational sponsor. This was not the case with many interest group–sponsored issue ads because the groups funneled most of their soft money activities through "front" organizations bearing patriotic or innocuous names. This tactic increased the ads' credibility with voters and protected the identity of the ads' financiers. For example, during the 2002 elections, some of the nation's major pharmaceutical companies joined behind the name United Seniors Association to spend $8.7 million on televised issue advocacy ads in support of Republican candidates who favored the drug industry's interests. The ads, featuring actors playing the roles of healthy and attractive senior citizens, had more credibility and influence than they would have received had they been attributed to a list of large drug companies. This strategy also enabled the companies to avoid a potential backlash from voters, consumers, and congressional incumbents.[6]

Soft money and issue advocacy were the major targets of the reformers backing the BCRA. The law's enactment bore similarities to that of other campaign finance reform legislation. Soft money contributions and issue advocacy advertising increased concern about the role of money in politics. Media coverage of White House sleepovers, weekend getaways with national political leaders for some wealthy individual and interest group donors, and private policy briefings for others added a whiff of scandal. Finally and more specifically, the Enron scandal put names and faces to questions about the influence of corporate contributions on government regulatory decisions. These factors were instrumental in leading some members of Congress to conclude that a vote for the BCRA was a good vehicle for showing their willingness to take action against corporate abuses and encouraged President George W. Bush to sign the BCRA into law.[7]

The BCRA had fairly modest goals. It did not introduce public financing or even propose a return to the immediate post-1974 FECA regulatory environment wherein virtually all money spent in federal elections originated as contributions or expenditures that were voluntarily made by individuals and disclosed to the public.[8] Instead, it sought to institute three major changes. First, it prohibited parties from raising or spending soft money for use in federal elections. Second, it created a new category of campaign spending called *electioneering communications,* which, for all practical purposes, are interest group issue advocacy ads that are aired 30 days before a primary or 60 days before the general election, and it required groups to disclose to the FEC the names of the individuals and organizations funding those ads. The third major change required all voter registration drives conducted during the last 120 days of a federal election that mention a federal candidate be financed with federally regulated funds. Among other things, the law also increased the limits for contributions to parties to partially compensate for the ban on party soft money.[9]

Despite its modest provisions, opponents of the BCRA began preparing to mount legal challenges while the bill was still being debated in Congress. During his filibuster against the law, Sen. Mitch McConnell (R-Ky.), stated, "Should the bill become law, I will be the lead plaintiff."[10] True to his word, McConnell was a party to the first court challenge to the BCRA.

In 2003, in *McConnell v. FEC*, the court upheld most of the law, but overturned some provisions, including one prohibiting political parties from making both coordinated and independent expenditures. Four years later, in *FEC v. Wisconsin Right to Life, Inc.*, the Court dealt the BCRA a serious blow when it ruled unconstitutional the BCRA's disclosure requirements for electioneering communications. This freed corporations, unions, and other groups to broadcast these ads without disclosing their funding sources throughout the duration of an entire primary and general election cycle. In January 2010, in *Citizens United v. FEC*, the Court ruled on the issue of whether a partisan documentary (*Hillary the Movie*) financed by corporate money was prohibited under federal law. In this sweeping and highly controversial decision, the Court struck down the provisions of the law prohibiting corporations, unions, and other groups from spending general treasury funds to expressly advocate the election or defeat of a federal candidate. Almost as significant as the substance of the ruling was its impact on corporations, unions, and other groups that had previously been hesitant to spend general treasury funds in federal elections. The ruling gave these organizations a green light to do so. Indeed, several of them spent heavily in the 2010 midterm election.

Organizing for Influence

The shifting regulatory environment increased the opportunities for organized interests to participate in federal elections.[11] From the mid-1970s through the dawn of the twenty-first century, political action committees (PACs) carried out virtually all interest group spending in federal elections. The exceptions were internal communications to group members, which could be financed with funds taken from a group's treasury. As a result of the decline of the regulatory regime, there is now a plethora of interest group entities that participate in these contests. These include independent expenditure-only committees (commonly referred to as *super PACs*), 501(c) organizations, and 527 committees, as well as traditional PACs and interest groups that use their internal communications to try to influence the political participation of their members. In addition, corporations, trade associations, labor unions, and other groups now are free to spend general treasury funds to influence the outcomes of federal elections. Some interests use a cluster of interrelated legal entities in order to influence congressional and other elections, and each form of entity offers different financial and political advantages.

Political Action Committees

Initially mentioned in the Introduction to this book, a PAC is an organization that collects funds via voluntary, individual donations, and redistributes those funds to federal, or in some cases state or local, candidates with the goal of influencing election outcomes, the formation of public policy, or both. Some PACs also contribute to political parties or make independent expenditures for or against federal candidates. Most PACs have a sponsoring, or parent, organization, such as a corporation, labor union, trade association, or other group, but for *nonconnected* PACs, the PAC itself is the organizing group.

To qualify as a PAC (referred to as a *multicandidate committee* under the FECA) an organization must raise money from at least fifty donors and spend it on at least five candidates for federal office. Qualified groups can contribute a maximum of $5,000 per candidate in each stage of the election.[12] The ceilings that federal campaign finance statutes establish for individual contributions to candidates and the $5,000-per-year limit set for individual contributions to any one PAC make PAC contributions a popular vehicle among interest groups and wealthy individuals who wish to influence congressional elections.

The major advantages that PACs currently offer over other entities that participate in elections are that a PAC can directly contribute cash or in-kind services to a candidate and coordinate its efforts with that candidate or a party committee. The exception to the rule is independent expenditures, which must be made without the knowledge or consent of the candidate or anyone involved in the candidate's campaign. The major disadvantage associated with PACs concerns the limits on the sources and amounts of the contributions they can accept.

Between 1974 and the 2010 elections, the PAC community grew from more than 600 to 5,431 committees. Most of the growth occurred in the business sector, with corporate PACs growing in number from 89 in 1974 to 1,592 in 2010. Labor unions, many of which already had PACs in 1974, created the fewest new PACs, increasing the number from 201 to 295 during this period. The centralization of the labor movement into a relatively small number of unions greatly limited the growth of labor PACs. In addition, three new species of political action committees emerged on the scene in 1977—(1) the nonconnected PAC (these groups are mostly ideological, issue oriented or, in the case of leadership PACs, associated with politicians), (2) PACs whose sponsors are cooperatives, and (3) PACs associated with corporations without stock. The nonconnected PACs are the most important of these. By 2010 their number had grown to 1,923; in contrast, the combined total for the two other types of PAC had reached only 143.[13]

The growth in the number of PACs was accompanied by a tremendous increase in their activity. PAC contributions to congressional candidates grew from $12.5 million in 1974 to approximately $402.4 million in 2010. Corporate and other business-related PACs accounted for most of that growth. In 2010, corporate PACs accounted for more than 37 percent of all PAC contributions to congressional candidates, followed by trade association PACs, which accounted for about 27 percent. Labor PACs gave about 15 percent of all contributions received by congressional candidates, leadership PACs contributed 9 percent, and nonconnected PACs (excluding leadership PACs) gave 8 percent. PACs sponsored by cooperatives and corporations without stock contributed a mere 3 percent.

A very small group of PACs is responsible for most PAC activity. A mere 397 PACs, about 8 percent of the entire PAC community, contributed roughly $285.4 million during the 2010 election cycle, representing approximately two-thirds of all PAC money given in that period. Each of these committees contributed over $250,000 to congressional candidates. They include PACs sponsored by corporations, trade associations, and unions, such as Boeing, the American Medical Association, and the Service Employees International Union (SEIU) Committee on Political Education, as well as nonconnected PACs such as the League of Conservation Voters (LCV), which supports pro-environmental candidates. The next 9 percent of all PACs contributed between $100,001 and $250,000, accounting for 17 percent of all PAC contributions. These include PACs associated with Amway, the U.S. Chamber of Commerce, the Utility Workers Union of America, and EMILY's List, which seeks to elect Democratic, pro-choice women candidates.[14] Most of the PACs in the top two groups (corporate or business-related and trade PACs) were in a position to support all of their preferred candidates. Few of the 9 percent of PACs making contributions ranging from $50,001 to $100,000 were in this position, but they could make their presence felt in the world of campaign finance. The 43 percent of all PACs that contributed less than $50,000 were clearly constrained by their size. They made donations that were significantly smaller than those of the larger PACs, and their managers routinely had to tell candidates that they would have liked to support them but they did not have the money. Finally, 31 percent of all PACs registered with the FEC were dormant, making no contributions during the 2010 elections.

527 Committees

Nonprofit interest groups have been in existence for a long time, but their conspicuous presence in congressional elections is only a recent phenomenon. The deteriorating system of regulations governing federal campaign finance led some existing nonprofit entities to use unregulated soft money to run outside campaigns, in the form of coordinated grassroots voter mobilization efforts and independent media expenditures (discussed subsequently) to influence federal elections. Others created new entities for this same purpose. These developments resulted in 527 committees and 501(c) organizations becoming highly visible players in congressional elections.

Traditionally, candidate campaign committees and other groups participating in federal elections were governed by section 527 of the federal tax code, which exempts political organizations from paying income taxes. This provision was originally designed to cover candidate campaigns, PACs, and party committees that registered with and disclosed their finances to the FEC, making it unnecessary for the Internal Revenue Service (IRS) to monitor them. In 1997 some interest groups began to create 527 committees solely to raise and spend unregulated soft money on voter mobilization and issue advocacy ads similar to those broadcast by political parties. These activities were considered outside of the scope of campaign finance regulations because they did not expressly advocate the election or defeat of a federal candidate.

At first, 527 committees that declined to register with the FEC were not legally obligated to report their financial transactions to any federal agency. But beginning in January 2001, they were required to publicly disclose their funding sources and provide an overview of their expenditures, including an overview of issue advocacy ads, to the IRS. The enactment of the BCRA strengthened some reporting requirements for 527s and created a new category of reportable activities referred to as *electioneering communications,* which, for all practical purposes, are issue advocacy ads that air thirty days before a primary or sixty days before the general election. Following some FEC rulings and Supreme Court cases, provisions of the BCRA concerning electioneering communications and prohibitions against using soft money to finance independent expenditures were either weakened or overturned.

Currently, 527 committees are required to provide the IRS with an overview of their activities and the names of their donors (which the agency does not release to the public). They also are obligated to disclose to the FEC their independent expenditures and electioneering communications and the names and contributions of any individuals or groups who stipulate their donations are to be used to finance these activities. Thus, there are two major advantages associated with 527s. First is their ability to raise and spend sums from sources and in amounts that are prohibited to PACs. Second is the less stringent reporting requirements imposed on them. Unlike PACs, 527s are not required to publicly disclose who helped finance many of their activities, including research, payroll, daily operations, or issue advocacy ads (excluding electioneering communications). The disadvantages associated with 527s are prohibitions against their making contributions directly to federal candidates, political parties, or PACs.

Federally oriented 527 committees spent more than $1.1 billion in the four elections held since 2004. Some 338 of them spent $211.6 million with the goal of influencing the 2010 congressional elections. The top spender among federally focused Democratic/liberal leaning groups was the SEIU at $15.5 million, and the top spender among Republican/conservative-oriented groups was American Solutions for Winning the Future, a group formed by former Republican House Speaker and 2012 presidential candidate Newt Gingrich, which spent $28.4 million. As is the case with PACs, a few groups were responsible for most 527 spending. During the 2010 elections, the top ten 527 committees were the source of almost half of it. Where 527s differed from PACs in 2010 is in the sizes of the contributions that accounted for much of their revenues. The top personal donations to 527s were given by Fred Eshelman, executive chairman of Pharmaceutical Product Development Inc., who contributed $3.4 million to a group called RightChange.com, and Senate candidate Carly Fiorina (R-Calif.), whose Carly Fiorina enterprises contributed $2.5 million to a group called Carly for California. The top organizational donor to a 527 was the SEIU, which transferred $18.7 million of its treasury funds, most of it to its 527 committee.[15]

501(c) Organizations

Tax-exempt organizations defined in section 501(c) of the internal revenue code have become increasingly visible in electoral politics since the 2002 elections and were very active in 2010. There are four important players here: (c)(3), (c)(4), (c)(5), and (c)(6) organizations. As defined, *501(c)(3) organizations* are tax-exempt groups organized for charitable purposes. They are prohibited from becoming directly involved in federal campaigns, including endorsing or contributing to candidates or organizing a PAC—a major disadvantage for groups that want to be directly involved in elections. Nevertheless, these organizations can conduct research and educational activities, carry out nonpartisan voter registration drives and get-out-the-vote drives, and sponsor candidate forums. Two major advantages enjoyed by 501(c)(3) groups are that their donors can deduct group contributions from their federal taxes and that the IRS does not disclose their names, an important consideration for those who wish their association with a group to remain anonymous. Established in 1990, Rock the Vote is an example of a 501(c)(3) organization that is concerned with politics.

The internal revenue code defines *501(c)(4) organizations* as nonprofit social welfare organizations. These groups are allowed to rate candidates, promote legislation, sponsor PACs, broadcast issue advocacy ads (including electioneering communications), and make independent expenditures as long as partisan activities are not their primary purpose. The line between partisan and nonpartisan activities is somewhat fuzzy, however. Campaign finance lawyers, tax attorneys, and experts in these fields typically advise their clients not to spend more than 50 percent of their funds on independent expenditures or electioneering communications.[16] Groups with (c)(4) status, similar to (c)(3)s, are prohibited from making campaign contributions, are exempt from federal taxes, and can collect contributions from undisclosed sources. Unlike 501(c)(3) groups, donors to 501(c)(4) organizations cannot deduct their donations from their federal tax returns. Labor groups that enjoy *501(c)(5) status* and trade associations that organize as *501(c)(6) organizations* are allowed to conduct similar activities and receive similar tax benefits as 501(c)(4) organizations.

The major benefits associated with a 501(c)(4), (c)(5), or (c)(6) organization concern fundraising. These entities can raise funds from sources and in amounts prohibited to PACs, and the names of the individuals and groups that finance their election activities are not publicly disclosed.[17] One of their comparative disadvantages relative to 527 committees and PACs is the expectation that a 501(c)(4), (c)(5), or (c)(6) spend less than half of its funds on partisan activities. Nevertheless, this limitation may not be overly burdensome to groups that wish to advertise on radio or television because they are still allowed to broadcast unlimited issue advocacy communications that have obvious partisan implications. Finally, prohibitions against their contributing to federal candidates, party committees, or PACs constitute a significant disadvantage for groups that wish to influence elections.

It is virtually impossible to determine exactly the amounts 501(c)s spend to influence congressional elections because they are required to disclose only some of their election activities to the FEC.[18] But these groups' spending easily exceeded $100 million in 2010. The top five groups, alone, spent approximately $95 million on independent expenditures and electioneering communications.[19] All of these organizations were associated with conservative Republican-allied groups. Spending by 501(c) organizations provided GOP congressional candidates with a huge advantage over Democratic opponents.

Super PACs, Corporations, Labor Unions, and Other Groups

Corporations, trade associations, labor unions, and other incorporated groups long have participated in congressional elections. Even though the FECA and the BCRA prohibited them from using treasury funds to contribute to or make independent expenditures for or against federal candidates, it allowed them to use those funds to finance internal political communications to their members. Groups of all types continue to devote portions of their newsletters, e-mails, and other correspondence to raise money for their PAC, make political endorsements, and urge their members to support their preferred candidates with votes, contributions, or by volunteering on their campaigns. Groups spent $13.4 million on internal political communications during the 2010 congressional elections.[20]

Interest group internal communications are a pittance compared to the new form of spending activity that became available for the first time in 2010. Unleashed by the court rulings in *Citizens United v. FEC* and *SpeechNow.org v. FEC,* corporations, unions, and other incorporated groups can use funds from their treasuries to make independent expenditures or to finance separate super PACs for this purpose.[21] Handed down in January 2010, the *Citizens United* ruling resulted in organizations spending $71.8 million from their treasuries on independent expenditures before election day. Super PACs spent an additional $59.2 million. Regardless of whether they are funded directly from a group's treasury or by a super PAC, these expenditures and their funding sources must be fully disclosed to the FEC. Of course, and as is the case with 527s, 501(c)s, and PACs, a super PAC can use a name with widespread appeal to mask the interests of its financial backers. The financiers of American Crossroads, for example, read like a who's who of industrialists and corporations, and those of Commonsense Ten are major labor unions.

Independent spending from interest group treasuries or by super PACs offer these organizations some advantages. First, unlike PAC independent expenditures, they can be financed with funds from sources and in amounts prohibited to PACs. Second, unlike 501(c) organizations, these organizations do not have to be concerned with spending at least half of their assets on the charitable or educational activities associated with nonprofit organizations. Of course, the major disadvantages associated with independent expenditures by super PACs and incorporated groups are associated with their disclosure requirements and prohibitions against their making contributions directly to a federal candidate, party committee, or PAC.

Multifaceted Groups

Some interest groups develop complex interconnected organizational structures to participate aggressively in the political process without violating the federal campaign finance law or tax statutes. These groups adapt to changing regulations and political conditions by creating new legal entities to accomplish different purposes. In some ways, interest group organizational development, like party development, is analogous to some basic principles of architecture: new needs are met by adding new rooms to existing structures or by building new structures to complement existing ones, and a group's resources, goals, and regulatory codes influence the forms these improvements take.[22] As the preceding review of the advantages associated with the different political entities that participate in elections demonstrates, the importance of regulatory codes cannot be overstated. A brief comparison of the regulations governing political parties and interest groups reinforces this point. In the case of parties, any party aide or consultant involved in making party independent expenditures is prohibited from discussing them with other party officials. By contrast, coordination is permissible among the personnel associated with one sponsoring interest group. Indeed, it is legal for the same personnel who work for one of a group's legal entities to be employed by some or all of the others, including the group's PAC, 501(c) organizations, 527 committee, or super PAC. When this occurs, which is often the case, each participating organization in the group's family pays a portion the salaries of the overlapping personnel.

The League of Conservation Voters is an example of a group that pursues its mission using several entities. Founded in 1969, the LCV "run[s] tough and effective campaigns to defeat anti-environment candidates, and support those leaders who stand up for a clean, healthy future for America."[23] It is probably best known for its National Environmental Scorecard, Environmental Champions, and Dirty Dozen lists, which thrust environmental issues onto the political agenda and inform voters of the environmental records of members of Congress. Its entities, known as the LCV "family of organizations," include: the LCV, its core 501(c)(4) organization; the LCV Education Fund, a 501(c)(3) that conducts research and educational activities; the LCV Accountability Project, a 501(c)(4) that carries out media and grassroots educational campaigns about the environmental records of members of Congress; the LCV Action Fund, the group's PAC; the LCV Victory Fund, a super PAC; and the LCV Political Engagement Fund, a 527 organization that supports the LCV's national election-oriented groups and some state-level LCV affiliates, freeing these organizations to spend more of their funds to influence elections. Many of the personnel employed by one these organizations work for several of them. The LCV also has more than thirty-five state-level affiliates.

The 2010 Election

Interest groups used a more diverse array of legal entities to participate in the 2010 midterm elections than in any previous federal election cycle, totaling about $700 million (see Figure 1.1).[24] Relative newcomers on the political scene financed most of the increased spending. First, and foremost, are the $139.7 million in independent expenditures financed by corporations, unions, trade associations, other organized interests and the 527s committees, 501(c) organizations, and super PACs they fund. These accounted for approximately 20 percent of the interest group spending reported in the election cycle.[25] Interest group electioneering communications increased substantially, amounting to $80 million or about 11 percent of total spending. Contributions and expenditures by traditional PACs reached a record $403 million and $62.5 million, 58 percent and 9 percent, respectively, of all interest group spending. These sums increased over previous years, but their rate of increase pales next to the growth in spending by the newer interest group entities. Finally, the internal communications by corporations, unions, trade associations, and other groups, totaling about $13.4 million (less than 2 percent of the total), actually fell slightly from the record levels set in 2006.

FIGURE I.I   Interest Group Spending in Congressional Midterm Elections, 1994–2010

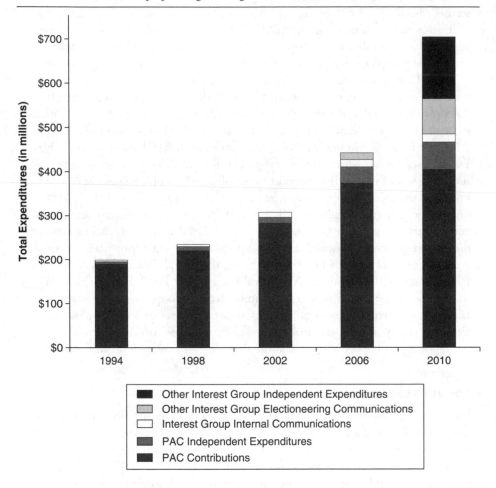

Source: Compiled from Federal Election Commission and Center for Responsive Politics data.

Notes: "Other interest group independent expenditures" consist of spending by 527 committees, 501(c) organizations, super PACs, corporations, unions, and other interest group entities. Other interest group electioneering communications consist of spending from the general treasuries of corporations, unions, and other groups as well as by 527 committees, 501(c) organizations, and super PACs. Other Interest Group Independent Expenditures consist of spending from the preceding sources. Some interest group spending in congressional elections is not disclosed and thus not included in the figure.

Campaign Contributions

PAC contributions were not equally distributed across different types of PACs. Corporate PACs accounted for 37 percent of all PAC contributions made to congressional candidates in two-party contested elections. They were followed by trade associations (27 percent), labor committees (15 percent), leadership PACs (9 percent), and nonconnected PACs (8 percent). PACs sponsored by corporations without stock or cooperatives contributed the least (just 3 percent of the total). Incumbents have laid claim to the lion's share of PAC money since the PAC boom of the 1970s. Since the mid-1980s, business-related PACs have been among the most incumbent-oriented committees, adhering more closely to an access strategy than do labor, leadership, or ideological PACs.

In 2010, corporate PACs made 89 percent of their House contributions to incumbents, and distributed more than half of those funds to candidates who won with more than 20 percent of the vote (see Table 1.1).[26] These committees

TABLE 1.1   Allocation of PAC Contributions to House Candidates in the 2010 Elections (in percent)

	Corporate	Trade, Membership, and Health	Labor	Leadership	Nonconnected
Competitive races					
Incumbents					
Democrats	31	33	49	40	32
Republicans	5	5	1	6	5
Challengers					
Democrats	–	1	4	2	1
Republicans	5	7	–	27	11
Open-seat candidates					
Democrats	1	1	5	4	2
Republicans	2	2	–	6	2
Uncompetitive races					
Incumbents					
Democrats	21	20	32	2	19
Republicans	32	27	5	6	23
Challengers					
Democrats	–	–	2	0	–
Republicans	–	–	–	–	1
Open-seat candidates					
Democrats	–	1	3	1	1
Republicans	2	3	–	5	2
Total House contributions ($, thousands)	$110,577	$79,596	$50,656	$24,284	$20,536

Source: Compiled from Federal Election Commission data.

Notes: Figures are for general election candidates in major-party contested races.
Corporate PACs included corporations with and without stock. Competitive races are those that were decided by 20 percent or less of the major-party vote or in which an incumbent was defeated. Uncompetitive races constitute the remainder. Dash (–) = less than 0.5 percent. Some columns do not add up to 100 percent because of rounding. $N = 812$

donated 5 percent of their House contributions to challengers and another 5 percent to open-seat candidates. Corporate PACs made only 44 percent of their House contributions to candidates in competitive races. Similarly, corporate PACs distributed 61 percent of their Senate contributions to incumbents, including many incumbents in one-sided contests, 32 percent to candidates for open seats, and a mere 5 percent to Senate challengers (see Table 1.2). PACs sponsored by trade associations, which also represent businesses interests, also dedicated few resources to challengers. The overall patterns of PAC contributions associated with businesses were consistent with their goal of maintaining good relations with congressional incumbents.

Labor PACs have consistently pursued highly partisan, mixed strategies. They contribute the vast majority of their money to Democrats. In 2010, labor PACs favored Democratic incumbents with 81 percent of their contributions to House candidates, including 49 percent to Democrats who were shoo-ins for reelection. Labor committees gave 57 percent of their Senate contributions to Democratic incumbents, including 17 percent to Democratic incumbents whose victories were all but assured. Labor's contributions to House and Senate challengers and open-seat candidates, however, were tilted toward those in competitive races. Both access-oriented and election-oriented goals appear to have motivated labor contributions to candidates in both chambers.

Nonconnected PACs, which have traditionally followed the ideological strategy of spending most of their money in close races, largely continued this pattern in 2010.[27] They made 58 percent of their Senate contributions and 54 percent of their House donations to candidates in close races. Nevertheless, the flows of nonconnected PAC money to Democratic and Republican candidates differed sharply. Nonconnected PACs gave more money to Democratic candidates in competitive races than uncompetitive ones, and Democratic incumbents in both the House and Senate were the major beneficiaries of these PACs' largess. When contributing to Republicans, on the other hand, nonconnected PACs targeted relatively more of their resources to nonincumbents. The contours of the 2010 political environment informed these contributions, and put the Democratic Party in the position of having to defend many Democrat-held seats while presenting the Republican Party with strong opportunities to win them.

Campaign Services

Although most of the journalistic reporting on interest groups focuses on the money they raise and spend, many groups also carry out activities that political parties have traditionally conducted. Some wealthy groups, including some labor unions and the U.S. Chamber of Commerce, try to influence the political agenda in close races. Many ideological organizations, including various groups on both sides of the abortion rights issue, recruit candidates.[28] Some PACs provide

TABLE I.2   Allocation of PAC Contributions to Senate Candidates in the 2010 Elections (in percent)

	Corporate	Trade, Membership, and Health	Labor	Leadership	Nonconnected
Competitive races					
Incumbents					
Democrats	21	24	25	19	22
Republicans	9	7	–	5	5
Challengers					
Democrats	–	–	2	–	–
Republicans	4	6	–	11	4
Open-seat candidates					
Democrats	4	6	37	15	12
Republicans	18	17	1	18	15
Uncompetitive races					
Incumbents					
Democrats	12	20	32	2	19
Republicans	19	27	5	6	23
Challengers					
Democrats	1	1	5	3	1
Republicans	–	–	–	–	–
Open-seat candidates					
Democrats	1	1	11	5	3
Republicans	9	9	1	7	8
Total Senate contributions ($, thousands)	$31,795	$18,598	$6,201	$10,410	$6,894

Source: Compiled from Federal Election Commission data.

Notes: Figures are for general election candidates in major-party contested races. Dash (–) = less than 0.5 percent. Competitive races are those that were decided by 20 percent or less of the major-party vote or in which an incumbent was defeated. Uncompetitive races constitute the remainder. Some columns do not add up to 100 percent because of rounding. $N = 72$ Percentages and totals do not include Lisa Murkowski.

candidates with in-kind contributions of polls, voter targeting, issue research, or campaign staff. PACs belonging to a few groups, including the National Federation of Independent Businesses (which supports candidates advancing the goals of small business) and EMILY's List, host campaign training schools. Many groups provide endorsements, which can help uninformed voters learn about the candidates and the issues.

One of the most important forms of assistance that a group can give to a candidate, particularly a nonincumbent, is help with fundraising. Many groups make their donors aware of the candidates they are supporting. Some also post contact information for preferred candidates in their direct mail, e-mails, websites, and social media. ActBlue, which bills itself as "the online clearinghouse for Democratic action," enables donors to contribute to candidates through its website.[29] It directed well in excess of $24 million in contributions to Democratic candidates for Congress in 2010.[30] Other PACs get their members to buy tables at candidates' fundraising events or "bundle" checks from individual donors and deliver them to the candidate. The maturation of the Washington interest group community has led to the development of several networks of PACs, other organizations, and individual donors that often assist each other in selecting candidates for support and helping those candidates raise money.

Other organized interests provide a range of assistance to candidates in congressional elections. Think tanks, such as the Heritage Foundation, on the right, and the Center for American Progress, on the left, provide issue research with a partisan angle. Labor unions and church-based organizations in African American and ethnic communities have long histories of political activism and have made decisive contributions to Democratic candidates' field activities; they also have conducted their own voter registration and get-out-the-vote (GOTV) campaigns. Business leaders, including those associated with the Chamber of Commerce, have traditionally assisted Republicans.

Virtual groups, sometimes referred to as *netroots* associations, are relative newcomers to electoral politics, but, as noted in Chapter 10, they play increasingly important roles in congressional elections. Netroots associations have some similarities to traditional grassroots organizations but their membership is internet-based rather than defined by geography. ActBlue, RightRoots, and some other groups serve as financial conduits individuals can use as vehicles to make campaign contributions to their preferred candidates.[31] Other groups, including Democracy for America and the Progressive Change Campaign Committee, provide websites that, among other things, enable volunteers to download lists of voters for the purpose of making GOTV calls.[32]

Coordinated Grassroots Campaigns

Interest groups also carry out voter mobilization and advertising activities that traditionally have been associated with political parties. In 2010, labor unions, the LCV, EMILY's List, and a raft of other left-leaning organizations invested hundreds of millions of dollars and countless volunteer hours registering Democrats and Democratic-leaning voters, informing them of opportunities for early and absentee voting, and telephoning, e-mailing, and personally visiting them to make sure they cast their votes. Conservative groups, including the Chamber of Commerce, the National Rifle Association, and Crossroads GPS, also conducted impressive voter mobilization campaigns, although they were somewhat less volunteer based.

Finally, some grassroots campaigns are carried out by local groups or groups that are founded locally and then loosely affiliate with one another and receive guidance from more structured organizations. The Tea Party movement, examined in Chapter 9, exemplifies this. Beginning with a few local protests, there were an estimated 1,400 local Tea Party groups by election day. These groups attracted the attention and leadership of a number of GOP luminaries, including former Alaska governor and GOP vice presidential nominee Sarah Palin, Sen. Jim DeMint of South Carolina, and congressional Tea Party Caucus founder Rep. Michele Bachmann (R-Minn.). They also received support from several Republican-leaning 501(c)(4) groups and PACs, including the Tea Party Patriots; FreedomWorks, led by former House majority leader Dick Armey; and the Tea Party Express, which was associated with a PAC created by a prominent Republican consulting firm in California. The Tea Party movement provided an outlet for conservative voters, activists disgruntled with the Republican Party, and independents happy with neither party to channel their energies and votes in support of a subset of Republican candidates. It helped the GOP win control of the House and make gains in the Senate.

Independent Media Campaigns

During the 2010 election cycle, interest groups spent an unprecedented $287 million advertising directly to voters—almost five times more than in the previous midterm election. Much of this activity was funded from sources that were previously prohibited under federal law. Traditional PACs and interest group internal communications accounted for $62.5 million and $13.4 million, respectively (about 26 percent of the total). The new players in federal elections accounted for considerably more: corporate, trade association, union, and other group treasuries (including the super PACs they sponsored) and 501(c) organizations provided roughly $131 million and $80 million (the remaining 74 percent).

Moreover, the messages these new entities disseminated were decidedly more negative than those of their predecessors: 68 percent of all independent spending by PACs and 84 percent of all spending on internal communications financed positive messages, but the same is true of only 44 percent of the independent expenditures financed by interest group treasuries and the super PACs they financed. Although the disclosure requirements for electioneering communications do not require groups to characterize them as positive or negative, it is safe to

TABLE 1.3   Distribution of Interest Group Spending in Independent Media Campaigns in 2010 Congressional Elections (in percent)

	House		Senate	
	Democrats	*Republicans*	*Democrats*	*Republicans*
Competitive races				
Incumbents	86	8	60	2
Challengers	4	78	–	47
Open-seat candidates	8	8	34	41
Uncompetitive races				
Incumbents	1	1	1	1
Challengers	–	1	–	–
Open-seat candidates	1	3	5	9
Total ($, thousands)	**$48,950**	**$49,570**	**$28,233**	**$69,519**

Source: Compiled from Federal Election Commission data.

Note: Figures include all independent spending designed to help a candidate (i.e., those for a candidate or against an opponent). They comprise independent expenditures and internal communications made by PACs, super PACs, 527 organizations, 501(c) committees, and other groups in support of or in opposition to major-party general election candidates in contested races. – = less than 0.5 percent. Some columns do not add to 100 percent because of rounding. N = 812 for the House; N = 72 for the Senate.

assume that most of the $70 million spent by conservative groups and the $9 million spent by liberal groups was overwhelmingly negative.[33]

Most groups that carried out independent media campaigns supported either Democrats or Republicans; few supported candidates of both parties. Virtually all of the groups' media spending was in elections for the House; it was heavily concentrated in competitive races and divided fairly equally between Democratic and Republican candidates (see Table 1.3). It also was influenced heavily by the national political agenda. In their attempts to help Republican challengers ride the emerging electoral tidal wave to victory, pro-Republican groups spent 78 percent of their outside funds mainly to blame Democratic incumbents for the state of the economy and to link them to unpopular Democratic leaders, policies, and the federal government. The spending pattern for pro-Democratic groups was reversed, as pro-Democratic groups committed 86 percent of their expenditures to preventing Democratic incumbents from being drowned by that same tidal wave; strategies to protect those in jeopardy often included attacking the qualifications and experiences of competitive GOP challengers. Groups on both sides committed roughly equal sums to the races of open-seat prospects.

Interest group media spending in the Senate elections favored the Republicans substantially. For every $1 an organization spent to improve the chances of a Democrat, an opposing group spent $2.46 cents to help a Republican. Interest groups communicated messages in the Senate contests that were similar to those used in races for the House: Republican-leaning groups focused on national issues and Democratic-leaning groups highlighted local concerns. The distribution of outside spending in elections for the upper chamber also was comparable to that for the lower chamber in that most spending to help Democrats was committed to incumbents in competitive contests and most pro-Republican spending was dedicated to challengers in these same races. One noteworthy difference between interest media spending in elections for the upper chamber and the lower chamber is that groups distributed considerably larger percentages of their funds on close open-seat contests for the Senate. Another difference concerns the high levels of pro-Republican spending that occurred in lopsided open-seat contests for the Senate. These were largely the result of the three-way races in Florida and Alaska.

The heavy concentration of interest group spending in the same elections and the overlap in messages come as little surprise. Political parties go to great efforts to signal to interest groups their priority races and the nature of the expenditures they intend to make in them. Many allied interest groups routinely follow their leads.[34] Such signaling is not necessary among interest groups that make independent, electioneering, or issue advocacy expenditures because they can legally coordinate their efforts. Many do, and as a result the messages broadcast by allied interest groups are similar to each other and to those broadcast by their preferred candidates and party.

Conclusion

Although the laws governing contemporary campaign finance were challenged almost as soon as they were enacted, the 2010 congressional elections were the first to take place after the Supreme Court struck down provisions of the law prohibiting corporations, trade associations, labor unions, and other groups from spending funds from their general treasuries to expressly call for the election or defeat of a federal candidate. Many wealthy groups and individuals found the Court's ruling liberating and responded using existing legal entities, or new ones, to make independent expenditures and issue advocacy ads to influence the outcomes of congressional races. This resulted in interest groups making record expenditures in the 2010 elections, including substantial expenditures by entities that had not previously played a significant role in federal campaigns. Moreover, some of the new entities, particularly those associated with corporate interests, followed strategies that contrasted sharply with those used by their PACs.

As is the case with any major change in the regulations governing campaign finance, it is challenging to speculate about their long-term impact because the nation's foremost political and legal talent continually probe campaign finance laws. Moreover, because of the recent unraveling of the regulations governing interest group participation in federal elections, many groups have not had the opportunity to respond to the new legal environment. Given a chance to adjust, interest group efforts in future congressional elections may be different from that exhibited in 2010. Moreover, organized interests have yet to participate in a presidential election in the post–*Citizens United* era. Nevertheless, some predictions are possible. First, one can anticipate that many of the business and labor groups that directly financed independent expenditures or issue advocacy ads for the first time will continue to do so in future federal elections. Second, given that they will have more lead time to prepare for upcoming elections, their spending will probably increase. Third, because organization usually begets counter-organization, some groups that did not adapt to the new state of affairs during the 2010 election cycle will probably do so in upcoming elections. Future elections will probably involve more fundraising and spending by interest group entities that raise large sums from corporations, unions, and other groups and do not provide full and timely disclosure of their campaign activities. Fourth, given that most members of Congress "run scared," including those who hold what many would regard as safe seats, it is likely that incumbents will step up their fundraising efforts in response to the uncertainty that the new forms of interest group spending have injected into congressional campaigns.

Should these predictions prove correct, they likely will lead to a number of undesirable outcomes. The costs of elections undoubtedly will increase. The time incumbents spend fundraising probably will grow at the expense of the time they devote to meeting with constituents and performing other congressional duties. Of course, anything that increases the amount of money needed to contest an election works to the disadvantage of challengers, most of whom already face major obstacles when fundraising. Under this scenario, many potential quality challengers of modest or middle-class means may choose not to run for Congress. This will do little to enhance representation in a legislature that already has a disproportionate number of wealthy individuals.

Endnotes

1   *Citizens United v. FEC,* 558 U.S. 08-205 (2010).
2   For a fuller discussion of the dynamics of campaign reform, see Diana Dwyre and Victoria A. Farrar-Myers, *Legislative Labyrinth: Congress and Campaign Finance Reform* (Washington, DC: CQ Press, 2001).
3   See, for example, Paul S. Herrnson, *Congressional Elections: Campaigning at Home and in Washington,* 6th ed. (Washington, DC: CQ Press, 2011), ch. 1.

4 See the Supreme Court's ruling in *Buckley v. Valeo*, 424 U.S. 1 (1976).
5 See David B. Magleby, *Outside Money: Soft Money and Issue Advocacy in 1998 Congressional Elections* (Lanham, MD: Rowman & Littlefield, 2000).
6 David B. Magleby and J. Quinn Monson, *Campaign 2002: The Perfect Storm* (Provo, UT: Center for the Study of Elections and Democracy, 2003).
7 Anthony Corrado, "Money and Politics," in *The New Campaign Finance Sourcebook,* ed. Anthony Corrado, Thomas Mann, Daniel Ortiz, and Trevor Potter (Washington, DC: Brookings Institution Press, 2003).
8 The exception was individual contributions of less than $200.
9 For more on the BCRA, see Anthony Corrado, "Money and Politics," in *The New Campaign Finance Sourcebook,* ed. Anthony Corrado, Thomas Mann, Daniel Ortiz, and Trevor Potter (Washington, DC: Brookings Institution Press, 2003); and Dwyre and Farrar-Myers, *Legislative Labyrinth.*
10 Adam Clymer, "Foes of Campaign Finance Bill Plot Legal Attack," *The New York Times,* February 17, 2002.
11 This section draws from Herrnson, *Congressional Elections,* ch. 5.
12 PACs that do not meet these requirements are subject to the same $1,000 contribution limit as are individuals.
13 Leadership PACs, which the Federal Election Commission categorizes as nonconnected PACs, are omitted from the figures and discussion of nonconnected PACs. For a discussion of leadership PACs and their roles in the 2010 elections, see Herrnson, *Congressional Elections,* chs. 4–5.
14 The EMILY in EMILY's List is an acronym for Early Money Is Like Yeast to which the group sometimes adds: It raises the dough.
15 Center for Responsive Politics, www.opensecrets.org.
16 Federal Election Commission, Political Committee Status 11 CFR Part 100 [Notice 2007–3], Federal Register, Vol. 72, No. 25, Wednesday, February 7, 2007, 5595–606.
17 The exception is that a 501(c) organization that accepts a contribution earmarked for an independent expenditure calling for the election or defeat of a specific federal candidate, must publicly disclose the source of that contribution to the FEC.
18 On 501(c) organizations and 527 committees, see for example, Stephen R. Weissman and Kara D. Ryan, *Soft Money in the 2006 Election and the Outlook for 2008* (Washington, DC: Campaign Finance Institute, 2007).
19 Based on figures compiled from the Center for Responsive Politics, www.opensecrets .org.
20 Figures compiled from FEC data.
21 *Citizens United v. FEC,* 558 U.S. 08-205 (2010); *Speechnow.org v. FEC;* U.S. Court of Appeals for the D.C. Circuit, No. 08-5223 (2010).
22 Paul S. Herrnson, "The Roles of Party Organizations, Party-Connected Committees, and Party Allies in Elections," *Journal of Politics* 71 (2009): 1207–1224.
23 League of Conservation Voters, www.lcv.org/about/mission/.
24 This section draws from Herrnson, *Congressional Elections,* ch. 5.
25 It is impossible to report on the activities of every interest group entity because of the limited disclosure requirements imposed on some of them, but it is possible to estimate the relative expenditures of each.

26 Figures discussed in connection with Tables1.1–1.3 are for general election candidates in major-party contested races only.

27 See note 13.

28 On abortion rights PACs, see, for example, Christine L. Day and Charles D. Hadley, *Women's PACs.*(Upper Saddle River, NJ: Prentice Hall, 2005).

29 ActBlue, https://secure.actblue.com/.

30 This figure excludes contributions of less than $200, which are not itemized in the PAC's disclosure reports. Center for Responsive Politics, www.opensecrets.org.

31 ActBlue, https://secure.actblue.com/; Rightroots, www.rightroots.com.

32 See http://calloutthevote.com/.

33 The groups are required to report the candidates portrayed in an ad, but not the ad's tone. Dollar estimates compiled from the Center for Responsive Politics, www.open secrets.org. On the tone of the ads, see Michael M. Franz, Erika Franklin Fowler, and Travis N. Ridout, "Citizens United and Campaign Advertising in 2010," paper presented at the Annual Conference of the Midwest Political Science Association, Chicago, March 31–April 3, 2011.

34 Herrnson, "The Roles of Party Organizations, Party-Connected Committees, and Party Allies in Elections."

CHAPTER 2

The Voice of American Business

The U.S. Chamber of Commerce and the 2010 Elections

Robert G. Boatright

In October of 2010, a frustrated President Barack Obama joined many other Democrats in criticizing the United States Chamber of Commerce for its $50 million voter education campaign, alleging that the Chamber was channeling foreign money into its advertisements.[1] Four months later, Obama delivered a speech to the Chamber, promising to work cooperatively with the Chamber in the upcoming two years, praising many of the Chamber's programs, and highlighting areas of agreement between Obama and the Chamber.[2]

Obama's *volte face* says much about the "shellacking" his party received in 2010 and the steps Obama sought to take to reposition himself for the 2012 election. Yet it also says much about the Chamber of Commerce. As the self-described "voice of American business," the Chamber is easily the largest and most politically influential American business organization. The Chamber is what is known as a *peak organization,* a group that represents a large number of smaller groups. Some peak organizations, such as the American Hospital Association, represent particular trades, professions, or business sectors. The Chamber seeks to represent all businesses. Its size and reputation enable it to speak authoritatively about which policies will benefit American businesses. Yet its size and clout also present risks. On the one hand, like many other peak organizations, the Chamber can go where its members cannot—it has the expertise to conduct research about matters that affect its members and it can advocate for policies about which its member corporations might prefer to remain silent. It can do this in part because it is not required by law to disclose the names of its donors, so corporations can contribute to the Chamber's political activities without being publicly linked to these actions. On the other hand, the Chamber is constrained by its large and diverse membership, so it must be very selective in the issues it addresses. And when politicians wish to cast aspersions on "big business," the Chamber is an easy target.

All of these features were on display in the 2010 elections. As had been the case for the past decade, the Chamber of Commerce spent the most money on election-related activities of any business organization, and most (but certainly not all) of this spending was on behalf of Republican candidates. And, as has been the case in each of the past ten years, the Chamber spent more money on lobbying than any other organization.[3] The Chamber's activities in 2010, then, were hardly unexpected, but the Chamber was arguably more visible in 2010 than it has been in past elections.

The Chamber plays a unique role in American elections. Most of the other organizations that were among the top spenders on the 2010 elections were either new organizations created solely to channel members' contributions into election-related advertising (as was the case for groups such as American Crossroads) or were groups that had long-established ties with only one party. The Chamber, on the other hand, has existed since 1912, and historically has worked closely with presidents and congressional leaders of both parties. To some, the Chamber's prominence in the 2010 election is a sign of the increased politicization of umbrella business groups such as the Chamber, the National Federation of Independent Businesses (NFIB), and many other industry-specific groups. To others, it is a consequence of the Democratic Party's increased hostility toward business.

Putting the Chamber's 2010 Activities in Context

The U.S. Chamber of Commerce is composed of over three million member companies and seven thousand different local or state chambers.[4] Member companies pay dues to the U.S. Chamber on a sliding scale based on their size. Thus, while the Chamber reports 96 percent of members are small businesses, large and medium-sized businesses provide the majority of the Chamber's operating funds, and the leaders of larger businesses dominate the Chamber leadership. Few of the companies that join the Chamber join for political reasons; in many communities, membership in the local chamber is a standard way of developing professional connections and ensuring access to community business events. The federal Chamber has twelve different policy committees, as well as a small business advisory committee, a corporate leadership advisory committee, and committees of 100 different corporate executives and state and local chamber executives. The Chamber also appoints temporary task forces and special councils. This organizational structure ensures that the Chamber can provide helpful information to member companies and can provide guidance on the sorts of problems that might be specific to a small number of members.

The Chamber has a complicated governing structure, designed to minimize conflict between the group leadership and its members. According to most analyses of the Chamber, the group provides minority factions with a veto over Chamber decisions and requires near-unanimity among members before taking policy positions.[5] The Chamber thus must spend much of its time discovering what sorts of issues demonstrate this sort of consensus. As explained by Mark Smith, the Chamber cannot take a particularly proactive role in lobbying Congress—it may make the views of its membership known, but it is unable to take a lead role in helping to craft or amend legislation.[6] This is a crucial difference between the Chamber and associations that represent particular industries or types of businesses (such as the National Association of Realtors or the National Beer Wholesalers Association) or associations that represent CEOs of a small number of elite businesses (such as the Business Roundtable). The Chamber's size also is problematic for political action in that members may have a greater allegiance to industry-specific groups than to the Chamber; for instance, an automobile dealer may make greater use of its membership in the National Automobile Dealers Association than of its membership in the Chamber. Accordingly, the political action committees (PACs) of groups like the automobile dealers are more successful at raising hard money contributions than is the Chamber's PAC.[7]

For all of these structural reasons, the U.S. Chamber of Commerce historically has been able to speak authoritatively when it does speak, but it was not a dominant player in election financing until the late 1990s. The Chamber was one of several large business associations that became more politically active, and more partisan, during the 1990s.[8] The Chamber's political spending increased substantially during this time. The Chamber's PAC, for instance, spent nothing from 1992 through 1996, and then went from spending $75,000 in 1998 to spending over $380,000 in 2000.[9] Similarly, lobbying expenses increased from approximately $17 million in 1998 and 2000 to $41 million in 2002. To hear the leaders of business groups tell it, this increase was sparked by the AFL-CIO's decision to spend heavily in an effort to help the Democratic Party retake Congress in 1996. Following the announcement of the AFL-CIO's effort, a number of business groups, including the Chamber, the NFIB, the Business Roundtable, and a few industry-specific groups, created a group called The Coalition: Americans Working for Real Change. Members of this group shared information about which districts the AFL-CIO was targeting and how each would respond. Although the Coalition disbanded after the election, the groups that were involved in the Coalition remained active in subsequent years.

Many of the major business groups also hired far more aggressive leaders during this time. In 1999, the Business-Industry PAC (BIPAC) hired a new CEO, Greg Casey, who immediately sought to reorganize the group's political operations to emphasize grassroots communication with members. Earlier, in 1995, the NFIB hired Jack Faris, who had been a major fundraiser for the Republican National Committee. Tom Donahue, who had reoriented the American Trucking Association in a more political and partisan direction, became the Chamber's president and CEO in 1997. Faris, Casey, and Donahue all were leaders with a background in politics, and all sought to strengthen ties with the Republican Party. The goals of these leaders dovetailed with the Republican congressional leadership's emphasis on cementing close ties with the business community and raising PAC money from business associations.

Although the Chamber's lobbying and PAC expenditures tell part of the story, they do not quite capture the scale of the Chamber's role in elections. The Internal Revenue Service classifies the Chamber as a 501(c)(6) organization, which, as explained in Chapter 1, is a tax-exempt organization whose aim is to promote the common interest of its members.[10] A 501(c)(6) group can raise money from individuals or businesses in unlimited amounts, but it cannot contribute this money to a candidate or spend it in coordination with a candidate. By its own accounting, in 2000 the Chamber raised approximately $25 million for its 501(c)(6) fund from members, a substantial increase over fundraising in the 1990s, and perhaps a sign of its concern about the consequences of union spending.[11] Much of this money was spent on advertising; studies of the 2000 election pegged Chamber spending on ads at between $4 million and $5.5 million.[12]

The 2000 election set the template for what the Chamber would do in subsequent years, and it help put the Chamber's 2010 activities in context. Whatever category of spending one considers—PAC expenditures, lobbying expenditures, advocacy through its 501(c)(6) fund, or spending through its 527 fund—the Chamber clearly increased its spending, and increased its support of Republican candidates, from 2000 to 2010.

Figure 2.1 shows the increase in lobbying expenditures by the Chamber and its affiliates (at the national level; the figure does not include state and local chambers). The increase in lobbying expenditures provides one example of the Chamber's increasing clout. By 2010 it had become virtually the only peak business association of consequence; the Chamber spent $144 million on lobbying in 2009 and $132 million in 2010, while the second-highest spending peak association, the Business Roundtable, spent only $13 million and $8 million in those years, and the NFIB, the third-highest spender, spent $3 million and $6 million. The increase in spending by the Chamber also far outstripped the overall increase in lobbying expenditures over that period; total lobbying expenditures for all groups increased 142 percent from 1998 to 2010, while the Chamber's lobbying expenditures increased almost 700 percent.

Figure 2.2 shows total PAC receipts, expenditures, and the partisan breakdown of expenditures through the 2000s. The PAC is not particularly consequential in determining election outcomes, but it does signal the priority races. And, as was the case for many business associations, the Chamber's contributions

FIGURE 2.1   Lobbying Expenditures by the US Chamber of Commerce and Its Affiliates, 1998–2010

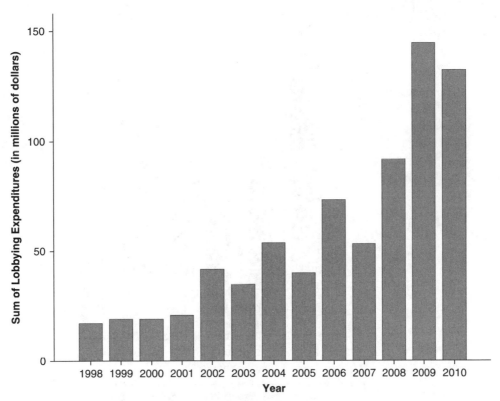

Source: Center for Responsive Politics, www.opensecrets.org.

tend to go to Republicans, but tilted somewhat more toward the Democrats during the one election here (2008) where Democrats held power and were expected to keep it. Business PACs conventionally are divided into those that seek to use their contributions to influence election results and those that use contributions as a means of gaining access to politicians.[13] The Chamber has never been an access-oriented PAC; it generally contributes money to candidates who are in close races. Figure 2.3 shows, however, that while the Chamber has favored Republicans throughout the past decade, it has sought to secure some access to policymakers by increasing its giving to Democrats in years such as 2006 and 2008 when it had reason to expect Democrats to wield power in Congress, and correspondingly its increase in Republican support in 2010 may be read as an adaptation to the fact that it expected Republicans to win a majority in one or both chambers of Congress.

FIGURE 2.2   U.S. Chamber of Commerce PAC Receipts and Expenditures, 1998–2010

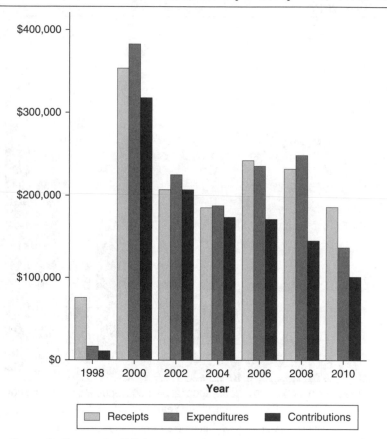

Source: Center for Responsive Politics, www.opensecrets.org.

Most of the Chamber's spending, however, has not come in the form of contributions, and it is therefore difficult to measure. We must rely on the Chamber's own estimates of the spending originating from its 501(c)(6) fund. This has been the principal vehicle for most of the Chamber's election-related spending in every election over the past decade except 2004, when the Chamber organized a 527 group, the November Fund, to distribute information about Democratic vice presidential nominee John Edwards and, more broadly, to criticize trial lawyers.[14] Like many other business and advocacy groups, the Chamber abandoned its 527 in 2006, following an FEC challenge to many of the more prominent 527 groups.[15]

The Chamber dramatically increased its 501(c)(6) spending in 2006, and even further increased it in 2008. Although we cannot get exact figures, we can

FIGURE 2.3   Partisanship of U.S. Chamber PAC Contributions, 1998–2010

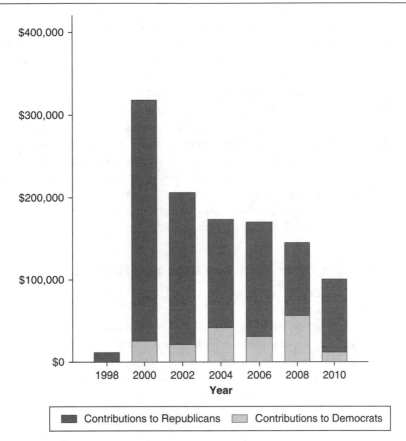

Source: Center for Responsive Politics, www.opensecrets.org.

rely on the Chamber's own descriptions of its spending, on IRS reports, and on efforts to measure the quantity of political advertising. One such study by the Campaign Finance Institute indicates that the Chamber spent over $20 million on the 2006 election, including $10 million on television advertising, another $10 million on direct mail and telephone calls, and a bus tour to fifteen different states.[16] The Chamber focused on defending Republican incumbents in competitive races, with the goal of retaining the Senate majority for the Republicans. In 2008 the Chamber almost doubled its spending yet again, surpassing $36 million in total spending.[17] The Chamber's 2008 expenditures included $16 million in television advertising, this time aimed at preventing the Democrats from reaching sixty Senate seats and being able to invoke cloture against filibuster attempts.[18] The advertising buys suggest that the Chamber was concerned more with Senate races than with the presidential race; states such as New Hampshire and Minnesota saw an influx of Chamber ads criticizing the Democratic Senate nominees, but the Chamber was entirely absent in the presidential election swing states. PAC contributions also reflect the Chamber's concerns; its contributions to House candidates in 2008 were evenly divided between Democrats and Republicans, but its contributions to Senate candidates went almost entirely to embattled Republican incumbents.

The Chamber has contributed to several different groups throughout the decade; its beneficiaries include a few different nonprofit groups, organizations such as the Republican and Democratic Governors Associations,[19] and different issue-specific business coalitions. It also maintains several charitable affiliated funds, including the Business Civil Leadership Center, a group that promotes engagement between businesses and their communities, and the Institute for a Competitive Workforce, which promotes cooperation between businesses and primary and secondary schools.[20] These affiliates have stayed clear of campaign politics.

Analyzing the Chamber's Spending in the 2010 Elections

The Chamber increased its spending further in 2010. Although 501(c)(6) groups are not required to report all of their political expenditures, they are required to report money spent on what are known as electioneering communications, introduced in Chapter 1, which are advertisements or other communications with the public that refer to candidates for office.[21] The Chamber's 501(c)(6) fund spent $33.2 million on electioneering communications alone, and most estimates of its total spending (including the Chamber's own) placed it at $50 million or more.[22] Tom Donahue, still the Chamber's president, described the 2010 effort as "the largest, most aggressive voter education and issue advocacy effort in our nearly 100-year history."[23] The Chamber far outspent other established conservative organizations; the only bigger spender was the newly formed American Crossroads, which lagged behind the Chamber in spending until the final week of the campaign.

Characteristics of Chamber Expenditures

The Chamber's political spending has little to do with gaining access to politicians or policymakers; instead, it invested in races that were competitive in an effort to affect the election results. Although the Chamber was involved in a large number of races in 2010—a total of sixty-seven—this is more indicative of the large number of competitive races than it is of the Chamber's efforts to spread its money around.[24] That is, the Chamber tends to pick its races carefully, to avoid backing two candidates in the same race or investing in races that will not be close. As is the case for most group-sponsored political advertisements, the majority of the

Chamber's ads were attack ads: a total of $27.3 million was spent on ads opposing incumbents or open-seat candidates (all Democrats, with the exception of one independent open-seat candidate, Florida governor and Senate candidate Charlie Crist), while only $5.9 million was spent on ads in support of candidates.[25]

Although groups are not required to state whether they support or oppose the candidates discussed in these communications, in the case of the Chamber it is relatively easy to conclude from its PAC contributions and the tone of its advertisements which candidates it supports and which it opposes. Table 2.1 presents a breakdown of the Chamber's electioneering activity in 2010, with reference to which party's candidate was the intended beneficiary of the ad. As the table shows, the Chamber's electioneering spending roughly parallels its PAC contributions[26] in regards to ideology—in the House, the Chamber did not entirely give up on Democrats, and it backed a few Democrats (such as Rep. Bobby Bright, D-Ala.) whose opponents were arguably just as good or better on the Chamber's issues of concern. The Chamber also did not stint in its support of these Democrats; for House candidates, a quick look at the table shows that the proportion of Democratic candidates supported and the proportion of funds spent on advocacy for Democrats are similar. And most of these Democrats were running in competitive races, as evidenced by the fact that eight of the eleven lost their reelection bids. To be sure, the Chamber may not have had reason early in these races to suspect that they would become competitive,[27] but the Chamber appears, despite news coverage to the contrary, not to have gone into the election cycle with the single-minded goal of securing a Republican majority in the House.[28] The Democrats it did support, however, were conservative Democrats—all of them were to the right of the House's center according to *National Journal*'s vote rankings.[29] The Chamber opposed several Democrats who were just as conservative as those it supported. For instance, it supported Frank Kratovil (D-Md.), who stood exactly at the center of the House in terms of liberalism, and Jim Matheson (D-Utah) and John Barrow (D-Ga.), who were immediately to Kratovil's right, but it ran advertisements against Gabrielle Giffords (D-Ariz.), who was more conservative than each of these three. This suggests that the Chamber was concerned with particular votes, not merely overall ideology. To take the most obvious possibility here, Giffords voted for the Patient Protection and Affordable Care Act (the health care reform bill), while Kratovil, Barrow, and Matheson did not. All of the Chamber's ads for Democrats were ads encouraging viewers to support the Democrat. The Chamber did not air ads critical of the Republican candidates in these races.

The Chamber was more partisan in its spending on Senate races, with Sen. Blanche Lambert Lincoln (D-Ark.) the lone Democrat supported by the Chamber. Lincoln benefitted from a Chamber advertising campaign in the Democratic primary, a race she narrowly won against a more liberal challenger. Other than Lincoln, the Chamber had little interest in Senate Democrats. The Chamber's

TABLE 2.1   Chamber of Commerce Electioneering Expenditures, 2010

Chamber	Party	N	Total Expenditures
House	Democrat	11	$2,049,614
	Republican	41	9,232,160
	Total	52	11,281,774
Senate	Democrat	1	600,000
	Republican	14	21,289,574
	Total	15	21,889,574
Total	Democrat	12	2,649,614
	Republican	55	30,521,734
	Total	67	33,171,348

Source: Author's calculations, using data from Center for Responsive Politics, www.open secrets.org.

Note: Numbers listed here are for races, not for expenditures. The Chamber reported expenditures for or against sixty-nine different candidates; in two instances the Chamber reported expenditures opposing one candidate and expenditures supporting that candidate's opponent.

spending against Democrats relates to the competiveness of the race and the size of the state. For instance, as Table 2.2 shows, it spent nearly $5 million against incumbent Barbara Boxer (D-Calif.), approximately $2 million in Colorado and Florida, and over $1 million in Illinois, New Hampshire, Missouri, Kentucky, and Pennsylvania. Of these, all but New Hampshire were highly competitive. The Chamber spent somewhat less in Washington and Wisconsin—races that did not become competitive until later in the election cycle, and in Connecticut and Indiana, states where the Senate races were less competitive.

The Chamber's partisan preferences were more evident in its choices about open-seat races. All of the Democrats the Chamber supported were incumbents, while none of the Republicans the Chamber supported were. The Chamber did not support any Democratic open-seat candidates. In the House, the Chamber spent slightly over $7 million on ads supporting thirty different Republican challengers, but only $2.2 million in support of twelve different Republican open-seat candidates. This, again, may simply be a function of the election—there were a large number of competitive Republican challengers, so it seems unlikely that the Chamber made a decision to support challengers at the expense of open-seat candidates, or to avoid backing Republican incumbents, few of whom were threatened. Spending in the Senate was more balanced, with $12.9 million spent in favor of challengers and $8.4 spent in favor of open-seat candidates. The difference here may simply have to do with the states that fall into each category; California alone accounts for this difference.

TABLE 2.2   Top Five Senate and House Races for Chamber, 2010

Candidate	State	Total Spent	Type of Candidate Supported	Party of Beneficiary
Senate				
Against Barbara Boxer	California	$4,911,122	Challenger	Republican
Against Michael Bennet*	Colorado	2,045,526	Challenger	Republican
Against Charlie Crist	Florida	2,000,000	Open Seat	Republican
Against Robin Carnahan/for Roy Blunt	Missouri	1,759,741	Challenger	Republican
Against Alex Giannoulias	Illinois	1,682,856	Open Seat	Republican
House				
Against Dina Titus	Nevada	549,850	Challenger	Republican
Against Top Perriello	Virginia	442,765	Challenger	Republican
For Frank Kratovil	Maryland	437,524	Incumbent	Democrat
Against Harry Teague	New Mexico	436,953	Challenger	Republican
Against Martin Heinrich	New Mexico	416,882	Challenger	Republican

Source: Author's calculations, using electioneering communication data from Center for Responsive Politics, www.opensecrets.org.

*Excludes money spent on behalf of candidates in the Republican primary to challenge Bennet.

The Chamber was not particularly active in competitive primaries. It did air some advertisements in uncompetitive Republican primaries, but these were advertisements clearly aimed at helping the eventual nominees in the general election. The two primaries it did take a role in, however, are worthy of some attention. Blanche Lambert Lincoln's primary opponent, Bill Halter (D-Ark.), was the beneficiary of over $7 million in spending by labor unions and other liberal groups determined to unseat Lincoln. Lincoln was not expected to win the general election were she to survive the primary. The Chamber's support of Lincoln, then, can be read either as an effort to show that it could counter labor's clout, or to curry favor with Lincoln in the short term. The Chamber did not purchase any advertisements in the general election—either because it viewed Lincoln as a lost cause or perhaps because it did not see a substantial difference between Lincoln and her Republican general election opponent, John Boozman, to whom she lost.

The other primary candidate the Chamber supported was Jane Norton (R-Colo.), who was the more mainstream or establishment candidate for the Republican nomination in Colorado. Norton was defeated by the Tea Party–supported candidate in the race, Ken Buck (R-Colo.). The Chamber turned around and spent money against the Democratic incumbent in the general election, but Buck was clearly not its first choice. The Colorado race provides an interesting contrast to the Nevada Senate race. The Republican primary there provided a similar contrast among candidates, but the Chamber stayed entirely out of the Republican primary and the general election. Indeed, this is the only high-profile Senate race where the Chamber was not active. Senate majority leader Harry Reid (D-Nev.) emerged victorious from this race; the Chamber may have been leery of supporting any challenger to Reid.[30]

Finally, the Chamber also invested heavily in special elections, supporting unsuccessful Republican candidates for the House in special elections in New York and Pennsylvania, and providing slightly over $1 million for Scott Brown's (R-Mass.) successful Senate campaign in early 2010. The Chamber proudly noted that it was the most active outside group in the Scott Brown race.[31]

The Trajectory of the Chamber's Involvement in the 2010 Election

The Chamber spent its money relatively early in the election cycle. It spent $11.8 million in the final three weeks of the election—a large amount, to be sure, but only slightly more than one-third of the total money it spent on electioneering. This decision makes the Chamber look a little bit more like labor unions in its strategic calculus than like the newly formed pro-Republican groups. American Crossroads, for instance, spent over 60 percent of its electioneering funds in the final three weeks, while the Service Employees International Union (SEIU) and the American Federation of State, County, and Municipal Employees (AFSCME), the two highest-spending labor unions, each spent less than a third of their electioneering budget late in the race.[32] This strategy befits a group that has spoken not only of winning elections but of shaping campaign dialogue, that is, of influencing which issues get talked about in the campaign and which races become competitive. The Chamber had the money to make races competitive early, and it had the resources to run advertisements that injected business issues into campaigns. In referring to one race where the Chamber spent money early, Bill Miller, senior vice president for political affairs noted that "we got in early in crucial states like Pennsylvania, and helped put Joe Sestak (and his Pelosi politics) on the defensive."[33] Miller's explanation clearly shows the Chamber's intent to establish the issues and the tone of the 2010 elections.

In March of 2010, the Chamber announced a $50 million election spending goal.[34] This announcement came after several months in which Chamber president Donahue publicly expressed his frustration with the reluctance of Congress and the Obama administration to work more closely with the Chamber on health care, credit card regulation, and Wall Street reform. The Chamber framed its high lobbying expenses as a sign that it had made a real effort to communicate with the administration and that it had been repeatedly rebuffed.[35] From the Obama administration's point of view, the Chamber had been insufficiently appreciative of Democrats' efforts to work with it on the stimulus bill, and the White House responded to the Chamber's claims of their efforts to communicate by pointing out that the Chamber always supported Republicans.[36] The relationship between the Chamber and Democrats had clearly soured by the time the election campaign began, although given the Chamber's spending in prior elections and its aggressive support for Scott Brown in early 2010, it is not at all clear whether a better relationship would have affected Chamber spending.

Before the magnitude of the expected Republicans gains became clear, however, the Chamber in September allied itself with several conservative Democrats, and among its earliest major expenditures was the announcement of the Campaign for Free Enterprise, an effort to use online media to push congressional candidates to reject new regulations and pledge to cut spending and taxes.[37] The Campaign for Free Enterprise established a Facebook page, which ultimately attracted over 100,000 supporters.[38] The Chamber's campaign was announced with little reference to specific campaigns, and it was presented as a tool that voters could use to quiz candidates about their priorities. The Chamber also sponsored a DC "fly in" for Chamber members to meet with their senators and representatives to emphasize the Campaign for Free Enterprise.[39] This is a tactic the Chamber frequently uses, but in the framework of the campaign it seems, again, like the prelude to an electioneering effort.

The Chamber ramped up its advertising in late September and early October, spending over $10 million in the first week of October.[40] By this time the scope of potential Republican gains had become clear, and other conservative groups such as Crossroads also had invested heavily in the election. The amount of spending by other groups, the fact that some of these groups received large donations that the Chamber thought it would receive,[41] and the possibility that that many Republican candidates simply did not need the Chamber's help appears to have reduced Chamber spending during the campaign's final weeks. The Chamber responded by coordinating its spending with other major conservative groups,[42] increasing its web advertising,[43] and seeking to rally Chamber members through, among other things, a speaking tour to visit local chambers.[44] According to one account, the Chamber even developed and distributed to members a board game in which players would seek to avoid "burdensome regulations."[45] The Chamber also invested steadily in phone calls to members, direct mail, e-mail, and so forth, on a scale (at least according to the Chamber) much greater than what the Chamber had done in the past.[46]

These activities fall well within the playbook business groups developed during the 2000s. Peak associations like the Chamber, the NFIB, and BIPAC all had been emphasizing member contact, the use of the Internet to rally members, and the benefits of microtargeting since the 2000 election.[47] No doubt these methods have proven effective, but it is important to note that the majority of Chamber expenditures were on television advertising. If we accept the Chamber's $50 million estimate of its 2010 spending, this means that the Chamber spent two-thirds of its election-related budget on advertising in 2010, as opposed to approximately 40 percent in 2008. Just as was the case for other groups, 2010 was for the Chamber far more about advertising than it was about the sorts of more personalized voter contacting methods that had been so prevalent in the past three election cycles.

Just as the total spending data show that the Chamber preferred Republicans but maintained a loyalty to the Democrats it had cultivated in the past, so media reports show that the Chamber tilted toward Republicans but had not turned completely against the Democrats. The Chamber publicly endorsed Democrat Joe Manchin (D-W.Va.) in the late-breaking West Virginia Senate race (although it did not spend any money on Manchin's behalf), and it also remained neutral or endorsed Democrats in several other high-profile races where it did not spend money, including the race in the Chicago suburbs between Melissa Bean (D-Ill.) and Joseph Walsh (R-Ill.), and in the South Dakota race between Stephanie Herseth Sandlin (D-S.Dak.) and Kristi Noem (R-S.Dak.).[48] Several accounts of the election noted, however, that the Chamber now opposed several Democrats it had supported in the past, including three (Joe Sestak, D-Pa.; Paul Hodes, D-N.H.; and Brad Ellsworth, D-Ind.) who were seeking to move from the House to the Senate.[49] Some Democrats and Democratic supporters also complained that the Chamber had lobbied Democrats on the stimulus bill, but had then turned around and criticized many sympathetic Democrats for failing to create jobs.[50] More broadly, some Democrats, and some journalists as well, alleged that the Chamber was airing a number of misleading advertisements and a number of advertisements that criticized Democrats for ethical transgressions or other things that had little or nothing to do with the Chamber's priorities.[51] As the election progressed, the Chamber had to walk a thin line between advancing its larger goals—which clearly depended upon changing the party that controlled the House and Senate—and showing support or at least consistency in its treatment of legislators with whom it had an existing relationship. This is something the newer groups did not need to worry about, and it is something that groups that do not lobby do not have to consider. The large sums the Chamber spent on lobbying in 2010, however, meant that earlier on in the election it clearly had spent much time lobbying the same members of Congress that it later was criticizing.

To summarize, the Chamber did not do anything radically different from what it had done in the past. Its electioneering ads were, on the whole, no more harsh than they had been in past elections, and the Chamber was more restrained in its attacks on Democrats than were other groups. It did the same things it had done in the past, but it just did more of them. As the highest-spending group in the election—or, at least, the highest-spending group with a proven track record and an established identity—the Chamber drew a fair amount of scrutiny from the media and from Democrats, and it came to exemplify, in the eyes of many, the consequences of the deregulation of interest group electioneering catalyzed by the Supreme Court's *Citizens United v. FEC* decision. This was ironic because the Chamber did not obviously change its strategy in response to *Citizens United*. The Chamber's activities were not even an adaptation to the Republican wave that was building during 2010. They appear, instead, to be a more aggressive version of what the Chamber had done in the past, driven by the Chamber's unhappiness with the treatment it felt it had received from the Democratic House leadership and from the White House.

Consequences of the Chamber's Role in 2010

Why, then, did the Chamber draw so much attention in 2010? One could argue that the Chamber of Commerce spent as much time creating the political environment of the 2010 elections as it did responding to that environment. That is, the Chamber had announced its intention to spend lavishly in 2010 long before it became apparent that the Republican Party would be so successful in the midterm elections, long before it was apparent that groups such as American Crossroads would also spend heavily in support of Republicans, and slightly before the Supreme Court's *Citizens United v. FEC* decision increased the ability of businesses to spend money on advertising. The Chamber was only indirectly a beneficiary of the new spending environment, insofar as its favored candidates also received support from groups that did adjust their strategies to take advantage of *Citizens United*, and the Chamber arguably could spend less on some candidates or shift its funds around because of what other groups were doing.

The *Citizens United* decision affected who could spend money on political advertisements and what could be said in the ads. As explained in Chapter 1, advertisements that directly ask viewers to vote for or against a candidate, or use similar words such as *support, oppose, elect,* and *defeat* are considered to be express advocacy and could only be used in ads paid for with PAC money before *Citizens United*. Groups that are not PACs instead ran issue advocacy ads, also discussed in Chapter 1, that are advertisements that say positive or negative things about candidates but do not make any direct reference to whether they should be elected. These types of ads were permissible, with some restrictions, before *Citizens United*.[52] The *Citizens United* decision permits business not only to pay for issue advocacy but also to pay for express advocacy. Despite its new freedom to use its 501(c)(6) account to buy ads that use such language, the Chamber did not engage in direct advocacy. In most instances, the Chamber's ads stayed well within the confines of issue advocacy, as this example, from the California Senate race, shows:

Without water, the Central Valley can't work. Barbara Boxer is famous for protecting the three-inch smelt instead of protecting California jobs and farms. She voted to cut water to the Central Valley, killing jobs and driving unemployment as high as forty percent. Check the facts for yourself at uschamber.com. And tell Barbara Boxer the Central Valley needs water to create jobs.[53]

The Chamber clearly coordinated with other conservative groups that took greater advantage of the *Citizens United* decision, but the Chamber itself did not do anything differently. Tables 2.3 and 2.4 show the partisan breakdown of Chamber electioneering expenditures and the top races for the Chamber in 2008. When compared with Tables 2.1 and 2.2, it is evident that the Chamber spent more money in sum and in its highest priority races, but the increase is not dramatic. The changes from 2008 and 2010 are clear signs of the shift in the political context: the Chamber spent a larger percentage of its money on House races in 2010 because the chance of a change in majority control in the House was greater than it had been in 2008, and it was arguably greater than was a change in Senate control. Recall that the Chamber's main concern in 2008 was ensuring that the Democratic Party did not hold enough seats to invoke cloture; the emphasis on the Senate in 2008 is thus understandable. The Chamber actually supported *more* Democrats in 2010, and spent a larger fraction of its money on their behalf, than it had in 2008. This does not mean that the Chamber was more enthusiastic about

TABLE 2.3   Chamber of Commerce Electioneering Expenditures, 2008

Chamber	Party	N	Total Expenditures
House	Democrat	3	$250,000
	Republican	24	2,218,723
	Total	27	2,468,723
Senate	Democrat	0	0
	Republican	11	13,814,914
	Total	11	13,814,914
Total	Democrat	3	250,000
	Republican	35	16,033,637
	Total	38	16,283,637

Source: Author's calculations, using electioneering communication data from Center for Responsive Politics, www.opensecrets.org.

Note: Numbers listed here are for races, not for expenditures. The Chamber reported expenditures supporting or opposing forty-six different candidates.

TABLE 2.4   Top Five Senate and House Races for Chamber, 2008

Candidate	State	Total Spent	Type of Candidate Supported	Party of Beneficiary
Senate				
For John Sununu/ against Jean Shaheen	New Hampshire	$3,105,246	Incumbent	Republican
For Norm Coleman/ against Al Franken	Minnesota	2,438,844	Incumbent	Republican
For Gordon Smith/ against Jeff Merkley	Oregon	1,504,478	Incumbent	Republican
Against Mark Udall	Colorado	1,472,646	Open Seat	Republican
Against Mary Landrieu	Louisiana	1,195,580	Challenger	Republican
House				
For Peter Roskam	Illinois	320,590	Incumbent	Republican
For Vern Buchanan/ against Christine Jennings	Florida	275,000	Incumbent	Republican
For Dave Reichert/ against Darcy Burner	Washington	173,185	Incumbent	Republican
For Melissa Bean	Illinois	150,000	Incumbent	Democrat
For Jeb Bradley	New Hampshire	150,000	Challenger	Republican
For Tom Feeney	Florida	150,000	Incumbent	Republican
For Robin Hayes	North Carolina	150,000	Incumbent	Republican
Against Tim Mahoney	Florida	150,000	Open Seat	Republican

Source: Author's calculations, using electioneering communication data from Center for Responsive Politics, www.opensecrets.org.

the Democratic Party in 2010; it may indicate that fewer of the Democratic allies of the Chamber needed help in 2008.

Because of its vocal commitment to helping to defeat the Obama agenda in 2010, the Chamber earned early criticism from the President, from congressional Democrats, and from U.S. Chamber Watch, a group formed by Change to Win, the coalition of labor unions that broke away from the AFL-CIO in 2005. Chamber Watch sought to expose what it considered questionable dealings on the part of the Chamber and criticized both the policy positions and campaign tactics of the Chamber.[54] Chamber Watch scored several points against the Chamber during the campaign, and the Chamber took Chamber Watch seriously; e-mails and other documents hackers made public after the election revealed what the Chamber's law firm described as a concerted effort by the firm "to degrade [Chamber Watch's] messaging capabilities and credibility."[55] Although the Chamber denied any knowledge of the effort, the firm at the least felt it would find a receptive audience at the Chamber for its tactics.

The liberal critique of the Chamber, pushed by Chamber Watch, other interest groups, and by Democratic politicians, included two main allegations. First, MoveOn.org and other organizations aired advertisements in several states accusing the Chamber of serving as a front for large donors. The disclosure during the campaign of several large donations, including media magnate Rupert Murdoch's $1 million contribution, as well as multimillion dollar donations from Prudential Financial, Goldman Sachs, Chevron Texaco, and Dow Chemical, clearly put the donors on the defensive, if not the Chamber.[56] *The Wall Street Journal* alleged that attempts by liberal groups such as MoveOn, Chamber Watch, Public Campaign, and Public Citizen to publicize the names of these donors and to link these donations to federal policies were efforts not only to curb such donations, but to also cause media outlets to question the legality of the ads they were running.[57] These groups sought to push the Chamber to make its donor lists public or to push the Department of Justice or the IRS to investigate the Chamber. Again, the Chamber was not the only group singled out for criticism, but it was arguably the largest and most recognizable to the public. These criticisms also were linked by many Democrats to the party's DISCLOSE (Democracy Is Strengthened by Casting Light On Spending in Elections) Act, an effort to respond to *Citizens United* by requiring advertisers to, among other things, disclose their donors to the FEC and to include with their ads a statement identifying the advertisement's funding source.[58] According to the Chamber, the threat the DISCLOSE Act posed was one of the major reasons for its substantial lobbying expenditures in 2010.[59]

Second, and more consequentially, *Think Progress*, the blog of the Center for American Progress, a left-leaning think tank, alleged in early October that the Chamber was using foreign funds to pay for its electioneering advertisements. The blog based its allegation on the fact that the Chamber maintains a number of *AmChams*, business councils headquartered in foreign countries that are affiliated with the U.S. Chamber.[60] Although the *Think Progress* post could identify only relatively small amounts of money contributed from these foreign groups to the U.S. Chamber—about $100,000—the allegations were quickly picked up by the president, the vice president, presidential adviser David Axelrod, and Sen. Al Franken (D-Minn.), and *Think Progress* broadened its claims to include reference to U.S. affiliates of foreign companies, or multinational companies that derived revenues from other countries.[61] By the end of the campaign, *Think Progress* was estimating that the Chamber raised at least $885,000 in foreign funds for its 501(c)(6) account.[62] The Chamber angrily responded that it separated foreign funds from the funds it used in campaigns, but the claim persisted through the remainder of the campaign. The response from the right included claims by conservative operatives Karl Rove and Ed Gillespie that Obama was maintaining an "enemies list" and was seeking "to criminalize" the actions of those who opposed him.[63]

Although the Chamber clearly won at the ballot box in 2010, and although Donahue continually argued, when attacked, that the Chamber would "ramp up" its spending in order to counter its critics, the Chamber found itself playing much more of a villain's role than it had become accustomed to in past elections.[64] To address the first set of allegations, the Chamber has always sought to protect the anonymity of donors. There is a long paper trail of claims by 501(c)(6) political directors that their members will be punished if their contributions are disclosed.[65] The Chamber, according to some analysts' interpretation of its amicus brief in the *Citizens United* case, foresaw that criticism of its secrecy about donors would increase in 2010, but generally has considered this sort of criticism the price it must pay in order to protect the anonymity its donors expect when they give.[66] In regards to the allegations about foreign money, there is again a lengthy history of claims about the ways in which interest groups of all sorts are able to segregate funds. If one assumes that the Chamber does rigorously separate contributions from foreigners from those it uses for political advocacy, this means that the Chamber simply can reallocate its money—that it can shift toward political purposes money that came from domestic sources and was to be used for nonpolitical purposes. Any group that engages in electioneering can use this sort of approach, so it was in no way particular to the Chamber. In the absence of a finding of any sort of quid pro quo—a finding, for instance, that the Chamber received a large foreign contribution and then immediately turned that money toward advertising—there is no reason to think that the AmCham money had any effect on the Chamber's electioneering. Furthermore, because the Chamber did not engage in direct advocacy, it muddied the waters to suggest that the Chamber was using its money for "partisan" purposes.

The angry tone of the Chamber's responses to Democratic attacks may have been a piece of political theater, but it seems likely that the Chamber would have preferred not to be at the center of such controversies. It certainly had not been the focal point of the 2008 campaign, despite its high spending then. The Chamber appears to have suffered relatively little among voters, however, despite criticism of its activities. A postelection poll by Douglas Schoen and Scott Rasmussen found that 45 percent of respondents held a favorable view of the Chamber while 26 percent had an unfavorable view. While this poll provides no benchmark numbers on support for the Chamber before the election, the numbers certainly do not indicate substantial hostility toward the Chamber, and they do not seem to obviously reflect different attitudes toward the Chamber than one might see outside of the election cycle.[67]

There was some internal fallout from the Chamber's role in 2010, however. As noted earlier, the need to achieve near-consensus among its members constrains the Chamber's advocacy, and this need prevents the Chamber from speaking on issues that pit some sectors of the business world against others. The Chamber had endured a contentious internal debate in 2009 over whether it should take a position on climate change, and some of the Chamber's more progressive members, including Apple, Nike, and the power companies Pacific Gas and Electric, PNM Resources, and Exelon had quit as a consequence of this debate.[68] These sorts of internal conflicts continued after the Chamber's 2010 campaign. Local Chamber groups in left-leaning cities such as Seattle, Philadelphia, and Manchester, New Hampshire considered disaffiliating from the Chamber after the election, and liberal groups pressured many large corporations to resign from the Chamber or limit their contributions.[69] While none of these groups did leave, it was expected that they would encourage the Chamber to tone down its partisanship and its rhetoric in the future. The year of 2010 was certainly one in which the congressional elections were nationalized; the result of this was that the national Chamber found itself at odds with local chambers in a number of races.

After the Election

Many business groups seek to avoid letting the public know about their campaign expenditures. The Chamber of Commerce was very open about its goals in 2010, the amount of money it was spending and planned to spend, and the places it was spending the money. This has not always been the case for the Chamber, but the Chamber clearly wanted to receive credit in 2010 for its role in defeating Democratic members of Congress. The Chamber took much of the credit for the Republican victories after the election, and Donahue vowed that the conflicts with Obama were far from over: "Hell no, they are in the second inning."[70] The Chamber clearly now had a large number of new allies in Congress, both in that the newly elected Republicans could be expected to be more business-friendly and in that a number of these candidates benefitted from the Chamber's electioneering.

Many groups also tout their won/loss records after every election. In the case of the Chamber, such numbers are not particularly revealing. An access-oriented PAC can back winners simply by contributing mainly to safe candidates; likewise, a group can have a substantial effect on an election yet lose a large number of close races. The Chamber clearly falls into the latter category. Almost all of the Democrats it supported lost, which can be read more as a sign of the tenor of the election than of the value of a Chamber endorsement—not even business-friendly Democrats were safe. The Chamber spent over $7 million on the unsuccessful Senate challengers in California and Colorado, a sign that it is willing to take risks. The California race, despite the Chamber's investment, was never among the most competitive Senate races, but the Chamber clearly saw defeating Barbara Boxer (D-Calif.) as a high enough priority that it would continue to try to alter the dynamics of the race.

Finally, many groups seek to make postelection amends with candidates they agree with but did not back in the election. In many instances, Republican challengers defeated Democrats with whom the Chamber had had a friendly relationship. The Chamber is a large enough group, however, that one would not expect these Republican victors to hold a grudge against the Chamber, nor would one expect the Chamber to have a need to make postelection PAC contributions to these candidates. While many business groups were holding fundraisers for the new class of Republicans in November and December,[71] the Chamber's PAC made a postelection contribution to only one of these members of Congress, newly elected Rep. Raul Labrador (R-Wyo.). The Chamber's PAC never has prioritized access and the Chamber never has sought to spread money around to all of the candidates it supports or lobbies, as do larger PACs such as the National Association of Realtors. Chamber leaders did participate in several postelection roundtables, however, and sought to make clear their priorities for the 112th Congress and for the lame duck session that concluded the 111th Congress.

In terms of policy, the Chamber clearly now had the votes to stymie President Obama's agenda in the next Congress, and during the lame duck session it lobbied for several more immediate goals, including the extension of the Bush tax cuts. The biggest immediate consequence of the election, however, was the President's effort at rapprochement with the Chamber. Treasury Secretary Timothy Geithner met with Tom Donahue during the week following the election and Obama made plans to give a speech to the Chamber in February.[72] By the time Obama delivered that speech, both sides were busy making positive overtures toward each other: Obama had hired several new staff members who were well regarded by the Chamber, and both the President and the Chamber had identified shared priorities for the upcoming two years.[73] After Obama's speech, the Chamber announced that it was "committed to the priorities laid out by the President."[74] With the next election nearly two years away, neither side had any reason to attack the other, but of course the positive comments say little about the tenor of the 2012 election. It should be noted, however, that the speech was Obama's first visit to the Chamber as president, so it may well have been a harbinger of a less confrontational relationship.

What should one expect of the Chamber in the upcoming election cycles? Many postelection reports discussed the Chamber's close collaboration with the new conservative super PACs and 501(c)(4) organizations. Some accounts also noted the Chamber's involvement in events such as a gathering of Republican donors sponsored by the Koch brothers in October that was geared toward developing a 2012 strategy.[75] If one is trying to infer the Chamber's strategy in future elections from its activities in 2010, however, there is little evidence that 2010 provides any new information. The Chamber has never been particularly active in presidential elections; in 2008, for instance, its primary concern was the Senate. Although the Chamber has spent some money on independent expenditures attacking Barack Obama, it may well turn its attention to the Senate again as long as party control of the Senate remains tenuous. While a preponderance of Chamber leaders would likely prefer a Republican in the White House, the Chamber's resources are best expended in races further down the ballot, and such an approach runs less of a risk of antagonizing members. The size of the Chamber's expenditures may create a ripple effect among other groups—like-minded groups can expect to spend money that complements what the Chamber is doing, which might mean that conservative groups other than the Chamber could take more of an interest in the presidential election than they would were the Chamber not there. On the Democratic side, it is clear that the role the Chamber and other Republican-leaning groups played in 2010 has forced Democrats to rethink their stance on outside group spending.[76] That is, there will surely be more money on the Democratic side as a result of Democratic leaders' evaluations of the role money played in 2010, and the Chamber is a big part of that evaluation.

In 2010, the Chamber clearly wanted to be a central part of the election. It got its wish, for better (mostly) but also for worse. The Chamber did what it has done in past elections, but it did a lot more of it. While the Chamber clearly will be a major force, the vehemence of its opposition to the Democratic agenda in 2010 was stronger than usual, and there is certainly much that may happen over the upcoming years that will determine how aggressive the Chamber is in 2012 and beyond.

Endnotes

Thank you to Amanda Gregoire for research assistance.

1   Dan Eggen and Scott Wilson, "Obama Continues Attack on Chamber of Commerce," *The Washington Post*, October 11, 2010.
2   Tom Hamburger, "Obama Courts Business with Chamber of Commerce Address," *Los Angeles Times*, February 7, 2011.
3   Center for Responsive Politics, www.opensecrets.org/lobby/top.php?indexType=s.
4   This, and all subsequent information about Chamber organization, is drawn from the Chamber's website, www.uschamber.com.
5   Philip A. Mundo, *Interest Groups: Cases and Controversies* (Chicago: Nelson Hall, 1992).
6   Mark A. Smith, *American Business and Political Power* (Chicago: University of Chicago Press, 2000), 47–48. As Smith notes, this can be observed in the testimony provided by Chamber lobbyists to congressional committees—spokespersons for the Chamber are generally not able to respond orally to questions, but must submit written responses after getting approval from the Chamber leadership or relevant policy committees.
7   Incidentally, this is a problem that labor unions have as well; the PACs of individual unions tend to be stronger than the AFL-CIO's PAC.
8   For discussion, see Robert G. Boatright, Michael J. Malbin, Mark Rozell, and Clyde Wilcox, "BCRA's Impact on Interest Groups and Advocacy Organizations," in *Life After Reform: When the Bipartisan Campaign Reform Act Meets Politics,* ed. Michael J. Malbin, (Lanham, MD: Rowman & Littlefield, 2003), 17–43.

9   This and all subsequent campaign finance data is drawn from the Center for Responsive Politics, www.opensecrets.org, unless otherwise noted.

10 A full explanation is available at www.irs.gov/charities/nonprofits/article/0,,id=96 107,00.html.

11 Don Van Natta Jr. and John M. Broder, "With Finish Line in Sight, An All-Out Race for Money," *The New York Times*, November 3, 2000.

12 David B. Magleby, "Election Advocacy: Soft Money and Issue Advocacy in the 2000 Elections," in *Election Advocacy: Soft Money and Issue Advocacy in the 2000 Congressional Elections*, ed. David B. Magleby (Salt Lake City, UT: Center for the Study of Elections and Democracy, Brigham Young University, 2001); *Issue Advertising in the 1999-2000 Election Cycle* (Philadelphia: Annenberg Public Policy Center of the University of Pennsylvania).

13 For more on the access vs. influence distinction see John R. Wright, *Interest Groups and Congress* (New York: Pearson, 2003), 153–157.

14 527 groups, named for the section of the U.S. tax code under which they were organized, are political organizations that do not contribute money, and thus are not subject to contribution limits. Although some such groups existed in the 1990s, many were formed in 2004 as a response to the Bipartisan Campaign Reform Act's restrictions on contributions to the political parties and on interest group advocacy. For discussion, see Robert G. Boatright, "Situating the New 527 Organizations in Interest Group Theory," *The Forum* 5, no. 2 (2007).

15 See the FEC statement on the matter, http://eqs.nictusa.com/eqsdocs/29044223819.pdf.

16 Stephen R. Weissman and Kara D. Ryan, *Soft Money in the 2006 Election and the Outlook for 2008: The Changing Nonprofits Landscape* (Washington, DC: Campaign Finance Institute, 2007).

17 Campaign Finance Institute, *501(c) Groups Emerge as Big Players Alongside 527s* (Washington, DC: Campaign Finance Institute, October 31, 2008).

18 Campaign Finance Institute, *Soft Money Political Spending by 501(c) Nonprofits Tripled in 2008 Election* (Washington, DC: Campaign Finance Institute, February 25, 2009).

19 These are both categorized by the Internal Revenue Service as 501(c)(4) groups, organizations that can engage in some political activities but the majority of whose spending is nonpolitical.

20 These are classified by the Internal Revenue Service as 501(c)(3) groups, charitable groups that do not engage in politics.

21 For the official Federal Election Commission discussion of electioneering, see www .fec.gov/pages/brochures/electioneering.shtml#Electioneering_Communications.

22 Eric Lipton, Mike McIntire, and Don Van Natta Jr., "Top Corporations Aid US Chamber Campaign." *The New York Times*, 21 October, 2010; see also the Annenberg Fact Check page on the Chamber, http://factcheck.org/2010/08/us-chamber-of-commerce/; and Dan Eggen, "U. S. Chamber of Commerce Sets Sights on Democrats Ahead of Midterm Elections," *Washington Post*, March 16, 2010, on the Chamber's goal of spending at least $50 million.

23 Lipton, McIntire, and Van Natta, "Top Corporations Aid US Chamber Campaign."

24 This number includes special elections (discussed later), and one state (Colorado, also discussed later) where the Chamber backed a candidate in the primary and then backed another in the general election.

25 For discussion of the tone of interest group advertising, see Michael M. Franz, Paul B. Freedman, Kenneth M. Goldstein, and Travis N. Ridout, *Campaign Advertising and American Democracy* (Philadelphia: Temple University Press, 2008).

26 A detailed breakdown of PAC contributions in 2010 is not provided here largely because the amount contributed by the PAC is dwarfed by the amount spent through the 501(c)(6) on electioneering. The basic patterns described subsequently here—a greater tilt toward Republicans in the Senate than in the House, an emphasis on competitive races, and a preference for some Democratic incumbents but no Democratic challengers or open-seat candidates—hold for PAC contributions as well.

27 It is conventional in studies such as this to provide data on support for candidates in competitive and uncompetitive races. This is not provided here for two reasons. First, independent expenditures are rarely made in uncompetitive races, while PAC contributions sometimes are; second, the extremely fluid nature of the 2010 race and the lopsided margins in so many elections where Democrats were at one point viewed as safe makes competitiveness measures questionable for this election cycle.

28 See Eggen, "U.S. Chamber of Commerce Sets Sights on Democrats ahead of Midterm Elections" for claims about the Chamber's interest in defeating Democrats.

29 See Ronald Brownstein, "Pulling Apart," *National Journal*, February 26, 2011, 18–25, and the vote rankings that accompany Brownstein's article.

30 See Brody Mullins, "Candidates Hustle to Get Out Nevada's Vote," *The Wall Street Journal*, November 1, 2010 for a discussion of the Chamber's relationship with Reid.

31 Bill Miller, "On the Verge of a New Beginning for Business," *Chamber Post*, November 1, 2010, www.chamberpost.com/2010/11/on-the-verge-of-a-new-beginning-for-business/

32 See *The Washington Post*'s election spending tracker, www.washingtonpost.com/wp-srv/politics/campaign/2010/spending/committee_list.html.

33 Miller, "On the Verge of a New Beginning for Business."

34 Alex Isenstadt, "Third-Party Election Spending Surges," *Politico*, May 5, 2010.

35 Dan Eggen and Michael D. Shear, "Chamber of Commerce Losing Battles Against Obama," *The Washington Post*, July 22, 2010.

36 Michael D. Shear, "Rift Between Obama and Chamber of Commerce Widening," *Washington Post*, October 20, 2009.

37 Scott Wong, "U. S. Chamber Takes Aim at Dems," *Politico*, September 9, 2010.

38 Tom Collamore, "CFE Hits Social Media Milestone," *Chamber Post*, December 2, 2010, www.chamberpost.com/2010/12/cfe-hits-social-media-milestone-takes-over-cap-south-metro-station/.

39 U.S. Chamber of Commerce, "U.S. Chamber and Business Leaders Blitz Capitol Hill," U.S. Chamber of Commerce press release, September 15, 2010, www.uschamber.com/press/releases/2010/september/us-chamber-and-business-leaders-blitz-capitol-hill.

40 Jim Kuhnhenn, "US Chamber Spends More Than $10 Million on Ads," *The Washington Post*, October 7, 2010.

41 Brody Mullins, "Impact of Money Mixed in Midterm," *The Wall Street Journal*, November 8, 2010; Bennett Roth and Alex Knott, "Chamber Ramps up Political Spending but Will Likely Miss Goal," *Roll Call*, November 1, 2010.

42 Jeanne Cummings, "GOP Groups Coordinated Spending," *Politico*, November 3, 2010.

43　Tom Hamburger and Kathleen Hennessey, "Conservatives Struggle to Unify Voter Outreach," *Los Angeles Times*, October 26, 2010.

44　Chris Frantes, "Chamber: Dem Regulations Onerous," *Politico*, October 6, 2010.

45　Ibid.

46　Bill Miller, "We've Come a Long Way."

47　For discussion see Robert G. Boatright, *Interest Groups and Campaign Finance Reform in the United States and Canada* (Ann Arbor: University of Michigan Press, 2011), 115–27.

48　James Warren, "Tea Party Pure, With Idiosyncrasies," *The New York Times*, September 25, 2010; Nathan Gonzalez, "Friend of Foe, U.S. Chamber Plays Both Roles for Democrats," *Roll Call*, October 9, 2010.

49　Kevin Freking, "Spin Meter: Business Group Turns on Past Allies," *The Washington Post*, October 4, 2010.

50　Martin Vaughn, "Some CEOs Defend Stimulus." *Wall Street Journal*, October 28, 2010.

51　Greg Sargent, "Many Chamber Ads Attacking House Dems Contain Debunked Falsehoods, Distortions," *The Plum Line Blog, Washington Post*, October 18, 2010, http://voices.washingtonpost.com/plum-line/2010/10/many_chamber_ads_attacking_hou.html; see also Kim Geiger, "U.S. Chamber of Commerce Launches Boxer Attack Ads," *Los Angeles Times*, October 19, 2010.

52　For discussion, see Trevor Potter and Kirk L. Jowers, "Speech Governed by Federal Election Laws," in *The New Campaign Finance Sourcebook*, ed. Anthony Corrado, Thomas E. Mann, Daniel R. Ortiz, and Trevor Potter (Washington, DC: Brookings Institution, 2005), 205–231.

53　"Turn California Around – Central Valley Water," www.youtube.com/watch?v=FF594R-YhHA.

54　See the group's website, www.fixtheuschamber.org/.

55　Kenneth P. Vogel, "To Left, Leaked e-mails Validate Aggressive Tactics," *Politico*, February 23, 2011.

56　Jim Rutenberg, "With Another $1 Million Donation, Murdoch Expands His Political Sphere," *The New York Times*, October 1, 2010; Eric Lipton, Mike McIntire, and Don Van Natta Jr., "Top Corporations Aid U.S. Chamber of Commerce Campaign," *The New York Times*, October 21, 2010.

57　Elizabeth Williamson, "Democrats Aim to Curb GOP Donors," *The Wall Street Journal*, October 12, 2010.

58　See, for instance, Eric Licthblau, "Democrats Sue to Force U.S. Election Agency to Reveal Political Donations," *The New York Times*, April 22, 2011.

59　U.S. Chamber of Commerce, "DISCLOSE Act is Partisan Effort to Silence Critics and Gain Political Advantage," U.S. Chamber of Commerce press release, May 20, 2010, www.uschamber.com/press/releases/2010/may/us-chamber-disclose-act-partisan-effort-silence-critics-and-gain-political-a.

60　Lee Fang, "Exclusive: Foreign-Funded 'U.S.' Chamber of Commerce Running Partisan Attack Ads," *Think Progress*, October 5, 2010, http://thinkprogress.org/2010/10/05/foreign-chamber-commerce/.

61　Helene Cooper, "Obama Calls for Voters to Outweigh Outside Money," *The New York Times*, October 7, 2010; Scott Wong, "Franken Seeks Probe of Foreign Cash," *Politico*,

October 6, 2010; "Axelrod: U.S. Chamber Using Foreign Cash to Fund GOP Campaigns," *The Wall Street Journal*, October 10, 2010; Michael Rubinkam, "Biden Criticizes GOP Outside Fundraising Effort," *The Washington Post*, October 11, 2010; Faiz Shakir, "How the Chamber Gets Its Foreign Money," *Think Progress*, October 9, 2010, http://thinkprogress.org/2010/10/09/nyt-wp-on-chamber/.

62 Lee Fang, "How the 'US' Chamber Uses its Money to Pay Pundits, Manipulate Google, and Create Fake News Outlets," *Think Progress*, October 28, 2010, http://think progress.org/2010/10/28/thinkprogress-media-chamber/.

63 Mike Allen, "Rove Claims Obama 'Enemies List,'" *Politico*, October 10, 2010; Glenn Thrush, "W.H. Villain Hurls Charges at Obama," *Politico*, October 11, 2010.

64 Michael D. Shear, "Chamber of Commerce Vows to 'Ramp Up' Political Activity," *The New York Times*, October 12, 2010.

65 See, for instance, Edward L. Monroe, Deposition of Plaintiffs Associated Builders and Contractors in the U.S. District Court (District of Columbia) Three Judge Court, *McConnell et.al. v. Federal Election Commission et.al.*, Case No. 02-0582, September 12, 2002.

66 Sam Stein, "Chamber Argued that Public Skepticism Was Proper Price to Pay for Donor Secrecy," *The Huffington Post*, October 11, 2010, www.huffingtonpost .com/2010/10/11/chamber-argued-that-publi_n_758435.html.

67 Douglas Schoen, "2010 Election Survey," www.douglasschoen.com/pdf/schoen_ survey_questionnaire_2010_election.pdf.

68 See David A. Farenthold, "Apple Leaves U.S. Chamber Over Its Climate Position," *The Washington Post*, October 6, 2009; for a copy of Apple's letter to Tom Donahue, see http://graphics8.nytimes.com/packages/pdf/business/apple-chamber.pdf. For dis- cussion, see Devin Leonard, "Tom Donahue: Obama's Tormentor," *Bloomberg Businessweek*, November 3, 2010.

69 Jeanne Cummings, "Angry Member Groups Shun Chamber," *Politico*, December 7, 2010; Ross Kerber, "Activcists Pressure U.S. Companies on Political Money," *Reuters*, November 5, 2010; Katrina vanden Heuvel, "Chamber of Commerce Backlash," *The Washington Post*, November 2, 2010.

70 Devin Leonard, "Tom Donahue: Obama's Tormentor."

71 See, for example, Elizabeth Williamson, "Businesses Seek to Sway Incoming Wave of Republicans," *The Wall Street Journal*, November 3, 2010.

72 Mike Allen, "Obama Plans Truce With Chamber," *Politico*, November 20, 2010; Michael D. Shear, "After Months of Feuding, Obama Makes Overture to Business Group," *The New York Times*, November 4, 2010.

73 John Harwood, "Obama and U.S. Business Sheath Weapons for Now," *The New York Times*, February 7, 2011.

74 Tom Collamore, "President Obama Address U.S. Chamber: Our View," *Chamber Post*, February 7, 2011, www.chamberpost.com/2011/02/president-obama-addresses-us- chamber-our-view/.

75 Jim Rutenberg, "Conservative Donor Groups Lay a Base for 2012 Elections," *The New York Times*, October 31, 2010; Kate Zernike, "Secretive Republican Donors are Planning Ahead," *The New York Times*, October 19, 2010.

76 See, for example, Jim Kuhnhenn, "Election of 2012 Promises to Push Campaign Money Boundaries; Past Two Elections Set the Stage," *Los Angeles Times*, November 8, 2010.

CHAPTER 3

Drugs, Doctors, and Hospitals

Campaigning Post–Health Care Reform

Suzanne M. Robbins

On March 23, 2010, the Patient Protection and Affordable Care Act became law. This landmark legislation overhauled the American health care system, guaranteeing health insurance for millions of previously uninsured Americans. Specifically, more children would gain access to health care, young adults would maintain coverage via their parents until age twenty-six, and those with preexisting conditions would no longer face discrimination in insurance coverage. In addition, seniors gained discounts on prescription drugs and small businesses received tax credits to cover their employees.[1] In short, health care became more accessible to more people. The drama leading up to the president's signature included the rise of the Tea Party, discussions of death panels, and extensive partisan maneuvering, with the act earning the irreverent name "ObamaCare" from its more conservative opponents.[2] Organized interests—including those representing the drug industry, medical professionals, and health institutions—chose to work within the political process to protect their constituents' interests. Despite the discordant political atmosphere during policy formation and 2010 midterm elections, the key players representing these industries chose to continue a pattern of working within existing governmental and legal frameworks. Since the election, these same organizations have forged relations with newly elected members, while maintaining preexisting relationships.

This chapter focuses on the legislative and electoral behavior of three crucial groups representing these drug, medical doctor, and health care institutions: the Pharmaceutical Research and Manufacturers Association (PhRMA), the American Medical Association (AMA), and the American Hospital Association (AHA).[3] All three organizations supported health care reform in part due to some of the deals they struck with the Obama administration. For example, through PhRMA, the drug industry bargained for rules that would limit competition from generic drugs.

Through their respective organizations, medical doctors and hospitals agreed to lower Medicare payments in the short term in return for the bigger windfalls reform promised.[4] In particular, AMA's "support for the principles" of the legislation was an important political win for supporters of the legislation, given AMA's historical opposition to health care reform.[5] The AMA and PhRMA joined the coalition Healthy Economy Now, with PhRMA providing a "substantial investment" in the multimillion-dollar advertising campaign to push for passage of the Affordable Care Act.[6]

The three groups were powerhouse lobbying forces during the 111th Congress (2009–2010). Moreover, all three organizations were active in the 2010 elections, following the traditional strategy of supporting individuals likely to win (incumbents) and the party in power, while making strategic choices in open-seat races. In other words, they followed an investment strategy that appeared partially independent of partisanship, consistent with research on established nonideological groups and businesses.[7] They also acted traditionally, in that they did not take advantage of newer legal structures such as 527s or super PACs described in Chapter 1. These groups played insider politics, or supported the status quo, rather than pursue an ideological pattern to encourage a shift in the majority party or a major shake-up in who makes policy.

Organization and Behavior

PhRMA, AMA, and AHA represent drugs, doctors, and hospitals. By many accounts, they are considered among the most powerful organized interests electorally and legislatively, or the lead organizations for their respective sectors of the economy, though they are not the only organizations to represent these interests.[8] For example, over fifty other organizations represent hospitals, hospices, and nursing homes in the electoral process, such as the American Health Care Association (representing nursing homes) and the Federation of American Hospitals. Likewise, health professionals can choose to join any other of over one hundred professional and specialty organizations, such as the American Chiropractic Association, the American Nurses Association, or the American Academy of Pediatrics. The most important players among health professionals though, include medical doctors (the AMA), dentists (the American Dental Association) and anesthesiologists (American Society of Anesthesiologists). The pharmaceutical industry is interesting, in that not only does it find representation through trade associations like PhRMA, the American Herbal Products Association, or the National Wholesale Druggists Association, but directly through the various companies manufacturing drugs and drug products. In fact, Pfizer, Merck, AstraZeneca, and others all contribute more to campaigns as individual companies than PhRMA does, though the group outlobbies its member companies. These groups, like many organized interests, do not rely solely on money and campaigns to achieve their goals; they also direct their resources toward providing quality political and policy information to their membership as well as policymakers.[9]

Group Resources and Information

The three organizations have much in common, differing primarily in the resources they bring to bear. Both the medical doctors and hospitals are long-established organizations, in existence for more than 100 years. The American Medical Association is federated, with member societies across the fifty states, which can better facilitate individual membership, while AHA maintains regional offices. PhRMA, however, is a newer trade association, primarily representing businesses, such as Glaxo-Smith Kline or Eli Lily, with interests in drugs worldwide. The doctors' group has the largest revenue of the three, topping $273 million dollars in 2010; they likewise have the largest staff available.[10] Politically, all three lobby government and participate in federal elections. All three own a separate political action committee (PAC) and have subsidiary units including charitable foundations. Of the three, only PhRMA maintains a 527 organization. In terms of the 2010 election, the American Hospital Association's PAC had the largest budget for expenditures, followed by the doctors' PAC (see Table 3.1 for details).

The American Medical Association represents physicians and local medical societies, focusing on liability reform, physician payments, patient safety, as well as overall health care and Medicare reform. In general, it uses multiple tactics to achieve its goals, not all related to advocacy or electoral activity, including maintaining professional standards for the practice of medicine. In particular, this professional association disseminates scientific information through conferences and publications such as *American Medical News* and the *Journal of the American Medical Association*, to inform doctors and the public. It educates members regarding the potential consequences of policy change to the profession while also informing decision makers about potential political and policy outcomes from government action.

The American Hospital Association represents hospitals and other health care provider organizations with a primary focus on improving public health. Also active in research-oriented information, it focuses on emerging trends in the area of hospitals, including provider payment, health care costs, information technology, as well as health care reform and Medicare/Medicaid issues.

The Pharmaceutical Research and Manufacturers Association focuses on the regulatory facets of drug manufacturing, sales, and use. It too relies on information-based techniques, on issues such as existing and pending governmental policies, including patents, manufacturing practices, research standards and quality control issues, though not on specific drugs its members produce.

TABLE 3.1   Organizational Characteristics

	American Medical Association (AMA)	American Hospital Association (AHA)	Pharmaceutical Researchers & Manufacturers Association (PhRMA)
Headquarters	Chicago,	Chicago,	Washington, D.C.
Other offices	Washington D.C., NJ; federated	Washington D.C.; nine regional offices	Albany, Atlanta, Baton Rouge, Boston, Denver, Indianapolis, Olympia, St. Paul, Sacramento, Amman, and Tokyo
Founded	1847	1898	1958
Legal structure			
Tax status	501(c)(6)	501(c)(6)	501(c)(6)
PAC	AMPAC	AHA PAC	PhRMA Better Government Committee
Super PAC	No	No	No
527	No	No	PhRMA
Other	Yes	Yes	Yes
Members	297,000	37,000	63
Primary member type	Individuals	Organizations	Organizations
Staff	1045	502	80
Organizational revenue	$273,800,000	$98,700,000	$2,500,000
PAC budget, 2010	$3,600,000	$3,900,000	$210,700

Source: AMA Staff and Revenue Data from AMA 2010 Annual Report "Moving Medicine Forward," www.ama-assn.org/resources/doc/about-ama/2010-annual-report.pdf; AMPAC budget available from AMPAC, last modified 2011, www.ampaconline.org/about-us/ampac-election-report/; AHA Staff and Revenue Data from AHA 2009 Form 990, www.aha.org/aha/about/Organization/index.html; PhRMA Revenue Data from *National Trade and Professional Associations of the United States* (Bethesda: Columbia Books, 2010); PAC Budget Data for AHA and PhRMA from the Center for Responsive Politics, "Influence and Lobbying: Political Action Committees," www.opensecrets.org/pacs/index.php, based on data released by the FEC on April 25, 2011; all other data from Associations Unlimited, Gale Databases, 2011.

Advocacy and Electioneering

While all three associations focus on different aspects of health care, the strategies for representing their respective memberships are similar. Like most interest groups, they spend time keeping their membership informed about the latest developments in the substantive field of interest (i.e, medical or pharmaceutical research) as well as informing decision makers of what will best advance their member interests, which includes public health. They do so using both electoral and legislative strategies.

The three groups lobby the federal government extensively, as noted in Figure 3.1. From 1999–2010, spending on lobbying combined has nearly doubled, from $35.6 to $68.4 million.[11] The groups have roughly tracked one another in spending. PhRMA's spending started modestly, relative to medical professionals (one-third) and the health institutions (one-half), eclipsing both organizations in lobbying by 2006. Spending for all three is increasing on average. Each group relies extensively on in-house lobbyists to disseminate its message, though they also make use of contract lobbyists, particularly PhRMA.

The groups differ over time in how much they invest in federal elections, as seen in Figure 3.2.[12] The PACs for both doctors and hospitals are big players in the

FIGURE 3.1   Total Lobbying Expenditures, 1999–2010

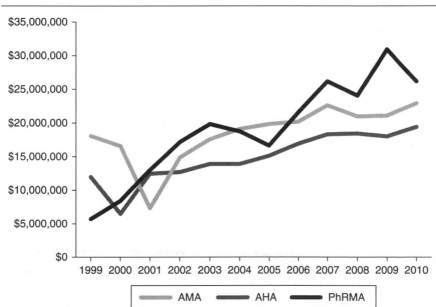

Source: Data compiled by author from the U.S. Senate Lobbying Disclosure Database, http://senate.gov/legislative/Public_Disclosure/LDA_reports.htm.

campaign finance game. Since 1998, the doctors (through AMPAC) have spent more than $23.5 million dollars on congressional elections, while the hospitals' organization has spent slightly more than half that amount, or about $13.4 million. In contrast, PhRMA's Better Government Committee has spent only $685,000 over the same time period. What Figure 3.2 does not show is that PhRMA's spending is increasing—it just does not match the scale of the other two political action committees. Notice, too, that AMPAC has been reducing its campaign finance expenditures in recent elections, most notably in the 2010 elections. According to its website, this was intentional: "AMPAC made a strategic decision to husband resources for the critical 2012 redistricting elections to ensure a significant role by organized medicine."[13] This strategy echoes findings regarding quality challengers' choices to forgo running for election prior to redistricting.[14] From a business perspective, it is perfectly rational to wait, as less uncertainty simplifies decision making.

These expenditure amounts include both regulated or disclosed funds to candidates (hard money, discussed in Chapter 1) as well as disclosed independent expenditures on behalf of candidates. During this time period, the doctors led in independent expenditures, averaging over $1.5 million per electoral cycle—except in 2010, when they chose not to use this type of spending, which accounts for some

FIGURE 3.2   Total Electoral Expenditures for Federal Candidates, 1998–2010

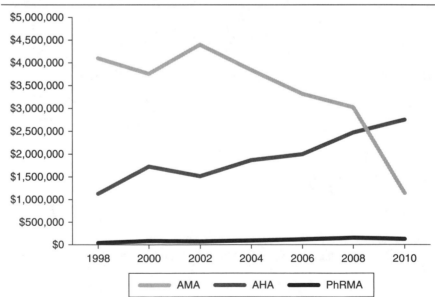

Source: Data compiled by the author from the Center for Responsive Politics, www.open secrets.org.

of the steep decline in 2010 expenditures. The hospital PAC's use of independent expenditures on behalf of a candidate is increasing, moving from approximately $98,000 in 1998, to nearly one million dollars in 2010. PhRMA's Better Government Committee did not use this form of expenditure during this time period, and while it has a 527, the last time it spent money from its 527 was in 2006.[15]

The 2010 Federal Elections

Electoral strategies are much less direct in terms of legislative influence. Giving money to candidates may be considered a form of buying votes or buying access, though the evidence remains clouded in answering the question of influence.[16] More simply, electoral contributions may be conceived as investments—to either maintain a favorable coalition or to change the cast of characters to achieve a legislature more in tune with a group's desires.[17] The former strategy suggests that groups give to the party in power, as well as those most likely to win. In practice, this means contributing to incumbents, and contributing more to those incumbents who are in the majority.

In the 2010 midterm elections, all three organizations had something to protect; they had won significant gains in their bargains over the Patient Protection and Affordable Care Act. Though each still desired modifications, none wanted to completely overhaul the law. This differed in significant ways from the last major attempt to overhaul health care, under President Clinton (1993–1994). President Clinton's initiative failed to pass; and many organizations, notably the AMA, did not support the legislation. The election that followed also was historic in nature, as the Republicans took control of Congress then as in 2010. In both elections, health care organizations participated broadly in the elections, primarily supporting incumbents, but also were active in key races. Their electoral strategies did not change much after federal rule changes (such as the *Citizens United* case); in fact, they reflect a great deal of path dependence, or doing what they have always done before.[18]

Some preelection analyses suggested that groups such as the hospital organizations favored Democrats in incumbent races, but favored Republicans in open-seat campaigns, suggesting either partisan balance or protection of those who voted for the Affordable Care Act. Evidence from early contribution data suggested that all three organizations avoided supporting challenges to incumbents, especially Democrats, who voted in favor of the law. The American Hospital Association specifically denied having a partisan leaning in its contribution patterns or for rewarding members for their support for the health care legislation. In fact, its electioneering communications, discussed subsequently, suggest otherwise. In an interview with the *National Journal*, Mark Seklecki, AHA vice president for political affairs, stated: "Our giving is not based on, 'Did you support health care reform, yes or no?' We have never been a single-issue group. I don't think we will ever be. We have far too many issues at play in one cycle."[19] The evidence from the final election reports suggests that all three groups were doing what most astute business organizations do: supporting bipartisan incumbents, or those in office, rather than following an ideologically motivated giving strategy.[20]

Giving, the Old-Fashioned Way

In 2010, all three of the organizations' PACs chose to use the most transparent of activities, hard money contributions, for their electoral investments. Of the three, only the hospital association chose to use independent expenditures or in-kind contributions, while the medical association had some communications costs related to working with its state societies. Maintenance strategies suggest protecting investments across chambers, though House incumbents are generally less vulnerable than senators.[21] Because incumbents rarely lose, it also is possible to invest early, such as during the primary season.

The health care institutions sector, which includes hospitals, spent more than $8 million dollars in the 2010 midterm elections. The American Hospital Association easily outspent other organizations in the sector, with $2.7 million. In comparison, the other hospital organization within this sector, the Federation of American Hospitals, spent $425,000. The next closest spender to AHA, the American Health Care Association, spent $1.2 million.[22] The hospital PAC used about two-thirds of its donations in hard money form, those contributions limited to $5,000 per candidate, per election. Individual candidates then spend these funds at their own discretion. The sector as a whole favored Democrats, in particular, three senators: Charles Schumer (D-N.Y.), Harry Reid (D-Nev.), and Ron Wyden (D-Wash.). All three retained their seats, with only Reid encountering any real opposition. Regardless of the election year, however, the hospital PAC provides 77 to 88 percent of its funds in House races, and generally backs candidates early in the primary season.

The health professionals sector was the most generous with donations in 2010, spending $28.6 million, or more than three times as much as the other two sectors (this is the largest of the three as well). The medical doctor's PAC was not the largest donor within this sector, spending only $1.1 million in the election. Eight other specialty organizations spent more than AMPAC, with the American Society of Anesthesiologists disbursing almost double that of the doctors. In general, this sector as a whole supported Democrats in 2010, though they generally favor Republicans. The top three recipients from this sector were in Senate races, including independent candidate Charlie Christ's (I-Fla.) unsuccessful Senate race, and two successes, Majority Leader Harry Ried's (D-Nev.) fight with Tea Party candidate Sharon Angle (R-Nev.) and Rep. Mark Kirk's (R-Ill.) open-seat bid for President Obama's old seat. Like AHA, the medical doctors generally have favored

House races over Senate races, though they prefer to wait and invest in the general election.

The pharmaceutical and manufacturing sector paid out slightly more than the hospitals, at $8.5 million. Like the doctors though, other PACs outspent PhRMA's Better Government Committee (a mere $124,000 in hard money contributions). Fifteen corporations, twelve of which belong to the trade association, disbursed far more in 2010, amounting to 82 percent of the entire sector's spending. Pharmaceuticals as a whole favored Democrats only slightly more than Republicans; the top three candidates receiving support were all incumbents, representing both chambers: Sen. Richard Burr (R-N.C.), Sen. Harry Reid (D-Nev.), and Rep. Steny Hoyer (D-Md.). Unlike the doctors and hospitals, PhRMA sometimes focuses on the House, other times, as in 2010, on the Senate; they also invest early—backing candidates before they faced any real opposition.

Protecting Earlier Investments: Support Incumbents!

Incumbents are generally a safe bet in normal electoral cycles, and early investments can ward off quality challengers, insuring the bet.[23] In 2010, twelve senators and thirty-seven representatives chose to retire, creating open-seat contests. In the Senate, only twenty-five incumbents were up for reelection—twenty-three at the end of their full terms and two completing shorter terms created by vacancies—as opposed to the entire House.[24] When the dust settled, the Republicans had gained six seats in the Senate, with three each coming from open-seat races and defeated incumbents, though the Democratic party remained in the majority. In the House, Republicans gained fifteen seats from open-seat contests and defeated fifty-two Democratic incumbents to win back the chamber. Similarly, in 1994, Republicans picked up eight Senate seats and fifty-four House seats, giving them control of both chambers for the first time since 1952.

Impressive as this sounds, incumbents still won handily: in 1994, 90 percent of all incumbents won reelection (as opposed to 88 percent in 1992); in 2010, 85 percent won (as opposed to 94 percent in 2008). In all four elections, hospitals and pharmaceuticals invested at least 80 percent of their expenditures on incumbents. In 2008 and 2010, PhRMA chose this "sure" bet for 90 percent of its expenditures. Only the medical doctors appear to have a more open approach to spending, though not much more: 70 percent of its PAC resources also go to incumbents. AMPAC found open-seat races more compelling in 2010 than in 2008, allocating 22 percent of its resources to these races; in 2008 it supported more challengers. This is in part due to the fact that AMPAC often supports its physician members who choose to run for office such as state senator Andy Harris (R-Md.) and Democrat Ami Bera of California. In these races, AMPAC backed both candidates with communications to its local membership, winning the seat in Maryland. [25]

Support in these open-seat races did not always correlate with support for the Affordable Care Act, as both the medical doctors and health care institutions donated to Rand Paul (R-Ky.) in his successful Senate candidacy, despite his strong opposition to the law. Other candidates receiving financial support from these two groups, despite their issue positions, include former Florida Gov. Marco Rubio (R-Fla.) and Rep. Pat Toomey (R-Pa.), each of whom won their Senate races. The Pennsylvania Medical Society publicly endorsed Toomey, despite the national organization's no endorsement policy. In all three races, polls showed clear leads for these candidates near the time of contributions, suggesting that both organizations were desirous of establishing friendly relations with likely winners in these open-seat contests. In the Toomey race versus Rep. Joe Sestak (D-Pa.), AMPAC justified its financial support with Toomey's proposed positions on other issues of concern to the organization, including litigation and physician reimbursement. In an interview with the *National Journal*, AMA president Wilson noted, "This would be an easy job if everyone had a 100 percent record on issues we support. I think the important thing to emphasize is that it's not as simple as one issue or the other. It's a matter of where candidates stand in general."[26]

If business and nonideological PACs generally support incumbents, then that support also should be bipartisan, with a slight tilt toward the majority party. But a close look at giving patterns over these four elections reveals some partisan leanings (see Figure 3.3). Historically, the American Hospital Association supports Democratic candidates, with as much as 70 percent of its funds allocated to them in 1992; however, that support has waned over time, to just over 57 percent in 2010, even though the Democratic party held both chambers in all four elections. Both AMA and PhRMA have increased support for Democrats since 1992, with PhRMA investing 73 percent of its funds in Democratic candidates in 2010, up from 47 percent in 1992. In an interview with the *National Journal*, PhRMA indicated that increased support for Democrats simply correlates with the fact that more of them are in office, and that they try to "be politically relevant in a bipartisan way."[27] In another interview, PhRMA president Castellani noted that "[o]ur mantra is to work with whomever is in charge."[28] In other words, these organizations purport to act pragmatically, not ideologically.

The American Hospital Association PAC also spent $910,000 in independent expenditures on behalf of candidates. They supported seven different candidates, with 60 percent of expenditures on behalf of Republicans. Still, with the exception of two Senate races, these independent expenditures were for relatively safe incumbents—all won reelection by at least 14 percentage points. The two races with any real political interest were Rep. Mark Kirk's (R-Ill.) open-seat Senate bid and Sen. Blanche Lincoln's (D-Ark.) unsuccessful reelection.

Much of the political interest in the Lincoln race was in her highly contested primary, which she eventually won. Her primary opponent, Lt. Gov. Bill Halter,

FIGURE 3.3   Percent of Investment in Democratic Candidates

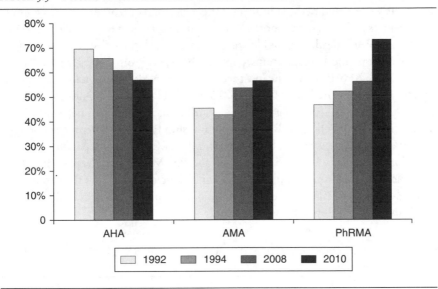

Source: Data compiled by author from the Center for Responsive Politics Bulk Data, www.opensecrets.org/myos/index.php.

had the support of many labor unions as well as MoveOn.org due to Lincoln's more conservative positions on health care and the environment. Lincoln withheld her support for the health care bill until the last minute, before finally voting in favor, despite its unpopularity in Arkansas. In the primary race she ran ads touting her "courageous vote" in favor of the legislation in an effort to win back supporters.[29] The American Hospital Association's PAC supported her reelection in the primary with both cash contributions and $251,000 in independent expenditures. In the general election, however, they chose to contribute to both Lincoln ($2,500) and her Republican opponent Rep. John Boozman ($1,000); Boozman went on to win the election with 57.9 percent of the vote.

The special election to fill President Obama's Senate seat between Kirk and state treasurer Alexi Giannoulias (D-Ill.) was much closer in outcome, with the race focusing more on character issues than on policy. Both candidates generally avoided the health care issue, though Kirk noted that he would lead an effort to repeal health care, and Giannoulias suggesting the timing, given the economy, was not appropriate.[30] Still, hospitals devoted $123,500 to Kirk in independent expenditures, though not until very late in the general election campaign.

Groups spend on other groups as well—not just candidates. They can contribute to party committees, leadership PACs, and other ideological committees; each of these groups can then help finance candidates. The motivations for doing so are beyond the scope of this chapter, but one can assume that organizations are attempting to curry favor, and perhaps indirectly affect electoral outcomes. Spending limits differ here, as groups can give more to party committees than to candidate committees or other PACs (leadership or ideological). In 2010, all three PACs gave to various types of other political organizations, particularly to party committees and leadership PACs, though AHAPAC was the most active in this type of campaign finance, spending $617,000, compared to AMPAC's $226,500 and PhRMA's $63,000. Unlike the hospital associations' spending patterns regarding party and chamber control discussed thus far, AHA favored Republican leadership PACs over Democratic leadership PACs (those PACs owned by current members of Congress, separate from their reelection campaigns). Meanwhile AMPAC and PhRMA favored the party in power, or Democratic leadership committees. When it came to supporting the two parties, however, both hospitals and medical professionals supported their traditional allies, the Democrats and Republicans, respectively.

TABLE 3.2   Contributions From AHAPAC, AMPAC and PhRMA to Other Political Organizations

PAC	AHA	AMA	PhRMA
Conservative PACs	$4,500		$5,000
Liberal PACs	14,500	10,000	2,500
Ideological PACs	10,750		
Democratic Leadership Committees	220,500	38,500	27,500
Republican Leadership Committees	242,500	22,500	24,000
Republican Joint Committees	15,000		4,000
Republican Party	45,000	90,000	
Democratic Party	60,000	60,000	
Other	4,500	5,500	
Total	617,250	226,500	63,000

Source: Data compiled by author from the Center for Responsive Politics Bulk Data, www .opensecrets.org/myos/index.php.

Various watchdog organizations were particularly concerned about third-party spending in the 2010 elections, especially in the wake of the *Citizens United* decision. *Third-party spending* is that which does not go directly to the candidates or parties, but to other organizations or on behalf of or in opposition to a candidate. This includes independent expenditures and communications costs, as well as electioneering communications, or advertising directly about a candidate within proximity to an election. The Center for Responsive Politics reported that outside organizations of all types spent more than $489 million dollars to engage in electioneering communications and involve the public in the midterm election. In addition to independent expenditures, the American Hospital Association also spent $585,000 for electioneering communications in support of five incumbent Democrats, only one of whom voted for the Affordable Care Act.[31] Only two of these incumbents, Rep. Mike Ross (D-Ark.) and Rep. Jason Altmire (D-Pa.) were reelected.

While not listed as an outside group with the Center for Responsive Politics, other news sources indicate that PhRMA spent $2.5 million in advertising to support six vulnerable Democratic representatives, only two of whom were reelected. In its advertising blitz, PhRMA defended its expenditures noting that they were "committed to helping build greater consensus and support for reform that ensures all Americans have access to high-quality and affordable healthcare coverage."[32] In other words, the group was attempting to improve support in the next congress for continuation of the new policy. Public Citizen also took on PhRMA in a "Stealth PAC" report alleging donations to third party groups in previous elections. Public Citizen asserted that PhRMA funneled "stealth" donations to groups such as the United Seniors Association, America 21, and 60 Plus Association.[33] Of these three organizations, however, only the 60 Plus Association was active in 2010, spending more than $7 million against fifty-two Democrats, twenty-eight of whom were defeated. The group does not disclose its donors; therefore it is difficult to verify PhRMA's involvement. But given the spending patterns of PhRMA elsewhere, it does not seem likely. Other sources indicated that, in the 2010 election, this support was for Democrats in highly contested races, such as Sen. Harry Reid (D-Nev.) and Sen. Patty Murray (D-Wash.).[34]

The Results: Did the Investments Pay Off Electorally?

The 2010 elections exhibited interesting dynamics leading up to November. Early prognostications suggested the Democrats would hold on to the House (which they did not) and the Senate (which they did). But the rise of the Tea Party movement influenced the health care debate and Republican primary dynamics. Many of these races garnered national media attention, such as the Delaware and Nevada Senate races. In general, however, how did the PACs do in terms of their investments?

When it came to incumbents, all three gave more on average to losing incumbents than to winning incumbents, as reported in Table 3.3. This suggests that these organizations were attempting to help shore up incumbents in trouble, as the previous discussion notes. The hospitals appear to have done a better job in targeting winning open seats and challengers— investing on average $4,870 and $3,275 per winning candidate, as opposed to $1,820 per incumbent. Doctors and pharmaceuticals also gave more on average to individual open-seat and challenger races, though not quite with the same success rate (in terms of dollars). Thus, while these organizations may give the lion's share of their budget to incumbents, they give more on average to those few races that may help improve their chances of favorable legislation in the future. That is, these organizations pursue a mixed strategy of maintaining access, while continuing to support like-minded legislators when the investment is likely to pay off.

TABLE 3.3   Average Expenditures on Winners and Losers, by Candidate Type, 2010

	AHA		AMA		PhRMA	
	Winner	*Loser*	*Winner*	*Loser*	*Winner*	*Loser*
Incumbent	$1,820.29	$2,434.17	$1,787.60	$2,040.82	$1,200.00	$1,153.85
Open seat	4,870.69	2,519.23	3,590.91	3,588.24	1,666.67	
Challenger	3,275.00	1,700.00	2,976.92	3,333.33		1,500.00

Source: Data compiled by author from the Center for Responsive Politics Bulk Data, www.opensecrets.org/myos/index.php.

Post–2010 Election and Lobbying Activity

Thus far, campaign contributions in the 2012 elections have been limited to hard money contributions, overwhelmingly to incumbents. Overall, the amounts thus far have been relatively small, with the AMA contributing $125,200 to forty-three representatives and ten senators. The AHA has contributed $595,000 to 225 representatives and forty senators. PhRMA has donated the least ($56,500) to twenty-eight representatives and eight senators. Generally, the AHA is giving slightly more (55 percent) to Democrats than to Republicans, while the AMA and PhRMA are financing Republicans by a heavier margin (60 percent and 56 percent respectively). Both the AHA and AMA have donated equally to the party congressional campaign committees. Closer inspection shows that the AHA is supporting Democrats in both chambers, while both the AMA and PhRMA are pursuing the age-old investment strategy of giving money to those who control power (see Figure 3.4).

Early on in the electoral cycle, both doctors and hospitals continued to support established members of Congress; they also are investing in freshmen members, though not necessarily using the same strategies. Hospitals appear to be investing more heavily in longer term incumbents, both in total dollars, and average contributions size. As such, they continue to cultivate relationships over time. They are giving more to newly elected Republicans than to newly elected Democrats, in part because there are simply more new Republicans than Democrats, suggesting that they are hedging their bets and cultivating new relationships. Doctors, on the other hand, appear to be returning to supporting newly elected Republicans exclusively. While they have been conservative in the amount of financing distributed thus far, 87 percent of their contributions to Republicans have been to new members.

Not surprisingly, all three organizations also reported extensive lobbying activity in 2011 following the 2010 midterm elections. Together, the three organizations spent $58.8 million dollars on health care related issues, about 10 million less than the year before. While health care issues certainly were on the agenda in 2011, the reduction in spending recognizes that the status quo in Washington usually wins.[35] In 2011, the Patient Protection and Affordable Care Act was part of the status quo, and not likely to disappear during the current Congress, especially under divided government. Early reports suggested that although repeal measures would be introduced, the Affordable

FIGURE 3.4   Contributions by Chamber and Party, 2012

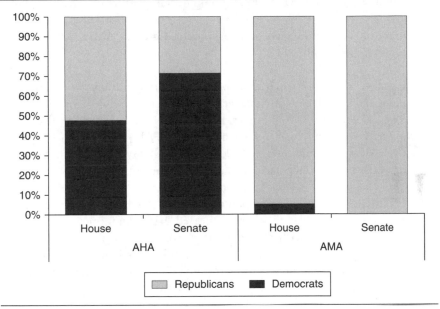

Source: Data compiled by author from U.S. Federal Election Commission files, downloaded May 15, 2011, from http://fec.gov/finance/disclosure/ftp_download.shtml. The data reflect first quarter 2011 filings only.

Care Act was more likely to be attacked one piece at a time. Dave Camp (R-Mich.), chair of the House Ways and Means Committee, explained the Republican strategy colorfully, "The tree is rotten, you cut it down—and if we can't cut it down and succeed doing that all at once, we'll prune it branch by branch."[36]

Moreover, recall that each organization bargained for favorable status with the legislation; repealing the legislation would be a net loss for these organizations. Instead, each has focused, and is likely to continue focusing upon, maintaining the gains while striving for improvements at the margins. PhRMA is likely to change direction in some ways, after criticism it received for its support for the Affordable Care Act, including spending over $150 million on issue advocacy to increase support for the legislation. Its director, former representative Billy Tauzin (R-La.), resigned in 2010, after the legislation passed, and was replaced with a more business-friendly individual. Still, though PhRMA was criticized for participation, the deal— and regulatory certainty—was a victory for Tauzin and PhRMA.[37]

In 2011, the AHA reported $18.4 million in lobbying expenses. In particular, the AHA reported lobbying on a multitude of health care issues. These include lobbying on specific legislation before congress, such as HR 541, Pay for All Your Procedures (PAYUP) Act and HR 452 Medicare Decisions Accountability Act. In addition, they have lobbied on labor issues, specifically HR 972, The Secret Ballot

Protection Act.[38] In general, the AHA is active on all dimensions of health care related to hospitals, from Medicare and billing to liability reform and employee relations.

On the one-year anniversary of the Affordable Care Act, AMA president Cecil Wilson said this about the law:

> Expanded health coverage, insurance-market reforms, administrative simplifications and initiatives to promote wellness and prevention are key parts of the new law that reflect AMA priorities. Improvements to the law are needed, and the AMA is working for major changes in the IPAB [Independent Payment Advisory Board] framework, expanded medical liability reforms, and elimination of the IRS 1099 reporting requirement, among other issues.[39]

This is reflected in the issues upon which they have been lobbying since the 2010 elections. In particular, they have supported legislation former physician and Rep. Phil Gingrey (R-Ga.) has introduced regarding medical liability and tort reform. The organization spent $21.5 million dollars lobbying government on these and other issues of interest to them, including physician payment, health system and managed care reform, and patient safety.[40]

PhRMA lobbied the federal government to the tune of $18.9 million. They have a slightly broader agenda than the other two groups. Specifically, they have lobbied on the budgets (both 2011 and 2012) with respect to funding the Food and Drug Administration, showed direct interest in patent reform and intellectual property issues, and make themselves heard on Medicare prescription versus generic drug policies. In addition, they have lobbied extensively on legislation to curb prescription drug abuse. PhRMA's international interests are evident in their interest in international free trade agreements on the agenda, such as with Korea.[41]

A Look to the Future

Going forward, all three groups will be paying attention to changes in government spending. In particular, groups are concerned about changes to Medicaid, Medicare, and the Affordable Care Act. In particular, the American Hospital Association is concerned about the uncompensated services under a new voucher style program for Medicare that has the potential for increasing costs for insured patients. Specifically, "If coverage is not expanded and the government does not pay its fair share, hospitals will be forced to 'cost shift,' or pass along the difference to the privately insured."[42] Moreover, the AHA began running issue advocacy ads early in 2011 arguing that additional cuts to Medicare will result in less efficient services, including shutting down emergency departments.[43] The American Medical Association also has much at stake in approaches to Medicare, only recently signaling support for the Obama administration's suggestions for overhauling "fee-for-service" and recognizing quality of service over volume of service in reimbursements.[44]

These groups will continue to build relations with new and senior members of Congress and lobbying on the issues that are central to their core mission. In addition, the organizations will work on building relations with their own membership, as in the case of the AMA, or building relations on Capitol Hill. During the debates leading up to passage of the Affordable Care Act, Representative Boehner (R-Ohio) accused PhRMA of "appeasement" stating that it "rarely works as a conflict resolution strategy," in making its deal with the Obama administration over prescription drug importation and patents.[45] The new president of PhRMA noted the following in an interview: "One of the things incumbent on us as an industry and us as an association is to rebuild bridges with people who were sore about the politics of health care reform. I am absolutely committed to do that."[46] In the meantime, expect these three organizations to continue to use every resource at their disposal, from political and policy information to campaign contributions to promote their organizations' goals and acquire access to the decision-making process.

Endnotes

1   "Understanding the Law," U.S. Department of Health and Human Services, www.healthcare.gov/law/introduction/index.

2   Lawrence R. Jacobs and Theda Skocpol, *Health Care Reform and American Politics: What Every American Needs to Know* (New York: Oxford University Press, 2010).

3   Throughout this chapter, short-hand terms refer to the three organizations, such as *drugs*, *doctors*, and *hospitals*, even though other organizations also represent these interests. This is to reduce confusion when relying on the alphabet soup of acronyms common with respect to these groups.

4   Jacobs and Skocpol, *Health Care Reform and American Politics*, 70–71.

5   Jeffrey Young, "AMA Conditionally Backs House Health Bill," *The Hill*, November 5, 2009, http://thehill.com/homenews/house/66569-ama-conditionally-backs-house-healthcare-bill.

6   Ben Smith and Kenneth P. Vogel, "Dem Officials Set Stage for Corporate Backed Health Care Campaign," *Politico*, October 16, 2009, www.politico.com/news/stories/1009/28362.html; Susan Crabtree, "PhRMA Defends Itself From Boehner Criticism," *The Hill*, August 18, 2009, http://thehill.com/homenews/administration/55331-phrma-defends-itself-from-boehner-criticism.

7   Paul Herrnson, "Interest Groups and Campaigns: The Electoral Connection," in *The Interest Group Connection: Electioneering, Lobbying and Policymaking in Washington*, 2nd ed., ed. Paul S. Herrnson et al. (Washington, DC: CQ Press, 2002); Margaret M. Conway, Joanne Connor Green, and Marian Currinder, "Interest Group Money in Elections," in *Interest Group Politics*, ed. Allan. J. Cigler and Burdett. A. Loomis

(Washington, DC: CQ Press, 2002); Marion Currinder, *Money in the House: Campaign Funds and Congressional Party Politics* (Boulder, CO: Westview Press, 2009); John R. Wright, *Interest Groups and Congress: Lobbying Contributions and Influence* (Boston: Allyn & Bacon, 1996).

8 See, for example, "Heavy Hitters: Top All Time Donors, 1989-2010," Center for Responsive Politics, last modified 2011, based on data released by the FEC on April 25, 2011, www .opensecrets.org/orgs/list.php?order=A; "Lobbying: Top Spenders," Center for Responsive Politics, last modified 2011, www.opensecrets.org/lobby/top.php?indexType=s; CQ Press, *Public Interest Group Profiles 2006-2007* (Washington, DC: CQ Press, 2006).

9 See, for example, John R. Wright, *Interest Groups and Congress: Lobbying Contributions and Influence*; Richard L. Hall and Alan V. Deardorff, "Lobbying as Legislative Subsidy," *American Political Science Review* 100 (2006): 69–84.

10 "Moving Medicine Forward: 2010 American Medical Association Annual Report," American Medical Association, www.ama-assn.org/resources/doc/about-ama/2010-annual-report.pdf.

11 U.S. Senate Lobbying Disclosure Database, http://senate.gov/legislative/Public_ Disclosure/LDA_reports.htm.

12 Data for this paragraph compiled by the author from the Center for Responsive Politics, www.opensecrets.org. Dollar amounts here and in Figure 3.2 reflect hard money, in-kind contributions, independent expenditures, and communications costs.

13 "AMPAC Election Report," AMPAC, www.ampaconline.org/about-us/ampac-election-report/.

14 Marc J. Hetherington, Bruce Larson, and Suzanne Gobletti, "The Redistricting Cycle and Strategic Candidate Decisions in U.S. House Races," *Journal of Politics* 65 (2003): 1221–34.

15 "Influence and Lobbying: Political Action Committees," based on data released by the FEC on April 25, 2011, www.opensecrets.org/pacs/index.php.

16 For a review, see Frank R. Baumgartner and Beth L. Leech, *Basic Interests: The Importance of Groups in Politics and Political Science* (Princeton, NJ: Princeton University Press, 1998).

17 Conway, Green and Currinder, "Interest Group Money in Elections."

18 All data from this section except data from the 2012 cycle compiled by author from the Center for Responsive Politics Bulk Data, www.opensecrets.org/myos/index.php. Data for the first quarter of the 2012 elections compiled by author from U.S. Federal Election Commission files, http://fec.gov/finance/disclosure/ftp_download.shtml.

19 Mark Seklecki, in Matthew DoBias, "Health Care Groups Do Balancing Act With Donations," *National Journal,* October 9, 2010.

20 Herrnson, "Interest Groups and Campaigns: The Electoral Connection"; Conway, Green, and Currinder, "Interest Group Money in Elections."

21 Barbara Sinclair, *The Transformation of the U.S. Senate* (Baltimore: Johns Hopkins University Press, 1989).

22 All data from this section except data from the 2012 cycle compiled by author from the Center for Responsive Politics Bulk Data, www.opensecrets.org/myos/index.php. Note that the figures in this section differ from the values on the Center for Responsive Politics. They note that the hospital sector spent $19.8 million in the election. This is

because they also include all individual contributions greater than $200 as part of that sector, if the individual is employed in that sector.

23 Gary Jacobson, "The Effects of Campaign Spending in House Elections: New Evidence for Old Arguments," *American Journal of Political Science,* 00 (1990): 334–62.

24 Five Senate vacancies had occurred over the previous two years, largely due to the advent of the Obama administration. Three of the appointed incumbents chose not to run during the 2010, adding to the number of open Senate seats. In total, therefore, thirty-seven Senate seats were contested, including two in New York.

25 Bera garnered 43.2 percent of the vote against Republican incumbent Dan Lundgren, though the Democrats entertained hopes of winning this seat; Harris beat Democratic incumbent Frank Kratovil with 54.2 percent of the vote.

26 Cecil Wilson, in Matthew DoBias, "AMA Endorses Candidate Seeking to Repeal Reform Law," *National Journal,* September 18, 2010.

27 Wes Metheny, in Matthew DoBias, "Health Care Groups Do Balancing Act With Donations," *National Journal,* October 9, 2010.

28 Ylan Q. Mui and Jia Lynn Yang, "Cooperation with Democrats May Haunt Firms," *The Washington Post,* November 2, 2010, Metro Edition.

29 Shailaigh Murray, "In Ad, Blanche Lincoln Showcases Her Vote for Unpopular Health Care Overhaul," *Washington Post Online Edition,* May 10, 2010, http://voices .washingtonpost.com/44/2010/05/in-ad-blanche-lincoln-showcase.html.

30 Jeff Coen, "Giannoulias, Kirk Quiet on Health Care," *Chicago Tribune,* October 26, 2010, http://articles.chicagotribune.com/2010-10-26/news/ct-met-senate-issues-healthcare-20101026_1_giannoulias-and-kirk-health-care-medicare-services.

31 "Outside Spending," Center for Responsive Politics, www.opensecrets.org/outside-spending/index.php.

32 Aaron Blake, "PhRMA Ad Buy for Six Dems Totals $2.5 Million," *The Hill,* July 1, 2009, http://thehill.com/blogs/blog-briefing-room/news/campaigns/49193-phrma-ad-buy-for-six-dems-totals-25-million.

33 Taylor Lincoln and Neal Pattison, "Big PhRMA's Stealth PACs: How the Drug Industry Uses 501(c) Nonprofit Groups to Influence Elections," Public Citizen Congress Watch (2004), www.stealthpacs.org/documents/092004Phrma.pdf.

34 Chris Frates, "PhRMA Quietly Spends Big in 2010," *Politico,* November 10, 2010, www.politico.com/news/stories/1110/44917.html.

35 For a discussion, see Frank R. Baumgartner, Jeffrey M. Berry, Marie Hojnacki, David C. Kimball, and Beth L. Leech, *Lobbying and Policy Change: Who Wins, Who Loses, and Why* (Chicago: University of Chicago Press, 2009); or Ronald G. Shaiko, "Making the Connection: Organized Interests, Political Representation, and the Changing Rules of the Game in Washington Politics," in *The Interest Group Connection,* ed. Paul S. Herrnson, Ronald G. Shaiko, and Clyde Wilcox (Washington, DC: CQ Press, 2002).

36 Dave Camp, in Emily Ethridge and Ben Weyl. "Next for GOP: Piecemeal Repeal." *CQ Weekly,* January 24, 2011.

37 Rebecca Adams, "PhRMA Casualty." *CQ Weekly,* February 15, 2010, 376. See also, Meghan McCarthy, "Castellani Might Help Mend PhRMA's Fences With GOP," *National Journal,* July 17, 2010.

38 American Hospital Association, *First Quarter Lobbying Report* (April 20, 2011), Senate Lobbying Disclosure Act Database, http://soprweb.senate.gov/index.cfm?event= selectfields.

39 Althea Fung, "Health Care Birthday Wishes," *National Journal Online*, March 24, 2011.

40 American Medical Association, First Quarter Lobbying Report (April 20, 2011), Senate Lobbying Disclosure Act Database, http://soprweb.senate.gov/index.cfm?event= selectfields.

41 Pharmaceutical Research and Manufacturing and Manufacturers Association, *First Quarter Lobbying Report* (April 20, 2011), Senate Lobbying Disclosure Act Database, http://soprweb.senate.gov/index.cfm?event=selectfields.

42 Rich Umdenstock, in Carol Eisenberg and Emily Ethridge, "Casting a Narrower Safety Net," *CQ Weekly,* April 11, 2011.

43 "N2K Health Care: Senate Rejects Ryan Budget Plan; List of Dems Who Want IPAB Repeal Grows," *National Journal Online*, May 26, 2011.

44 Matthew DoBias, "Health Care Providers This Week Signaled Surprising Support for Obama's Vision of How to Tame Rising Medical Costs," *National Journal Online*, May 5, 2011.

45 Susan Crabtree, "PhRMA Defends Itself From Boehner Criticism," *The Hill*, August 18, 2009, http://thehill.com/homenews/administration/55331-phrma-defends-itself-from-boehner-criticism. See also, Ylan Q. Mui and Jia Lynn Yang, "Cooperation With Democrats May Haunt Firms."

46 John Castellani, in Chris Frates, "PhRMA Quietly Spends Big in 2010," *Politico,* November 10, 2010, www.politico.com/news/stories/1110/44917.html.

CHAPTER 4

More Bang for the Buck?

Defense Industry Contributions and the 2010 Elections

Jake Haselswerdt and Christopher J. Deering

Capitol South is the closest Washington, DC Metro stop to the U.S. Capitol, on the House side of the Hill. To the casual observer exiting from this station, it also would appear to be the lobby of the Northrop Grumman corporate headquarters—festooned as it is with advertisements for Northrop's products. Not too far away, the Navy Yard station, near the new Washington Nationals stadium, appears to be owned by the Lockheed Martin Corporation. Although the casual observer has little reason to notice, tourists gazing across the Potomac River toward Arlington Cemetery might be distracted by a sleek futuristic building—sometimes called the airfoil building—in downtown Rosslyn, Virginia. Atop the building facing directly east toward downtown Washington, they will see Northrop Grumman spelled out in large, lighted, letters.[1] Just a few blocks away another Rosslyn edifice shouts out EADS (European Air Defense Systems) while still another advertises BAE Systems North America (a British defense company).

And that is not all. Episodically, a burst of full-page display ads appear in *The Washington Post, The Hill,* and *Roll Call* touting the virtues of various weapons systems produced by Northrop, Lockheed, Boeing, United Technologies, EADS, and General Electric. For the past year or so, these ads have focused on competition to provide a new air-refueling tanker and an alternate engine for the F-35 joint strike fighter. Meanwhile, commuters listening to National Public Radio will hear promotional spots for Lockheed, General Dynamics, and Finnmeccanica (an Italian defense conglomerate). Surely somebody is listening (or reading). All told, the ad blitz amounts to a multimillion-dollar campaign by the nation's largest defense contractors anxious to secure billions of dollars in defense contracts from the Pentagon.[2] For Washingtonians these are but the most visible signs of the competition. Not that the competition stops there.

Defense contractors are not just about "advertising." During the 2010 election cycle, Boeing's political action committee (PAC) contributed $2.2 million to political campaigns, while Lockheed's put up $2.1 million, Raytheon $1.8 million, Northrop Grumman $1.34 million, General Dynamic $1.2 million, and United Technologies $1.1 million.

In the aggregate, defense sector PACs put $14.3 million into the 2010 elections. This election cycle featured sweeping Republican victories sufficient to retake the House of Representatives and nearly the Senate as well. So surely these companies gave overwhelmingly to the GOP and helped to cement this landslide victory, right? They did not. Of the aforementioned $14.3 million, 55 percent went to Democrats and 45 percent went to Republicans.

How could that be? What drives the contribution strategies of these defense companies? Would they not be far more comfortable with the generally pro-defense attitudes of most Republicans? Or are they more interested in access, on the assumption that reelection-minded members will support them regardless of party? This chapter examines these questions in the context of the role and strategies of defense industry PACS. Although the group is composed of some of the largest corporations in the United States, they were latecomers, but not strangers, to campaign finance and are more balanced in their contributions to Republicans and Democrats than other industries.

This Is the Defense Industry

The total U.S. budget for fiscal year 2010 was $3.5 trillion. Of that total, 23 percent ($793 billion) went to fund Medicare and Medicaid and another 20 percent ($701 billion) went to social security—the two largest components of what is called *non-discretionary* spending.[3] The third largest component was the defense budget at 20 percent of the total—a bit under $700 billion.[4] It is worth noting that nearly the entire defense budget is authorized and appropriated each year – and, hence, is *discretionary.* This is the result of the so-called Russell Amendment, which Congress adopted in 1959 (and subsequently substantially expanded). Under the Russell Amendment, no appropriations for defense procurement are permissible in the absence of an authorization, which, in turn, must be made on an annual basis.[5]

To fund these authorized programs, Congress then passes two appropriations bills each year. The larger of the two bills, a defense appropriations act, has five major components: (1) operations and maintenance, (2) personnel, (3) procurement, (4) research, and (5) defense health programs.[6] The second appropriations bill is for military construction and veterans' affairs.[7] With the exception of funds for personnel, which is largely pay and benefits, the billions of dollars represented by the defense budget flow more or less directly into the hands of thousands of private sector defense contractors. Thus, they have an enormous stake in the decisions made annually by the president, Congress, and the Pentagon.

Without exception, the ten largest government contractors are all defense contractors. (The top ten U.S. defense contractors appear in Table 4.1.) And, not surprisingly, the nation's largest defense contractors rank among the nation's largest corporations. Boeing, United Technologies, Lockheed Martin, Northrop Grumman, General Dynamics, and Raytheon, the six largest domestic defense contractors in terms of total company size, ranked twenty-eighth, thirty-seventh, forty-fourth, sixty-first, sixty-ninth, and ninety-fifth on the Fortune 500 list of the largest U.S. companies in 2010. Equally unsurprising, the PACs of these same corporations, excepting United Technologies, ranked forty-second, fifty-seventh, thirty-sixth, sixty-third, sixty-sixth, and seventy-fourth respectively among OpenSecrets's Heavy Hitters—the largest contributors to political campaigns since 1989 as recorded by the Federal

TABLE 4.1   Top Ten U.S. Government Defense Contractors, Fiscal Year 2010

Company	Primary Product	Total U.S. Government Contracts ($ billions)	Percent of Total	Fortune 500 Rank
Lockheed Martin Corporation	Aircraft	$35.8	6.78%	44
The Boeing Company	Aircraft	19.5	3.69	28
Northrop Grumman Corporation	Aircraft, electronics	16.8	3.18	61
General Dynamics Corporation	Aircraft, submarines	15.2	2.89	69
Raytheon Company	Electronics	15.2	2.89	95
United Technologies Corporation	Aircraft engines, helicopters	7.7	1.46	37
L-3 Communications Holdings Inc.	Electronics	7.4	1.41	148
Oshkosh Corporation	Military vehicles	7.2	1.37	nr
SAIC Inc.	Systems engineering technical services	6.8	1.29	nr
BAE Systems PLC	Aircraft	6.6	1.24	nr

Source: Federal Procurement Data System, General Services Administration, www.fpds.gov.

Election Commission (FEC). Although United Technologies did not rate a position among the Heavy Hitters, it nonetheless contributed $1.3 million during the 2010 election cycle—an amount quite comparable to its competitors.

The nation's, indeed the world's, leading defense contractors include a number of household names – such as General Electric (GE), Boeing, and United Technologies. Not surprisingly, these three are better known at least in part because they do considerable business in the commercial, nondefense sector. GE is the twenty-second ranked government contractor but defense contracting (mostly engines) is only 3 percent of its overall business. United Technologies' defense contracts are only 27 percent of its total revenues, and less than half of Boeing's total business is defense related as it also makes commercial airliners. By contrast, 80 percent of Northrop's business and 80 percent of General Dynamics' business is derived from defense. But the list also includes more than a few that are far less well known to the American public—including the alphabet soup group of L3, BAE, SAIC, KBR, and CH2M Hill—all of which are in the top twenty government contractors.[8]

It is worth noting that this is not strictly a domestic affair. Consider that three of the top ten arms-producing companies in the world in 2009 were European companies.[9] These include BAE Systems (a merger of Marconi Electric and British Aerospace) of the United Kingdom ranked second, a European consortium EADS (European Aeronautic Defence and Space Company) ranked seventh, and Finmeccanica of Italy ranked eighth. In addition, Rolls Royce, which makes jet engines in addition to luxury automobiles, ranked nineteenth. BAE Systems, which deals in aircraft, electronics, military vehicles, and shipbuilding, ranks tenth among all *U.S.* government contractors. Under campaign finance laws, these companies may not establish PACs in the United States, but their American-based subsidiaries can do so and receive donations from their American employees. And so they do, with BAE (second), Rolls Royce (eleventh), and EADS (twenty-third) ranked among the top "foreign-connected PACs" during the 2010 cycle. Although Finmeccanica has a North American subsidiary headquartered in Washington, DC, it does not currently sponsor a PAC. But, as with the other European firms, it has a lobbying and public relations presence in the United States.

In sum, these are large corporate entities with a huge stake in government contracting. The contracts themselves can be worth tens, even hundreds, of billions of dollars. One nuclear aircraft carrier costs about $10 billion while the new F-35 joint strike fighter program will run about $300 billion for procurement alone.[10] Are these corporations equally large participants in campaign finance and lobbying? Their presence on the Heavy Hitters list suggests at least a qualified yes. But as we will see, the form of their participation is distinctly traditional and far more bipartisan than for other groups discussed throughout this volume.

Theories of PAC Giving

At first blush, one might expect that defense PAC donations will be invested in Republican candidates. The military is, by and large, conservative. The Pentagon leadership, despite changes in party control of Congress and the White House, is likewise much more conservative than it is liberal. And, one presumes, defense company executives are likely to (1) have military backgrounds and/or (2) support bigger military budgets. That is, defense companies will be hawkish on defense and that generally has meant Republicans over Democrats. Beyond this predisposition, one also might expect corporations more generally to be inclined toward the Republican party, given its stance on taxes, regulation, and free markets. Call this a *preference theory* of campaign donations. In effect, according to the preference theory, PACs are either buying votes or investing in candidates who already agree with them. To date, the evidence for PACs buying votes is mixed, at best, with some scholarly work showing some affirmative evidence but rather more work showing no particular relationship.[11]

But there is an alternative, *constituency-based theory* that sees members of Congress as single-minded seekers of reelection.[12] As such, members aim to please their constituents with policies that redound to local advantage—earmarks or pork barrel legislation—particularly where jobs and the economy are concerned. That is to say, partisanship and ideology are of lesser importance than bringing home the bacon. By this view, defense contractors likely will put aside their true preferences politically and simply invest in incumbents, who should have the increased advantages of seniority, contacts, and expertise especially if they are on the right committees. And, the evidence backs this up as an increasing share of PAC contributions, particularly by labor and corporate donors, has gone to incumbents.[13] In fact, certain committees in Congress are distinctly more *constituency oriented,* featuring lower levels of partisan conflict and policy jurisdictions with lower national salience.[14] The agriculture, transportation, public works, and armed services committees fall neatly into this category. And in one study, a significant relationship emerged between the contributions of defense industry PACs and membership on the House Armed Services Committee and the Defense Appropriations Subcommittee—a point to be returned to later.[15]

Additional research makes a strong case that interest groups are "buying time" rather than "buying votes."[16] This argument is based on the assumption that most policymaking—especially on less controversial, less salient, constituency type issues—is accomplished in committee. And this is true particularly in the House. Taken all together, therefore, we would expect defense PACs to prefer Republicans to Democrats, all else equal. But, all else not being equal, they will prefer incumbents to challengers, the majority party to the minority party, and members on relevant committees (regardless of party). This is not necessarily true for PACs across the board. For example, labor PACs give disproportionately to Democrats regardless of circumstances. In addition, energy PACs give disproportionately to Republicans (see Table 4.2). But the pork barrel, constituency-based nature of defense contracting suggests a far more balanced approach by defense PACs as PACs rather than as corporate PACs more generally.

Defense Campaign Contributions in Context

The vast majority of information that we have about campaign finance comes from the Federal Election Commission (FEC), which was established pursuant to the Federal Election Campaign Act Amendments of 1974. Pursuant to the act, candidates, parties, and political action committees are required to report amounts they raise and spend to the Commission. That information is available to the public through the FEC. And scholars, journalists, and a variety of research organizations further disseminate it through their work. One of these organizations, the Center for Responsive Politics, established a website, OpenSecrets.org (mentioned in previous chapters), after the 1996 elections to make public access easier. As explained in Chapter 1, the FEC divides PACs into six broad categories: (1) corporate, (2) labor, (3) trade/membership/health, (4) nonconnected, (5) cooperative, and (6) corporations without stock. Designating these categories, unfortunately, does not readily lend itself to isolating defense PACs as a separate category.[17] OpenSecrets is helpful, however, because they employ a somewhat richer thirteen-category scheme that isolates defense PACs.[18]

Although defense PACs donate large sums of money, and include the aforementioned Heavy Hitters, they collectively donate the lowest amount relative to the other sectors—a bit over $14 million compared to $63.5 million by labor PACs, $62.3 million by financial PACs, and just under $60 million by ideological and single issue PACs in the 2010 election (see Table 4.2 for details). And this consistently has been the case: in each election cycle since 1998, defense PACs collectively raised and donated the least amount of money.

One reason for this is that defense PACs also are the fewest in number at just over 50, while ideological and single issue PACs number nearly 800 and financial PACs over 450. In fact, the correlation between the number of groups in a sector and the total contributions by that sector is a robust 0.75 (significance < .003). The four smallest groups—defense, construction, transportation, and lawyer/lobbyist PACs, respectively —all rank at the bottom. Size alone does not predetermine total giving, however, as labor organizations donate the most but are the fifth smallest group of PACs, just ahead of construction, transportation, and lawyer/lobbyist PACs.[19]

Having said this, it is worth recalling that, save for General Electric (forty-second), defense PACs fail to crack the top fifty Heavy Hitters in terms of the largest hard money

TABLE 4.2   PACs by Industry and Donation Levels, 2010 Election Cycle

Sector	Total	Total to Democrats	Total to Republicans	Democratic Share (%)	Republican Share (%)	Party Difference (%)*
Labor	$63,544,962	$59,294,890	$4,071,522	93	6	87
Finance, insurance & real estate	62,335,865	29,317,048	32,752,617	47	53	−6
Ideological/single-issue	59,379,783	29,259,535	29,666,642	49	50	−1
Health	54,293,458	29,885,513	24,107,795	55	44	11
Misc business	37,449,330	17,260,241	19,920,232	46	53	−7
Energy & natural resources	28,529,601	12,041,178	15,903,873	42	56	−14
Communications/electronics	24,625,278	13,218,306	11,280,222	54	46	8
Agribusiness	22,748,905	11,208,143	11,424,727	49	50	−1
Transportation	20,952,856	10,256,121	10,505,235	49	50	−1
Lawyers/lobbyists	15,700,096	11,043,664	4,509,396	70	29	42
Construction	15,390,204	$6,193,865	9,045,339	40	59	−19
Defense	**14,145,464**	**7,889,447**	**6,190,517**	**56**	**44**	**12**
Other	1,289,161	$877,861	407,800	68	32	36

Source: OpenSecrets.org.

Note: A negative sign indicates more donations to Republicans than to Democrats.

contributors to political campaigns.[20] Top spots are instead dominated by large membership organizations such as labor unions (six of the top ten), issue groups (two), and a trade association (National Association of Realtors). Only one corporation appears in the top ten (AT&T) and only three (add UPS and Goldman Sachs) in the top thirty. So, both as a sector and as individual entities, corporations employ distinctly different campaign finance strategies when compared to the larger field of participants.

Who Gives and How?

In the rich and evolving environment of PACs, super PACs, 527s, and 501(c)s, and union, corporate, and trade association direct spending in electoral politics, the defense industry, to date, remains very traditional in its organization and donation patterns. That is to say, for defense firms that participate in the electoral process, they do so through PACs and direct employee contributions alone. There is only a single defense related 527, the National Interest Security Company (and an affiliated PAC), which raised $16,000 in the 2010 cycle with expenditures of almost $12,000.[21] In addition, there is only a single 527 listed in the foreign policy sector, associated with the Public Affairs Alliance of Iranian Americans. Likewise, defense sector donations to organizations engaged in *outside spending*—spending that is not coordinated with candidate campaigns—are but a trace amount—$74,000 of the $490 million in outside spending during the 2010 cycle—of the totals spent in recent elections.[22] (See Chapter 1 regarding the rich and evolving array of outside spending vehicles.) Donations to these organizations do not have to be reported, of course, but there is little reason to think that defense companies are contributing large amounts of unreported donations. Finally, there are no super PACs associated with the defense industry and none of the groups engaged in outside spending is identifiably defense oriented.[23]

As noted previously, fifty-four defense PACs made contributions during the 2010 election. This is about average as sixty did so in the 1998 cycle and forty-nine in the 2004 cycle. It is difficult to determine what proportion of "defense companies" participate in the electoral process because there is no clear list of such companies and no single trade association that represents the defense industry—no "Defense Industries Trade Association."[24] As a rough baseline, however, one might use the Aerospace Industries Association (AIA) motto: "Aerospace and Defense: The Strength to Lift America," which certainly goes well beyond defense. Nonetheless, AIA currently has 147 "full" members and 198 "associate" members. So there is no reason to think that anything approaching all defense companies actually have PACs. OpenSecrets lists only twelve defense aerospace PACs, for example.

Given the range in size and resources, it occasions no surprise that defense PAC contributions ranged rather widely. Mechanical Technology, a relatively small electronics firm based in Albany, New York donated $1000 to Rep. Paul Tonko (D-N.Y.) of Albany and another $1,000 to Sen. Charles Schumer (D-N.Y.) during the 2010 cycle. Dynetics Inc., of Huntsville, Alabama donated $48,500 in the 2010 cycle. Nearly all of it went to Republicans and 75 percent went to candidates within the state of Alabama.

By contrast, the largest givers in the 2010 cycle—Boeing, Lockheed Martin, Northrop Grumman, General Dynamics, and Raytheon—donated an aggregate of nearly $11 million out of $14 million total for the industry (see Figure 4.1 for details on the top five). Needless to say, this group made donations to a much larger group of candidates. On average the top five contractors donated to 280 House candidates and 60 Senate candidates in the 2010 cycle, up from 202 and 42 respectively in the 1998 cycle. Boeing gave to the largest number of House candidates (368) and Raytheon the largest number of Senate candidates (74).[25] Given that thirty-seven Senate seats were up for grabs in the 2010 elections, large spending PACs like these supported both candidates (and, in some cases, primary challengers) in a number of races. For example, Boeing, General Dynamics, Northrop Grumman, and Lockheed

FIGURE 4.1 Total Contributions by Major Defense Contractors and Employees by Electoral Cycle (1990–2010)

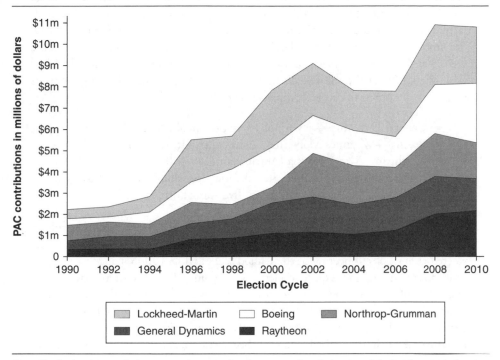

Note: Each election cycle is a two-year period prior to a national election. Hence the 1990 election cycle is 1984–1990. Totals are the sum of PAC and employee contributions.

Source: OpenSecrets.org.

Martin all contributed to both Kendrick Meek (D) and Marco Rubio (R) in the open-seat Florida Senate contest. And all four gave *more* to Meek, who came in a distant third in the race, than to Rubio (who won). Northrop also contributed to former Republican Gov. Charlie Crist, who ran as an independent and polled second in the general election. Raytheon donated only to Rubio.

PAC donations are not the only way that defense firms play a role in campaign finance. Individual employees (including top managers) also are free to make donations directly to candidates' campaigns. Since the FEC asks individual donors to list their employer, it is possible to compile the amounts that individuals working for a particular company donate to federal campaigns. These individual contributions are included in the totals reported in Table 4.3. While PAC contributions make up the lion's share of those totals, individual contributions are not an insignificant portion. From 1990 to 2010, Lockheed Martin employees contributed $3.7 million, Boeing employees $3.4 million, Northrop Grumman employees $2.2 million, General Dynamics employees $1.6 million, and Raytheon employees $1.4 million.[26]

These individual contributions play a particularly important role because PAC contributions to any one candidate are capped at $10,000 per cycle; individual contributions offer a way for a defense contractor to give extra money to particularly favored legislators (see the proceeding section, "Who Gets?"). All that said, the amounts the CEOs of these large corporations give pale in comparison to the well-healed backers of MoveOn.org or Crossroads who pony up. During the 2010 cycle the CEOs of the top five domestic contractors gave the following amounts (exclusive of contributions to company's own PAC):

- General Dynamics—Jay Johnson: eight contributions, $14,300
- Boeing—W. James McNerney: eight contributions, $11,700
- Northrop—Wes Bush: six contributions, $9,400
- Lockheed Martin—Robert Stevens: four contributions, $7,900
- Raytheon—William H. Swanson: five contributions, $6,351

With one exception, BAE Systems, "foreign" funds play rather little role in national elections. As noted earlier, the Italian defense firm Finmeccanica has, to date, steered clear of electioneering in the United States, while EADS' participation is of quite recent vintage and is quite modest relative to its defense brethren—rising from about $60,000 during the 2006 election cycle to nearly $300,000 during the 2010 cycle. Almost all of these donations went to incumbents and it was split quite evenly between Republicans and Democrats. Rolls Royce, which has both domestic and defense interests in the United States, has been a player, albeit a very modest one, for a longer period of time—donating only about $13,000 during the 1994 cycle and rising to $378,000 in 2010. By contrast, BAE has been a much bigger player in American elections. They were the second biggest foreign contributor to candidates in the 2010 cycle (behind Anheuser-Busch) at $745,000. Overall, their PAC spent $1.2 million. As with most defense PACs, they sent more money to Democrats than to Republicans during this cycle but they were quite evenhanded with respect to the four partisan campaign committees—donating $30,000 to each. And though not as aggressive as Lockheed, Boeing, or Raytheon, their contribution patterns and amount are quite comparable to those of Northrop and General Dynamics.

Who Gets?

An analysis of the list of the top recipients of defense campaign cash in the 2010 election cycle confirms the notion that defense firms, both through their PACs and through employee contributions, are in the business of buying time rather than buying votes. Table 4.3 displays the top twenty recipients of defense PAC and employee contributions during that cycle. The total amount received by their campaign committees from defense sources is displayed under "Campaign Committee," while the amount received by their leadership PACs is displayed

TABLE 4.3   Top Recipients of Campaign Contributions from Defense Contractor PACs and Employees, 2010 Election Cycle

Candidate	House/ Senate	Campaign Committee	Leadership PAC	Relevant Position
Shelby, Richard C (R-Ala.)	Senate	$482,200	$602,200	Appropriations, Defense Subcomte
Inouye, Daniel K (D-Hawaii)	Senate	418,000	138,500	Appropriations (Chair), Defense Subcmte (Chair)
Skelton, Ike (D-Mo.)	House	433,311	60,000	Armed Services (Chair)
McKeon, Howard P (Buck) (R-Calif.)	House	336,500	132,400	Armed Services (Ranking Member)
Mikulski, Barbara A (D-Md.)	Senate	289,500	159,000	Appropriations, Defense Subcmte
Murray, Patty (D-Wash.)	Senate	258,300	34,000	Appropriations, Defense Subcmte
Sestak, Joseph A Jr (D-Pa.)*	Senate	204,760	12,500	Armed Services (while in House)
Moran, Jim (D-Va.)	House	195,250	32,500	Appropriations, Defense Subcmte
McCain, John (R-Ariz.)	Senate	180,900	17,000	Armed Services (Ranking Member)
Reyes, Silvestre (D-Tex.)	House	172,950	38,000	Armed Services
Burr, Richard (R-N.C.)	Senate	177,200	30,000	Armed Services
Wittman, Rob (R-Va.)	House	166,100	0	Armed Services
Critz, Mark (D-Pa.)*	House	163,919	0	Armed Services (once elected in May special election)
Dicks, Norm (D-Wash.)	House	157,300	52,800	Appropriations, Defense Subcmte (Chair after Murtha's death)
Ruppersberger, Dutch (D-Md.)	House	156,250	42,000	Armed Services
Hoyer, Steny H (D-Md.)	House	152,000	100,000	Majority Leader
Young, C W Bill (R-Fla.)	House	147,000	10,000	Appropriations, Defense Subcmte (Ranking Member)
Granger, Kay (R-Tex.)	House	142,350	18,500	Appropriations, Defense Subcmte
Giffords, Gabrielle (D-Ariz.)	House	140,000	0	Armed Services
Murtha, John P (D-Pa.)	House	139,550	60,000	Appropriations, Defense Subcmte (Chair)

Source: Data from OpenSecrets's list of top recipients for the defense industry, www.opensecrets.org/industries/recips.php?cycle=2010&ind=D.

*Nonincumbent

Note: These numbers are subject to change as more data is released by the FEC and as more information is coded by OpenSecrets. In some cases (e.g., Senator Shelby), OpenSecrets's individual member pages had more recently updated data on the dollar amounts received from defense sector sources. In those cases, the number from the member page was used.

under "Leadership PACs."[27] The recipients' relevant institutional positions (e.g., committee assignments) are displayed under "Relevant Position."

In terms of partisan split, this list echoes the observations of the previous section: defense sector giving favored Democrats (the reigning majority party in both chambers) but was not wildly unbalanced by any means. Seven of the top twenty recipients were Republicans, including Sen. Richard Shelby, a Republican from Alabama, who amassed the most defense money for both his own campaign committee and leadership PAC of any legislator in 2010 according to the most recent data available.

Almost all of the recipients listed above ran as well-established incumbents in 2010. The only exceptions were Joseph Sestak (D-Pa.), a sitting House member, Armed Services Committee member, and retired navy vice admiral who ran unsuccessfully for the Senate, and Mark Critz, a longtime staffer for the chair of the Defense Appropriations Subcommittee, John Murtha (D-Pa.), who won a May special election to replace his boss following Murtha's death in February (Murtha himself had accumulated enough defense sector contributions before his death to make the top twenty list). In other words, the defense sector was primarily interested in funding the campaigns of incumbents and far less interested in funding those of political outsiders.

Furthermore, each of the top twenty recipients occupied an institutional position of importance. Ten sat on their chamber's defense committee (the House committee in Sestak's case, though he was a Senate candidate), nine sat on their chamber's military appropriations subcommittee, and one (Steny Hoyer, D-Md.) was the House majority leader. This pattern is much more consistent with buying time than buying votes, for the defense sector clearly directed disproportionate support to members with special influence over the *content* of key legislation (namely, the annual defense authorization and appropriations measures) rather than those who might determine the outcome of a floor vote. This is an obvious strategy for a sector primarily interested in the distribution of funds for contracts rather than in the type of hot-button issues that result in contested floor votes.

Defense sector giving to members of these key committees was not limited to these top recipients. In total, during the 2010 cycle the defense sector contributed a whopping $5.2 million to the campaigns of House Armed Services members, $3.7 million to those of Senate Armed Services members, $3.6 million to House Appropriations members and $4 million to Senate Appropriations members.[28] This generosity was fairly well distributed; of the dozens of members of the defense committees and funding committees, all but three (Todd Platts [R-Pa.] and Vic Snyder [D-Ariz.] of Armed Services and Zach Wamp [R-Tenn.] of Appropriations) received at least some money from the defense sector. A look at the giving patterns of the top five Heavy Hitters mentioned previously confirms the importance of these committees to their political activities: all five gave heavily to committee members.

Of course, these legislators did not come to occupy positions of importance to the defense sector purely by chance. For every single member of Congress on this list, defense-related economic activity and jobs are a major part of the economy back home in the district or state (see Table 4.4). From Fort Leonard Wood and Whiteman Air Force Base in the western Missouri district of former House Armed Services Chair Ike Skelton (D) to the numerous defense contractors headquartered in the southwestern Pennsylvania district represented by Murtha and Critz to the plethora of military facilities in Democratic Sen. Daniel Inouye's strategically located home state of Hawaii, defense is an important business to the constituencies of all of these legislators.[29] This is why they have sought out posts that allow them to keep the defense money, including contracts, flowing to their districts and states.

TABLE 4.4   Constituency Connections to the Defense Industry for Top Recipients of Campaign Contributions from Defense Contractor PACs and Employees, 2010 Election Cycle

Candidate	House/ Senate	State or District Defense Connections
Shelby, Richard C. (R-Ala.)	Senate	Defense contracts to Alabama-based companies from FY 2000–2010 totaled almost $64 billion. Northrop Grumman has a significant presence in Alabama and Shelby supported their (ultimately unsuccessful) bid with Airbus to construct the air force KC-30 tanker there.
Inouye, Daniel K. (D-Hawaii)	Senate	Defense contracts to Hawaii-based companies from FY 2000–2010 totaled over $13 billion. Hawaii-based defense projects supported by Inouye through appropriations include an army high-tech intelligence center, the Maui Space Surveillance System, and the Pacific Missile Range Facility.
Skelton, Ike (D-Mo.)	House	Missouri's 4th district includes counties or parts of counties (e.g., Jackson, Webster) that are home to thousands of defense contractors, as well as Fort Leonard Wood and Whiteman Air Force Base.
McKeon, Howard P. (Buck) (R-Calif.)	House	The China Lake Naval Air Weapons Station, the Goldstone deep-space communications complex, and the battlefield training center at Fort Irwin are all located in California's 25th district.
Mikulski, Barbara A. (D-Md.)	Senate	Defense contracts to Maryland-based companies from FY 2000–2010 totaled over $118 billion. Numerous military installations, including Andrews Air Force Base, Fort Meade, and Fort Detrick, are also located there.
Murray, Patty (D-Wash.)	Senate	Defense contracts to Washington-based companies from FY 2000–2010 totaled almost $37 billion. Boeing has a large presence in Everett, and the Army; Navy/Marine Corps and Air Force all have multiple facilities in the state.

(Continued)

TABLE 4.4   (Continued)

Candidate	House/ Senate	State or District Defense Connections
Sestak, Joseph A. Jr. (D-Pa.)*	Senate	Defense contracts to Pennsylvania-based companies from FY 2000–2010 totaled over $92 billion.
Moran, Jim (D-Va.)	House	Virginia's 8th district includes the DC suburbs Arlington and Alexandria, home to the Capital-area headquarters of many defense contractors.
McCain, John (R-Ariz.)	Senate	Defense contracts to Arizona-based companies from FY 2000–2010 totaled over $90 billion. The Yuma Proving Grounds, Fort Huachuca, Marine Corps Air Station Yuma and three air force installations are also located there.
Reyes, Silvestre (D-Tex.)	House	Texas's 16th district is home to Fort Bliss, the army's second-largest installation and the place of performance for 5,449 defense contracts totaling almost $1.6 billion from FY 2000–2010.
Burr, Richard (R-N.C.)	Senate	Defense contracts to North Carolina–based companies from FY 2000–2010 totaled over $19 billion. Fort Bragg and numerous other military installations are also located there.
Wittman, Rob (R-Va.)	House	The Navy and Army facilities located just outside of Virginia's 1st district in the Hampton Roads area are major employers of residents in the district.
Critz, Mark (D-Pa.)*	House	Pennsylvania's 16th district is home to many defense contractors. In Johnstown alone (population 23,906 in the 2000 census), fifty-nine defense contractors garnered almost $1.9 billion in contracts from FY 2000–2010.
Dicks, Norm (D-Wash.)	House	Bremerton Naval Shipyard is located in Washington's 6th District and Boeing employs thousands of people in Everett (also in the 6th). Dicks was instrumental in the air force KC-30 tanker going to Boeing (see Shelby).
Ruppersberger, Dutch (D-Md.)	House	Maryland's 2nd district includes the Aberdeen Proving Ground, the place of performance for 2,228 defense contracts totaling over $1 billion from FY 2000–2010. Nearby Fort Meade is a major employer, though not located in the district.
Hoyer, Steny H. (D-Md.)	House	The Patuxent River Naval Air Station Complex and the Naval Surface Warfare Center at Indian Head are both located in Maryland's 5th district.

Candidate	House/ Senate	State or District Defense Connections
Young, C. W. Bill (R-Fla.)	House	Pinellas County, which includes all of Florida's 10th district, is home to 645 defense contractors who garnered almost $9.8 billion in contracts from FY 2000–2010.
Granger, Kay (R-Tex.)	House	Lockheed Martin has a major plant in Texas's 12th district. Carswell Air Force Base and a Bell Helicopter Textron plant are both located nearby.
Giffords, Gabrielle (D-Ariz.)	House	Within Arizona's 8th district is Cochise County, home to Fort Huachuca and 326 defense contractors who received almost $529 million in contracts from FY 2000–2010.
Murtha, John P. (D-Pa.)	House	See Critz (Pennsylvania's 16th district).

Source: District/state information gathered from the National Journal's *The Almanac of American Politics* and Government ContractsWon.com.

Taking a step back, we can see a dynamic, constituency-based pattern of interest group and legislator behavior at work in the defense sector. Reelection-oriented politicians from defense-heavy constituencies seek out institutional posts (e.g., seats on the defense committees or military funding subcommittees) that allow them to champion issues and projects important to those constituencies, which include defense contractors and their employees. Contractors, recognizing the value of such well-placed and favorably disposed legislators to their own interests, donate to their campaigns. This helps to ensure the legislators' reelection, which in turn increases their seniority and makes them even more powerful within Congress and their respective committees—and therefore even more valuable to the contractors.

Are these members more supportive of defense interests because of campaign contributions? Conventional wisdom would suggest that they are, but it is important to keep in mind that most if not all of these legislators began their political careers as supporters of defense projects and jobs in their states and districts. Thus, defense contractor contributions to their reelection campaigns are unlikely to change their minds on many issues. In all likelihood, defense contractors get something more subtle in exchange for their cash: access to the member's office for their lobbyists and a willingness on the part of the member to put in the staff time necessary to write and insert favorable legislative provisions, or to support the bid of one contractor over another through both public and backchannel influence at the Department of Defense. In other words, defense contractors are most likely buying time.

A case in point is the story of the competition for the $35 billion contract to replace the U.S. Air Force's aging fleet of aerial refueling tankers. The ten-year process, which finally concluded in early 2011, developed into a bitter and politicized struggle between Boeing on the one hand and Northrop Grumman and European partner EADS (the parent company of Airbus, Boeing's top competitor) on the other. Boeing proposed to build the tankers at its plant in Everett, WA and convert them for military use at its Wichita, KS facility, while Northrop-EADS proposed to do the initial building in France and finish in Mobile, AL.[30]

With billions of dollars and thousands of jobs at stake, it was perhaps inevitable that legislators from the three states in question would get involved. Nonetheless, it is instructive to note those that took the lead. Sen. Patty Murray (D-Wash.), Rep. Norm Dicks (D-Wash.), and Rep. Todd Tiahrt (R-Kans.) all threw their weight behind Boeing, while Sen. Richard Shelby (R-Ala.) tenaciously backed the Northrop-EADS proposal.[31] All were powerful members of the defense appropriations subcommittees of their respective chambers. Each had a compelling interest from the point of view of their geographic constituencies to support the bids that they did. And, each also received very generous campaign support from the contractors they supported. Murray was the top recipient of campaign funds from Boeing's PAC and employees in the 2010 cycle with an impressive $85,860, Tiahrt received $32,900, and Dicks, known on Capitol Hill as "Mr. Boeing,"[32] received $22,000. Shelby received $19,250 from Northrop Grumman's PAC and employees during the 2010 cycle, and the Center for Public Integrity estimates that he has received at least $108,000 in Northrop PAC donations alone since his first Senate election in 1986.[33]

Dicks and Shelby in particular went to extraordinary lengths to support their favored bids. Dicks vocally backed Boeing's official protest of the Air Force's initial decision to award the contract to Northrop-EADS in 2008.[34] After the Government Accountability Office sustained that protest in June of 2008 and required the Air Force to reopen the bidding process, Dicks questioned Department of Defense officials at a July hearing on the criteria by which bids would be evaluated. The existing criteria had required the Air Force to consider the cost of operating the aircraft over a twenty-five-year life cycle. Dicks, realizing that the less fuel-efficient Northrop-EADS tankers would be comparatively more expensive over a longer life cycle, successfully pressed for a change requiring the Air Force to use an arguably more realistic forty-year life cycle in their calculations.[35]

Shelby, outraged at what he viewed as an attempt to rig the process in Boeing's favor, used the considerable parliamentary powers granted by Senate rules to hit back at the executive branch. In April of 2009, he placed a hold on the nomination of Ashton Carter as Pentagon acquisition chief, demanding assurances that the tanker competition be conducted fairly. This was a notable step, but what followed was truly remarkable. In early 2010, Shelby, still unsatisfied with the direction of the bidding process, placed a "blanket hold" on *all* pending presidential nominations. Essentially, Shelby used Senate rules to hold seventy Obama administration nominees hostage to his demands, attracting a great deal of negative attention into the bargain.[36] Shelby ultimately dropped the holds, declaring them successful in "get[ting] the White House's attention,"[37] but his scorched-earth tactics turned out to be for naught. In March of 2010, Northrop-EADS dropped its bid. In the words of Northrop CEO Wes Bush, the process "clearly favor[ed]" Boeing's tanker and that to pursue the contract further would violate the companies' "fiduciary responsibility" to shareholders.[38] The contract was officially awarded to Boeing in early 2011.

If Boeing and Northrop Grumman did not donate to legislators' campaigns, would Dicks still have wanted thousands of new tanker construction jobs in Washington? Would Shelby still have wanted those jobs in Alabama? Without question, yes. But given that defense interest groups appear to pursue a buying time strategy, this is not really the pertinent question. Instead, the question is whether or not Dicks and Shelby would have made the tanker competition such a priority, whether they would have expended such extensive time and effort and placed their credibility on the line so publicly (especially in Shelby's case). Or, alternately, perhaps the real question is whether Boeing and Northrop would have had such stalwart and powerful congressional champions in the first place if they had not invested so heavily in their electoral careers over the course of decades, helping them to become firmly entrenched senior incumbents. The story of the aerial refueling tanker is instructive not only because it shows the importance for contractors of enlisting political allies but also because it illustrates the dynamic and almost symbiotic relationship between defense contractors and their congressional champions. It is not necessarily that campaign money buys congressional support; instead, campaign money and congressional support are mutually reinforcing components of a long-term relationship.

Defense Contractors Inside the Beltway

On May 25 and 26 of 2011, Section A of *The Washington Post* featured full page ads placed by General Electric and Rolls Royce announcing: "F136 engine development is on our dime." A large dime dominates the ad. It was not the first time the ad had appeared and it would appear three or more times in the following weeks. What were GE and Rolls Royce up to? The backstory is that in 2001 the GE–Rolls team had lost out to Pratt & Whitney in a competition to produce a new engine for the F-35 joint strike fighter when Lockheed was selected to produce the airframe. The so-called alternate engine program, which dated back to 1994, was congressionally mandated—a means of keeping two engine producers in the game of designing power plants for high performance aircraft. But when the airframe competition came to an end, GE supporters saw to it that the alternative engine program continued. In 2006, the Bush administration requested termination of the program for fiscal year (FY) 2007—a request renewed for the next four years into the Obama administration. Each time Congress refused, and by FY 2009 GE and Rolls had received $2.9 billion total for their work. Finally, in a free-for-all of floor voting on HR1, an omnibus FY 2011 appropriations bill for defense and other programs, the House approved an amendment sponsored by Rep. Tom Rooney (R-Fla.) to terminate the program. It passed on a fairly narrow bipartisan 233-198 vote.[39] On March 26, 2011 the Pentagon issued a "stop work" order for the program.

The floor vote itself was not a surprise; a similar vote had failed to halt the program in the previous Congress. And intense lobbying by representatives of both sides preceded it. But the outcome of the vote surely was a surprise, as a majority of freshman Republicans backed termination and thirty-two other members of both parties switched their votes to do so as well. GE–Rolls and its congressional supporters, led by chair of the Armed Services Committee Howard "Buck" McKeon (R-Calif.), vowed to revisit the issue in the FY 2012 budget. But what could not be achieved in the cozy confines of the defense committees or appropriations subcommittees could be achieved on the House floor in the midst of widespread panic about mounting deficits and debts. Hence the ads, which appeared the same week that the FY 2012 defense authorization bill hit the House floor. (Subsequent ads appeared in weeks coincident with further House and Senate action on defense.) GE–Rolls had, clearly, shifted their strategy by offering to foot the bill for 75 percent of the *remainder* of the development program. Moreover, House Armed Services Committee forces friendly to the GE–Rolls cause saw to it that an amendment was included in the FY 2011 defense authorization bill that could revive the program if the Pratt & Whitney engine failed to meet certain performance standards.

The "off the shelf" price for the aforementioned *Post* ads approaches $150,000 per day, meaning GE–Rolls spent nearly three quarters of a million dollars "lobbying" inside the beltway policymakers in this fashion alone over a period of just a few weeks.[40] But that is not all. GE–Rolls also had numerous online advertisements and a highly polished website, F136.com, that includes on every page, a "Tell Congress you support the F136 engine program" field: "Click on the contact button and you can register your support – or do so via Twitter or Facebook." The alternate engine case is but one example of this sort of inside-the-beltway advertising, Internet grassroots lobbying, and old fashioned shoe-leather lobbying that can occur when these large contracts are at stake.[41] Very similar types of activity took place during the competition for the air refueling tanker competition and for programs before that.

All told, in fact, the defense sector spends far more on various forms of lobbying than it does on electioneering. This is, in fact, true for all twelve sectors reported in Table 4.2 with the near exception of labor. Since 1998 the total reported to the secretary of the Senate by the defense industry is $1.3 billion, with $238 million in 2009 and 2010 alone. Unlike PAC donations, these amounts place the defense industry closer to the middle of the sectors listed in Table 4.2 rather than dead last—with health and financial institutions again ranking near the top but labor and ideological groups falling to the bottom.

The top contractors once again led the way in 2010: United Technologies, $18.2 million; Boeing, $17.9 million; Northrop Grumman, $15.7 million; Lockheed Martin, $12.7 million; General Dynamics, $10.8 million; and Raytheon, $6.9 million. These numbers put United Technologies, Boeing, and Northrop among the top twenty spenders during calendar year 2010. And they employ a small army of lobbyists. Defense sector reports filed with the Senate name 755 lobbyists (in-house and outside hires) employed to advance their various causes. The European group is similarly active in advancing its causes on Capitol Hill. BAE Systems reported spending $4.7 million in 2010 while EADS reported $3.4 million, and Finmeccanica, after being a virtual nonparticipant prior to 2007, reported $3.4 million.

The Federal Election Campaign Act, notwithstanding the *Citizens United* case, caps regular PAC contributions while lobbying expenditures are unlimited, so it is not surprising that lobbying expenditures exceed campaign contributions. Nonetheless, these figures show that the defense sector reports spending something approaching $20.00 on lobbying for every dollar donated to federal campaigns during the 2010 election cycle. By contrast, labor spent less than $1.50 on lobbying for every (hard) dollar contributed.   Still, the defense sector does not have the largest campaign-to-lobbying imbalance, as the health industry spent $110.00 on lobbying for every campaign dollar. At bottom, neither lobbying nor campaigning ever stops as election seasons and party control of Congress and the White House come and go. Thus, we conclude with a look ahead to 2012.

Looking Ahead to 2012

This analysis of defense sector firms' giving patterns in 2010 and previous years suggest some obvious expectations for their strategy in the congressional races of 2012 and beyond. First and most obvious, we can be sure that defense sector contributions will heavily favor incumbents, especially in the House. With rare exceptions (such as Mark Critz, see earlier discussion), defense firms clearly see little value in backing new candidates who, even if elected, will wield little influence over the all-important defense authorization and appropriations measures.

Second, campaign contributions will remain relatively balanced between the parties, but tilt modestly toward Republicans in the House and Democrats in the Senate. This follows both because majority legislators are more influential (and hence more useful in a buying time strategy) and because of incumbency. Most incumbents in the House are Republican, while more Democrats than Republicans are up for reelection in the Senate in 2012.

Third, defense firms will continue to back legislators that wield the most influence over the issues of most interest to them. This means the members of the defense committees and funding subcommittees. In particular, while none of the relevant committee leaders in the Senate are up for reelection in 2012, giving on the House side should favor committee leadership: on the Armed Services Committee, chair Buck McKeon (R-Calif.) and ranking member Adam Smith (D-Wash.); and on the Defense Appropriations Subcommittee, chair Bill Young (R-Fla.). The subcommittee's ranking member, Norm Dicks (D-Wash.), decided not to stand for reelection in 2012, leaving potential contributors in the position of trying to figure out who his successor would be. Still, recent experience suggests that committee members need not be chairs or ranking members to garner considerable support from the defense sector (e.g., Richard Shelby in 2010). For the most part, the recipients of these donations will be receptive not just to the money itself, but also to the pleas for assistance coming from the donors. This is because members serving on these committees are self-selected, and defense-related economic activity is important to their constituents.

PAC disclosures to the FEC since the 2010 election seem to confirm these expectations regarding defense sector contributions. First, they confirm that the usual Heavy Hitter suspects remain active: Lockheed Martin ($617,000), Raytheon ($498,283), Boeing ($497,000), General Dynamics ($319,473), and Northrop Grumman ($163,500) all jumped out of the gate with substantial giving before 2011 was even half over.[42] The desire to maintain some partisan balance is evidenced by the fact that Lockheed, Boeing, General Dynamics, and Northrop all have contributed to the Democratic Congressional and Senatorial Campaign Committees (DCCC and DSCC) on the Democratic side and the National Republican Congressional and Senatorial Committees (NRCC and NRSC) on the Republican side. Raytheon differs in that it has not yet contributed to the DCCC, though it has contributed to the other three. Lockheed and Raytheon also have contributed to the campaigns of all four relevant House committee leaders (McKeon, Smith, Young, and Dicks), while the remaining three Heavy Hitters have each contributed to at least two of them, and may yet contribute to the others before election day.[43] In short, it looks like business as usual so far for the defense sector in the 2012 congressional races.

Turning to the 2012 presidential contest, if the 2008 presidential election is any guide, defense firms will not be major players. The defense industry contributed about $1 million to Barack Obama's campaign in 2008 and $649,000 to John McCain's. While these amounts are certainly more than the sector gave to any single legislator, they pale in comparison to the support both candidates received from other sectors and industries; Obama received a staggering $43 million from lawyers and law firms and almost $23 million from the education sector, while McCain reaped almost $33 million in contributions from retirees.

In the realm of campaign finance, the defense sector simply cannot compete with these numbers, nor would it likely care to try. The distributive politics of defense contracting are largely conducted not in the Oval Office, but in the committee staff offices of Capitol Hill and the program offices of the Pentagon. While the defense sector can never be very important to the campaign of a president or presidential candidate, it can be very important indeed to those of a few well-placed members of Congress, who in turn can promise much more time and attention to defense sector firms' priorities.

Endnotes

1 In September 2011, Northrop moved its corporate headquarters from Los Angeles to Falls Church in Northern Virginia, occupying a large modern building formerly owned by Verizon —replete with large lighted letters on two sides. In January 2012, the Northrop Gumman signage was removed from the building in Roslyn.

2 Paul Farhi, "Influx of Ads for Military Weapons Throwing Commuters for a Loop," *The Washington Post*, June 25, 2010.

3 Mandatory because preexisting statutes determine who is eligible to receive benefits and thereby determine total spending.

4 Defense spending is considered discretionary because it is authorized and appropriated each year. Total discretionary spending is a bit under 40 percent of the FY 2010 budget. It also is worth noting that the military efforts in Iraq and Afghanistan generally have been funded through "off budget" supplemental and emergency appropriations bills. They were off budget inasmuch as the funding was not included in the president's budget message or in the normal appropriations bills, for the most part. Hence, the funding also was not included in deficit projections. Renamed Overseas Contingency Operations, these funds now are included in the annual budgets commencing in FY 2010.

5 The text of the original Russell Amendment (Sec. 412, subsection (b), of PL 86-149) read: "No funds may be appropriated after December 31, 1960, to or for the use of any armed force of the United States for the procurement of aircraft, missiles, or naval vessels unless appropriation of such funds has been authorized by legislation enacted after that date." This requirement was expanded eleven times through 1982—by which point all but about 2 percent of the defense budget was annually authorized. For additional details, see Barry M. Blechman, The Politics of National Security: Congress and U.S. Defense Policy, (New York: Oxford University Press, 1990), 29–31.

6 These are listed in descending order of size. Technically, defense health is in an "other" category but it is overwhelmingly the largest component.

7 Military construction was long a stand-alone appropriations bill but Veterans Administration (VA) programs were recently folded into it as part of a reorganization of the appropriations process. Family housing has somewhat recently been added as a category of defense spending but it is less than one percent of the total defense budget and is, essentially, construction.

8 Of the top twenty FY 2009 government contractors listed by the General Services Administration only three are unambiguously not defense firms—Oshkosh Truck Corporation and two health firms, McKesson Corporation and Humana Incorporated.

9 See the SIPRI's (Stockholm International Peace Research Institute) "Top 100 Arms Producing Companies 2009," www.sipri.org/research/armaments/production/Top100.

10 Additional costs for research and development and for operations and maintenance for the F-35 may drive total program costs above $1 trillion according to Government Accountability Office (GAO).

11 There is quite a bit of work here so a few examples on each side should suffice. On the affirmative side: William Welch, "Campaign Contributions and Legislative Voting: Milk Money and Dairy Price Supports," *Western Political Quarterly* 35 (1982): 478–495; Sam Peltzman, "Constituent Interest and Congressional Voting," *Journal of Law and Economics* 27 (1984): 181–210; and Laura Langbein, "PACs, Lobbies, and Political Conflict: The Case of Gun Control." *Public Choice* 75 (1993): 254–271. On the negative side: Janet Grenzke, "Political Action Committees and the Congressional Supermarket: The Currency is Complex," *American Journal of Political Science* 33 (1989): 1–24; John R. Wright, "Political Action Committees, Campaign Contributions, and Roll Calls," *American Political Science Review* 79 (1985): 400–414; and John R. Wright, "Contributions, Lobbying, and Committee Voting in the U.S. House of Representatives," *American Political Science Review* 84 (1990): 417–38.

12 Most famously, by David R. Mayhew, *Congress The Electoral Connection* (New Haven: Yale University Press, 1974).

13 On this point, see Kevin B. Grier and Michael C. Munger, "Comparing Interest Group PAC contributions to House and Senate Incumbents: 1980–1986," *Journal of Politics* 55 (August 1993): 615–43.

14 Christopher J. Deering and Steven S. Smith, *Committees in Congress* (Washington, DC: CQ Press, 1997).

15 J. David Gopoian, "What Makes PACs Tick? An Analysis of the Allocation Patterns of Economic Interest Groups," *American Journal of Political Science* 28 (1984): 259–81.

16 The seminal piece on this is Richard L. Hall and Frank W. Wayman, "Buying Time: Moneyed Interests and the Mobilization of Bias in Congressional Committees," *American Political Science Review* 84 (1990): 797–820.

17 Corporate PACs have the largest share of the total (38 percent), followed by nonconnected (31 percent), trade/membership/health (22 percent), labor (6.4 percent), corporations without stock (2.3 percent), and cooperatives (less than 1 percent).

18 The categories appear in Table 4.2. OpenSecrets also has a fourteenth, "other", category but it contains only a relative handful of organizations, mostly related to education.

19 To some extent, this relationship is "true by definition" because the FECA limits contributions to individual candidate PACs. The correlation reported here is for the 2010 election cycle but is consistent over time. For the 2006 cycle, for example, it is .78 (sig. < .002).

20 General Electric does rank forty-second, but with only 3 percent of its business in the defense sector it is not even categorized with the other defense companies.

21 The 527 and PAC are affiliated with National Interest Security Corporation (NISC), an information technology company based in Virginia that has defense, intelligence, and homeland security components. IBM purchased the company in 2010. All of

NISC's receipts for the 2010 cycle came from company officers. Their PAC donated predominantly to Democrats during the cycle.

22 Labor accounted for the largest share of donations in the most recent cycle ($25 million) with ideological and single-issue donations not too far behind ($16.5 million). Note that not all donations to groups engaged in outside spending, various 501(c) organizations, are disclosed.

23 There is an organization called Combat Veterans for Congress that spent just under $8,000 in favor of Republican candidates during the 2010 cycle.

24 There is a Pentagon initiated Coalition of Defense and Space Industry Associations that has seven member associations—from the broadly defined Chamber of Commerce to the more narrowly defined Aerospace Industries Association.

25 General Dynamics donated to the fewest Senate candidates (38) and Northrop Grumman donated to the fewest House candidates (196).

26 These totals include soft money contributions made by individuals prior to the 2002 election cycle, when the Bipartisan Campaign Reform Act banned such contributions. Only Boeing and Lockheed Martin employees contributed a notable amount of soft money ($116,905 and $108,046 respectively, across all cycles), though even these amounts were small.

27 Leadership PACs are chaired by members of Congress, and donate to the campaign committees of the members' copartisans. Running a successful leadership PAC is a way for members to accumulate influence and prestige within their legislative parties. They also offer a way for donors to give to a favored legislator beyond the legal limits on contributions to their campaign committee.

28 All numbers in this paragraph reflect total contributions by defense PACs and donations by individuals employed by defense firms.

29 Defense contractors tend to geographically concentrate around military installations, and such installations are often the official place of performance for defense contracts.

30 Les Blumenthal, "Boeing Has Inside Track for Tanker as Northrop Steps Aside," *McClatchy Newspapers,* March 8, 2010, www.mcclatchydc.com/2010/03/08/90034/boeing-has-inside-track-for-tanker.html.

31 Les Blumenthal, "Northrop Charges That Tanker Bidding Skewed Toward Boeing," *McClatchy Newspapers,* November 1, 2009, www.mcclatchydc.com/2009/11/01/78107/northrop-charges-that-tanker-bidding.html.

32 According to Dicks's entry in the *National Journal Almanac of American Politics* for 2010.

33 Josh Israel and Nick Schwellenbach, "Senator Richard Shelby Goes to Bat for Major Financial Benefactor," *Center for Public Integrity iWatch News,* February 6, 2010, www.iwatchnews.org/2010/02/05/2735/senator-richard-shelby-goes-bat-major-financial-benefactor.

34 Dana Hedgpeth, "Boeing to File Protest on Lost Tanker Deal," *The Washington Post,* March 11, 2008, www.washingtonpost.com/wp-dyn/content/article/2008/03/10/AR2008031002777.html.

35 Rob Hotakainen, "How One Lawmaker Gave Boeing a Boost in Tanker Contest," *Los Angeles Times,* February 28, 2011, http://articles.latimes.com/2011/feb/28/business/la-fi-tanker-bid-20110228.

36 Shelby was also attempting to secure a $45 million earmark to build an FBI improvised explosive device testing lab in Alabama. For more information on Shelby's holds, see Sam Stein, "Richard Shelby Senate Hold Puts Spotlight on Defense Contractor Ties," *Huffington Post*, February 5, 2010, www.huffingtonpost.com/2010/02/05/shelbys-blanket-hold-puts_n_450934.html

37 Evan McMorris-Santoro, "Richard Shelby Drops Blanket Holds, Says They Were A Success," *TPMDC*, February 9, 2010, http://tpmdc.talkingpointsmemo.com/2010/02/richard-shelby-drops-blanket-holds-says-they-were-a-success.php

38 Blumenthal, "Boeing Has Inside Track for Tanker as Northrop Steps Aside." EADS could have continued in the competition alone but without Northrop their chances had essentially evaporated.

39 Democrats supported the amendment with a 123-68 vote; Republicans opposed it 110-130. For further details see Charlene Carter, "F-35 Alternative Engine Funding Stripped by House," *CQToday Online*, February 16, 2011.

40 In all likelihood, they paid somewhat less inasmuch as the *Post* has lower rates for "contract" customers. On the other hand, all the major contractors make routine use of the *Post* and other key publications (such as *Roll Call* and *The Hill*, both targeted to Capitol Hill readers) in much the same fashion. So, certainly, total ad budgets just for advertising in the Washington area run in the millions of dollars.

41 At $2.9 billion to date, the engine program is not all that large by defense standards. But it is just the development phase. GE and Rolls Royce stand to earn billions more if the engine is actually used in some part of the F-35 fleet at a future date. Moreover, with Rolls as its partner, GE figures to garner a large share of the foreign market, mostly European initially, if there is an optional engine with European content.

42 All numbers cited here are total PAC contributions according to the FEC website as of May 24, 2011. Note that since OpenSecrets has not yet begun to code FEC data for the 2012 cycle, information about the giving patterns of defense sector *employees* is not yet available. These numbers are for contributions by PACs only.

43 Northrop Grumman might well not assist in Dicks's reelection after his involvement on Boeing's behalf in the air force tanker controversy (noted previously).

CHAPTER 5

Past as Prologue

The Electoral Influence of Corporations

Michael M. Franz

For over a century, there has been a fear about the role of corporations in American elections. In early 2010, when the Supreme Court issued its opinion in *Citizens United v. FEC*,[1] which, as detailed in the Introduction, cleared the way for corporations, unions, and other groups to spend directly for the support or defeat of federal candidates, these concerns were amplified to a fever pitch. The 2010 congressional elections were the first major test of the *Citizens United* impact, and outside interests spent more money on express candidate advocacy than in any previous election in American history. Corporations played a unique role in those elections. They did not sponsor or run a single campaign ad on behalf of a federal candidate—which might surprise some—but many were aggressive funders of other groups that did. The rules for electioneering ushered in with the Court's historic decision in 2010 made it far easier for corporations to fund political activities, and the absence of commensurate disclosure rules made it simple to keep those investments hidden.

These developments vis-à-vis corporations are the focus of this chapter. Of course, corporations always have played a role in American politics and elections, and that perspective should be considered carefully. As such, the chapter is organized into three main sections. It begins first with a consideration of an ongoing avenue of corporate politicking, contributions to federal candidates. The ability to donate to candidates through political action committees (PACs) was unaffected by *Citizens United*, but looking at the activity of corporations in this area is essential to understanding their mind-set as they approach electoral politics. The chapter then shifts to a discussion of an outlawed area of influence, contributions from corporate treasuries to party committees—a form of electoral investment that situated corporations at the center of the contentious politics of the late 1990s. This discussion clarifies that corporations are not shy about influencing elections when the rules permit it. Finally, the chapter considers an evolving area of corporate influence, the sponsorship of direct candidate advocacy efforts. The rules in that regard have undergone considerable change in recent years, punctuated by the *Citizens United* decision in January 2010. The chapter concludes by reviewing the role of corporations in state elections (in which there is considerable diversity of rules for corporate involvement) and speculates on the implications of corporate electioneering in future cycles.

Ultimately, the question posed here is simple: how do corporations play a role in American politics and is that role too big? As the evidence will show, there is real reason to believe the answer to the second question may be yes. Corporations always have found the means to influence the political and electoral process, and this is no more true than now. Getting a real handle on the influence of corporations is no easy task, however. Whether the millions corporations invest has a distorting effect on policy outcomes after the election, for example, is a matter of considerable debate in political science, and reasonable people disagree on the ultimate power corporate America holds in the electoral process. There is no denying, however, that *Citizens United* reduced the barriers to entry, and as the campaign finance system strains under the weight of evermore challenges, it seems investing in federal elections is a growth industry.

PACs and Corporations

The initial consideration here is the role of corporate money in directly funding the electoral efforts of federal candidates. At first blush, that influence would seem limited. As discussed in previous chapters, corporations are prohibited from directly contributing to candidates and their campaigns, and they have been since the Tillman Act of 1907. Corporations are, however, legally permitted, and have been since the 1970s, to form PACs and collect donations from employees (subject to contribution limits of $5,000 per employee), which can then be redirected to candidates.[2] Unions, trade associations, membership groups, and ideological organizations can do the same. Contributions to candidates from a PAC are capped, however, at $5,000 per election. This prevents the use of corporate treasury funds for candidate contributions, on the one hand, but allows employees of the corporation to act more cohesively—although in a limited fashion—in supporting or advocating for federal candidates.

In addition to contributing directly to candidate coffers, PACs can advocate independently for the election or defeat of candidates. These are called *independent expenditures* and can take the form of advertisements, phone banking, direct mail, canvassing, billboards, and so forth. Any attempt to convince voters that a federal candidate should be elected or defeated is classified as an independent expenditure, and these costs cannot be coordinated with the candidate.[3] Moreover, while the PAC must use money raised under the caps to sponsor these efforts, there are no upper limits on what the PAC can spend in that regard.

The data on PAC contributions and expenditures are telling as to what role corporate PACs play in American politics. The evidence is clear that corporate PACs prefer to contribute directly to candidates as opposed to spending independently on their behalf (see Table 5.1). In any given election in the last twenty years, corporate PACs account for over 36 percent of the total. In general, corporate PACs account for about a third of the PAC population,[4] and this translates into proportionate contribution totals. For independent expenditures, though, PACs consistently sponsor less than 1 percent in any specific election.

TABLE 5.1   Corporate PAC Activity, 1990–2010

Election Cycle	Contributions to Candidates	Independent Expenditures (IEs)	Contributions as Percent of All PACs	IEs as Percent of All
2009–2010	$165,455,021	$31,909	38.34%	0.00%
2007–2008	158,323,496	221,207	38.35	0.16
2005–2006	135,925,970	250,345	36.53	0.66
2003–2004	115,641,547	223,729	37.24	0.39
2001–2002	99,577,798	52,190	35.31	0.37
1999–2000	91,525,699	137,535	35.23	0.65
1997–1998	78,018,750	54,268	35.47	0.58
1995–1996	78,194,723	375,797	35.90	3.56
1993–1994	69,610,433	38,289	36.71	0.75
1991–1992	68,430,976	47,883	36.22	0.45
1989–1990	58,131,722	16,519	36.53	0.32
	$1,118,836,135	$1,449,671		

Source: Federal Election Commission.

Why the discrepancy between contributions and expenditures? In general, corporations prefer not to advocate for the election or defeat of federal candidates under the banner of the corporate entity. In that sense, corporations are "risk averse," preferring to contribute to influential incumbents, by and large, as opposed to the risky game of public electioneering. Political scientists generally sort the electoral motives of interest groups into two camps: *access* and *replacement.*[5] Interest groups with access goals prefer to curry favor with legislators through campaign contributions, hoping for a seat at the table in the drafting and passage of legislation. Groups with a replacement strategy use elections to defeat unfavorable legislators. Because independent expenditures are more direct evidence of replacement goals, the evidence in Table 5.1 suggests that corporations are more immediately interested in access.[6]

This has consequences for the role of corporations in the aftermath of *Citizens United*. Some were concerned that corporations beginning in 2010 would use their treasury funds to advocate publicly for federal candidates. Imagine, for example, if Starbucks were to put "Vote McCain" on their coffee cups or McDonald's offered a "Vote Obama" Happy Meal. Corporations engaging in such behavior would risk alienating potential customers, a price too high to pay. Corporate executives much prefer the more subtle politics of campaign contributions, which are disclosed publicly but little noticed by the voting electorate. The historic absence from corporations in the world of independent expenditures suggests then that they will not be direct campaigners using general treasury funds in future elections.

Corporations, on the other hand, are not absent from direct electioneering— far from it, in fact. They may hope to avoid a public airing of their political preferences, but it does not mean they have no stake in the outcome. To that effect, membership and trade association PACs, many of which organize to represent corporate interests, contribute heavily to candidates as well as sponsor independent expenditures.[7] For example, the National Beer Wholesalers Association, which is one of the top PACs in the country, organizes to represent corporate interests in that industry. Over the last twenty years, membership and trade PACs have contributed an additional 26 to 28 percent of all PAC contributions to candidates, and from 1990 to 2008 they sponsored between 32 and 58 percent of independent expenditures in any given election (see Table 5.2)—though it should be noted that the ratio of contributions to expenditures for these PACs is nearly 6 to 1 in 2010, suggesting that access is still the primary concern. (Note further the drop in 2010, to just 12 percent of independent expenditures, explained later in this chapter.)

Moreover, the category of trade or membership PACs is not exclusively committed to corporate interests. Some PACs in this category, such as the National Rifle Association, count citizens as members, not corporate entities. As such, not every dollar in this category of PACs should be treated as pro-corporation. Still, trade associations and membership groups form another line of attack for corporate interests to pursue replacement or access goals, and because they can better shield specific corporations from the media spotlight, trade PACs are far more likely than corporate committees to act toward replacing unfavorable legislators.

Both sets of PACs also count as noteworthy investors in elections even if we factor in the role of private citizens, who also can contribute directly to candidates and who donate the bulk of campaign contributions in American politics. In 1990, corporate PACs accounted for 18 percent of all candidate receipts, while trade and membership PACs added an additional 13.8 percent. In 2002, the totals were 13.5 percent and 10.2 percent, respectively. By 2010, corporate PACs made up 12.6 percent of House and Senate candidate coffers, with trade PACs pitching in 8.8 percent.[8]

TABLE 5.2   Trade and Membership PAC Activity, 1990–2010

Election Cycle	Contributions to Candidates	Independent Expenditures (IEs)	Contributions as Percent of All PACs	IEs as Percent of All
2009–2010	$115,335,850	$25,756,047	26.73%	12.14%
2007–2008	112,897,919	44,911,854	27.35	33.22
2005–2006	101,803,507	19,050,740	27.36	50.37
2003–2004	83,221,870	18,138,069	26.80	31.61
2001–2002	75,146,673	8,092,148	26.64	57.77
1999–2000	71,802,756	11,143,902	27.63	52.96
1997–1998	62,322,845	5,312,135	28.34	56.90
1995–1996	60,153,725	4,628,414	27.61	43.86
1993–1994	52,853,630	1,826,292	27.87	35.93
1991–1992	53,870,702	3,517,187	28.51	33.05
1989–1990	44,804,886	1,840,324	28.16	35.71
	834,214,363	144,217,112		

Source: Federal Election Commission.

The percentage drops between 1990 and 2010 were likely the consequence of two key factors: (1) the increasing relevance of Internet fundraising, which has made collecting contributions from individuals a lot easier; and (2) higher contributions limits for individuals, which were raised from $1,000 per election to $2,000 (indexed to inflation) with 2002's Bi-Partisan Campaign Reform Act. The critic at this point might hold these PAC declines as evidence for the reduction in corporate influence in federal elections, and this claim would have some truth to it. But the preceding numbers include all candidates in the totals, including challengers and long shots who appeal very little to corporate interests. Corporate PACs, along with all PACs, play a prominent role in the campaign financing of *specific* members of Congress.

In 2010, for example, House Speaker Nancy Pelosi (D-Calif.) raised $2.6 million for her reelection, 60 percent of which came from PACs. Some contributors included the Credit Union National Association, Mortgage Bankers Association, the Florida Sugar Cane League, and General Electric. Majority Leader Steny Hoyer (D-Md.) raised over $4.5 million, with 63 percent coming from PACs, including the National Restaurant Association, the American Health Care Association, and Coca-Cola. And Eric Cantor (R-Va.), who served as the minority whip in the House in 2010, raised just under $6 million for his reelection efforts, and 41 percent of that total came from political action committees such as Goldman Sachs, T-Mobile, and Bank of America.

In fact, a quick search of any prominent member of the House or Senate, either in party leadership or on key committees, demonstrates the prominent role of PACs in fundraising. This is an ongoing, and unchanged, component of American politics that greatly amplifies the role of the corporate voice in congressional policymaking.

Corporate Soft Money and Parties

In line with the ban on direct candidate contributions, corporations are similarly prohibited from using any general treasury funds for contributions to parties that help federal candidates. A loophole in the 1990s, however, seriously undermined the efficacy of that ban. This came in the form of soft money, which, as explained in Chapter 1, was officially outlawed for parties with the Bipartisan Campaign Reform Act of 2002. Between roughly 1980 and 2002, however, parties were allowed to raise unregulated funds from any source to help with their nonfederal efforts, ranging from support for state and local candidates to the purchase of office space.[9] This became an issue in the 1990s, however, when the parties stepped up their use of soft money for issue advertising that often mentioned federal candidates but stopped short of explicitly endorsing them for election or defeat. Corporations, as will be demonstrated, took full advantage of the opportunity.

It is important to pause here and once again consider the implications of the soft money loophole. Before 1996, parties were prevented from independently advocating for federal candidates in any way, under the assumption from Congress that parties could not advocate for such candidates without some collusion. (Parties could coordinate with candidates, but such efforts were capped.) In 1996, the Supreme Court invalidated that logic in *Colorado Republican Federal Campaign Committee v. FEC* and freed the parties to use contributions for independent expenditures. Between 1996 and 2002, however, parties spent only about $19 million total on such efforts, compared to $63 million from PACs. The Democratic and Republican Party committees did, however, spend over $280 million on television ads between 1998 and 2002, according to estimates from the Wisconsin Advertising Project.

What did they say in such ads? During this time period, if an ad from an interest group or party included a set of particular words or phrases (what came to be termed "magic words"), the ads were considered independent expenditures subject to stringent funding guidelines. These magic words, first listed in the 1976 Supreme Court decision in *Buckley v. Valeo* were as follows (and identified in Chapter 1): *vote for, elect, support, cast your ballot for, Smith for Congress, vote against, defeat,* or *reject.* Absent them, the ad was considered issue education or issue advocacy. The parties could use their soft money accounts for such efforts. In principle, however, the parties crafted ads that walked close but stopped short of the magic word bright line. Consider one ad from the Republican National Committee that aired in 2000:[10]

Female Narrator: Under Clinton/Gore, prescription drug prices have skyrocketed and nothing's been done. George Bush has a plan. Add a prescription drug benefit to Medicare.

George Bush: Every senior will have access to prescription drug benefits.

Female Narrator: And Al Gore, Gore opposed bipartisan reform. He's pushing a big government plan that lets Washington bureaucrats interfere with what your doctors prescribe. The Gore Prescription Plan: Bureaucrats Decide. The Bush Prescription Plan: Seniors Choose.

The ad does not tell the viewer how to vote, opting instead to compare the policy positions of Bush and Gore on prescription drugs for seniors, meaning the Federal Election Commission (FEC) considered the ad issue education and not electioneering.

How important were corporations to party finances in this soft money period? The FEC mandated that the party committees report their soft money receipts starting in 1992, meaning there are data on six election cycles through the 2002 ban. The data are stored in the FEC's detailed files on contributions by individuals.[11] As will be demonstrated later in this chapter, available data on corporate contributions to outside groups are limited, making this analysis of party contributions all the more relevant to understanding how corporations behave politically when the rules permit it. Between 1992 and 2002, parties raised over $1.4 billion in soft money. A soft money contributor could be anyone, from a wealthy individual to a union or a Fortune 500 company.

Figure 5.1 shows corporate investments in each election as a percentage of all soft money to parties and as a percentage of interest group soft money.[12] All told, corporations played a critical role in funding the parties during the soft money period. The vast majority of those funds were allocated to the Republican Party, about 75 percent of the corporate total. The following are some of the biggest donors in this time period:

- Freddie Mac—$3.5 million in 2002 and $2 million in 2000
- AT&T—$3.3 million in 2002 and $3.3 in 2000
- Phillip Morris Company—$3 million in 1996 and $2.7 million in 2002
- Amway Corporation—$2.5 million in 1994
- Microsoft—$2.5 million in 2002 and $1.7 million in 2000
- Pfizer—$1.5 million in 2000 and $1.3 million in 2002

Keep in mind that corporations have been permitted for nearly forty years to form PACs and make contributions to party committees (in addition to candidates),

FIGURE 5.1   Corporate Soft Money Contributions, 1992–2002

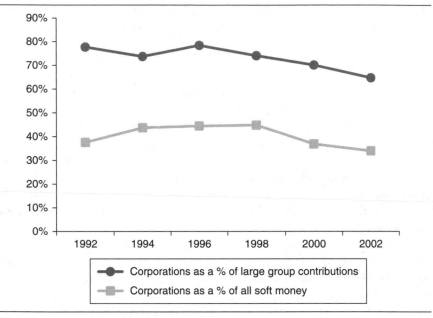

Source: Federal Election Commission.

but such contributions are limited to $30,000 in total for an election cycle. During the soft money period, then, corporate donors leveraged the parties' desire for large soft money donations to become central to the party network, especially for the GOP. Unlike the world of candidate fundraising, in which corporate PACs are now a smaller share of overall receipts than they were twenty years prior (as noted earlier), corporate money in the soft money world exceeded 33 percent in every election cycle between 1992 and 2002, and over 40 percent in three of those election years (along with making up about 75 percent of large interest group donations). That suggests a powerful role for these donors in setting the party's policymaking agenda. The data here do not demonstrate actual influence on party agendas, of course, but because corporations were so critical a source of funds for parties in sponsoring their issue advocacy messages, it only stands to reason that large donors would have some say in crafting what party leaders pushed in Congress.

Soft money is now illegal, and corporations are limited to helping parties directly through their corporate PACs, which would suggest some diminished power for corporations.[13] This may be true—though the evidence in the next section might suggest otherwise—but the lesson of soft money is the extent to which corporations will go to be important players in American politics. When the regulations are not in place to blunt that influence, corporations and other interest groups will take full advantage.

Campaign finance reformers have fought hard in the last ten years to prevent the soft money loophole from blowing back open. One court case from 2010, *RNC v. FEC*, considered a challenge from the Republican Party on whether to overturn the party soft money ban in light of *Citizens United*. If corporations, the plaintiffs argued, have free speech rights to spend independently advocating for candidates, why not extend the logic to contributions to parties? The U.S. District Court for the District of Columbia rejected that logic, and the Supreme Court refused to hear the case. In 2011, two pro-Democratic groups—as a consequence of a Republican plan—asked the FEC whether federal candidates could raise unlimited funds for interest groups working outside the party structure. Critics worried that such groups would become parallel party soft money engines. The FEC argued that this innovative proposal was not permitted relative to soliciting directly corporate or union contributions. Both developments were victories for the opponents of party soft money, but the outcome in both cases was not immediately clear, especially in light of the deregulatory trend suggested by the Court in *Citizens United*.

Corporate Electioneering and Disclosure

Thus far, the evidence suggests first that corporate PACs play an important role in funding candidates (about 38 percent of all PAC contributions and about 13 percent of all candidate contributions, with much higher investments in powerful legislators). Second, while corporate PACs are nearly nonexistent in the funding of independent expenditures, many pro-corporate trade associations eagerly fill the void. Finally, corporations played a central role in the financing of the parties' soft money operations throughout the 1990s, and although this was finally outlawed after the 2002 elections, the ban has faced pressure in the courts and in the regulatory process.

Corporate influence is not restricted to these areas, however. Although now prohibited from using general treasury funds to donate to parties, they can sponsor directly their own electioneering messages (as a consequence of *Citizens United*), as well as aid the efforts of a host of other interest groups. As with PACs, and as will be demonstrated, corporations generally eschew the former, but have embraced the latter, though assessing the level of this activity is a bit hampered by holes in disclosure mandates.

The laws and regulations structuring corporate electioneering have undergone a bit of turmoil in recent years, moving in a libertarian direction since the BCRA reforms of 2002. To best understand the role of corporations as of 2010, it may be useful to consider three key time periods over the last twenty years. Each period brought with it a unique profile of groups and corporate involvement.

Group Profile and Corporate Involvement, 1994–2002

Between about 1994 and 2002, all interest groups were free to sponsor issue advocacy messages, much like the parties, with unregulated funds.[14] Moreover, during most of this period, there was almost no disclosure for such groups. This can be demonstrated by looking at the political advertising data in two of these years, 2000 and 2002. The data come from the Wisconsin Advertising Project and include all ads aired on broadcast television in the top 75 (in 2000) or top 100 (in 2002) media markets in the United States. One challenge in using the data is that the project does not identify the campaign account that paid for the political ads, making note only of the sponsor as identified in the disclaimer at the end of the ad. Some groups have PACs that register with the FEC, as well as parallel nonprofit groups that fund issue advocacy. Nonetheless, one can cross-check whether the group had a PAC and whether it reported independent expenditures in that election cycle.

The top twenty groups airing political ads in 2000 and 2002 are listed in Table 5.3—meaning some groups are repeated if they were active in both years—excluding labor unions.[15] To be clear, this shows the number of ads on television sponsored by groups that mentioned or pictured federal candidates at any point in the election year, noting also the estimated cost of the total ad buys.[16] The last two columns indicate whether the group also had a PAC that registered with the FEC in that election cycle and the total amount in independent expenditures reported to the FEC by the PAC.

The data are striking. Only eleven of the twenty groups had a PAC, and seven of those groups reported some independent expenditure efforts in the noted year. That total amounted to only $7.4 million, however, over $5.7 million of which was from the League of Conservation Voters in 2000 and 2002. In contrast, the Wisconsin Advertising Project data identifies nearly $50 million in pro-candidate advertising. By implication, the vast majority of those funds, in not being reported to the FEC, were issue advocacy messages that stopped short of directly advocating for or against candidates but nonetheless contained some mention of them. Consider the following example from the Citizens for Better Medicare in 2000:[17]

> Announcer: Congressman Shaw believes Florida seniors deserve the best health care so he is fighting to improve Medicare with an affordable prescription drug plan that gives seniors peace of mind. Congressman Shaw believes seniors should have real choices because he recognizes that every senior has different health care needs. Real choice. Quality. Affordability. Congressman Shaw has the right plan to bring Florida's seniors peace of mind. Support Clay Shaw's prescription for Florida's seniors.

TABLE 5.3   Top 20 Interest Groups in Political Advertising, 2000 and 2002

Group	Cost	Ads Aired	Year	Ind. Exp.	Have a PAC?
United Seniors Association	8,134,358	13,984	2002	0	Yes
Citizens for Better Medicare	6,777,291	10,876	2000	0	No
Chamber of Commerce	5,480,846	7,574	2000	0	Yes
Planned Parenthood	5,340,506	5,916	2000	66,862	Yes
Women Voters, Project of EMILY's LIST	3,639,189	2,665	2000	27,552	Yes
Americans for Job Security	3,084,484	5,555	2000	0	No
Business Roundtable	2,962,192	4,884	2000	0	No
Handgun Control	2,067,654	3,311	2000	1,243,567	Yes
Americans for Job Security	1,588,227	2,172	2002	0	No
Alliance for Quality Nursing Home Care	1,439,888	2,033	2000	0	No
Sierra Club	1,383,758	2,168	2000	330,271	Yes
Republicans for Clean Air	1,355,679	1,722	2000	0	No
Republican Leadership Council	1,180,048	1,807	2000	0	Yes
EMILY's List	971,321	896	2002	0	Yes
League of Conservation Voters	900,601	1,705	2000	3,324,178	Yes
Coalition for the Future American Worker	710,900	739	2000	0	No
Voters for Choice	699,024	683	2000	0	No
League of Conservation Voters	660,140	1,398	2002	2,391,518	Yes
American Family Voices	628,219	447	2000	0	No
Club for Growth	558,399	1,574	2002	7,049	Yes
Totals	49,562,724	72,109		7,390,997	11 of 20

Source: Wisconsin Advertising Project and Federal Election Commission.

Because these messages were not reportable to the FEC, they could be funded rather liberally with large donations from wealthy individuals, unions, and corporations. Of the twenty groups in Table 5.3, twelve of them sponsored ads that aided Republican candidates and are presumably the most likely to have accepted large contributions from corporate treasuries. (The groups aligned with the Democrats were Planned Parenthood, EMILY's List, Handgun Control, the Sierra Club, the League of Conservation Voters, and Voters for Choice.) Consider the brief profiles of a handful of them:[18]

- United Seniors Association—often described as a conservative alternative to the AARP. It was reportedly backed by a prescription drug lobby group, the Pharmaceutical Research and Manufacturers of America.
- Citizens for Better Medicare—an advocacy group formed and backed by the pharmaceutical industry; affiliates included the United Seniors Association.
- Chamber of Commerce—a trade group that advocates for corporations and maintains local chapters across the country. (See Chapter 2 in this volume for more information.)
- Americans for Job Security—a pro-business advocacy organization that is thought to have spun off of the Chamber of Commerce. Among rumored donors were Microsoft and the American Insurance Association.
- Business Roundtable—a pro-business lobbying group comprised of CEOs of large corporations.

Because Congress had not mandated the disclosure of these groups' efforts in 2000 and 2002, we have no real handle on the level of investments from outside interests absent the Wisconsin Advertising Project.[19] Still, even with the ad-buy data, we can make very reasonable inferences that corporate donors funded many of these groups. The data on party soft money from the previous section make clear that corporations do not forego significant investment in electoral politics, even if they do not sponsor pro-candidate messages directly. And while corporations may have felt pressure from party leaders in contributing to the parties' soft money accounts, so as to secure access to policymakers, corporate funding of pro-business groups is more intentional, motivated more obviously by the goal of tipping close elections in favor of pro-business candidates.

Group Profile and Corporate Involvement, 2003–2007

As noted earlier, Congress passed the party soft money ban with BCRA in 2002, but a parallel provision mandated that all ads sponsored by interest groups within sixty days of a general election and thirty days of a primary be funded only by individuals or PAC dollars. This was intended to stymie the efforts of groups like the ones listed in Table 5.3. In 2003, a number of groups organized as political organizations under Section 527 of the tax code and pledged publicly to accept large contributions to fund issue advocacy efforts in the 2004 elections. In 2004, 527s became a household name, as a variety of groups, such as MoveOn.org, Swift Boat Veterans, and Progress for America actively aired political ads that year—in much the same way as in previous elections, stopping short of explicitly calling for the election or defeat of federal candidates. For many, this was a glaring loophole in BCRA, one that neither Congress nor the FEC was able to sidestep. Ironically, however, the 2004 and 2006 elections might be the ones where corporate influence was at its weakest in the last twenty years.

How is this the case? Most importantly, 527s sponsoring television or radio ads during this time could not accept any contributions from corporations or unions for the purpose of funding advertising efforts. This was directly proscribed in BCRA. The real loophole for 527s was in the permission to accept large contributions from individuals. Table 5.4 demonstrates this by examining the top conservative-leaning 527s in 2004 and 2006, as identified by the Center for Responsive Politics. The table shows seventeen groups in both years, of which only the Club for Growth sponsored a PAC. It also shows the amount spent on independent expenditures (in this case, only the Club for Growth's efforts), and electioneering communications, the new term (first defined in Chapter 1) used by the FEC starting in 2004 referring to radio or television ads aired within the thirty or sixty day windows. To review, electioneering communications are ones that do not explicitly advocate for the election or defeat of federal candidates, but merely mention or picture them in ads. Table 5.4 also shows the total receipts reported to the IRS by each group and the percentage contributed by individuals.

The listed groups raised over $90 million in both years and bought nearly $58 million in electioneering communications. Of particular importance is the dominance of individuals in the contributor pool for these listed groups. Over 98 percent of the total came from individuals. The last column in the table also shows the largest contributor for each group, and these donations were of considerable size. Bob Perry, a Texas homebuilder, bankrolled four groups in 2006 to the tune of $9.4 million, and he was a major backer of the Swift Boats in 2004 with over $4.3 million. Other large donors included Alex Spanos, a real estate developer and owner of the San Diego Chargers and Dawn Arnall, cochair along with her husband of Ameriquest in 2004, as well as the cochair of the Republican National Convention.

Large contributions from individuals are concerning, but these contributions were not given in the name of any specific corporation, nor were they from a corporate treasury account. Whether this is good or bad for the democratic system is a matter of debate, but it is worth reemphasizing that in 2004 and 2006, the efforts

TABLE 5.4 Contributions and Expenditures of Conservative 527s, 2004 and 2006

	Independent Expenditures	Electioneering Comm.	Have a PAC?	527 Receipts	% of 527 Funding from Individual	Largest Contributor
Top Conservative-Leaning 527s in 2006						
Club for Growth	$2,753,238	$530,596	Yes	$6,375,280	100	Virginia Manheimer, $860,000
Americans for Honesty on Issues	$0	$3,188,095	No	$3,030,221	99	Bob Perry, $3,000,000
Economic Freedom Fund	$0	$1,938,286	No	$5,050,450	100	Bob Perry, $5,000,000
Free Enterprise Fund Committee	$0	$1,038,682	No	$1,239,003	100	Bob Perry, $1,000,000
Softer Voices	$0	$915,149	No	$1,403,300	100	Jack Templeton, $630,000
Free Enterprise Committee	$0	$350,000	No	$400,124	100	Bob Perry, $400,000
New Yorkers for Responsible Leadership	$0	$188,228	No	$128,250	76	21st Century Freedom PAC, $25,000
Republicans Who Care Individual Fund	$0	$182,561	No	$599,300	93	Robert D Ziff, $75,800
Americans for Conservation	$0	$78,000	No	$705,000	100	David Bonderman, $225,000
Totals	$2,753,238	$8,409,597	1 of 9	$18,930,928	99	

Top Conservative-Leaning 527s in 2004

	Independent Expenditures	Electioneering Comm.	Have a PAC?	527 Receipts	% of 527 Funding from Individual	Largest Contributor
Progress for America Voter Fund	$0	$26,493,866	No	$44,929,178	98	Alex Spanos and Dawn Arnall, $5,000,000
Swift Vets & POWs for Truth	$0	$17,209,137	No	$17,008,090	99	Bob Perry, $4,350,000
Club for Growth	$1,499,446	$3,715,730	Yes	$6,530,939	99	GJ Jensen, $1,038,000
Americans United to Preserve Marriage	$0	$916,947	No	$1,192,090	100	Aubrey McClendon, $625,000
Softer Voices	$0	$474,570	No	$671,100	100	Bruce Kovner, $195,000
Colorado Conservative Voters	$0	$354,635	No	$525,500	100	Terry Considine and Bill Armstrong, $100,000
Americans for Peace Through Strength	$0	$100,000	No	$240,000	83	Lawrence J Ellison, $200,000
Greater New Orleans Republicans Fund	$0	$68,525	No	$90,000	100	Walter Gray, $30,000
Totals	$1,499,446	$49,333,410	1 of 8	$71,186,897	98	

Source: Federal Election Commission and Center for Responsive Politics.

of direct corporate money were stymied. Soft money to parties was banned, and 527s sponsoring issue advocacy in the final two months of the election were forced to look elsewhere for funding. Of course, corporations could still contribute to nonprofit groups using issue advocacy outside the thirty- and sixty-day windows, but Congress argued in BCRA in 2002 that these efforts were less of a concern than the ads aired in the immediate run-up to election day.[20]

Group Profile and Corporate Involvement, 2008 and 2010 (and Beyond)

If 2004 and 2006 represented a triumph, of sorts, in blunting the role of corporate money in elections, then the most recent elections are a decided step backwards. Two Supreme Court cases have upended the rules and opened the door to unprecedented corporate influence. As noted at the beginning of the chapter, *Citizens United v. FEC* overturned all bans on corporate and union sponsorship of direct candidate advocacy. A 2007 case, however, *Wisconsin Right to Life v. FEC*, may have been more important.[21] In that case, the Court argued that the ban on corporate and union sponsorship of electioneering communications—the "good news" noted in the previous section—was unconstitutional if it prevented groups from raising funds to do genuine lobbying. The Court said, for example, that not all ads aired within the thirty- and sixty-day windows should be considered electioneering just because the ad mentions a federal candidate. If the intention of the ad is to lobby citizens to act on a policy issue, the Court asserted, the ad should be considered exempt from the corporate and union ban.

The next question is obvious: what constitutes an election ad that can be regulated and a lobbying ad that cannot? The Court offered no real guidance, opening the door for corporations and unions to once again sponsor ads that attacked or supported candidates but that were cloaked in enough policy language to be considered issue advocacy. The vagueness in that supposed distinction was enough to move the Court toward its more drastic opinion in *Citizens United*.

Consider, first, the advertising efforts of the Chamber of Commerce in 2006 (when the corporate ban was in effect) and 2008 (when issue advocacy was again permissible in the final two weeks). Chapter 2 in this volume focuses more explicitly on the Chamber's efforts in recent elections, while the example here serves only to make clear the effect of the changing rules. Figure 5.2 plots the Chamber's House and Senate television advertising in both years, showing the total ad buys per day between the first ads aired and election day.[22]

In 2006, the Chamber was on the air aggressively in early August and then again in late August and early September. All ads stopped, however, on September 7th, the beginning of the sixty-day window. And because the Chamber accepts corporate contributions, they were prevented in 2006 from using those funds in

FIGURE 5.2   Timing of Chamber of Commerce Political Ads, 2006 and 2008

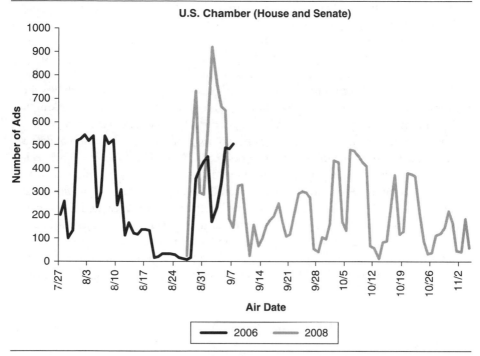

Source: Wisconsin Advertising Project and Wesleyan Media Project.

the two-month period before the elections. In 2008, however, with *Wisconsin Right to Life* changing the parameters for when corporate funds could be applied to pro-candidate advertising, the Chamber went on the air in late August and advertised through election day.

A quick look at the Chamber's ads in 2008 points to their issue advocacy frame. One ad, which aired in Maine during the reelection campaign of Susan Collins, said the following:

Announcer: Health care is vital. That's why Susan Collins voted to ensure Maine seniors have better access to health care and affordable prescriptions. Collins supported funding for health technology and cutting-edge scientific research so Maine families can live longer, healthier lives. And Collins supports doctors and patients making health care decisions, not government bureaucrats. Call Susan Collins. Tell her to keep working for better health care.

The tag line urging voters to call Collins establishes the Chamber's issue advocacy goal, freeing its use of corporate donations in purchasing the airtime. That Collins was facing a tough challenge from Democratic Rep. Tom Allen was irrelevant to the test outlined in *Wisconsin Right to Life*.

By 2010, interest groups had truly been "unleashed," to borrow from this book's title, and were no longer required to shade their language to avoid calling for the election or defeat of candidates. This is clearly evidenced in Table 5.5, which lists the top twenty interest groups involved in the 2010 elections. Perhaps most striking is the dominance of reported independent expenditures over electioneering communications, the former being messages that call expressly for candidates' election or defeat and the latter being ads that merely mention candidates. The *Citizens United* decision, in that regard, freed groups to be more direct in how they communicated to the broader public. A second inference from the table is the absence of any for-profit corporation in the list of top groups. As noted with respect to PACs, and as was true for the period from 1994 to 2002, corporations are not inclined to sponsor electioneering messages directly, preferring to fund trade groups or ideological nonprofits.

From the perspective of the campaign finance reform community, the 2004 and 2006 elections were preferable because corporations were prohibited from

TABLE 5.5   Expenditures of Top Interest Groups, 2010

	Independent Expenditures	Electioneering Comm.	Disclose Donors?	Why?
U.S. Chamber of Commerce	$0	$32,851,997	No	501(c)(6) business group
American Action Network	5,669,821	20,418,210	No	501(c)(4) social welfare group
American Crossroads	21,553,277	0	Yes	Super PAC
Crossroads GPS	16,017,664	1,104,782	No	501(c)(4) social welfare group
SEIU	15,692,364	0	Partial	501(c)(5), PAC and 527, though its 527 receives only transfers from SEIU affiliates
AFSCME	11,995,182	68,539	Partial	501(c)(5), PAC and 527, though its 527 receives only transfers from AFSCME affiliates
National Education Association	7,239,105	105,724	Yes	527, PAC, and super PAC

	Independent Expenditures	Electioneering Comm.	Disclose Donors?	Why?
American Future Fund	7,387,918	2,211,888	No	501(c)(4) social welfare group
Americans for Job Security	4,406,902	4,584,307	No	501(c)(4) social welfare group
National Association of Realtors	7,122,031	0	Yes	PAC and super PAC
National Rifle Association	7,263,028	0	Yes	PAC
Club for Growth	8,240,060	0	Yes*	PAC, super PAC, 527
60 Plus Association	6,698,287	397,838	No	501(c)(4) social welfare group
America's Families First Action Fund	5,878,743	0	Yes	Super PAC
League of Conservation Voters	5,496,070	0	Yes*	PAC, super PAC, 527
Americans for Tax Reform	4,140,044	0	No	501(c)(4) social welfare group
AFL-CIO	3,319,984	0	Partial	501(c)(5), PAC, super PAC, 527, though its latter two accounts receive only transfers from affiliated unions
EMILY's List	3,894,402	74,299	Yes	PAC, super PAC, 527
Commonsense Ten	3,257,033	0	Yes	Super PAC
VoteVets.org	2,360,867	858,004	No	501(c)(4) social welfare group
	147,632,782	62,675,588		

Source: Federal Election Commission and Center for Responsive Politics.

*These groups also have a 501(c)(4) that does not disclose, though the extent to which that account was utilized is unclear.

funding groups airing ads in the final sixty days of the election. In the absence of that prohibition currently, many would call alternatively for strong disclosure laws to clarify which groups are receiving large contributions from wealthy individuals or corporate treasuries. One consequence of *Citizens United*, however, was in empowering groups to sponsor pro-candidate ads that did not also have to disclose donors publicly. PACs and 527s have been the primary focus of this chapter, and both types disclose donors, but a number of other groups are now relevant players. These include the following:

- 501(c)(4) social welfare nonprofits
- 501(c)(5) unions; unions typically funded their federal electioneering through their affiliated PACs, but can now sponsor ads with funds from their parent (c)(5) organization
- 501(c)(6) business leagues and chambers of commerce
- Independent expenditure–only PACs (super PACs); groups that pledge only to independently electioneer for candidates and make no direct contributions to federal candidates

The first three in the preceding list do not make public their donor lists, while the last one is a new group created in the aftermath of *Citizens United* that does disclose to the FEC. All are now dominant players in electoral politics. Recall again the trade PAC totals from Table 5.2, whereby the percentage of independent expenditures from said groups dropped to only 12 percent in 2010. The steep decline was the consequence of these new groups entering the scene and sponsoring pro- or anti-candidates ads.

Of the top twenty groups, eight were not required to reveal any donors (Table 5.5), accounting for over $109 million in electioneering, which is 51 percent of the total expenditures in the table. Another nine groups did reveal donors behind $70 million in expenditures. Finally, three groups—all unions—are best classified under partial disclosure because so much of their funding comes from transfers between affiliated unions and other accounts, and how much of those underlying funds come from union dues or other sources is unclear.

Overall, one of the most critical consequences of the Supreme Court's decision in 2010 was the empowerment of groups to sponsor independent expenditures and electioneering communications without commensurate disclosure laws. Congress's attempt to rectify that imbalance—the DISCLOSE Act—stalled under a Republican filibuster in 2010. In 2011, President Obama considered, but dropped, an executive order that would have required corporations with federal contracts to make public their contributions to any group engaging in pro-candidate electioneering. As with the period from 1994 to 2002 discussed earlier, outdated disclosure provisions make it exceptionally difficult to quantify the likely large influence of corporations in this arena of electioneering. But this may be exactly the preferable outcome for corporations. Because they are averse to direct electioneering, corporations motivated to participate in electoral politics would likely prefer to make large and nondisclosed contributions to front organizations like American Action Network or American Future Fund.[23]

One other critical consequence of *Citizens United* may be the further weakening of the formal party committees relative to super PACs or 501(c) groups. While these latter organizations are now free to raise and spend unlimited amounts on independent expenditures or electioneering communications, the formal party committees (i.e., the Democratic National Committee) are constrained to hard money limits as proscribed in BCRA. As noted earlier, the parties were formally prolific in their raising and spending of soft money, but the BCRA limits potentially further alienate party leaders in the execution of campaigns. As large corporate, union, or individual checks increasingly fund super PACs, 527s, and 501(c) groups, they will take on more prominent roles in competitive elections. These groups can also coordinate amongst themselves, as many already do. The formal party committees, however, have very limited opportunities to coordinate with their own candidates and no such opportunities to work with outside groups who are otherwise their allies. These developments produce a fragmented campaign finance system in which the new central players are often untraceable front organizations with no clear and formal linkage to the party system. This outcome may not concern many, but from the perspective of democratic theory, it is a system that no one would likely design a priori.

A Word on State Elections

It is worth noting that state election laws vary considerably in the allowances given to corporations to participate in elections for state legislative, judicial, and executive offices. After *Citizens United*, all twenty-four states with corporate expenditure bans were overturned; instructively, twenty-six states even before 2010 allowed for some corporate electioneering. The ruling did not affect state contribution limits, and as of 2012, twenty-eight states allowed corporations to contribute directly to state candidates, though the limit on such contributions varies across states.[24] For example, four states allow for unlimited contributions to candidates directly from corporate treasury funds—Missouri, Oregon, Utah, and Virginia. In most other states, the limits are usually the same as those that apply to individuals and range from $250 in Maine for legislative candidates to $10,000 in Illinois. In a few states—Alabama, Indiana, and Mississippi—contributions from individuals are unlimited but are capped for corporations. And in a number of states, the rules for corporations are more restrictive than those for unions.[25]

States are often considered the laboratories of democracy, and the considerable variation in corporate regulations on electioneering allow for some assessment of the possible impact of *Citizens United* on federal elections.[26] Of course, one caveat in that regard is that comparing the impact of unlimited corporate electioneering in a state like Utah is not ideally suitable to assessing the impact on unlimited corporate electioneering at the federal level. The scale of issues considered and moneys allocated in Washington, DC are way beyond those in Salt Lake City. On the other hand, if states with and without corporate restrictions do not vary considerably in the partisan slant in the state or the success of corporations at securing favorable policies, we might more justifiably infer that the impact of *Citizens United* at the federal level will be slight.

A number of studies have looked for such effects, though more work is needed. The initial evidence suggests that states with a corporate contribution ban look similar to states without such a ban. For example, one study examined states using fifteen different metrics of political outcomes, from the business climate in various states to the progressive nature of their tax code and partisan slant of their elected legislature.[27] Across the metrics, the results showed that states with and without corporate limits tended to have similar outcomes. It should be noted that the analysis was limited to a bivariate investigation, and did not take into account other factors that might mask key differences across states. Another study compared four states in 2008, two with a corporate ban on electioneering and two without. The results similarly suggested little difference between the states on electoral and policy outcomes.[28]

Both sets of results are counterintuitive, and incredibly important. They complicate the narrative that corporate electioneering efforts have deleterious effects on the electoral process. Nonetheless, the research here is still new, and these initial findings may not hold up in subsequent elections.

Implications and Conclusions

At the end of the day, assessing the role of corporations in American politics is not an easy task. The evidence from this chapter indicates that corporate funds, while no longer a dominant component of the parties' fundraising and not a particularly noteworthy portion of 527s's receipts in 2004 and 2006, are nonetheless important players in the electioneering campaigns of nonprofits, especially post–*Citizens United*. Of course, the ability to assess the level of that influence, and to search for the donations of specific corporations, is limited by the lack of disclosure laws. One can only assume that when the Chamber of Commerce spends $33 million in 2010 on electioneering communications that their primary funding comes from the corporate members who contribute to the Chamber's budget. Again, the experience of state politics is instructive. When Target contributed $150,000 in 2010 to a political group advocating for a gubernatorial candidate that opposed gay rights, the subsequent media firestorm embarrassed the corporation. When disclosure calls attention to corporate electioneering, citizens have the chance to reward or punish corporations. Absent disclosure, corporations can avoid direct candidate advocacy but remain in the shadows with their support of nonprofit groups. As the actions of these nonprofits extend in future elections, and in the absence of better disclosure laws at the federal level, the stealth role of corporations is likely to grow.

There are two principle criticisms of the analysis in this chapter, though, both coming from different perspectives. First, any assessment of the "role of business" in American elections should be careful to note that corporations do not speak with a single voice. They are not, as some might suggest, in uniform agreement on political goals. In fact, when one scholar used corporate PAC contributions to incumbent House members to estimate the ideology of the PAC, the results revealed considerable diversity—with some PACs far more conservative than others.[29] A different analysis using an alternative methodology demonstrated that Massey Energy, for example, is far more conservative than Google, Apple, and Intel.[30] Because of this, any claim that corporations play too big a role in American politics misses the conflicts and contentions that can and often do arise when corporations engage in politics and policymaking.[31]

On the other hand, a second criticism starts with the counterclaim that even if the universe of corporations has disagreements, there may be uniformity among them on supporting free market principles at the expense of pro-labor policies, redistributive policies that include higher corporate taxes, and environmental regulations. Moreover, as political scientist Tom Ferguson argues, any analysis that looks only at corporate treasury investments misses the role of large individual contributors who use their vast wealth to push political policies that better the bottom line of their corporate employer.[32] For example, Bob Perry and others have invested millions in political groups that have electioneered for federal candidates. The discussion of 527s in 2004 and 2006 implies that contributions from wealthy individuals are less worrisome. Although these individuals did not use corporate treasury money in pursuing these goals, wealthy investors are very likely now hoping to accomplish policy ends in line with their business interests. As such, any discussion that ignores large contributions from individuals to interest groups likely underestimates corporate influence. One recent study to that effect demonstrated that contributions from individuals to federal candidates are often directed to those politicians serving on committees that regulate their employers, suggesting that contributions are motivated toward particularistic economic ends.[33] Notably, the study did not limit the analysis to members of the firms' boards, but to all donors reporting their employer on standard campaign finance disclosure forms.

There is one final consideration as well. The discussion in this chapter has focused on the role of corporations in elections, but the lobbying world is another avenue of influence. In this arena, corporations can invest general treasury dollars without limit—something that was true long before the rules liberalized for elections with *Citizens United*. And, there is some concern that lobbying investments from corporations skew policy outcomes. E. E. Schattschneider famously argued, in that regard, that "the flaw in the pluralist heaven [where competing interests cancel out and prevent any single interest from consistently winning] is that the heavenly chorus sings with a strong upper-class accent."[34] That is, poor people, labor, and citizens' groups are not often able to effectively organize or compete with the weight of big business. Two scholars have presented suggestive evidence of this by showing that across a random sample of over 130 issues on which interest groups lobbied in the mid-1990s, business and trade groups made up the lion's share of lobbying efforts.[35] Moreover, on the vast majority of issues, only a handful of groups lobbied and businesses dominated these groups.

The evidence is not definitive, however. Some earlier empirical work showed that on important issue considerations in Congress, there was often a "hollow core" to the debate, with no hegemonic player—like big business—pulling the strings.[36] A recent landmark study also argued that the real bias in the system is a firmly rooted status quo, implying that business groups or the wealthy find it very difficult to demand a policy change and expect results—though they may have had a hand in setting up the status quo.[37] Finally, a wealth of studies have failed to find consistent evidence that corporate PAC contributions facilitate lobbying by influencing the votes of incumbents on legislation.[38] Since the early 1980s, corporate PACs have totaled about 1,800 in any single election cycle, which are but a small reflection of the overall corporate universe in the American economy. According to one estimate, only about 60 percent of Fortune 500 companies in 2000 had PACs, and a more recent survey of Fortune 500 companies in 2010 identified 25 percent who did not.[39] As such, the claim that large contributors and corporate interests manage the policymaking process is a contested one.

Despite these caveats, the overall message is that corporations play an important and growing role in federal elections. Corporations have always sought to influence the political process, and *Citizens United* did not emerge out of thin air. Through PACs, party soft money, and issue advocacy, corporations have been at the center of electoral politics for a long time. What worries many is that any attempt by Congress to limit the influence of corporations moving forward faces a skeptical Supreme Court. Many worry further about the return of party soft money and the potential overturning of corporate bans on candidate contributions. One more recent case (*U.S. v. Danielczyk*, decided in U.S. District Court in May 2010) even went so far as to claim that corporations have the right to donate directly to federal candidates. That case signals that nearly all restrictions on the role of corporations in elections are at risk in years to come.

And interest groups may have used the 2010 elections to "gear up" for deeper investments—most shielded from public view—in the 2012 presidential election and beyond. A new trend for 2012 is the development of candidate-specific super PACs that are directed independently by allies of the candidate. While candidates like former House Speaker Newt Gingrich raise and spend money within federal campaign finance limits, close friends of his can raise large sums from corporate treasuries or from wealthy corporate executives to be spent independently on his behalf. As this book went to press, the GOP primary campaign was still in full swing, and by early March 2012, over thirty outside groups had aired more than 60,000 ads on behalf of the Republican candidates for president. This represented about 50 percent of all the ads aired in the campaign, by far the largest investment from outside groups in a presidential primary campaign in modern American politics. If interest groups were unleashed with *Citizens United* in 2010, the past may be but quaint prologue in the story of corporate electioneering.

Endnotes

The author is particularly grateful to Ken Goldstein at the University of Wisconsin Advertising Project (http://wiscadproject.wisc.edu/) for granting access to the political advertising data for the 2000, 2002, and 2008 elections. Political ad data from the 2006 and 2012 elections are from the Wesleyan Media Project (https://election-ad.research .wesleyan.edu/), of which the author is codirector.

1   *Citizens United v. FEC,* 558 U.S. 08-205, 2010.
2   More specifically, corporations can solicit contributions regularly only from executive and administrative personnel, as well as from stockholders; there are limited opportunities to solicit from additional corporate employees who are not executives or administrative personnel.
3   Corporate PACs are permitted to spend treasury funds in consultation with candidates to communicate persuasion messages to executive and administrative personnel, as well as to stockholders. These totals across all PACs are much lower than the contribution and independent-expenditure totals, and corporate PACs in particular spend next to nothing on these communications.
4   See Mark Rozell, Clyde Wilcox, and Michael Franz, *Interest Groups in American Campaigns: The New Face of Electioneering,* 3rd ed. (New York: Oxford University Press, 2012), ch. 3.
5   Michael Franz, *Choices and Changes: Interest Groups in the Electoral Process* (Philadelphia: Temple University Press, 2008), 54–55.
6   It is not always the case that contributions signal an access goal or that independent expenditures are always motivated to move votes on election day. Sometimes a contribution to a competitive candidate can be useful in helping the candidate build a much-needed war chest, and independent expenditures are sometimes used to signal to constituents that a candidate has done a good job at legislating. Nonetheless, each form of electoral investment is most naturally affiliated with either access or replacement.
7   These PACs cannot fundraise from corporate treasury funds, but they do collect contributions from the employees of their member corporations.
8   The denominator here excludes all contributions to candidates by individuals that aggregate to less than $200 per election. In practical terms, excluding those totals amplifies the corporate and trade PAC percentages.
9   Anthony Corrado, "Money and Politics: A History Of Campaign Finance Law," in *The New Campaign Finance Sourcebook,* ed. Anthony Corrado, Thomas Mann, Daniel Ortiz, and Trevor Potter (Washington, DC: Brookings Institution Press, 2005).

10   The ad is entitled "Priority MD RNC," and is accessible from the Living Room Candidate project, www.livingroomcandidate.org/commercials/2000.

11   Specifically, for the compilation of files between 1992 and 2002, see "Contributions by Individuals," www.fec.gov/finance/disclosure/ftpdet.shtml; transaction type 10, which identifies soft money receipts, is the relevant indicator. Each donor was then sorted by the author into individuals, unions, corporations, nonprofit groups, trade groups, and other.

12   The corporate donors that serve as the numerator in both lines are limited to contributors who gave in the aggregate at least $25,000 in soft money in any single election cycle. The denominator for the solid line is all interest group contributors giving at least $25,000 in an election cycle. This cutoff accounts for about 75 percent of all soft money contributions in each year. The denominator for the dotted line is all soft money, including small group contributions and contributions from individuals.

13   There is some evidence that corporate investors were not upset with that change and may instead have perceived party soft money in negative terms, often feeling compelled to give for fear of being shut out of party politics while also seeing little return on their investments. See Timothy Werner, "The Sound, the Fury, and the Non-Event: Business Power and Market Reactions to the *Citizens United* Decision," *American Politics Research* 39, no. 1: 118–41; Stephen Ansolabehere, James M. Snyder, Michiko Ueda, "Did Firms Profit From Soft Money?" *Election Law Journal* 3, no. 2: 193–98.

14   In principle, they were free to do so prior to 1994 as well, but did not because federal regulators and the federal courts interpreted the laws more strictly in the 1970s and 1980s (see Franz, *Choices and Changes: Interest Groups in the Electoral Process*, ch. 3 and ch. 7).

15   Unions, as might be expected, are unlikely to accept or make use of corporate donations. Parts of this table are reproduced from Rozell, Wilcox, and Franz, *Interest Groups in American Campaigns: The New Face of Electioneering*.

16   These are only ads aired on network television and exclude local cable buys and radio ads.

17   The ad was retrieved from the Wisconsin Advertising Project archive.

18   All information on each group is assembled from a web search and from each group's webpage, if still in operation, as well as from SourceWatch.org, which is maintained by the Center for Media and Democracy.

19   There are two other points worth noting in that regard. First, Congress did mandate the disclosure of contributions and expenditures by 527s in the 2002 election. Because the issue advocacy rules were so lax in 2002, not many groups funded their issue advocacy through these organizational arrangements. Second, the absence of good data on issue advocacy in this period is reflected in the discussion of outside spending on the Center for Responsive Politics' website, www.opensecrets.org/outsidespending/index.php. Their totals for 2000 and 2002 include only the reportable sum to the FEC and exclude the issue advocacy totals, which are not tracked outside the data discussed in this chapter.

20   One additional caveat to this discussion, though, is that corporations could still fund advocacy efforts close to the election in the form of direct mail or Internet activity, for example. This is nearly impossible to track systematically, but there is case study evidence

that many groups were involved in such efforts in 2004 and 2006. See Kelly Patterson and David Magleby, "Stepping Out of the Shadows: Ground War Activity in 2004," in *The Election After the Reform,* ed. Michael J. Malbin (Lanham, MD: Rowman & Littlefield, 2006); David Magleby, J. Quin Monson, and Kelly D. Patterson, "Dancing Without Partners: How Candidates, Parties, and Interest Groups Interact in the Presidential Campaign," in *Dancing Without Partners: How Candidates, Parties, and Interest Groups Interact in the Presidential Campaign* (Lanham, MD: Rowman & Littlefield, 2007). To the extent that corporate money funded many of these groups is unknown, however. It should be noted that one study categorized all independent expenditures in 2010, in order to assess the extent to which television advertising dominates. That analysis confirmed that the majority of funds were spent on media advertisements, and there is no reason to expect a significantly different distribution of expenditures by type in 2004 and 2006. See Michael Franz, "The *Citizens United* Election? Or Same As It Ever Was?" *The Forum* 8, no. 4 (2010): Article 7.

21   Franz, "The *Citizens United* Election? Or Same As It Ever Was?".

22   The totals in 2006 are only for ads aired in the top 100 media markets. The totals for 2008 are for all 210 media markets.

23   There is some evidence, however, that many corporations are feeling pressure from shareholders to disclose donations to 501(c) groups or super PACs that advocate for candidates. See Kim Dixon, "More Companies Shed Light on Political Spending," *Reuters*, October 28, 2011. This pressure comes independent of any government mandates.

24   Information on state campaign finance laws was obtained from National Conference of State Legislatures, www.ncsl.org/.

25   These states are West Virginia, Tennessee, New York, New Hampshire, Montana, Mississippi, Minnesota, Massachusetts, Kentucky, Iowa, Connecticut, and Alabama.

26   One might also consider a comparison across Western democracies, which also varies in the scope of campaign finance provisions. Robert Boatright instructively compares the comparatively libertarian framework of the U.S. system to the much more restrictive Canadian system. See Robert Boatright, *Interest Groups and Campaign Finance Reform in the United States and Canada* (Ann Arbor: University of Michigan Press, 2011).

27   John Coleman, "Citizens United and Political Outcomes," (working paper, University of Wisconsin-Madison, 2010).

28   Ray La Raja, "Will *Citizens United v. FEC* Give More Political Power to Corporations?" (paper presented at the Annual Meeting of the Midwest Political Science Association, Chicago, March 31–April 3, 2011).

29   Franz, *Choices and Changes: Interest Groups in the Electoral Process,* ch. 4.

30   Adam Bonica, "Citizens United and the Myth of a Conservative Corporate America," Ideological Cartography, http://ideologicalcartography.com/.

31   See also Jeffrey Berry and Clyde Wilcox, *The Interest Group Society,* 5th ed. (New York: Pearson Longman, 2009): 184–87.

32   Thomas Ferguson, *Golden Rule: The Investment Theory of Party Competition and the Logic of Money-Driven Political Systems* (Chicago: University of Chicago Press, 1995).

33 Alexei Ovtchinnikov and Eva Pantaleoni, "Individual Political Contributions and Firm Performance" (working paper, American Finance Association 2012 Chicago Meetings, http://papers.ssrn.com/sol3/papers.cfm?abstract_id=1732750.

34 E. E. Schattschneider, *Semi-Sovereign People: A Realist's View of Democracy in America* (New York: Holt, Rinehart and Winston, 1960): 34–35.

35 Frank Baumgartner and Beth Leech, "Interest Niches and Policy Bandwagons: Patterns of Interest Group Involvement in National Politics," *The Journal of Politics.* 63, no. 4 (2001): 1191–213.

36 John Heinz, Edward Laumann, Robert Nelson, and Robert Salisbury, *The Hollow Core: Private Interests In National Policy Making* (Cambridge: Harvard University Press, 1997).

37 Frank Baumgartner, Jeffrey Berry, Marie Hojnacki, and Beth Leech, *Lobbying and Policy Change: Who Wins, Who Loses, and Why* (Chicago: University of Chicago Press, 2009).

38 Stephen Ansolabehere, John De Figueiredo and James Snyder, "Why Is There So Little Money In U.S. Politics?" *Journal Of Economic Perspectives* 17, no. 1 (2003): 105–130.

39 Ibid; Werner "The Sound, the Fury, and the Non-Event: Business Power and Market Reactions to the *Citizens United* Decision," 134.

CHAPTER 6

Onward Union Soldiers?

Organized Labor's Future in American Elections

Peter L. Francia

Organized labor celebrated the results of two highly successful elections in 2006 and 2008. Democrats, many backed by labor, won majorities in the U.S. House and U.S. Senate in 2006 for the first time since the 1992 election. In 2008, unions supported Democratic presidential candidate, Barack Obama, who defeated Republican John McCain. Democrats also increased their majorities in the U.S. House and U.S. Senate, giving the party unified control of the federal government. Yet, organized labor could not prevent a historic electoral reversal in 2010 as Republicans stormed back to win majority control of the U.S. House and reduced the Democrats' majority in the U.S. Senate by six seats.

The dramatically different outcomes in these recent elections illustrate both the potential and the limitations of unions as a political force in the early twenty-first century. As this chapter discusses, the American labor movement has undergone significant changes over the past several decades that have affected which unions hold the most influence and which ones do not. Several factors, most notably increased global competition in the labor market, have transformed the present-day labor movement from one that was once concentrated in the manufacturing sector to one that is now strongest in the public and service sectors. Today's labor movement also is more diverse, but considerably smaller as a percentage of the U.S. workforce than it was during the so-called heyday of big labor, when unions represented one of every three American workers. These changes have had not only economic significance, but also have had political implications, which this chapter explains in the pages that follow.

In addition to these developments, recent changes in campaign finance law have created both opportunities and challenges for organized labor to influence the electoral process. The U.S. Supreme Court's ruling in *Citizens United v. Federal*

Election Commission has particular significance. As argued in this chapter, the impact of *Citizens United* is somewhat complex for labor. On the one hand, the ruling has made it more difficult for labor to compete against corporate interests. On the other hand, it has freed unions to spend more money in elections, allowing labor to take on a larger and potentially more influential role within the Democratic Party.

Finally, this chapter considers organized labor's future in the political arena in light of the changing economic and political developments that it has had to face in recent years. While the sweeping victories of Republicans in the 2010 election have put unions squarely on the defensive, these attacks also have served to mobilize union members, as protests in Wisconsin over collective bargaining rights for public employees demonstrated in early 2011. Nevertheless, despite some signs of renewed energy from the labor movement, significant tests remain for unions, notably in the area of organizing more workers. Labor's ability to respond to these challenges, as this chapter makes clear, will have significant implications for American elections.

The Major Players in the Labor Movement

The modern American labor movement became a significant force in American society with the passage of the National Labor Relations Act (NLRA) of 1935, also popularly known as the Wagner Act (named for its sponsor, Sen. Robert F. Wagner of New York). The NLRA made it illegal for an employer to discriminate against or fire a worker who attempted to organize or join a union, and created the National Labor Relations Board (NLRB) to supervise union certification elections and to penalize and remedy unfair labor practices. A surge in union membership followed: union membership increased from 3.6 million workers in 1935 to more than 12 million by 1945.[1] Significant growth in union membership continued for another decade, topping 16 million by the mid-1950s.[2]

During this peak period, workers in manufacturing, construction, mining, and transportation dominated the union ranks. The three largest unions by the end of the 1950s included the International Brotherhood of Teamsters (1.5 million members), the United Auto Workers (1.1 million members), and the United Steelworkers of America (945,000 members).[3] Although these individual unions wielded considerable influence, the most significant power brokers in the labor movement at this time were its two dominant federations: the American Federation of Labor (AFL) and the Congress of Industrial Organizations (CIO). By the mid-1950s, there were 10.6 million members who belonged to a union affiliated with the AFL and 4.6 million members who belonged to a union affiliated with the CIO.[4]

Yet developments such as the Taft-Hartley Act of 1947 (which placed more restrictive organizing laws into place),[5] advances in technology and automation, and increases in global economic competition presented a serious threat to the growth that organized labor experienced after the Wagner Act. To deal with these mounting challenges, the AFL and CIO merged in 1955 to become what is still the present-day AFL-CIO. Nevertheless, the merger could not prevent total employment in several heavily unionized sectors, notably in manufacturing, from decreasing by several million workers.[6]

The loss of U.S. manufacturing jobs also contributed to significant declines in union density in the private sector, which had reached a high of 35.7 percent in 1953, but fell to just 6.9 percent by 2010 (see Figure 6.1). Unions, however, have been able to offset some of these losses with large gains in the public sector where there have been increases in union membership rates from 10 to 12 percent in the 1950s to a peak of 40 percent in 1976, with levels stabilizing and settling at 36 percent in 2010.[7] Unionized public sector employees now outnumber unionized private sector workers, 7.6 million compared to 7.1 million, as of 2010.[8]

This "new unionism"—a term used by economist Leo Troy—has shifted the center of union power.[9] In 2010, three of the nation's largest unions were in the public and service sectors: the National Education Association (NEA); the Service Employees International Union (SEIU); and the American Federation of State, County, and Municipal Employees (AFSCME). The SEIU, which

FIGURE 6.1   Union Membership as a Proportion of the Private and Public Sector Labor Force

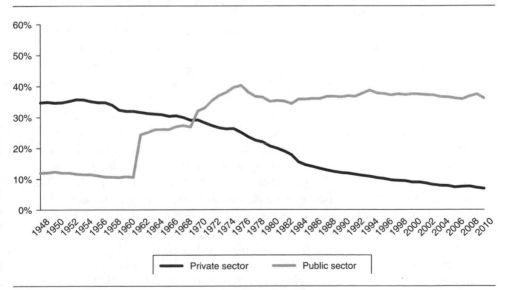

Source: Labor Research Association from 1948–1972; Barry T. Hirsch and David A. Macpherson, "Union Membership, Covrage, Density and Employment, 1973–2011," www.unionstats.com.

represents health care workers (nurses, doctors, lab technicians, nursing home and home care workers) and local and state government workers, public school employees, bus drivers, and child care providers, also has become the nation's fastest growing union.[10] Indeed, the SEIU's growth has led some to describe it as labor's "powerhouse."[11]

The SEIU, in fact, has grown so influential that, on the eve of the AFL-CIO's fiftieth anniversary convention in 2005, it led a revolt against the AFL-CIO, with its leadership arguing that more union resources needed to be devoted to member-organizing drives and less to political campaigns. With the support of textile, garment, hotel, and restaurant workers in UNITE-HERE, construction workers in the Laborers' International Union of North America (LIUNA), the United Brotherhood of Carpenters, the United Food and Commercial Workers (UFCW), the Teamsters, and the United Farm Workers (UFW), the SEIU formed the Change to Win (CtW) federation to focus resources on organizing more workers. Unions in the Change to Win federation disaffiliated themselves from the AFL-CIO; in the years since the split, however, the CtW federation has been unable to reverse overall declines in union membership and has lost some of its original members, which include the United Brotherhood of Carpenters (disaffiliated with CtW in 2009), UNITE-HERE (rejoined the AFL-CIO in 2009; although a third of the members in UNITE-HERE left to join the SEIU), and LIUNA (rejoined the AFL-CIO in 2010). As of 2011, the CtW federation continued to represent its four remaining unions, while the AFL-CIO represents workers in fifty-five affiliated unions (along with fifty-one state federations, including Puerto Rico's, and 543 central labor councils).

Despite the split between the CtW unions and those in the AFL-CIO, both federations and their member unions have continued to work together and to coordinate their political activities. The AFL-CIO, for example, set up Solidarity Charter programs, which allowed state-level federations and locals of disaffiliated unions to collaborate with the AFL-CIO during elections. To continue to improve coordination, the AFL-CIO and the CtW federation formed the National Labor Coordinating Committee in 2006 to help its local and state unions work together to share information, such as member lists, and to team up for grassroots political activities, such as phone banking, door-to-door canvassing, and related get-out-the-vote efforts. Nevertheless, some critics charge that despite efforts to coordinate, the AFL-CIO and CtW federation still operate two separate programs, creating inefficiency.[12]

In 2009, the AFL-CIO, the Change to Win federation, and the NEA joined forces to coordinate positions and to work together on issues of common concern through an association also called the National Labor Coordinating Committee. Discussions surfaced shortly afterward of a possible reunification of the labor movement. Merger efforts between the AFL-CIO and the CtW federation, however, ultimately broke down later that year.

Even with a labor movement that remains formally divided, there are still 14.7 million union members in the United States as of 2010.[13] While, as previously noted, this marks a decline from previous high marks in union membership, it is still a significant number. The National Rifle Association (NRA), regarded by some as one of the most influential interest groups in the nation, by comparison, has four million members. Union households also have made up a sizable portion the national electorate for more than a half-century, frequently topping the 20 percent marker—a high enough total for labor to remain a relevant force in American politics.[14]

Organized Labor's Political Strategies and Resources

The first president of the AFL, Samuel Gompers, advanced a straightforward strategy that unions protect their friends and punish their enemies. Individual unions and labor leaders, however, do not always agree on how best to accomplish this. Although there are decisions from central headquarters in Washington, DC that are certainly influential, the federated structure of the labor movement allows individual unions to be autonomous and to make their own decisions about political strategy. At times, this autonomy can lead to divisions within the labor movement.[15] Some unions also have a history of independence. The Teamsters, which operated outside of the AFL-CIO from 1957 to 1987 (and again from 2005 to the present), endorsed Republican presidential candidates Richard Nixon in 1972, Ronald Reagan in 1980 and 1984, and George H. W. Bush in 1988, despite the fact that most other unions supported their Democratic opponents.

Yet, such public breaks within the labor movement generally are rare when it comes to politics. Labor unions typically stand together and follow partisan, election-oriented strategies in which the goal is to maximize the number of pro-union candidates elected to public office by targeting resources in competitive elections. Nonetheless, some labor money does go to incumbents in safe contests to advance access-oriented goals (see Chapter 1).[16] Campaign finance records show that unions typically give more than 90 percent of their contributions to Democrats.[17] Indeed, the relationship between organized labor and the Democratic Party has been so strong that one scholar famously described organized labor as the Democratic Party's "most important functional arm in national elections"[18] with another scholar referring to the partnership as an "enduring alliance."[19]

Labor's rather long history of rewarding its "friends," mainly Democrats, first took formal shape when the CIO formed Labor's Non-Partisan League in 1936, and later, the CIO Political Action Committee (CIO-PAC) in 1943. During the same period, the AFL formed the Labor League for Political Education (LLPE). In 1955, the merged AFL-CIO created the Committee on Political Education (COPE), which remains active presently. COPE endorses candidates for public office, makes political contributions through its political action committee (PAC), and works to educate union members about political issues and to mobilize them to vote. COPE endorsements can be especially important because they often serve as a signal to other union PACs and groups to contribute to a candidate.[20]

Indeed, organized labor's financial resources are significant. Unions are regularly among the so-called Heavy Hitters of PAC donors in U.S. elections. According to the Center for Responsive Politics (CRP), twelve labor groups made its top twenty list of largest PAC donors from 1989 to 2009 (see Table 6.1). Six even made the top

TABLE 6.1   Top PAC Donors, 1989–2009

	Total	Dem %	Rep %
1. AT&T Inc.	$43,938,535	44%	55%
2. American Federation of State, County and Municipal Employees*	41,728,311	98	1
3. National Association of Realtors	35,376,883	48	51
4. Goldman Sachs	31,343,062	64	35
5. International Brotherhood of Electrical Workers*	31,287,957	97	2
6. American Association for Justice	31,232,479	90	9
7. National Educational Association*	30,035,417	92	6
8. Laborers Union*	28,705,400	92	7
9. Service Employees International Union*	27,830,017	95	3
10. Carpenters and Joiners Union*	27,650,183	89	10
11. Teamsters Union*	27,549,874	92	6
12. Citigroup Inc.	26,948,428	50	49
13. Communications Workers of America*	26,940,146	99	0
14. American Federation of Teachers*	26,282,221	98	0
15. American Medical Association	26,277,473	39	60
16. United Auto Workers*	25,767,002	98	0
17. Machinists and Aerospace Union*	25,002,277	98	0
18. National Auto Dealers Association	24,189,708	31	68
19. Altria Group	24,052,641	28	71
20. United Food & Commercial Workers Union*	24,027,833	98	1

Source: Center for Responsive Politics, www.opensecrets.org/orgs/list.php?order=A

*Denotes a labor organization.

ten: AFSCME (second on the list at $41.7 million), the International Brotherhood of Electrical Workers (fifth at $31.3 million), the NEA (seventh at $30 million), the Laborers Union (eighth at $28.7 million), the SEIU (ninth at $27.8 million), and the Carpenters and Joiners Union (tenth at $27.7 million). Labor groups also overwhelmingly gave their money to Democrats.

Labor groups were among the leaders in independent expenditures, discussed in Chapter 5 (campaign expenses that support or oppose a specific candidate, but are made without the candidate's cooperation, approval, or direct knowledge) and communication costs (money spent on internal political communications through phone banks, direct mail, and flyers to the group's members) over the same twenty-year period as well.[21] The SEIU spent $55.3 million, with $50 million spent in independent expenditures and $5.3 million in communication costs.[22] Two additional labor PACs rounded out the top five: AFSCME (third at $39.9 million) and the AFL-CIO (fourth at $36.5 million).[23]

As also noted in earlier chapters, another avenue for labor unions to funnel their financial resources into elections is through 527 and 501(c)(5) groups. Unlike PACs, which are restricted to raising regulated or hard money only, 501(c)(5) and 527 organizations are allowed to accept unlimited donations, although there are stricter rules governing how this money can be used and spent. Many labor unions contribute to 527 and 501(c) groups, including in some instances, their own 527s and 501(c)(5)s. The expenditures from these labor groups, particularly their own 527s, were again significant. In 2008, for example, the SEIU's Political Education and Action Fund and AFSCME's Special Account provided an estimated 30 percent of net pro-Democratic 527 funds.[24]

Money, however, is not labor's primary resource. Instead, labor's human resources are its top weapon. Indeed, research has confirmed that labor's grassroots activities have a greater effect on elections than its endorsements or campaign contributions.[25] As a union official explained, "Money is important, but if you haven't got the grassroots base, you ain't got it."[26] Perhaps not surprising given the importance of its members, labor unions are especially effective at mobilization efforts.[27] Research has shown that unions have a strong effect on political participation, with one study finding that areas with the highest concentrations of union members have significantly higher rates of voter turnout.[28]

To recruit union volunteers for get-out-the-vote (GOTV) activities and political education efforts in competitive congressional districts, the AFL-CIO sponsors the National Labor Political Training Center. The AFL-CIO also has attempted to reach beyond its membership to nonunion workers and the unemployed through a community affiliate organization, Working America, which includes 3.2 million members.[29] Working America connects nonunion members to the labor movement to expand the influence and power of working-class voters. It has been an important partner in the AFL-CIO's overall "ground war" in recent elections. Other unions, such as AFSCME, rely heavily on their 501(c)(5) organizations for spending on grassroots mobilization activities.

Unions in the CtW federation, likewise, have extensive ground operations. They have organizers to oversee voter canvas efforts and recruit thousands of volunteers for grassroots activities. In addition to these efforts, the SEIU has instituted an innovative program that it calls Walk a Day in My Shoes, which encourages candidates seeking the union's endorsement to spend an entire day with an SEIU member performing daily job duties. In 2008, Barack Obama spent the day with Pauline Beck, an SEIU homecare worker in California.[30]

Labor's mobilization activities have produced solid turnout numbers in recent elections. Those in union households were 23 percent of the electorate in 1996, 26 percent in 2000, 24 percent in 2004, and 21 percent in 2008.[31] Studies have shown further that union members are more likely to vote than nonunion members from the same socioeconomic backgrounds, with the union effect particularly strong among lower-income and middle-income voters.[32]

Moreover, unions place an emphasis on spreading word of important political issues through member-to-member contact. As a leader in a Steelworkers Local explained, "We want to break it down to one-to-one, because talking about issues and candidates really works better on the shop floor when people hear it from someone they know."[33] This approach has generally been followed with positive results for Democratic candidates. Since 1980, research shows that voters in union households have supported Democratic presidential candidates at rates around 10 percentage points higher than have those from nonunion households.[34] The differences separating union and nonunion household support for Democratic House and Senate candidates has been slightly higher, averaging between 10 percentage points and 20 percentage points since 1988.[35]

Changes in the union workforce are likely driving this strong support for Democrats. Specifically, unions have become considerably more diverse over the past several decades. Women comprise a larger segment of national union membership than ever before. In 2010, 46 percent of all union members were women compared to 35 percent in 1983—a rate of increase in percentage points about three times greater than the gains women made in their overall share of the workforce over the same period.[36]

Racial and ethnic minorities comprise a larger segment of national union membership as well. Over a twenty-five-year period from 1983 to 2008, whites went from 78 percent of the union workforce to 69 percent.[37] Latinos, by comparison, doubled as a percentage of the union workforce from 6 to 12 percent over the same period, mirroring their increases in the overall workforce.[38] There also were gains for Asian-Americans. African American representation in unions remained constant at 13 to 15 percent of the union workforce over this period;[39] African Americans, however, had the highest union membership rate in 2010 at

13.4 percent compared to 11.7 percent for whites, 10.9 percent for Asians, and 10 percent for Latinos.[40] Because the Democratic Party typically dominates the vote of minorities and does better among women than men, the changing demographics of the labor movement almost surely have played a role in its strong support for Democrats.

Nevertheless, despite these changes in the makeup of the union movement, one other constant for the labor movement has been the ever-declining percentage of union members in the workforce, which fell to 11.9 percent in 2010[41]—a low mark not seen since the days predating the Wagner Act.[42] While labor has been able to remain a relevant electoral bloc, its relative size in the workforce has reached a historic low, which has placed some limits its political power and influence. As the 2010 election ultimately exposed, unions by themselves are simply too small in number, especially in areas of low union density such as the South, Plains, and the Mountain states, to reverse overwhelming conservative momentum.

Background on the 2010 Election

As noted in the outset of the chapter, recent elections in 2006 and 2008 brought landslide national victories for Democrats, including for many labor-backed candidates. Unions played a significant role for Democrats in both elections. During the 2006 election, exit polls showed that nonunion voters provided a 2-point margin of victory for Democratic candidates compared to a significantly larger 5-point advantage for Democrats among voters in union households, resulting in what one account explained as "turning a modest victory into a wave."[43] A successful element of labor's effort was its decision to target "drop-off" voters (i.e., those who vote in presidential elections, but who usually do not vote in midterm elections). One report found that an impressive 79 percent of union drop-off voters in battleground states turned out to the polls in the 2006 election.[44] Even nonunion members that the AFL-CIO targeted through its community affiliate, Working America, turned out to vote in large numbers and strongly supported Democratic candidates.[45]

In 2008, union members were a bedrock of support for Barack Obama. Exit polls from Peter D. Hart Research Associates showed that 68 percent of union members in battleground states voted for Obama.[46] A similar margin of victory was reported for Working America members as well.[47] The Hart poll also revealed that Obama won an 18-point advantage among white men who belonged to a union compared to a net loss of 16 points among white men according to national exit polls.[48] Among veterans and gun owners, Obama lost both blocs nationally by 9 and 25 points respectively, but won them by 25 and 12 points respectively among union members.[49]

Union efforts in the 2008 election were extensive. Some estimates indicated that the AFL-CIO committed $250 million in the election to target union households in twenty-one states, while Change to Win spent $150 million, with the SEIU adding another $85 million.[50] One account reported that 80 percent of union members received union mail, 80 percent of union members received union publications, and 59 percent of union members reported that they received a live phone call during the election.[51] The precise placement of union communications was particularly sophisticated. The AFL-CIO, for example, claimed to have targeted more than 3 million undecided swing voters in August of 2008, helping the Obama campaign and congressional Democratic candidates in a number of competitive battleground states.[52] Even in states with very few union members, such as North Carolina, one study found that the grassroots efforts and television advertising campaigns of labor groups were still especially strong when compared to other outside groups.[53]

With a pro-union administration in the White House and huge majorities of Democrats in both the U.S. House and U.S. Senate following the 2008 election, the future looked brighter for organized labor than it had perhaps in any time since the days of the Wagner Act and the New Deal. Unions immediately pushed for their top legislative priority, the Employee Free Choice Act (EFCA), which would give workers the ability to form a union through the "card check" process in which the union is certified when a majority of workers sign a union card. EFCA would also require binding arbitration to set the terms of employment for workers if 120 days passed after the union was recognized without a collective bargaining agreement, and would increase penalties for employers who discriminate against or fire a worker who attempts to organize or join a union.

Business groups including the Chamber of Commerce, the Business Roundtable, the National Federation of Independent Business, and Wal-Mart, along with most Republicans, strongly opposed the legislation. The Chamber of Commerce alone spent more than $144 million in 2009 on lobbying with a significant share of that amount in opposition to EFCA.[54] By comparison, all labor groups combined to spend $44.2 million on lobbying in 2009.[55] The Chamber of Commerce also ran ads on EFCA targeting Sen. Arlen Specter after he left the Republican Party and joined the Democratic Party (see the box for an example of an ad that the Chamber of Commerce ran in Pennsylvania). Also assisting the Chamber's efforts were the Association of Builders and Contractors and the Retail Industry Leaders Association. These groups, along with the Chamber of Commerce, formed a partnership through the Coalition for a Democratic Workplace (CDW), which reportedly spent upwards of $30 million to defeat EFCA.[56]

Television Script of Chamber of Commerce Ad Targeting Sen. Arlen Specter

Person 1: We can't let Congress do this to our economy.

Narrator: Congress wants to strip away the secret ballot, and the bureaucrats dictate to Pennsylvania businesses.

Person 2: Pennsylvania needs jobs. We don't need government mandates. We need jobs.

Narrator: Senator Arlen Specter says it's a particularly bad time to pass card check.

Person 3: Card check won't just take away the secret ballot. Card check will wipe out jobs.

Person 4: Congress needs to fix the economy; not try to worry about trying to bail out the big unions.

Narrator: Tell Senator Specter to keep standing firm against card check.

Source: U.S. Chamber of Commerce, www.uschamber.com/wfl/default.

Ultimately, EFCA failed to muster the needed sixty votes to proceed in the U.S. Senate. Perhaps most disappointing to labor was that the bill failed to receive the support of a few Democrats. Senator Specter, who once cosponsored EFCA in the previous Congress as a Republican, oddly reversed his positions on the bill as a Democrat in 2009. Other Democrats including senators Mary Landrieu of Louisiana and Mark Pryor and Blanche Lincoln of Arkansas expressed reservations about the bill in the 111th Congress after previously supporting the legislation in 2007. The failure to enact EFCA, according to some accounts, left many union members less than enthusiastic about supporting Democrats in the 2010 election.[57]

Compounding labor's problems were continued rates of high unemployment and a weak economy—issues of top concerns to most Americans, but especially to union members. Record-high federal deficits and mounting government debt, as well as an unpopular government financial rescue package for the banking industry also dominated the headlines. Even the Democrats' signature legislative accomplishment—the passage of a controversial health care reform bill—lacked the so-called public option (a government health insurance plan), which labor strongly supported. Gerald McEntee, the president of AFSCME, conceded in the weeks leading up to the 2010 election, "It's hard to get [union] people juiced up."[58]

The 2010 election was also the first following the U.S. Supreme Court's controversial campaign finance decision in *Citizens United v. FEC*. In a controversial 5-4 ruling, the majority overturned *Austin v. Michigan Chamber of Commerce* and part of *McConnell v. FEC* by declaring prohibitions on corporations and labor unions from using general treasury funds in federal elections for independent expenditures and for electioneering communications to be unconstitutional. Critics of the decision charged that the decision would allow corporate and business interests to dominate U.S. elections or, as President Obama put it, "to drown out the voices of everyday Americans."[59] Then-Democratic Senatorial Campaign Committee (DSCC) chair, Sen. Robert Menendez of New Jersey, added, "Giving corporate interests an outsized role in our process will only mean citizens get heard less. We must look at legislative ways to make sure the ledger is not tipped so far for corporate interests that citizens' voices are drowned out."[60] Many political observers, in turn, viewed the decision as a net loss for organized labor because it would be unable to compete with the vast financial resources coming from the corporate sector. These new campaign finance rules, combined with unfavorable electoral conditions for Democrats, placed organized labor in an extremely difficult and challenging environment heading into the 2010 election.

The Agony of Defeat: 2010 Election

One of the first major actions from some key unions in the labor movement was to announce its plans to challenge Senator Lincoln of Arkansas in the 2010 Democratic primary by backing Lt. Gov. Bill Halter. In a state with just 6.4 percent of its workforce unionized[61] and with Bill Clinton actively supporting Lincoln's campaign, unions gambled that they could still win the election. While several polls showed Halter ahead, Lincoln ultimately prevailed in the election by a margin of just over 10,000 votes, 52 to 48 percent. Halter's loss generated a good deal of criticism of labor, with one union official calling the primary challenge strategy "mindless."[62]

Richard Trumka, AFL-CIO president, nonetheless defended the decision to challenge Senator Lincoln, calling the effort "priceless" and vowing to "do it again."[63] Trumka added, "You will see us doing more primary races in the future. Not less. More. And some of them will be successful and some of them won't. But people understand we are willing to fight for working people."[64] In the end, Lincoln's primary victory proved to be insignificant. The Republican nominee and challenger, John Boozman, went on to defeat Senator Lincoln in a 19-point landslide in the general election.

Senator Lincoln's troubles proved to be part of a much larger pattern for Democrats in 2010. A rising bloc of conservative activists and citizens, upset with the policies of the Obama administration, organized and mobilized for the election through a citizens' movement calling itself the Tea Party. The Tea Party made news in 2010 by first knocking off a few heavily favored incumbent Republicans, deemed too pragmatic and moderate by the movement, in several primary elections. This conservative energy flowed into the general election, creating momentum for Republicans, particularly right-wing, anti-union Republicans.

Organized labor responded to these circumstances by spending a reported $200 million to try to maintain Democratic majorities in the U.S. House and U.S. Senate in the 2010 election.[65] Given the difficult electoral environment for Democrats, unions targeted their resources to vulnerable Democratic incumbents (see Chapter 1). One union official summarized labor's "incumbency protection" strategy as a firewall to prevent even larger losses for Democrats in the election.[66]

The AFL-CIO focused its electoral resources on get-out-the-vote efforts to mobilize its members to turn out to the polls, scaling back its advertising budget. As Trumka explained, "We think this election requires more face-to-face contact."[67] In total, the AFL-CIO targeted eighteen Senate races and more than seventy House contests in twenty-six states, including the "firewall states" of California, Illinois, Nevada, New York, Ohio, and Pennsylvania.[68] It recruited more than 200,000 union volunteers, distributed 19.4 million flyers, placed 30 million phone calls, and knocked on 8.5 million doors during the 2010 election.[69]

Working America, likewise, assisted with more than 500,000 phone calls and had its volunteers knock on more than 800,000 doors.[70] Labor PACs also contributed $65.4 million to Democrats in 2010 (and another $4.5 million going to Republicans),[71] along with millions more donated from labor unions to federal 527 groups. Eleven of the top donors to federal 527s in 2010 were unions, with the SEIU leading all contributors (see Table 6.2). Unions also spent considerable sums on independent spending. Labor's three heavy hitters, AFSCME, the SEIU, and the NEA topped all liberal, Democratic-leaning organizations in outside money spent on independent expenditures, electioneering communications, and communication costs in 2010, combining for $39.4 million (see Table 6.3). Overall, AFSCME reportedly spent upwards of $82 million in the 2010 election cycle in seventeen Senate races, seventy to eighty House races, and twenty gubernatorial contests, including $2.5 million on direct mail and $2 million on phone banking.[72] Likewise, the SEIU spent $44 million on ten Senate races, thirty House races, and twenty gubernatorial contests.[73]

For the millions of dollars that labor spent to mobilize its members, some 74 percent of union members reported that they received election information from a union newspaper, magazine, or newsletter.[74] More than seven of out of ten union members also reported that their union mailed to their home an election pamphlet or flyer, and a majority received a personal telephone call from their union with election information.[75] Ultimately, 61 percent of those in union households voted for a Democrat to represent them in the U.S. House—a respectable total given that

TABLE 6.2   Top Contributors to Federally Focused 527 Organizations, 2010

Contributor	Total
1. Service Employees International Union*	$18,670,808
2. Democratic Governors Association	8,037,500
3. National Education Association*	6,305,425
4. United Food & Commercial Workers Union*	4,797,750
5. American Federation of Teachers*	4,398,545
6. Operating Engineers Union*	3,751,245
7. Pharmaceutical Product Development, Inc.	3,380,125
8. Laborers Union*	2,783,932
9. Am. Fed. of State, County, and Municipal Employees*	2,707,373
10. Carly Fiorina Enterprises	2,511,580
11. Friend of America Votes	2,328,361
12. Democratic Attorney Generals Association	2,185,000
13. Harold C. Simmons Family Trust	2,000,000
14. International Union of Operating Engineers*	1,677,300
15. City of New York, NY	1,652,656
16. International Brotherhood of Electrical Workers*	1,604,946
17. Tufts University	1,552,400
18. Public Storage Inc.	1,550,000
19. Sheet Metal Workers Union*	1,546,700
20. Carpenter and Joiners Union*	1,451,243

Source: Center for Responsive Politics, www.opensecrets.org/527s/527contribs.php.

*Denotes a labor organization.

nonunion households favored Republicans by a 53-44 advantage.[76] Among union and nonunion white women, the differences were especially large. White women who belong to a union favored the Democratic House candidates by a 36-point margin whereas those who are not in a union gave Republican House candidates a 17-point advantage.[77] Still, overall, just 17 percent of the national electorate came from union households in 2010[78]—a considerable decrease from previous elections and a low mark not seen since the 1994 election.[79]

Further creating problems for labor were the considerable sums of money now available to business and corporate interests in the aftermath of the *Citizens United* ruling. The U.S. Chamber of Commerce took full advantage of this new environment by running thousands of hard-hitting ads against Democratic

TABLE 6.3   Independent Expenditures, Electioneering Communications, and
            Communication Costs from Liberal, Nonparty Groups, 2010 Election

Organization	2010 Totals
1. SEIU	$15,952,331
2. AFSCME	13,185,800
3. National Education Association	10,245,561
4. America's Families First Action Fund	5,878,743
5. League of Conservation Voters	5,496,070

Source: Center for Responsive Politics, www.opensecrets.org/outsidespending/index.php.

candidates. Reports indicate that the Chamber spent $32 million in the 2010 election, with 93 percent of this money in support of Republican candidates.[80] The Wesleyan Media Project found that in the final sixty days of the 2010 election alone, the Chamber spent $21 million on 21,991 ads in twenty-eight House races and twelve Senate contests.[81] By comparison, the SEIU and AFSCME ran a combined 8,972 ads and spent nearly $7.5 million combined—significant totals, but little match next to the Chamber's efforts.[82]

In the end, the lackluster turnout from those in union households and the enormous financial advantage of business interests over labor contributed to devastating losses for Democrats. In the U.S. House, Democrats lost sixty-three seats and majority control of the chamber. On the Senate side, Democrats lost six seats, but did manage to maintain their majority.

Perhaps the lone benefit of the 2010 election for labor was that the *Citizens United* ruling did allow it to play a more significant role within the Democratic Party. Labor spent $17.3 million in treasury funds on independent expenditures—money that it would not have been able to spend absent the *Citizens United* ruling.[83] AFSCME led all unions with $7 million spent on independent expenditures from general treasury funds in 2010.[84] Overall, unions accounted for $59.55 million or 62 percent out of the $95.2 million spent by liberal, pro-Democratic groups in the 2010 congressional elections. This was up from 54 percent in 2008, 28 percent in 2006, and 17 percent in 2004 (see Table 6.4).

A second important campaign finance case, *SpeechNow.org v. FEC*, warrants mention. In March of 2010, the Washington, DC Circuit of Appeals ruled that federal political action committees that made independent expenditures and did not contribute to any candidates or political parties could raise unlimited sums of money. The result of this ruling was a new group of independent-expenditure committees, or super PACs. Unions responded to this ruling by donating nearly $14.6 million to super PACs in the 2010 election.[85] The NEA went a step further, setting up its own super PAC using $3.3 million from its general treasury.[86]

TABLE 6.4   Total Outside Spending by Liberal Groups

	2004	2006	2008	2010
Nonunion money	$100.31 (83%)	$27.81 (72%)	$72.49 (46%)	$35.65 (38%)
Union money	$20.79 (17%)	$10.89 (28%)	$86.31 (54%)	$59.55 (62%)

Source: Spencer MacColl, Center for Responsive Politics, www.opensecrets.org/news/2011/05/citizens-united-decision-profoundly-affects-political-landscape.html.

These new avenues allowed labor to spend more money in the 2010 election than it had in previous midterm cycles. With more resources available, labor took on an increasing share of the outside money spent on behalf of Democrats in the election. At the same time, as the 2010 general election proved, it also created the steep challenge of trying to compete with the expanded financial resources available to corporate interests.

After the 2010 Election: What's Next for Labor?

The results of the 2010 election exposed the consequences of labor's continuing problems with organizing more members. Organized labor, to its credit, has been able in the past to play an important role in national elections. The 2010 election results, however, illustrate the limitations of such a heavy reliance on its political ground operations to compensate for its membership declines. Under circumstances in which the political winds are blowing strongly against Democrats and unions cannot out-mobilize their opponents, the labor movement is vulnerable to dramatic swings like those that occurred in the 2010 election.

A stronger commitment to organizing more union workers, as the CtW leadership argued back in 2005, certainly remains a reasonable response for labor to follow and to prevent or at least mitigate election losses like those in 2010. This solution, however, runs up against the same difficulties and economic realities that have plagued the entire labor movement for decades. Organizing more workers, as the CtW federation's experience makes clear, is simply not accomplished easily even with additional resources.

Some union activists and labor scholars cite evidence that current organizing laws are a major obstacle for unions to overcome when organizing workers.[87] They cite evidence that employers routinely and willingly break organizing laws as a cost of doing business as well as long delays that often result from the current NLRB process to certify a union.[88] To correct these problems, labor has pushed hard for passage of the aforementioned Employee Free Choice Act. The inability of the Democratic Party to advance EFCA with huge majorities in the 111th Congress, however, exposed the limitations of a legislative strategy to rebuild the labor movement.

The EFCA setback and the continued inability of unions to organize within the current legal framework appear to leave organized labor with few viable options to reverse its membership decline. A small glimmer of hope may come from a recently passed rule by the NLRB to expedite union organizing elections—a provision that had been a part of EFCA. Business groups predictably denounced the change. Union leaders welcomed the proposal, but characterized it as only a "modest" step toward reform of organizing laws.[89]

Some scholars have called for "social movement unionism"[90] that would use protest tactics to advance labor's cause. Recent events in Wisconsin, where newly elected Republican Gov. Scott Walker pushed legislation to strip public workers of most collective bargaining rights, proved that American workers could be mobilized to engage in sustained protest activities. From mid-February to early March in 2011, tens of thousands of union protestors demonstrated in the State Capitol in Madison. Governor Walker was ultimately able to sign the bill into law, but the protests energized the union movement to such an extent that Richard Trumka, the president of the AFL-CIO, thanked Governor Walker and added that he deserved the "Mobilizer of the Year award."[91] Labor responded by gathering the necessary petition signatures to force a recall election for six Wisconsin Republican state senators who supported the legislation, and ultimately succeeded in ousting two of them.

A second option some labor scholars and union leaders endorse is to use the primary election to pressure more Democratic elected officials to respond to labor's legislative priorities.[92] Although this strategy failed in 2010 to defeat incumbent Sen. Blanche Lincoln, it has worked for unions in other instances. Current labor secretary, Hilda Solis, for example, won a seat in the U.S. House in 2000 with the strong backing of organized labor by defeating eighteen-year Democratic incumbent Marty Martinez, who had upset union members in his district for his support of free trade legislation. The effects of the *Citizens United* ruling, as noted earlier, also have increased labor's ability to funnel money into the electoral process. This has the potential to help unions expand their influence in the Democratic Party—a development that makes the primary strategy somewhat more viable.

Going forward into the 2012 election, labor leaders have expressed both optimism and pessimism. The energy coming from Wisconsin is a sign that union members could be especially mobilized in the next election. Unions also have more resources at their disposal in the aftermath of the *Citizens United* ruling, and will reportedly spend upwards of $400 million in local, state, and national elections in 2012.[93] There is, nevertheless, some real concern from union leaders that workers have grown frustrated by slow economic growth and what AFL-CIO president Richard Trumka has called "wasted energy" in Washington and "hysteria" about federal deficits rather than a sharper focus from Democrats on job growth.[94] President Obama's support for several free trade agreements could further dampen enthusiasm in some sectors of the union movement.[95] The 2012 election certainly presents yet another challenge for unions with ever-growing consequences for the influence and future role of the labor movement in American politics.

Concluding Thoughts

The American labor movement has had to adapt to significant transformations in the economy and workforce over the past several decades. These changes have presented major challenges that have resulted in losses to its membership and a weakening of once powerful unions such as the United Steelworkers of America and the United Auto Workers. With manufacturing unions in decline, public and service sector unions such as AFSCME, the NEA, and the SEIU, have become major players in the labor movement.

AFSCME, the NEA, and the SEIU now lead a labor movement that must operate in the post-*Citizens United* electoral environment. While many in the progressive community decried the *Citizens United* ruling for giving corporations the ability to spend previously restricted money in elections, the decision also freed unions to spend their treasury funds, which has allowed them to spend a greater share of outside money on behalf of Democrats than in previous elections. This may provide labor with an improved ability to shape nomination contests in Democratic primaries to replace incumbents who have wavered in the past on legislation important to the union movement. Conversely, as critics of the *Citizens United* ruling have argued, the decision also carries with it the very real possibility that the financial power and resources of corporate interests will simply drown out the voices of unions once the general election begins, further marginalizing labor interests in the political process.

While it is still too early to assess the full impact of the *Citizens United* ruling, recent election results reveal both the strengths and limitations of the labor movement. On the one hand, unions cannot, by themselves, prevent wave elections such as the one that swept anti-union candidates into office in 2010. On the other hand, unions still remain a critical component of a winning coalition for Democrats as the recent 2006 and 2008 elections proved. Nonetheless, many progressive critics have charged that even when labor "wins" in the electoral arena, unions often receive little in return afterward in the form of favorable legislation, as their recent defeat on EFCA illustrated.[96] Some scholars, however, have responded that the reasons for this have less to do with unappreciative Democrats than they have to do with the many checks and balances in congressional policymaking, which make it difficult for majorities to pass legislation.[97] Democrats also did provide some legislative victories for labor in the 111th Congress (e.g., passage of the Lilly Ledbetter Fair Pay Act) and they strongly supported the interests of autoworkers in the restructuring of General

Motors and Chrysler in 2009. Likewise, the controversial health care reform legislation of 2010, although ultimately falling well short of what unions ideally wanted, still received labor's backing, and became law only because of Democratic support. The large protests in Wisconsin against Gov. Scott Walker's budget and his efforts to restrict collective bargaining rights for public employees also saw Democratic state legislators stand steadfast with labor and its unionized workers in opposition to the bill. Perhaps, in the current volatile electoral environment that has witnessed wave elections in 2006, 2008, and 2010, another sweeping Democratic victory is possible that could bring with it a Wagner Act for the 21st century that could revitalize the union movement as it did in 1935.

The prospects for such a scenario, of course, seem slim, and membership declines only seem likely to continue based upon the trends of the past several decades. In the immediate future, a gradual drop in union density should have little impact on labor's political strength; however, continued and sustained decreases in membership are ultimately problematic for organized labor and its long-term future. The labor movement's response to this organizing challenge, as well as to other changes to the economic, electoral, and political environment undoubtedly will have meaningful political consequences for upcoming elections, public policy, and ultimately, political power in the United States.

Endnotes

The author wishes to thank Susan Orr for her helpful comments and suggestions.

1   Leo Troy, *Trade Union Membership* (New York: National Bureau of Economic Research, 1965), www.nber.org/books/troy65-1.

2   Ibid.

3   Ibid.

4   Ibid.

5   The Taft-Hartley Act of 1947, known officially as the Labor-Management Act, revised the National Labor Relations Act of 1935, giving increased power to employers. The law allowed states to pass so-called right-to-work laws that prohibit an employer from agreeing to hire only union members. It also banned secondary boycotts and gave the government the power to issue an eighty-day injunction against any strike that it determined to be a threat to national health or safety.

6   Employment data reveal a decrease from roughly 18 to 21 million manufacturing workers in the 1970s through the 1990s to just 13 million in 2010. Of these 13 million manufacturing workers, just 1.4 million are union members, down from as many as 7.8 million in 1973.

7   Several factors explain the growth and stabilization of public sector unionism. First, workers in the public sector were largely unaffected by the changes in the economy that harmed those in the manufacturing sector. Second, public sector unionism was helped by the actions of President John F. Kennedy, who signed Executive Order 10988 in 1961, which allowed public employees the right to bargain collectively on nonwage

issues in the federal sector. Because many of these workers belonged previously to employee associations, they were less difficult to organize into unions. Public sector workers have also proven to be easier to organize because they face less employer resistance to organizing campaigns than do workers in the private sector.

8   "Union Members Summary," Bureau of Labor Statistics, January 21, 2011, www.bls.gov/news.release/union2.nr0.htm.

9   Leo Troy, *The New Unionism in the New Society: Public Sector Unions in the Redistributive State* (Fairfax, VA: George Mason University Press, 1994).

10 Norma M. Riccucci, "The Changing Face of Public Employee Unionism," *Review of Public Personnel Adminsitration* 27 (2007): 71–78. See also "A Closer Look Inside Labor's Fastest Growing Union," Service Employees International Union, www.seiu.org/a/ourunion/a-closer-look-inside-labors-fastest-growing-union.php.

11 Peter Overby, "Union Operative Advocates and Gains Power," National Public Radio, August 6, 2008, www.npr.org/templates/story/story.php?storyId=93357018.

12 Kim Chipman, "Obama Turnout Priority in Labor's Bid to Revive Political Clout," *Bloomberg*, October 22, 2008, www.bloomberg.com/apps/news?pid=21070001&sid=aDqFqc1MabQ0.

13 "Union Members Summary."

14 Peter L. Francia, "Wither Labor? Reassessing Organized Labor's Political Power," *International Journal of Organization Theory and Behavior* 10 (2007): 188–212. See also Tracy Chang, "The Labor Vote in U.S. National Elections," *The Political Quarterly* 72 (2001): 375–85.

15 See for example, Steven Greenhouse, "The 1998 Campaign: The Unions; Split in Endorsements Deprives Candidates of Advantage," *The New York Times*, November 1, 1998. See also Peter L. Francia, *The Future of Organized Labor in American Politics* (New York, Columbia University Press, 2006).

16 Frank J. Sorauf, *Money in American Elections* (Boston: Scott, Foresman and Company, 1988). See also Theodore J. Eismeier and Philip H. Pollock III, "Strategy and Choice in Congressional Elections: The Role of Political Action Committees," *American Journal of Political Science* 30 (February 1986), 199–200; and Paul S. Herrnson, *Congressional Elections: Campaigning at Home and in Washington*, 5th ed. (Washington, DC: CQ Press, 2008), 141–44.

17 Michael Beckel, "Unions, Business Vie to Fill Democratic Pocketbook," Center for Responsive Politics, March 16, 2011, www.opensecrets.org/news/2011/03/unions-businesses-vie-to-fill.html.

18 J. David Greenstone, *Labor in American Politics* (New York: Alfred A. Knopf, 1969). Quote from updated edition, J. David Greenstone, *Labor in American Politics*, Phoenix ed. (Chicago: University of Chicago Press, 1977), xiii.

19 Taylor E. Dark, *The Unions and the Democrats an Enduring Alliance* (Ithaca, NY: Cornell University Press, 1999).

20 Clyde Wilcox, "Coping with Increasing Business Influence: The AFL-CIO's Committee on Political Education," in *Risky Business? PAC Decisionmaking in Congressional Elections*, ed. Robert Biersack, Paul S. Herrnson, and Clyde Wilcox (Armonk, NY: M.E. Sharpe, 1994).

21 Independent Expenditures and Communication Costs, 1989–2009," Center for Responsive Politics, www.opensecrets.org/orgs/indexp.php.

22 Ibid.

23 Ibid.

24 Steve Weisman, "Soft Money Political Spending by 501(c) Nonprofits Tripled in 2008 Election, Campaign Finance Institute, February 25, 2009, www.cfinst.org/Press/ PReleases/09-02-25/Soft_Money_Political_Spending_by_Nonprofits_Tripled_ in_2008.aspx.

25 Derek C. Bok and John T. Dunlop, *Labor and the American Community* (New York, Simon & Schuster, 1970).

26 Quoted in Robin Gerber, "Building to Win, Building to Last: AFL-CIO COPE Takes on the Republican Congress," in *After the Revolution: PACs, Lobbies, and the Republican Congress*, eds. Robert Biersack, Paul S. Herrnson, and Clyde Wilcox (Boston: Allyn & Bacon), 83.

27 Francia, *The Future of Organized Labor in American Politics*.

28 Benjamin Radcliff and Patricia Davis, "Labor Organizations and Electoral Participation in Industrial Democracies," *American Journal of Political Science* 44 (2000): 132–41.

29 "Trends in Union Membership," AFL-CIO, www.aflcio.org/joinaunion/why/union difference/ uniondiff11.cfm.

30 Jonathan Tasini, "Labor's Election Ground War–And How the Media Is Missing It," *The Huffington Post,* August 25 2008, www.huffingtonpost.com/jonathan-tasini/ labors-election-ground-wa_b_121208.html.

31 For 1996 through 2004 figures, see "GOP Makes Gains Among the Working Class, While Democrats Hold On to the Union Vote," Pew Research Center for People and the Press, August 2, 2005, http://people-press.org/2005/08/02/gop-makes-gains-among-the-working-class-while-democrats-hold-on-to-the-union-vote. For 2008, see National Exit Poll: President, CNN Election Center 2008, www.cnn.com/ ELECTION/2008/results/polls/#val=USP00p3.

32 Richard Freeman, "What Do Unions Do...to Voting?" (working paper, NBER Working Paper Series, September 2003, www.nber.org/papers/w9992). See also Jan E. Leighley and Jonathan Nagler, "Unions, Voter Turnout, and Class Bias in the U.S. Electorate, 1964-2004," *The Journal of Politics* 69 (2007): 430-41.

33 Quoted in Francia, *The Future of Organized Labor in American Politics*, 63.

34 "GOP Makes Gains Among the Working Class, While Democrats Hold On to the Union Vote," Pew Research Center for People and the Press.

35 Francia, *The Future of Organized Labor in American Politics*, ch. 3.

36 John Schmitt and Kris Warner, "The Changing Face of Labor, 1983–2008," Center for Economic and Policy Research, November 2009, www.cepr.net/documents/publica tions/changing-face-of-labor-2009-11.pdf. See also "Union Members Summary," Bureau of Labor Statistics.

37 Schmitt and Warner, "The Changing Face of Labor, 1983–2008."

38 Ibid.

39 Ibid.

40 "Union Members Summary."

41 Ibid.

42 Troy, *Trade Union Membership*.

43 Tula Connell, "The Union Vote's the Difference," AFL-CIO, November 8, 2006, http://blog.aflcio.org/ 2006/11/08/the-union-votes-the-difference.

44 Ibid.

45 Ibid.

46 Peter D. Hart Research Associates, "AFL-CIO Election Night Study # 8848," November 4, 2008.

47 "AFL-CIO Union Voters Help Drive Historic Victory for Obama," AFL-CIO, November 5, 2008, www.aflcio.org/mediacenter/prsptm/pr11052008a.cfm.

48 Ibid.

49 Ibid.

50 Chipman, "Obama Turnout Priority in Labor's Bid to Revive Political Clout."

51 Seth Michaels, "Union Voters Helped Propel Obama, Working Family Candidates to Victory," AFL-CIO, November 5, 2008, http://blog.aflcio.org/2008/11/05/union-voters-helped-propel-obama-working-family-candidates-to-victory.

52 "AFL-CIO Union Voters Help Drive Historic Victory for Obama."

53 Eric S. Heberlig, Peter L. Francia, and Steven H. Greene, "The Conditional Party Teams of the 2008 North Carolina Federal Elections," in *The Change Election: Money, Mobilization, and Persuasion in the 2008 Federal Elections* (Philadelphia: Temple University Press, 2011).

54 "Annual Lobbying by the U.S. Chamber of Commerce," Center for Responsive Politics, www.opensecrets.org/lobby/clientsum.php?id=D000019798&year=2009. See also Steve Spires and Cassandra La Russa, "OpenSecrets.org Offers 2010 Legislative Preview Ahead of Barack Obama's State of the Union Address," Center for Responsive Politics, January 27, 2010, www.opensecrets.org/MT/mt-search.cgi?search=EFCA &IncludeBlogs=8.

55 "Annual Lobbying by Labor," Center for Responsive Politics, http://www.opensecrets .org/lobby/indus.php?id=P&year=2009.

56 "Who Is Against the Employee Free Choice Act?" AFL-CIO, www.aflcio.org/ joinaunion/voiceatwork/ efca/against_list.cfm.

57 Sam Stein, "AFL-CIO President Trumka: 'We Did Our Job' in 2010," *The Huffington Post*, November 3, 2010, www.huffingtonpost.com/2010/11/03/aflcio-defend-election-2010-efforts-_n_778166.html.

58 Quoted in Peter H. Stone, "Inside the Shadow GOP," *National Journal*, October 27, 2010, www.nationaljournal.com/njonline/no_20101004_4486.php.

59 Quoted in David G. Savage, "Court Opens Up Election Spending," *The Baltimore Sun*, January 22, 2010, http://articles.baltimoresun.com/2010-01-22/news/bal-te.scotus22jan22_1_election-spending-corporations-and-unions-supreme-court.

60 Quoted in Kyle Trygstad, "Reactions to SCOTUS Campaign Finance Decision," RealClearPolitics.com, January 21, 2010, http://realclearpolitics.blogs.time .com/2010/01/21/reactions-to-scotus-campaign-finance-decision.

61 "Union Members Summary."

62 Quoted in Kevin Bogardus and Sean J. Miller, "Unions Taking on Dems Who Don't Toe Labor Line," *The Hill*, March 11, 2010, http://thehill.com/homenews/campaign/86127-unions-taking-on-dems-who-do-not-toe-labor-line.

63 Quoted in Sam Stein, "Trumka: Primarying Lincoln Was 'Priceless', Dems Will Realize Their Timidity," *The Huffington Post*, October 5, 2010, www.huffingtonpost.com/2010/10/05/trumka-primarying-lincoln_n_750740.html.

64 Ibid.

65 Holly Rosenkrantz and Frank Bass, "Labor Unions Face 'Huge Sinkhole' for Agenda," *Businessweek*, November 3, 2010, www.businessweek.com/news/2010-11-03/labor-unions-face-huge-sinkhole-for-agenda.html.

66 Chris Frates, "AFL-CIO's Fall Strategy: Less TV, More One-On-One," *Politico*, September 2, 2010, www.politico.com/news/stories/0910/41705.html.

67 Ibid.

68 Ibid.

69 James Parks, "Trumka: Be Proud of Union GOTV Effort, Get Ready Again to Fight for Jobs," AFL-CIO, November 3, 2010, http://blog.aflcio.org/2010/11/03/trumka-be-proud-of-union-gotv-effort-get-ready-again-to-fight-for-jobs.

70 Ibid.

71 "Business-Labor-Ideology Split in PAC & Individual Donations to Candidates and Parties: 2010 Overview," Center for Responsive Politics, www.opensecrets.org/overview/blio.php.

72 Frates, "AFL-CIO's Fall Strategy: Less TV, More One-On-One."

73 Ibid.

74 Peter D. Hart Research Associates, "AFL-CIO Election Night Survey 2010," November 2, 2010.

75 Ibid.

76 National Exit Poll: U.S. House, CNN Election Center 2010, www.cnn.com/ELECTION/2010/results/polls/#val=USH00p2.

77 Hart Research Associates, "AFL-CIO Election Night Survey 2010."

78 Ibid.

79 Francia, *The Future of Organized Labor in American Politics*, 75.

80 Matthew Murray, "Chamber Watch: Business Group 'Central' to GOP Gains," *Roll Call*, November 12, 2010, www.rollcall.com/news/-200473-1.html.

81 Michael M. Franz, "The *Citizens United* Election? Or Same As It Ever Was?" *The Forum* 8 (2010): Article 7.

82 Ibid.

83 Spencer MacColl, "Citizens United Decision Profoundly Affects Political Landscape," Center for Responsive Politics, May 5, 2011, www.opensecrets.org/news/2011/05/citizens-united-decision-profoundly-affects-political-landscape.html.

84 Ibid.

85 Ibid.

86 Ibid.

87 Dan Clawson and Mary Ann Clawson, "What Has Happened to the U.S. Labor Movement? Union Decline and Renewal," *Annual Review of Sociology* 25 (1999): 95–119.

See also Richard B. Freeman, "Why Are Unions Faring Poorly in NLRB Representation Elections?" in Challenges and Choices Facing American Unions, ed. Thomas Kochan (Cambridge, MA: MIT Press, 1985).

88 Kate Bronfenbrenner, "No Holds Barred: The Intensification of Employer Opposition to Organizing," Economic Policy Institute, May 20, 2009, www.epi.org/page/-/pdf/bp235.pdf. See also Morris M. Kleiner, "Intensity of Management Resistance: Understanding the Decline of Unionization in the Private Sector," *Journal of Labor Research* 22 (2001): 519–540.

89 Melanie Trottman and Kris Maher, "Plan to Ease Way for Unions," *The Wall Street Journal*, June 22, 2011, http://online.wsj.com/article/SB10001424052702304070104576399822234404508.html.

90 Dan Clawson, *The Next Upsurge: Labor and New Social Movements* (Ithaca, NY: Cornell University Press, 2003). See also Lowell Turner and Richard W. Hurd, "Building Social Movement Unionism: The Transformation of the American Labor Movement," in *Rekindling the Movement: Labor's Quest for Relevance in the 21st Century*, eds. Lowell Turner, Harry C. Katz, and Richard W. Hurd (Ithaca, NY: Cornell University Press, 2001).

91 Jennifer Epstein, "AFL-CIO President Richard Trumka 'Thanks' Scott Walker," *Politico*, March 10, 2011, www.politico.com/news/stories/0311/51049.html.

92 Francia, *The Future of Organized Labor in American Politics*, ch. 7. See also Kevin Bogardus and Sean J. Miller, "Unions Taking on Dems Who Don't Toe Labor Line," *The Hill*, March 11, 2010, http://thehill.com/homenews/campaign/86127-unions-taking-on-dems-who-do-not-toe-labor-line. For a different perspective, see Michael O'Brien and Kevin Bogardus, "AFL-CIO: Labor Will Stand by Obama," *The Hill*, August 18, 2011, http://thehill.com/homenews/campaign/177271-afl-cio-labor-will-stand-by-obama.

93 Steven Greenhouse, "Labor Leaders Plan to Apply New Clout in Effort for Obama," *The New York Times*, March 11, 2012, www.nytimes.com/2012/03/12/us/politics/unions-plan-a-door-to-door-effort-for-2012-election.html.

94 Quoted in Holly Rosenkrantz and Stephanie Armour, "Union Enthusiasm for Obama Re-Election Fades, AFL-CIO's Chief Trumka Says," *Bloomberg*, June 1, 2011, www.bloomberg.com/news/print/2011-06-01/union-enthusiasm-for-obama-re-election-fades-afl-cio-s-chief-trumka-says.html.

95 Ibid.

96 Michael Goldfield, *The Decline of Organized Labor in the United States* (Chicago: University of Chicago Press, 1987). See also Paul Buhle, *Taking Care of Business: Samuel Gompers, George Meany, Lane Kirkland, and the Tragedy of American Labor* (New York: Monthly Review Press, 1999). For a perspective on the EFCA defeat, see Peter L. Francia, "Assessing the Labor-Democratic Party Alliance: A One-Sided Relationship?" *Polity* 42 (2010): 293–303.

97 Tracy Roof, *American Labor, Congress, and the Welfare State, 1935–2010* (Baltimore: Johns Hopkins University Press, 2011). See also Taylor E. Dark, *The Unions and the Democrats an Enduring Alliance* (Ithaca, NY: Cornell University Press, 1999).

CHAPTER 7

It Wasn't Easy Being Green in 2010

The League of Conservation Voters and the Uphill Battle to Make the Environment Matter

Ronald G. Shaiko

There is an old political adage that in political campaigning, three-quarters of all the money spent on elections is wasted. That is, the campaign messages purchased with campaign funds often fall on deaf ears or reach citizens ineligible to vote for or against the particular candidate. Of course, the best political consultants and party operatives supposedly know which 25 percent works. This inexact science of campaign financing often leads to misspending, overspending, and less than stellar performances by campaign investors. This was clearly the case for those staking a claim for the environment in the 2010 election cycle. Far from getting a significant bang for their buck, national environmental organizations invested heavily in a large number of competitive congressional races across the nation, with little to show for their efforts. And, the new rules for campaign financing in the post–*Citizens United* era provided even more opportunities for overspending. The League of Conservation Voters (LCV), once again, led the environmental movement in fundraising and campaign spending in 2010 at $5.9 million in expenditures. Not only was LCV the largest environmental spender in the cycle, it was surpassed in nonparty outside spending efforts that overwhelmingly supported Democrats by only four groups—Service Employees International Union (SEIU); American Federation of State, County, and Municipal Employees (AFSCME); National Education Association (NEA); and America's Families First Action Fund, according to the Center for Responsive Politics.[1]

Like many of the more sophisticated nonprofit players in American politics, the League of Conservation Voters operates as a "full-service public interest organization."[2] LCV, Inc., the parent entity of the League "family of organizations," operates as a 501(c)(4) organization. The League of Conservation Voters

Education Fund, a 501(c)(3) entity, has a slightly smaller annual budget than LCV, Inc., but, interestingly, it does manage most of the lobbying activities for the organization. These two entities represent the core infrastructural aspects of LCV at the national level, although, in reality, there is one office staffed with one team of employees and leaders. As noted in Chapter 1, the Internal Revenue Service (IRS) regulates nonprofit organizations in the United States under Section 501(c) of the Internal Revenue Code. The largest percentage of nonprofits in the United States file as 501(c)(3) tax-exempt nonprofits. Such a tax status for an organization allows contributors to deduct these charitable contributions on their personal income tax forms. But 501(c)(3) status places limits on the amount of lobbying these groups can undertake; these groups also are banned from participating in any electioneering activities.

Organizations wishing to be more active in lobbying and to participate in electoral politics opt for 501(c)(4) nonprofit status with the IRS. These groups have no limits on lobbying expenditures and may spend organizational resources on influencing the outcomes of elections. The 501(c)(4) organizations also may have affiliated political action committees (PACs) and (independent expenditure only) super PACs, while 501(c)(3) groups may not. Contributors to 501(c)(4) organizations, however, may not deduct these contributions on their income tax filings. Both types of organizations must file IRS 990 organizational tax forms that report annual income and expenditures to the Internal Revenue Service.

LCV leaders and some staffers are paid by both the 501(c)(4) LCV, Inc. and the 501(c)(3) LCV Education Fund, according to the IRS 990 filings by the organizations. LCV also has a PAC—League of Conservation Voters Action Fund, and a super PAC—League of Conservation Voters Victory Fund. It also has a 527 organization—League of Conservation Voters Political Engagement Fund. There is one additional entity attributable to the League—LCV Accountability Project,[3] a subsidiary of the parent 501(c)(4) organization. Finally, there are thirty-five state LCV chapters, most of which are 501(c)(4) entities and file with the IRS individually. Collectively in 2011, LCV has roughly 210,000 members and contributors, with just over 4,000 donors to its PAC since 1997.[4] With this elaborate structure, LCV is able to package its campaign funding efforts in a variety of ways. In the 2009–10 election cycle, each of these entities (including the 501(c)(3) Education Fund) was engaged in the campaign process at the state or federal levels.

LCV Goals and Methods of Operation

Founded in 1970 as part of the first Earth Day celebration, the League of Conservation Voters "works to turn environmental values into national priorities. To secure the environmental future of our planet, LCV advocates for sound environmental policies, elects pro-environment candidates who will adopt and implement such policies, [and] provides the state LCVs with the resources and tools to accomplish and sustain their mission."[5] While LCV is known primarily for its impact on American electoral politics, the organization does have a lobbying presence in Washington, DC and is widely known for its National Environmental Scorecard and Presidential Report Card. For each session of Congress, LCV rates representatives and senators on key votes cast in each chamber on issues relating to energy and the environment. On average, ten-to-twenty roll call votes are scored with members and senators receiving scores from 0 (anti-environment) to 100 (pro-environment). Political activists as well as academics use LCV scores as proxies for environmental ideology.[6] Like other roll call–based measures of ideology for members of Congress (e.g., Americans for Democratic Action [ADA] and American Conservative Union [ACU] scores), LCV scores cluster at the extremes (0–20 and 80–100) in both chambers, with a comparative low percentage of members receiving scores between 40 and 60.[7] The LCV Presidential Report Card is issued periodically throughout the term of each president. The latest Presidential Report Card provides President Barack Obama and his administration with a grade of B+ for their handling of climate and clean energy issues.[8]

The lobbying activities of LCV are typical of most environmental groups and incorporate both direct lobbying efforts by the staff and grassroots lobbying efforts through media campaigns and membership mobilizations, all of which are reported through its 501(c)(3) entity. In terms of its overall operating budget, lobbying activities constitute a small percentage of LCV expenditures. For 2010, LCV reported, under the lobbying disclosure provisions set forth by Congress, $95,000 in lobbying expenditures; in 2009 it reported $90,000 in lobbying costs. Interestingly, in its IRS 990 filing for that year, LCV Education Fund reported $316,472 in direct lobbying expenditures and $110,090 in grassroots lobbying expenditures (not covered by lobbying disclosure requirements). This significant discrepancy highlights the inadequacy of current lobbying disclosure requirements as organizations are clearly underreporting their activities to Congress while, at the same time, providing a more comprehensive accounting of lobbying activities to the executive branch through the IRS.

While all of the lobbying expenditures are connected with the Education Fund, it appears that the LCV 501(c)(4) parent organization, LCV, Inc., contracts out for lobbying (and, perhaps, political campaigning) efforts as grants of more than $2.6 million were made to other lobbying or campaigning organizations in 2009, according its IRS 990 filing for that year. Recipients of the largest grants included the AFL-CIO, Building and Construction Trades Department ($512,000), Environmental Defense Action Fund ($200,000), Sierra Club ($300,000), Vote Vets Action Fund ($241,551), and the Partnership Project Action Fund through the Wilderness Society ($1,200,000).[9]

Beyond its policy advocacy efforts, LCV is a major player in American electoral politics. LCV operates on two fronts in the electoral arena—it punishes and it rewards. The LCV form of electoral punishment is its "Dirty Dozen" hit list. The Dirty Dozen had its origins in a feisty, little, heart-on-its-sleeve environmental group called Environmental Action. Formed at the same time as LCV in 1970, Environmental Action never attracted more than about 20,000 members in its twenty-six-year history, but it kicked and screamed louder than most groups. And, it went after those members of Congress who were deemed to be the worst environmental offenders. Overwhelmingly, Environmental Action targeted congressional incumbents with clear voting records against the environment. In 1994, in a desperate attempt to keep itself alive, Environmental Action jettisoned its 501 (c)(4) status for the tax-deductibility of membership contributions under 501(c)(3) status and renamed itself Environmental Action Fund. However, as a result of the switch, the Dirty Dozen hit list violated IRS prohibitions on electioneering by 501(c)(3) groups. So, by the 1996 election cycle, the Dirty Dozen left Environmental Action and moved to LCV.[10]

Since 1996, LCV has modified the approach to naming candidates to the Dirty Dozen list. Today, congressional challengers (even those with no voting records for or against the environment) are as likely to be named as incumbents. Between 1996 and 2008, "49 out of 79 of the Dirty Dozen have been defeated—a rate of 62%."[11] The 2010 cycle was a bit different for the hit list as it grew to be the Dirty (Baker's) Dozen. In addition to twelve actual candidates for the House or Senate, LCV added California Ballot Proposition 23—a statewide ballot proposition that would have suspended current state pollution control laws if passed—to the list (or at least those supporting Proposition 23).[12] LCV defeated six of the twelve candidates (50 percent success) on the list and declared victory in the defeat of Proposition 23 (see Table 7.1).

In addition to targeting anti-environment candidates for Congress for defeat, LCV also supports pro-environment candidates. In fact, the vast majority of LCV spending in the 2009–10 cycle was directed (largely through independent expenditures) toward supporting pro-environment candidates. Unfortunately for LCV, it had comparatively little electoral success in the congressional races where it invested most of its resources. In the twelve House and Senate races in which LCV spent $100,000 or more in support of the pro-environment candidates (all Democrats), it won only three, although it did win the race in which it invested the most money (see Table 7.2).

LCV Fundraising and Distribution

There exists in Washington, DC one physical structure that is the League of Conservation Voters. Its offices are located at 1920 L Street, NW and extend to much of the eighth floor of the building. In those offices one finds manifestations

TABLE 7.1   LCV Dirty (Baker's) Dozen, 2010

Targeted Candidate	Campaign	Voting Record	Election Outcome
Sharron Angle	Nev.-Senate	State Legislative Record	Defeated
Roy Blunt	Mo.-Senate	House Legislative Record	Elected
Ken Buck	Colo.-Senate	No Legislative Record	Defeated
Carly Fiorina	Calif.-Senate	No Legislative Record	Defeated
Ron Johnson	Wis.-Senate	No Legislative Record	Elected
Blanche Lincoln	Ariz.-Senate	Incumbent	Defeated
Christine O'Donnell	Del.-Senate	No Legislative Record	Defeated
Pat Toomey	Pa.-Senate	House Legislative Record	Elected
Michele Bachmann	Minn.-6	Incumbent	Elected
Steve Pearce	N.Mex.-2	Incumbent	Elected
Richard Pombo	Calif.-19	Incumbent	Defeated
Tim Walberg	Mich.-7	Incumbent	Elected
Proposition 23	Calif.	N/A	Defeated

Source: League of Conservation Voters; voting records and election outcomes compiled by author.

TABLE 7.2   2010 Congressional Races with LCV Spending Greater than $100,000

Candidate	State	Office	Total	Result
Michael Bennet	Colo.	Senate	$883,321	Won
Tom Perriello	Va.	House	608,270	Lost
Mark Schauer	Mich.	House	386,298	Lost
Martha Coakley	Mass.	Senate	350,667	Lost
Joseph Sestak	Pa.	Senate	548,314	Lost
Robin Carnahan	Mo.	Senate	264,461	Lost
John Boccieri	Ohio	House	250,018	Lost
Heath Shuler	N.C.	House	241,600	Won
Harry Reid	Nev.	Senate	228,429	Won
Dina Titus	Nev.	House	205,247	Lost
Ann McLane Kuster	N.H.	House	182,410	Lost
Alexander Giannoulias	Ill.	Senate	126,328	Lost

Source: Compiled by author using Center for Responsive Politics data, www.opensecrets.org.

of all of the various enterprises of LCV. The two main organizational entities of LCV, however, are the 501(c)(4) parent organization and the 501(c)(3) Education Fund. Each entity files separately with the IRS, although most of the staff members work for both organizations. The LCV senior executive team leads both entities and includes Gene Karpinski, LCV president;[13] Patrick Collins, senior vice president of finance and administration; Stephanie Kushner, senior vice president of development; Navin Nayak, senior vice president of campaigns; Mike Palamuso, vice president of communications; Tiernan Sittenfeld, senior vice president of government affairs; Rich Thomas, general counsel and senior vice president; and Ed Zuckerman, senior vice president of state capacity building. In addition to these eight LCV leaders, there are twenty-five staffers in the Washington, DC offices attributable to both entities. Two staffers work on political campaigns, three work on lobbying, while eight staffers are responsible for development and fundraising. Two staffers are on the communications team and two staffers work on coordinating state LCV efforts. The remaining eight staffers provide administrative and legal support. There are an additional seven employees found only on the LCV Education Fund staff directory—three in state capacity building, two in education programs, and two in development.

There are two boards of directors, with thirty members on the LCV, Inc. board and nine on the Education Fund board. Five of the nine Education Fund members, including its chair and treasurer, also serve on the LCV, Inc. board, in similar capacities. In addition to including key financial patrons on both boards, the senior board also includes representation from a sizeable number of allied environmental organizations, including the Natural Resources Defense Council (NRDC), Environmental Defense, Friends of the Earth, National Parks Conservation Association, the Wilderness Society, and the American Conservation Association as well as from four state LCVs.

For its 2009 IRS filings, LCV, Inc. reported total revenues of $14.3 million while LCV Education Fund reported total revenues of just under $9 million. So, together, the two entities have a collective income of $23 million. To place these figures in context, Sierra Club, Inc.— a 501(c)(4)—and Sierra Club Foundation—a 501(c)(3)—had a combined income of $125 million in 2009. Environmental Defense, both its 501(c)(3) and 501(c)(4), declared $145 million in revenues. And, the Nature Conservancy, 501(c)(3) only, reported income of $856 million in 2009.[14] Comparatively speaking, LCV cannot be considered among the most well healed of the environmental organizations in the United States, yet it is the largest spender in federal (and state) elections in the movement. Clearly, LCV is the leading electoral arm of the environmental movement today.

As a result of *Citizens United v. FEC*, LCV, Inc., the 501(c)(4) parent entity, was able to spend more than $3.9 million from its general treasury on independent expenditures during the 2009–10 election cycle. This amount represents more than two-thirds of the $5.9 million LCV, and its various electoral components at the federal level, spent in the cycle.[15] Therefore, 67 percent of LCV campaign contributions are not linked to any particular donors, as contributors to LCV, Inc. are not disclosed to Congress under the lobbying disclosure laws, to the Federal Election Commission (FEC) for election purposes, or to the IRS for tax purposes. It is possible, however, to find out where the money went in the cycle. Approximately $3.9 million went to independent expenditures on behalf of pro-environment Democrats running in congressional races; just under $200,000 in independent expenditure campaigns were targeted against Republicans running for Congress; and just under $20,000 went to fund independent expenditure campaigns in support of pro-environment Republicans. The remaining $1.5 million of the roughly $5.5 million in total independent expenditures by LCV came from the LCV PAC and super PAC.

In the mid-to-late 1980s, Common Cause and other government reform groups waged battles that targeted PACs as evil incarnate in the American campaign finance system. Now, a quarter century later, scholars and activists alike are pointing to PACs as *the* legitimate means through which campaigns are financed. The LCV Action Fund operates under the FEC rules governing PAC fundraising and spending. The PAC raised $1.6 million and spent $1.75 million in the 2009–10 cycle. The PAC was heavily reliant on the close to 100 donors who maxed out their PAC contributions to LCV and accounted for almost one-third of all funds raised in the cycle by the PAC. Of the $5.9 million in LCV's total federal campaign expenditures in the 2010 cycle, the only hard money contributions given directly to candidates totaled less than $400,000 (or less than 7 percent of total LCV spending). These direct PAC contributions to candidates were derived from the LCV Action Fund; the remainder of the PAC spending in the cycle came in the form of independent expenditures ($650,000) and payments to vendors ($700,000). The direct PAC contributions went to ninety-four House Democrats (challengers and incumbents) and six House Republicans as well as twenty-three Senate Democrats (challengers and incumbents). The PAC did support Republican Mike Castle in the Delaware Senate race where he lost in the primary to one of the Dirty Dozen— Christine O'Donnell.[16] In addition to these hard money contributions and independent expenditures, the PAC also bundled $1 million for congressional candidates, according to Mike Palamuso, vice president for communications.[17]

The LCV Victory Fund, its super PAC, raised $1.1 million and spent just under $1 million in the cycle. By definition, all of the Victory Fund campaign spending came in the form of independent expenditures ($908,660) because, as noted in earlier chapters, the FEC requires a special filing for super PACs that designates each to spend its resources in the form of independent expenditures only. Approximately 10 percent of the funds raised by the Victory Fund came in the form of transfers from LCV, Inc., totaling more than $110,000. The Victory

Fund also was reliant on several key patrons who each gave at least $50,000 as well as a larger group who contributed at least $10,000 to the super PAC. The lion's share of Victory Fund expenditures was targeted at two House races—Thomas Perriello, running for the Virginia District 5 House seat and Dina Titus, running for the Nevada District 3 House seat. Each Democratic candidate received just over $200,000 in independent expenditure support from the Victory Fund. Other Democratic candidates in the House and Senate who received significant support from the Victory Fund include: Harry Reid (Nevada Senate, $103,000), Martin Heinrich (New Mexico District 1, $95,000), Joseph Sestak (Pennsylvania Senate, $90,000), Harry Teague (New Mexico District 2, $60,000), Michael Bennet (Colorado Senate, $50,000), Patty Murray (Washington Senate, $30,000), and Robin Carnahan (Missouri Senate, $20,000). These nine House and Senate races account for 85 percent of the Victory Fund spending in the cycle.[18]

Finally, the LCV Political Engagement Fund, its 527 organization, raised over $600,000 and spent $1.1 million. To review, 527s, like 501(c) organizations, are creatures of the IRS. Section 527 of the Internal Revenue Code provides "political organization" status to entities who conduct political activities, broadly defined. Because 527 organizations provide the financial means to do whatever is necessary to keep the other affiliated organizations functioning properly and covering the overarching costs of operation, that frees up money to be devoted to the principal purposes of the groups (see Chapter 1 for more details on the history and role of 527s). From 2004 to 2010, LCV received individual contributions to its 527 totaling more than $10 million. This is where the truly serious money in political organizations is found. Table 7.3 lists the top ten LCV patrons during the four

TABLE 7.3   Top Ten LCV Patrons, 2004–2010

John A. Harris	Retired (deceased 2009)	$2,511,000 (2004–2009)
Alida Rockefeller Messinger	Philanthropist	1,597,000 (2004–2008)
John R. Hunting*	Philanthropist	1,298,000 (2003–2010)
Louis Moore Bacon	Moore Capital Mgt./CEO	1,038,000 (2004–2008)
Wendy Paulson	Teacher/Wife of Hank Paulson	614,000 (2003–2006)
Lynde Uihlein*	Brico Fund/Founder	592,000 (2004–2010)
David Bonderman	Texas Pacific Group/CEO	310,000 (2004–2010)
Fred Eychaner	Newsweb Corp./CEO	300,000 (2004)
Larry Rockefeller*	NRDC/Attorney	276,000 (2003–2010)
A. Scott Nathan*	Baupost Group LLP/Mgt. Dir.	232,000 (2009–2010)

Source: Compiled by author using data from www.CampaignMoney.com.
*LCV board member.

election cycles from 2004 to 2010. These ten individuals account for an astonishing $8.8 million in donations, the vast majority of which is funneled through the LCV Political Engagement Fund. These donors account for more than three-quarters of the $10 million raised by the 527 since 2004.

The more than $1 million spent by the 527 during the 2009–10 cycle includes a variety of payments for daily operations, data management, and support for state LCVs. In the 2004 election cycle, LCV's 527 organizations (they had two) ran afoul of the FEC for undertaking electioneering activities without registering with the FEC. The FEC ruled that "[a]mong other spending in the 2004 election, the League of Conservation Voters 527 groups funded door-to-door campaigns and phone canvassing activities that expressly advocated the election of Senator Kerry and the defeat of President Bush." LCV was fined $180,000 for its failure to register and file disclosure reports.[19]

During the 2009–10 cycle, LCV 527 spending was limited to operational costs and state LCV grants including more than $10,000 in American Express bills paid, $12,700 to Aristotle International for database management, $17,500 for subscription dues to America Votes, payroll and utility bills for the Washington State LCV totaling more than $35,000, as well as a grant to the Washington State LCV 527 of $175,000. The Nevada LCV received a $15,000 contribution while the Missouri LCV received $12,500. Montana LCV and Maine LCV received contributions of $30,000 and $25,000, respectively. Finally, the parent organization, LCV, Inc., received more than $86,000 to cover overhead costs.[20] While 527 expenditures do not have a direct impact on election outcomes, they do cover costs that make it easier for the electoral arms of the LCV to spend more of their money on influencing elections.

In addition to the organizational components attributable to the national LCV, there are state-level entities affiliated with LCV as well. While the LCV website lists thirty-five affiliated state LCVs, there is a significant range in organizational wealth and activities across these chapters. The largest in terms of budget and outlays, as one might expect, is the California LCV, with its 501(c)(4) political arm reporting $3.5 million in revenues in 2009 and its 501(c)(3) organization reporting just over $700,000 in revenues. In comparison, the New York LCV reported roughly $600,000 in revenues and the Arizona LCV reported approximately $100,000 in revenues for the same year. At least three state LCVs reported no income for 2009.

For the 2009–10 cycle, thirty-one state LCVs endorsed candidates for state offices and, for the first time, a state-level Dirty Dozen was issued by LCV. This Dirty Dozen list, selected through input from each of the state chapters, included gubernatorial candidates and candidates for state House and state Senate seats:

1. Al Melvin, Arizona State Senate District 26

2. Dean Cannon, Florida State House District 35

3. Timothy Cahill, Massachusetts Governor

4. John Pappageorge, Michigan State Senate District 13

5. Tom Emmer, Minnesota Governor

6. Roy Brown, Montana State Senate District 25

7. Don Gustavson, Nevada State Senate District 2

8. William Stachowski, New York State Senate District 58

9. Mark Crawford, North Carolina State House District 115

10. Frank Morse, Oregon State Senate District 8

11. John Perzel, Pennsylvania State House District 172

12. Rick Perry, Texas Governor

LCV declared victory in defeating half of the state Dirty Dozen candidates in 2010.

The state LCVs fared better in electing LCV-endorsed candidates in the cycle, however. According to LCV postelection analysis:

> Across the country 1134 out of 1619 (70%) state league endorsed candidates won! These successes illustrate the power of state leagues, and highlight the role the state leagues played in many of those races by strategically knocking on doors, airing television and radio ads, making phone calls, and targeting mail pieces. Collectively, state leagues engaged in 20 gubernatorial races, spent a *record-breaking* $7 million(!) and engaged in over 17 million voter contacts helping to get pro-conservation candidates elected.[21]

So, in addition to the $5.9 million LCV spent on federal elections in the cycle, state LCVs spent an additional $7.1 million on state-level elections. Clearly this dual-track strategy allowed state chapters to target and support candidates for state offices while LCV in Washington, DC orchestrated a federal campaign strategy.

Analysis of LCV Campaign Strategies and Tactics

The 2010 election cycle certainly will not be referenced as the "Year of the Environment." Far more pressing issues were on the minds of voters. According to 2010 exit polls, almost two-thirds of voters (62 percent) claimed that the economy was the most important issue, followed by concerns over health care (19 percent), illegal immigration (8 percent), and the war in Afghanistan (7 percent). Even among young voters (ages 18–29), the economy (59 percent) and health care (24 percent) were the dominant issues.[22] As a result, it was much more difficult to package the environmental issue agenda. All of the environmental groups active in the 2010 elections had to figure out the appropriate message and, as important, the appropriate messenger. LCV and several other groups (including National Wildlife Federation, NRDC, Environment America, Sierra Club, and Defenders of Wildlife) worked in concert to devise a plan to inject the environmental policy agenda into the congressional races they had targeted. In addition to crafting a message linking the environmental agenda to the more salient issues in the campaign cycle, they also found an interesting messenger to convey the repackaged message—VoteVets.org.

VoteVets.org did not exist prior to the 2006 elections. In the 2010 cycle, according to the FEC, VoteVets Political Action Committee was at best, a bit player, with reported expenditures of just over $200,000. The political reality, however, was quite different. It has risen to a prominent position in the liberal pantheon of political financiers. In 2010, its 501(c)(4) entity, VoteVets Action Fund, raised and spent more than $3.2 million, of which $2.3 million took the form of independent expenditures (40 percent for Democratic candidates and 60 percent against Republican candidates) and $860,000 in *electioneering communications* (broadcast advertisements aired within sixty days of a general election that mention a federal candidate but do not expressly advocate for or against his or her election, discussed in more detail in Chapter 1).[23] While, on its face, VoteVets.org appears to be a veterans organization with "over 100,000 members,"[24] it is largely bankrolled by organized labor and other liberal-leaning advocacy groups including environmental groups. (Remember that LCV, Inc. provided a grant of almost $250,000 to VoteVets Action Fund in 2009.) Virtually all of its $5,000 PAC contributions to VoteVets in 2010 came from labor unions.

Early in the cycle, LCV reached out to VoteVets.org to pursue a joint campaign strategy. Recognizing that their agenda was going to be difficult to sell, LCV leaders wanted to be "smart and strategic" in their efforts by packaging their message in the form of "energy security" and linking that message to candidates, both positively and negatively. They sought to frame their campaign first through an "economic message" and then as a "security message." They also needed a "credible messenger."[25] Hence, LCV reached out to VoteVets.org, allowing the veterans featured in the jointly funded campaign advertisements to articulate the energy security message. The partnership was most widely used in Pennsylvania, Ohio, and Minnesota where LCV and VoteVets.org aligned on candidate support and opposition.[26]

Beyond the alliances with VoteVets.org in competitive races, LCV also pursued several highly competitive races across the country, including the Colorado Senate race and the race for the Virginia District 5 House seat. In both instances, LCV's significant expenditures on behalf of the Democratic candidates in each race (see Table 7.2) "helped change the dynamic of the election," focusing voters on energy, climate change, and the environment.[27] LCV had targeted Ken Buck, the Republican candidate for the Colorado Senate race, as one of the Dirty Dozen and claimed victory with the election of Michael Bennet after having invested almost $900,000 in the race. But that large investment by LCV represented less than 3 percent of the more than $30 million in outside spending in the Buck–Bennet race.[28] In the Virginia District 5 House race, LCV sought to protect a vulnerable freshman Democrat, Tom Perriello, who had narrowly defeated the incumbent, Virgil Goode, in 2008. In this race, LCV poured in more than $600,000. This expenditure, comparatively speaking, was a bit more impactful as the entire race cost just over $6 million. Nonetheless, Republican Robert Hurt managed to defeat Perriello by less than 4 percentage points.

Throughout the cycle, LCV attempted to beat back the pro-Republican forces with a variety of campaign techniques including data mining to identify "persuadable voters," door-to-door canvassing (in Missouri, New Hampshire, Nevada, and Virginia), phone calling, and online campaigning. A variety of online videos were produced at a comparatively low cost of between $12,000 and $15,000 and posted on YouTube. *Googlebombing* efforts—attempts to manipulate HTML pages posted on the Internet in order to increase the likelihood of the page being placed at or near the top of search engine listings—were then undertaken in order for the videos to be placed in top positions when citizens searched for campaign information. For example, a video produced for the Sestak-Toomey Senate race by LCV (pro-Sestak) received over one million views. Approximately 10 percent of LCV advertising spending efforts went toward online advertising.[29]

In addition to LCV's expenditures in many competitive House and Senate races, LCV leadership decided, late in the cycle, to engage in the California Ballot Proposition 23 battle. If Proposition 23 had passed, California air pollution control laws that require polluters to report and reduce greenhouse gas emissions would have been suspended. It was not until October 14, 2010 that LCV placed Proposition 23 on its Dirty Dozen list and poured more than $1 million into the campaign to defeat it. In total, LCV spent $1.25 million to defeat Proposition 23 in California including $550,000 from LCV, Inc. LCV Education Fund also spent more than $650,000 on Proposition 23 as participating in ballot initiative campaigns is not considered electioneering under IRS 501(c)(3) regulations. The Nature Conservancy, with an $856 million annual budget, provided $800,000 to the effort. Only the National Wildlife Federation, with an annual budget of $100 million, spent more than LCV in the Proposition 23 battle (see Table 7.4). While polling on Proposition 23 showed an even split among voters throughout the summer months, later polls showed public opinion breaking consistently against Proposition 23. A Field Poll conducted from September 14–21 showed an 11-point lead for the opposition, more than three weeks before LCV decided to get involved in the battle.[30] And, the threat of "big oil" to dump tens of

TABLE 7.4   California Proposition 23 Funding and Votes

	Supporters	Opponents
Total contributions	$10,659,560	$31,307,744
Total votes	2,822,546 (38.9%)	4,4226,733 (61.1%)
Top contributors: ($1,000,000+)	Valero Services, Inc. $5,075,315	Thomas Steyer/Kathryn Taylor, $5,099,000
	Tesoro Companies $2,040,637	National Wildlife Federation, $3,000,000
	Flint Hills Resources $1,000,000	John/Ann Doerr, $2,100,000
		League of Conservation Voters, $1,250,000
		Vinod Khosla, $1,037,267
		Gordon Moore, $1,000,000
		Robert Fisher, $1,000,000

Source: Compiled by author using data from www.CampaignMoney.com.

millions of dollars into the campaign had not materialized. Despite these circumstances, LCV leaders believed that they "couldn't afford to take it for granted" that late oil money might flow into the campaign.[31] In the end, it seemed as though LCV was looking for a win to bolster its Dirty Dozen record and was willing to pay handsomely for the victory.

According to the Sunlight Foundation, more than $454 million was spent by outside groups to influence election outcomes in 2010. LCV accounts for about 1 percent of that undisclosed spending (or roughly $4 million). In tallying up this spending by individual House and Senate races, the Sunlight Foundation identified the top three Senate and House races for outside spending: in the Senate, it was Buck–Bennet in Colorado ($32 million), Toomey–Sestak in Pennsylvania ($25 million), and Rossi–Murray in Washington ($19 million); in the House, it was Walberg–Schauer in Michigan District 7 ($8.5 million), Heck–Titus in Nevada District 3 ($7 million), and Renacci–Boccieri in Ohio District16 ($6.5 million). (See Table 7.2; five of the six races are there.)[32] Outside money moved in waves in the 2009–10 cycle and LCV mirrored these waves of spending. In several of these races outside spending surpassed spending by the candidates themselves. For example, in Ohio District 16, James Renacci, John Boccieri and a third candidate spent a combined $4.1 million; outside spending in the race totaled $6.5 million.[33] While LCV participated in the outside spending fests, it became less and less clear how consequential each addition dollar of expenditure was in determining the final outcome. It would seem that, at least in these races, the point of diminishing returns on LCV's campaign expenditures had been reached.

Conclusion: Lessons from 2010 and a Look Ahead

By any measure, the 2010 cycle was not a terribly successful one for LCV, although the LCV efforts at the state level were quite effective in retaining pro-LCV state legislators across the nation. Half of the Dirty Dozen candidates won their elections and of the twelve races in which LCV invested most heavily, only three of its endorsed candidates were victorious. When one separates out the spending attributable to the traditional (pre–*Citizens United*) means of campaign financing by LCV in the cycle, the amount of money raised and spent was well below the level of spending in either 2006 or 2008. While LCV reported that their members were "angry" about the pro-Republican direction of the cycle and did contribute via online at rates higher than in previous cycles, they were not as engaged as in years past. As a result, and with the new freedom to spend organizational funds from the 501(c)(4) nonprofit corporation, LCV expended more than 25 percent of its 501(c)(4) annual revenues in 2010 on electioneering via independent expenditures in congressional races.

It is ironic that Rich Thomas, LCV general counsel, responding immediately to the *Citizens United* ruling by posting a YouTube video,[34] blasted the 5-4 ruling and laid out a potential scenario for ExxonMobil spending on elections as a result of the Supreme Court decision. If ExxonMobil had spent one-quarter of its annual revenues on electioneering from its general treasury (like LCV did) as a result of the *Citizens United* ruling, it would have spent $284 billion. Even if ExxonMobil had spent one-quarter of its *profits* from 2010, it would have spent $4.8 billion. When the dust finally settled on the 2010 cycle, LCV actually spent more than ExxonMobil in undisclosed expenditures.

The threat of unrestrained corporate campaign spending by the ExxonMobils of the country in the post–*Citizens United* era did have a significant impact on LCV and other group-based spending. This threat was particularly evident in the Proposition 23 battle. LCV jumped in late because they "couldn't afford to take it for granted" that big-oil money would not flow into the battle at the eleventh hour.[35] As a result of the potential threat of massive amounts of business money entering into the contest, disproportionate amounts of money on the opposition side were spent, even when the outcome seemed secure. This threat of unleashed corporate spending in federal elections, if it persists beyond the 2010 cycle, may drive some organizations into significant financial hardship in off-years and perhaps even to bankruptcy. Unions and cause groups (liberal or conservative) who tap into general revenues for electioneering purposes on a regular basis will not be sustainable.

Beyond the impact of post–*Citizens United* spending, this assessment of LCV sheds significant light on the regulatory scheme governing federal campaign financing. In addition to addressing the impacts of *Citizens United*, the existing system of carrots and sticks disproportionately constrains the more legitimate means of funding elections. The system is in dire need of a "nudge."[36] The current "choice architecture" in place drives money in directions that make candidates and their own campaigns less relevant, not more. That LCV chose to spend almost two-thirds of its PAC money on independent expenditures rather than on hard money contributions to candidates is quite telling. The current rule that limits the amount a PAC can give directly to a candidate in an election cycle results in the impact a PAC can have on directly supporting a candidate equal to rounding error in the larger accounting of all campaign expenditures in any particular congressional race. A maximum PAC contribution of $5,000 to a candidate in a multimillion-dollar congressional race is inconsequential. For candidates to have control over how their campaigns are conducted, then the PAC contribution limit needs to be raised significantly, perhaps by a factor of five ($25,000) or even ten ($50,000).

As for life after the 2010 elections for LCV, this multifaceted organization has survived and regrouped for the 112th Congress and the 2012 elections. It will continue to wage the battle on the congressional response to climate change. It will attempt to reenergize its base and mobilize greater resources for the 2012 election cycle in its continuing effort to fight the uphill battle in Congress.

Endnotes

1   Center for Responsive Politics, www.opensecrets.org/outsidespending/summ .php?cycle=2010 &chrt=V&disp=O&type=P.

2   Ronald G. Shaiko, "More Bang for the Buck: The New Era of Full-Service Public Interest Organizations," in *Interest Group Politics*, 3rd ed., eds. Allan J. Cigler and Burdett A. Loomis (Washington, DC: Congressional Quarterly Press, 1991).

3   According to the League of Conservation Voters, "The LCV Accountability Project was established as a new tool to educate the public about important environmental issues and to hold members of Congress and other politicians accountable for their votes and actions on the environment. The Accountability Project accomplishes its goals through strategic media and grassroots campaigns," www.lcv.org/about-lcv/ lcv-accountability/

4   Mike Palamuso (vice president, communications, LCV), telephone communication, June 3, 2011.

5   League of Conservation Voters, www.lcv.org/about-lcv/

6   See, e.g., Jon P. Nelson, "'Green' Voting and Ideology: LCV Scores and Roll-Call Voting in the U.S. Senate, 1988–1999," *The Review of Economics and Statistics* 84, no. 3 (2002): 518–29; Anwar Hussain and David N. Laband, "The Tragedy of the Political Commons: Evidence From U.S. Senate Roll Calls on Environmental Legislation," *Public Choice* 124 (2005): 353–64; Sarah Anderson, "Breaking the Green Gridlock," *PERC Reports* 36, no. 1 (2008): 1–4.

7   Anderson, "Breaking the Green Gridlock."

8   League of Conservation Voters, http://lcv-ftp.org/LCV/report_card/

9   The Internal Revenue Service requires that entities filing 990 tax forms must report grants of more than $5,000 to other organizations. The AFL-CIO is a 501(c)(5) organization; the remaining recipients are 501(c)(4) organizations. Unfortunately, 2010 IRS 990 filings are not yet available for public scrutiny. The $2.6 million in grants provided to other advocacy groups amounts to almost 20 percent of the LCV, Inc. budget for 2009.

10 The effort of Environmental Action to survive under 501(c)(3) status failed as it closed its doors in 1996. Ronald G. Shaiko, *Voices and Echoes for the Environment: Public Interest Representation in the 1990s and Beyond* (New York: Columbia University Press, 1999).

11 League of Conservation Voters, http://www.lcv.org/about-lcv/.

12 According to the *California Official Voter Information Guide,* California Ballot Initiative 23 "suspends air pollution control laws requiring major polluters to report and reduce greenhouse gas emissions that cause global warming until unemployment drops below specified level for full year. Fiscal Impact: likely modest net increase in overall economic activity in the state from suspension of greenhouse gases regulatory activity, resulting in a potentially significant net increase in state and local revenues," www.voterguide .sos. ca.gov/proposition23/.

13 According to the LCV, "Gene Karpinski joined LCV and LCV Education Fund in April 2006 after serving for many years as a member of the LCV and LCV Education Fund Boards of Directors and the LCV Political Committee. Prior to joining LCV and LCV Education Fund, Gene worked for 21 years as the Executive Director of the U.S. Public Interest Research Group (US PIRG), the national lobbying office for state PIRGs across the country, where he led many national environmental issue campaigns. Before his tenure at US PIRG, he was the field director for People for the American Way and Congress Watch, and Executive Director of the Colorado PIRG. He has served on the boards of Earth Share, the Partnership Project, the Beldon Fund, and the National Association for Public Interest Law. Gene is a graduate of Brown University and Georgetown University Law Center," www.lcv.org/assets/voterguide/ gene-karpinskis-biography.html.

14 2009 IRS 990 data for Sierra Club, Environmental Defense and Nature Conservancy, GuideStar, www2.guidestar.org/SearchResults.aspx.

15 All of the LCV spending in the 2009–10 cycle took the form of direct contributions to candidates through it PAC or through independent expenditures. LCV undertook no electioneering communications activities in the cycle.

16 Data for LCV Action Fund, CampaignMoney.com, www.campaignmoney.com/political/ committees/league-of-conservation-voters-action-fund.asp?cycle=10.

17 Mike Palamuso (vice president, communications, LCV), interview conducted at LCV Headquarters, Washington, DC, 1920 L Street, 8th Floor, December 16, 2010.

18 Data for LCV Victory Fund, CampaignMoney.com, www.campaignmoney.com/ political/committees/league-of-conservation-voters-victory-fund.asp?cycle=10.

19 Bob Biersack, "FEC Collects $630,000 in Civil Penalties From Three 527 Organizations," Federal Election Commission, December 13, 2006, www.fec.gov/ press/press2006/20061213murs.html.

20 Data for LCV Political Engagement Fund, CampaignMoney.com, www.campaign money.com/political/527/league-of-conservation-voters-political-engagement-fund .asp?spg=4.

21 League of Conservation Voters, 2010 State League Election Results, http://fscvl.org/ election-results/2010-state-league-election-results; the author is unable to verify independently the expenditure figure of $7 million by state LCVs in the 2009–10 cycle.

22 Rebecca Sinderbrand, "Exit Polls: Economy the No. 1 Issue," CNN Political Ticker, November 2, 2010, http://politicalticker.blogs.cnn/2010/11/02/first-exit-polls-economy/; Center for Information and Research on Civic Learning and Engagement (CIRCLE), "Fact Sheet: Young Voters in the 2010 Elections," CIRCLE, Tufts University, November 9, 2010, www.civicyouth.org/wp-content/uploads/2010/11/2010-Exit-Poll-Fact-Sheet.-corrected-Nov-10.pdf.

23 Center for Responsive Politics, www.opensecrets.org/outsidespending/detail .php?cmte=VoteVets.org&cycle=2010. VoteVets.org ranked ninth among liberal spenders in the 2009-2010 cycle.. BCRA banned electioneering communications within sixty days of a general election or thirty days of a primary election; the *Citizens United v. FEC* ruling overturned the ban.

24 VoteVets.org, www.votevets/org/about/

25 Palamuso, interview (2010).

26 Ibid.

27 Ibid.

28 Curtis Hubbard, "Outside Spending in Colorado's U.S. Senate Race Topped $30 Million," *The Denver Post,* January 21, 2011, http://blogs.denverpost.com/thespot/2011/01/21/ outside-spending-in-colorados-u-s-senate-race-topped-30-million/21293/.

29 Palamuso, interview (2010). Palamuso also noted that LCV online fundraising efforts yielded more contributions than in previous cycles.

30 Jon Walker, "Prop. 23: CA Voters Set to Reject Big Oil's Attempt to Suspend Climate Change Law," September 27, 2010, http://elections.firedoglake.com/2010/09/27/ prop-23-ca-voters-set-to-reject-big-oils-attempt-to-suspend-climate-change-law/.

31 Palamuso, interview (2010).

32 Patty Murray was not missed by LCV; she benefited from more than $40,000 in combined expenditures by LCV, including two maximum contributions from LCV Action Fund.

33 Bill Allison, "Daily Disclosures," Sunlight Foundation, November 2, 2010, http:// sunlightfoundation.com/blog/2010/11/02/daily-disclosures-19/.

34 Rich Thomas, general counsel, LCV, "Supreme Court Opens Floodgates for Corporate Expenditures," YouTube, January 21, 2011, www.youtube.com/watch?v=yIMFFWJU5GY

35 Palamuso, interview (2010).

36 Richard H. Thaler and Cass R. Sunstein, *Nudge: Improving decisions about health, wealth, and happiness* (New Haven: Yale University Press, 2008).

CHAPTER 8

Iron Law of Emulation

American Crossroads and Crossroads GPS

John J. Pitney Jr.

American Crossroads and Crossroads GPS are two nonparty groups that raised $71.4 million in the 2010 midterm campaign, helping Republicans retake the House and make major gains in the Senate.[1] These sister organizations were brand new and were working in ways that had become possible only in the past few years. "What they've cooked up is brilliant," one prominent Democrat told *Rolling Stone*. "Evil, but brilliant."[2]

Ironically, they were the spawn of Democratic strength and Republican weakness. Outside groups had aided Democrats with television advertising and voter mobilization in 2004, and played a major role in the Democratic takeover of Congress in 2006. They also were active in 2008, although the Obama campaign relied mainly on its own prodigious fundraising. The success of that campaign was a sobering moment for the GOP. The other side now had unified control of the federal government and was pushing an ambitious policy agenda. Many Republicans thought that they had to push back with something fresh. Because bad leadership was hobbling the Republican National Committee (RNC), the response would have to come from outside the formal party structure. Key GOP figures thus sought lessons from the outside-spending model that Democrats had developed.

Judicial and administrative actions also fostered the creation of the Crossroads groups. The most famous, of course, was the Supreme Court decision in *Citizens United v. Federal Election Commission*.[3] Perhaps almost as important, however, was *Federal Election Commission v. Wisconsin Right to Life, Inc.*, in which the Supreme Court expanded the ability of outside groups to run broadcast ads just before an election.[4] In the 2010 case of *SpeechNow v. Federal Election Commission*, the U.S. Court of Appeals for the District of Columbia Circuit struck down limits on what individuals could give to groups that only made independent expenditures.[5] In an advisory opinion stemming both from *Citizens United* and *SpeechNow*, the Federal Election Commission reasoned that "there is no basis to limit the amount of contributions to [an independent-expenditure committee] from individuals, political committees, corporations and labor organizations."[6]

With motive, model, and means in place, the Crossroads groups quickly became fundraising powerhouses. The 2010 election results brought a mind-bending role reversal, with Democrats talking about the need to create their own Crossroads. It would have been very hard to predict that development just two years earlier.

The Road to Crossroads

Karl Rove, former senior adviser to President George W. Bush, reportedly asked himself a big question after the 2008 election: "What is it that Democrats have that we don't have?"[7]

It was not an idle query. Just a few years earlier, Republicans had enjoyed great success, causing some Democratic analysts to worry that Rove's mystical (or demonic) powers were threatening American democracy.[8] But now Republicans were out of power, President Bush was in retirement, and Rove was on the sidelines. As the Obama administration got under way, Democrats were pulling ahead in organization and finance. The 2008 Obama campaign had raised an unprecedented $745 million, and now Democrats would draw even more contributions from interest groups seeking favor with the powerful. During the first half of 2005, Republican federal committees had raised 64 percent more money than the Democratic ones. During the same period in 2009, Democratic committees took in 5 percent more.[9] Moreover, Democrats seemed poised to extend their advantages to the policy battlefield. Obama for America, a committee that had been so effective during the 2008 campaign, moved into the Democratic National Committee as a project named Organizing for America. Though it would later prove to be a disappointment, political observers expected that it would mobilize grassroots support for health care legislation and other administration initiatives.

The GOP's plight had ample precedent. Three times in the past half-century, soul-crushing electoral defeats had left it in the political wilderness. Each time, a resourceful RNC chair had helped guide the party back.[10] After the LBJ landslide of 1964, Ray C. Bliss rebuilt the party's infrastructure and brought professionalism to its operations. In the late 1970s, Bill Brock repaired some of the Watergate damage by turning the committee into a valuable source of money and campaign services. And after 1992, when George H. W. Bush won the lowest popular percentage for any sitting president in eighty years, Haley Barbour revived the GOP at the state level and modernized the national party's efforts in research and communications.

Ever since the 2002 passage of the Bipartisan Campaign Finance Reform Act of 2002 (BCRA), out-parties have had a special need for strong leadership. Before that law, national party organizations maintained soft money accounts, which, as discussed in earlier chapters, could accept unlimited contributions from individuals, corporations, and unions. After BCRA banned party soft money, national committees now had to excel at raising a large number of contributions under federal caps. Presidents are money magnets, so RNC thrived as long as George W. Bush was in the White House. Now that the party was in the wilderness again, it would need a chair of the caliber of Bliss, Brock, and Barbour. Instead, it got Michael Steele.

In 2009, RNC chose the former Maryland lieutenant governor as its first African American leader, turning out incumbent Mike Duncan. Many Republicans were enthusiastic about Steele at first, but he soon proved an embarrassment, making odd remarks about gay marriage, abortion, Rush Limbaugh, and the war in Afghanistan, among others. His incompetence became the stuff of late-night one-liners when Federal Election Commission (FEC) filings showed that the committee had spent $2,000 at a bondage strip club. One Republican strategist told *The Washington Post* that contributors "just don't think the RNC is a smart place to invest their money right now."[11]

Developments outside the formal party structure also were turning against the GOP. Though BCRA had banned party soft money, it did not forbid independent organizations from spending large sums to influence elections and policy debates. Liberal groups had done more outside spending than conservative ones in the 2004, 2006, and 2008 elections (see Figure 8.1). Early signs suggested that the

FIGURE 8.1   Outside Spending in Federal Elections

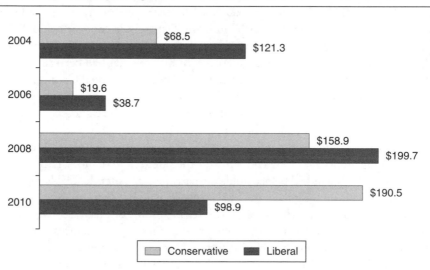

Source: Center for Responsive Politics, "Outside Spending," www.opensecrets.org/outside spending.

Note: Figures (in millions) include independent expenditures, electioneering communications, and communication costs.

imbalance would keep growing. In the 2009 battle on climate-change legislation, environmentalists actually outspent their opponents.[12]

In this setting, major Republican figures started discussions about the party's plight. [13] Rove was one of these figures. "In the coming year," he wrote in *Newsweek* right after the 2008 election, "we will be defined more by what we oppose than what we are for; the president-elect and the Democrats in Congress will control the agenda."[14] He concluded with an observation that seemed like graveyard-whistling: "In 1992, Bill Clinton stood atop the political world; in 1994, he stood defeated after Republicans took control of the House [and Senate]. We can't count on a replay of 1994, but we can take steps that will make 2010 a good year—and, with a bit of luck and skill, a very good year."

Another participant was Ed Gillespie, RNC chair during the 2004 campaign. Many Democrats and media commentators had called upon him to denounce the Swift Boat Veterans for Truth, an outside-spending group that had attacked John Kerry's war record. In a 2006 book, he contended that the media had ignored outside spending by liberal groups, "but when the Swifties spent a couple hundred thousand dollars, news organizations suddenly remembered how bad soft money was."[15] Gillespie was obviously aware of the Democrats' advantage in outside spending. "Where they have a chess piece on the board, we need a chess piece on the board," he said. "Where they have a queen, we shouldn't have three pawns."[16]

A third figure was Steven J. Law, chief legal officer and general counsel of the U.S. Chamber of Commerce. During the Bush administration, he had served as deputy secretary of labor. Law told *The Wall Street Journal* that this experience had taught him much about labor unions: "I was quite impressed by their courage, their dedication, their boldness, their willingness to put it all on the line to elect people who supported their political agenda."[17] Law studied books about the Democratic comeback, including David Plouffe's memoir of the Obama campaign and Matt Bai's *The Argument*, a 2007 portrait of wealthy liberals and online activists behind the outside-spending groups.[18]

Months of discussion culminated on March 29, 2010, when Law filed notice with the IRS that American Crossroads was organizing under section 527 of the tax code.[19] Law was president and CEO. Mike Duncan, the former RNC head whom Steele had defeated, was chair. Together with the presence of Rove and Gillespie as "informal advisers," Duncan's role signaled that American Crossroads would be a serious GOP player. Consultant Jim Dyke, a director of the group, said that its founders "recognized in 2004 that Democrats were using all the tools at their disposal to elect Democrats, something that became even more obvious in the 2006 and 2008 elections." He also said: "This is not a flash in the pan response to 2010 but something that will be around for cycles."[20]

Noting that the filing did not list an e-mail address, election law expert Richard Hasen told *The Washington Post*: "This is not based on mass appeal; it's a different model."[21] Indeed, it initially drew most of its money from a few big donors. B. Wayne Hughes, the chair of Public Storage, gave $250,000 on the day that the group turned in its papers, and Trevor Rees-Jones, president of Chief Oil and Gas, followed two weeks later with $1 million.[22] Two-thirds of its early money came from Texas. Communications director Jonathan Collegio said that "fundraising and membership isn't based on geography, though we happen to have some donors in Texas who believe strongly in what we're doing."[23] Some of the Texans were unhappy about the administration's policies on climate change. "It's like your doctor says you've got cancer and he pulls out a road map to recovery," said an associate to Rees-Jones. "People were anxious to be supportive. And praying that it would work."[24]

Organizational Evolution

The deliberations that led to American Crossroads had started well before the *Citizens United* decision. The creation of a pro-Republican outside organization would not hinge on the outcome of that case, because groups organized under Section 527 already had made their mark on the electoral landscape. They got a major boost in 2007, with the Supreme Court's decision in *Wisconsin Right to Life v. FEC*. The decision, noted in previous chapters as well, overturned a legal ban on the use of corporate or union money to buy broadcast ads identifying federal candidates during the sixty days before a general election (or thirty days before a primary). Section 527 groups, as well as other organizations, now could use corporate and union funds to run such ads, but only if they avoided express advocacy of the candidate's defeat or election, and instead emphasized issues. So rather than saying, "Vote against Senator Smithers," the ad would have to say something like "Call Senator Smithers and tell her to stop wasting taxpayer money." That requirement would not be a huge barrier: whatever the legal distinctions, ordinary voters see no difference between the two types of advertising.[25]

The Supreme Court handed down *Citizens United* about two months before the start of American Crossroads. The group's founders hoped that it would send a green light to contributors. "The principal impact of the *Citizens United* decision was to give prospective donors a general sense that it was within their constitutional rights to support independent political activity," Law later told *The New York Times*. "That right existed before, but this Supreme Court decision essentially gave a Good Housekeeping seal of approval."[26]

Nevertheless, early press reports suggested that the effort was lagging. Indeed, officials were not initially certain that they could meet their announced fundraising goal of $50 million. They met resistance from potential donors who said that the group lacked a track record. To build one, the group came to the rescue of

Sharron Angle, the Tea Party favorite who had won the GOP nomination to face Harry Reid (D-Nev.). After a tough primary, her warchest was empty. American Crossroads made a $120,000 television buy attacking Reid for backing the president's stimulus legislation. The ad did not directly call for Reid's defeat, instead saying that the "bailout" had failed to stop high unemployment in Nevada.[27] The ad reassured conservatives that American Crossroads would be an ally and convinced donors that it would be a sound investment. "It was like turning on a light switch," said Law.[28]

On the Democratic side, the lights were blinking red. Although Rove had no formal title, Democrats made him a rallying cry for attacks on the group. "Karl Rove's American Crossroads group just announced on Friday that it is turning the full force of its fundraising machine against no fewer than eleven Democratic candidates," warned a fundraising e-mail from the Democratic Senatorial Campaign Committee.[29] Jim Jordan, former executive director of the Democratic Senatorial Campaign Committee, told *The Washington Post* that with "talk of a hundred million dollars plus being raised by Republican independent groups, we're optimistic that our funding base will rally."[30] To counter the likes of American Crossroads, Jordan and other Democratic operatives formed the Commonsense Ten, an independent-expenditure PAC that would support Democrats and oppose Republicans in 2010.

Though the group would end up spending only a few million dollars, it did play a noteworthy—and ironic—role in the 2010 race. In March, the DC Circuit Court had handed down *SpeechNow*, the first major court ruling to apply *Citizens United.* The decision unanimously struck down limits on individual contributions to independent groups that spend money to support or oppose federal candidates. In the wake of *SpeechNow*, the Commonsense Ten secured an advisory opinion from the FEC confirming that it could gather unlimited contributions for independent expenditures. The Commonsense Ten advisory opinion, along with a similar one for the conservative Club for Growth, helped create a new kind of entity: the independent-expenditure PAC, better known as the super PAC, discussed in previous chapters in each particular context. Among the first super PACs was American Crossroads.

Soon after the advisory opinions, the group filed papers with the IRS and FEC changing its status. Jonathan Collegio, communications director for American Crossroads, told the OpenSecrets blog, "The FEC clarified that 527 groups like American Crossroads needed to file contribution and expenditure activity with the commission. Our filing is complying with that guidance issued by the FEC."[31] American Crossroads could now take unlimited contributions from individuals and corporations, and use them to *expressly* advocate the election of Republicans and the defeat of Democrats. Although the group would correctly note that hundreds of individuals contributed in 2010, more than 80 percent of its money came from a handful of sources:

- *Bob J. Perry* ($7 million), of Houston, is the owner of Perry Homes. He had given to many Republican candidates over the years, including George W. Bush and Mitt Romney. In 2004, he was the largest contributor to the Swift Boats Veterans for Truth.
- *TRT Holdings* ($4.84 million, $2.5 million from CEO Robert B. Rowling, $2.34 million from corporate funds), of Irving, Texas, owns the Omni Hotel chain and Gold's Gym International, and also has a stake in Gaylord Entertainment (owner of the Grand Ole Opry). The company is involved in oil and gas exploration.
- *B. Wayne Hughes* ($3.25 million), of Lexington, Kentucky, is the chairman of Public Storage, the country's largest self-storage company. In 2010, he also gave $88,000 in hard money contributions to GOP congressional candidates.
- *Alliance Resource Partners* ($2.42 million) of Tulsa, Oklahoma, is a diversified coal company with mining operations in Kentucky, Indiana, Illinois, West Virginia, and Maryland. In an SEC filing, the company indicated that it had a big stake in the "cap and trade" issue: "Increased regulation of greenhouse gas emissions could result in increased operating costs and reduced demand for coal as a fuel source, which could reduce demand for our products, decrease our revenues and reduce our profitability."[32]
- *Trevor Rees-Jones* ($2 million), of Dallas, is president of Chief Oil and Gas, as mentioned earlier.
- *The Harold C. Simmons Family Trust* ($2 million, half from Dixie Rice Agricultural Corporation and half from Southwest Louisiana Land), of Dallas, makes and markets beet sugar. In 2004, Simmons was a major backer of the Swift Boat Veterans, and in 2008, gave nearly $2.9 million to the American Issues Project, a group running advertisements linking Barack Obama to 1960s radical William Ayers.[33]
- *Jerry Perenchio* ($1 million from the Jerry Perenchio Living Trust), of Los Angeles, is the former chair and CEO of Univision, the nation's largest Spanish-language broadcasting company.

Many of the contributors had given to Republican candidates and causes. In addition to Perry and Simons, a number had supported the Swift Boat Veterans, a 527 group.[34] Indeed, the Swift Boat connection may help explain the new group's eagerness to become a super PAC. In 2006, FEC hit the Swift Boat Veterans with a civil penalty of $299,500 for breaking campaign finance laws. Potential contributors to American Crossroads may have initially worried that a 527 could run into legal trouble, but now the new super PAC vehicle seemed to have the triple blessing of *Citizens United*, *Speech Now*, and the Commonsense Ten advisory opinion.

In all, the group would raise about $27 million—but that sum was only part of the picture. On June 2, 2010, its founders formed a second organization, Crossroads Grassroots Policy Strategies (Crossroads GPS) as a Virginia corporation. In September, it applied with the IRS for 501(c)(4) status, allowing it to engage in issue advocacy, as well as political activities, as long as the latter did not become its primary purpose.[35] To review from earlier chapters, the rule of thumb is that no more than 50 percent of a 501(c)(4)'s activities can be political, though the line between issues and partisan politics can be blurry.[36]

Why a second organization? Law said: "The genesis of it from our perspective was that there are a number of things that are priorities for us that seemed to fit more into a 501(c)(4) than a 527, such as doing very legislatively focused issue advocacy activity which we will be undertaking in the next few months."[37] Law said that Crossroads GPS differed from American Crossroads by its long-term focus on "a suite of issues that are likely to see some sort of legislative response."[38] A concept paper for Crossroads GPS said that the group would "research, test, educate and galvanize citizens on high-resonance issues affecting the government and economy" and "shape citizen attitudes with hard-hitting issue advocacy and usable message tools for Republicans and their supportive activist communities." The "grassroots" part of the organization would build a "national grassroots network of center-right supporters who respond to our issue agenda and mobilize them to advocate effectively for policy change." It would work through "list exchanges, microtargeting techniques and other data enhancements, build the highest-quality national list of center-right advocates and sympathizers possible; then engage that community intensively with policy information and advocacy requests."[39]

Citizens United helped shape the activities of Crossroads GPS. Prior to the decision, a 501(c)(4) could run ads mentioning federal candidates, provided they did not explicitly advocate their election or defeat. Now, such a group could engage in independent expenditures, subject to the 50-percent rule of thumb. Crossroads GPS would be able to run ads very similar to those of its super PAC sister organization.

One motive for forming Crossroads GPS was that unlike a PAC, a 501(c)(4) does not have to make public disclosure of its donors. "There are some donors who are interested in anonymity when it comes to advocating for specific issues," Collegio told *The Washington Post*.[40] "Whether it's legitimate or not, there is this near-hysteria, this belief that the Democrats are going to come after us," said one potential contributor. "Everybody is truly afraid that the Obama administration is going to target them."[41] In a December 2010 panel discussion at the Annenberg Public Policy Center, *Politico*'s Ken Vogel asked why both organizational forms were necessary. Political director Carl Forti answered that "disclosure was very important for us, which is why the 527 was created. But some donors didn't want to be disclosed, and therefore, a (c)(4) was created." When Vogel asked if they would have eventually given anyway, Forti said: "I don't know. I know they were more comfortable giving to a (c)(4). And so we created one."[42] A Crossroads GPS fundraising memo drove home the point: "Any person or entity that contributes more than $5,000 to a 501(c)(4) organization must be disclosed to the Internal Revenue Service on Form 990. The IRS, however, does not make these donor disclosures available to the general public. Crossroads GPS's policy is to not provide the names of its donors to the general public."[43]

Crossroads GPS brought in about $43 million, substantially more than the take for American Crossroads.[44] But whether by chance or design, it made sense for American Crossroads to start first. Large contributions to the first group got a great deal of publicity, which one Republican operative said was "a way to energize others to give large amounts anonymously." The operative also said, "It has worked like a charm."[45]

Democrats looked on wistfully. During the 2008 campaign, a group of their operatives formed a 527 group, Progressive Media, to conduct and publicize opposition research against Republicans. After the Obama campaign let donors know that it wanted their money to go directly to the campaign, not outside groups, Progressive Media morphed into a pair of 501(c)(4) organizations. "It was a successful model and idea that the Democratic side shut down but the Republicans were smart enough to pick it up," said one former official.[46]

The Network

The Democrats' example inspired more than the two Crossroads groups. "I think the Democrats figured out how to collaborate and coordinate their efforts in a way that we'd never seen on the Republican side outside of the party apparatus," said Law. "They were very intentional about sharing plans, and information, and data."[47] Law was referring to a network of liberal organizations including the Democracy Alliance, an umbrella group founded by billionaire George Soros.[48]

At his Washington home in April 2010, Rove convened representatives of conservative and pro-Republican groups, both new and old.[49] All were involved in efforts to affect the 2010 election, and they agreed to work together. "A lot of what we're doing would normally be done with the RNC," said Mary Cheney, whose Alliance for America's Future was part of the gathering. "There's no money there."[50] The attendees called themselves the Weaver Terrace Group, after Rove's street address, and they would hold later meetings at the Washington headquarters of the Crossroads groups.

Aside from the meetings, there was a good deal of interaction and overlap among the groups. The American Action Network (AAN), headed by former senator Norm Coleman (R-Minn.), shared office space with them at 1401 New York Avenue. One of AAN's board members was B. Wayne Hughes Jr., son of Crossroads contributor B. Wayne Hughes. Carl Forti not only served as political director for the Crossroads groups, he handled media for the 60 Plus Association. Forti was a cofounder of the Black Rock Group consulting firm, headquartered in the same Alexandria office building as Americans for Job Security.[51]

Independent-expenditure committees may communicate with one another, but the law forbids them to coordinate with party organizations and candidates. Political professionals take this prohibition seriously. Said Erik Smith, head of the Soros-backed Media Fund in 2004, "One thing McCain–Feingold did was make criminal penalties for this stuff. I think John Kerry would be a great president, but I'm not going to jail for the guy."[52] Nevertheless, there are lawful ways around the ban. FEC says: "Persons may use publicly available information in creating, producing or distributing a communication."[53] Explained Collegio, "We work together as much as the law allows, though obviously you can glean information from what's in the public domain"[54] He also said: "If one group puts an ad on television in a certain congressional district, they let everyone else know that. This way they don't double up on the advertising."[55]

In 2010, the parties' House and Senate campaign committees used *microsites,* public websites to highlight opposition research that suggested attack themes. House Republicans used microsites that included the names of the Democratic incumbents. For instance, nyefacts.org contained information about Rep. Glenn Nye (D-Va.). The National Republican Senatorial Committee had sites that outsiders could easily find by entering a state as a subdomain—for example kentucky.nrsc.org.[56] Carl Forti told how the Crossroads groups used such material:

> I think over the last three cycles we've been getting smarter as to how to relay information. So the committees would probably make their buys earlier, I would hope. The NRSC recently launched its Harry Reid micro site with a bunch of research on it. That research then helps us on the outside have some sense of where to go.[57]

The independent groups were in sync with GOP candidates and organizations in another way. Each party has a community of operatives who rotate among campaigns, congressional staffs, party organizations, consulting firms, and outside spending groups.[58] Like members of a repertory company, they know everyone else's lines and can anticipate one another's moves. A telling example would be the formal and informal leaders of the Crossroads groups:

- Rove, Duncan, and Gillespie had all been national GOP figures. Among them, they knew every top person in the party, as well as many people further down the hierarchy.
- In addition to his previously mentioned posts at the Labor Department and the U.S. Chamber of Commerce, Steven Law had served as Sen. Mitch

McConnell's chief of staff and executive director of the National Republican Senatorial Committee (NRSC).

- Before founding the Black Rock Group, Carl Forti had served in several capacities at the National Republican Congressional Committee (NRCC), including communications director and issue advocacy director, where he ran an $80 million dollar independent-expenditure campaign. He kept in touch with fellow NRCC alumni: staffers who worked there during the disastrous fall of 2006 would gather for annual reunion dinners.[59]
- Jonathan Collegio was deputy chief of staff for Rep. Patrick McHenry (R-N.C.), then worked with Forti at NRCC.

Cooperation on the Republican side was neither perfect nor universal. FreedomWorks, a major force behind the tea party movement, saw the Crossroads groups as being too close to the GOP establishment.[60] Nevertheless, the extent of collaboration was striking. As Forti put it,

Combined with where the NRCC was, that was over 80 districts that we had somebody on TV for the final two weeks with absolutely no overlap. And that—you know, that's amazing. And that is—I think that is, by far, the untold story—not untold, I mean, you guys mentioned it—but that is—that is the highlight of what came out of this cycle—was the coordination.[61]

Strategy and Tactics in 2010

The Crossroads groups focused exclusively on federal races in 2010, leaving the gubernatorial contests to the Republican Governors Association (RGA). (Happily for GOP prospects, the chair of the RGA was Haley Barbour, governor of Mississippi, who had led RNC during the 1994 cycle.) In particular, it concentrated on Senate races (see Table 8.1), which made strategic sense. After Scott Brown's victory in the special election in Massachusetts, Senate Republicans had just enough seats to sustain filibusters, but only if they all voted together. Despite increasing polarization, they were always at risk of a few defections on certain roll call votes. Gaining a couple of seats would provide some cushion and greatly enhance their leverage. For contributors and activists who opposed measures such as cap and trade, this leverage would be well worth the investment. In the House, by contrast, the majority could still steamroll the minority even with a fairly narrow seat margin. Spending on House races would become urgent only if the GOP had a real chance at winning a majority.

As of midyear, that prospect did not yet seem highly likely. In June, American Crossroads had reportedly decided to put its chips on eleven Senate races.[62] In Florida, Missouri, Kentucky, New Hampshire, and Ohio, the departure of Republican incumbents had created takeover opportunities for the Democrats, so

TABLE 8.1   American Crossroads Spending in 2010 Senate Races

	TV	Mail	Phones	Production	Text, Online, Turnout	Total
Arkansas		$203,269				$203,269
Colorado	$4,712,506	757,590	$167,664	$73,365	$350,000	5,965,138
Florida		2,006,616	167,664			2,174,280
Illinois	1,101,072		7,981	18,177		1,127,230
Kentucky	1,007,384	370,433	30,049	48,899		1,456,765
Missouri	2,142,379	334,774	48,782	45,557	174,778	2,746,270
Nevada	1,736,078	343,892	29,883	72,243	215,626	2,397,722
New Hampshire	643,362	72,104		14,968		730,434
Ohio	787,759			32,846		820,605
Washington						1,080,835
West Virginia		245,460	19,3145			264,774

Source: American Crossroads, *2010 Performance Report.*

Crossroads worked to keep the seats in GOP hands. In Illinois and Pennsylvania (after Arlen Specter's primary defeat), strong Republican candidates vied for open Democratic seats. And in Arkansas, Colorado, Nevada, and Washington, Democratic incumbents looked vulnerable. (By autumn, Arkansas incumbent Blanche Lincoln had lost so much ground that Republicans appeared to have a lock on the seat and no longer made it a top priority.)

American Crossroads fired its first shot in the Nevada race, leading some to speculate that the move stemmed from a feud between Karl Rove and Harry Reid. Rove disliked Reid, but denied that this animosity had anything to do with the group's targeting decision.[63] There were other reasons to put Reid in the bulls-eye. First, as mentioned earlier, the ad buy established the group's credibility. Second, other Republicans loathed Reid, too: Rush Limbaugh called him "Dingy Harry."[64] Third, Nevada is a relatively small state where a given media buy can have more impact than in, say, California. Fourth, both parties long had followed strategies of "decapitation," meaning that they would try to take down each other's congressional leaders wherever possible. Republicans managed to beat House Speaker Tom Foley in 1994 and Senate Democratic leader Tom Daschle ten years later. Democrats nearly ousted Newt Gingrich (then House Republican whip) in 1990 and Senate Republican leader Mitch McConnell in 2008.[65] Fifth and perhaps most important, polls showed that Reid was vulnerable. In short, American Crossroads would have unloaded on Reid even if he and Rove had never met.

Some of the ads focused on candidates' characteristics. This spot, which ran in the Illinois Senate race, drew criticism from Factcheck.org for failing to put information in proper context: "Alexi Giannoulias is quite a driver. He helped drive his family's Broadway Bank into a ditch. Now, as Treasurer and head of the Bright

Start College Savings Fund, Alexi fell asleep at the wheel."[66] More often, the ads stressed national issues such as health care, energy, and the economy. As President Obama's approval ratings fell, the Crossroads groups exploited his unpopularity. In Kentucky, American Crossroads ran this spot against the Democratic Senate nominee: "Conway supports ObamaCare; billions in job-killing taxes; devastating small businesses; higher insurance premiums; gutting Medicare; slashing benefits for Kentucky seniors, which could jeopardize their care."[67]

The emphasis on the passage of the health bill and the purported threat to Medicare was in line with Rove's strategic philosophy. "Never go after someone's strength," he wrote in his memoirs, "go after what he thinks is his strength, but what is, in reality, a weakness."[68] At the start of the Obama administration, Democrats had thought that health care would be a winning issue, and they had always regarded Medicare as the GOP's weak spot, not theirs. This ad, and similar ones in other states, sought to upend these assumptions.

In California, a Crossroads GPS ad claimed that incumbent Democrat Barbara Boxer had voted to slash Medicare benefits.[69] Over a graphic showing the telephone number of Boxer's San Francisco office, the narrator said: "Call Boxer; stop the Medicare cuts."[70] Note that it did not ask voters to oppose her. Because the ad lacked express advocacy and because it aired more than sixty days before the general elections, it counted neither as an independent expenditure nor an electioneering communication (see Chapter 1). Crossroads GPS did, however, issue a news release saying that it spent $1 million on this ad buy, plus just over $1 million for similar spots in Kentucky and Pennsylvania.[71] Table 8.2 lists GPS spending by state, including House and Senate races.

American Crossroads entered the 2010 ground war, too. It promised to use "enhanced voter files and data on absentee ballot and early voting patterns to deliver absentee ballot mailers with chase calls, early voting notifications by mail and phone calls, and a 72-hour mail and phone call blitz prior to Election Day." The program's targets included "high, medium and low propensity Republican voters, as well as high propensity independent voters."[72] In Nevada and Colorado, American Crossroads deployed about fifty volunteers with iPads. The software directed each volunteer to preselected homes. As the volunteers spoke to potential voters, they entered data. "The old model is that volunteers would show up on a Saturday morning and do all of their get out the vote on a Saturday and Sunday morning. Now we will be in a situation where a voter will be able to download the app, download their walk book and they can do it in their spare time" said Collegio. "This new technology will allow us to regain the technological edge when it comes to contacting voters for elections."[73]

By autumn, it was clear that Republicans might take control of the House. In October, the Crossroads groups joined their allies in announcing a "House surge strategy." When describing this strategy, key figures used similar language:

TABLE 8.2   Crossroads GPS Aggregate Spending by State

Arkansas	$34,477
California	1,327,825
Colorado	1,344,664
Florida	763,535
Illinois	4,479,605
Indiana	352,089
Kentucky	1,378,569
Minnesota	48,546
Missouri	2,127,850
Nevada	3,307,979
New Hampshire	40,346
North Carolina	150,921
North Dakota	247,700
Ohio	629,997
Pennsylvania	1,361,885
Tennessee	272,100
Texas	331,600
Washington	3,718,043

Source: Crossroads GPS, *2010-2011 Interim Performance Report*. Data include all spending by state.

- Karl Rove—"The idea was to keep broadening the field and to make them fight in more places."[74]
- Carl Forti—"We were able to go places where Democrats were comfortable and require them to start spending money. For us, it was an effort to expand the field."[75]
- Steven Law—The effort aimed at "putting Republicans over the top by evening out the financial disparities and dramatically expanding the field of battle."[76]

Thus they applied Sun Tzu's advice to make the enemy prepare in a great many places. "And when he prepares everywhere he will be weak everywhere"[77] (see Table 8.3). The effort unnerved many Democratic incumbents who had been coasting in recent elections. For instance, Crossroads GPS and other groups ran ads attacking Jim Costa (D-Calif.) for his support of the stimulus bill. "California's economy is reeling," said a Crossroads GPS spot, "and Congressman Jim Costa is making it worse."[78] As in other districts, the incumbent and his party had to spend a great deal of money to hold the seat. In this case, they managed—just barely. Whereas Costa had won by a 48-point margin in 2008, challenger Andy Vidak held him to just 4 points in 2010. Other incumbents got ruder surprises. James Oberstar (D-Minn.), who first won his seat in 1974 and who had enjoyed a 36-point margin in 2008, narrowly lost in 2010.

TABLE 8.3   Crossroads Involvement in 2010 House Races

	Crossroads GPS Independent Expenditure & Electioneering	American Crossroads Independent Expenditure
California 3		$682,324
California 20	$337,825	
Colorado 3		45,389
Colorado 7		26,447
Florida 22		215,616
Georgia 2		137,856
Hawaii 1		179,727
Indiana 2	250,003	152,719
Missouri 3	250,225	28,629
Minnesota 8	48,546	
Nevada 3		65,174
New York 20		447,366
New York 22		533,584
New York 25		411,340
North Carolina 11		252,378
North Dakota AL	247,700	
Ohio 16	447,125	
Ohio 18		77,102
Tennessee 4	272,100	
Texas 17		164,086
Texas 23	331,600	
Washington 2		31,865
Washington 3		36,200
West Virginia 1		66,878
West Virginia 3		31,792

Sources: American Crossroads, *2010 Performance Report*; Center for Responsive Politics, "American Crossroads Recipients, 2010," www.opensecrets.org/outsidespending/recips.php ?cmte=American+Crossroads&cycle=2010; Center for Responsive Politics, "Crossroads Grassroots Policy Strategies Recipients, 2010," www.opensecrets.org/outsidespending/ recips.php?cmte=Crossroads+Grassroots+Policy+Strategies&cycle=2010. Where American Crossroads data differed from those of the Center for Responsive Politics, the table includes the former.

Many forces were at work in the 2010 campaign, so it is hard to quantify the impact of the Crossroads groups. But it is reasonable to suggest that they contributed to the GOP's showing. In all, Republicans scored a net gain of sixty-three House seats, their biggest pickup since 1938. Dozens of incumbent House Democrats lost, while only two Republican members went down. (Both came from heavily Democratic districts.) The GOP added six seats in the Senate. Although this result disappointed some Republicans who had yearned for a majority, it accounted for almost a third of the nineteen Democratic seats up that year. Of the Senate contests in which the Crossroads groups played a role, Republicans held open seats in New Hampshire, Florida, Ohio, Kentucky, and Missouri. It was no surprise that Democratic incumbent Barbara Boxer won in California, but Democratic retentions in Nevada, Colorado, and Washington had to be disappointments for the Crossroads groups. Meanwhile, they took satisfaction in seeing Republicans win Democratic seats in Arkansas, Illinois, Pennsylvania, and Wisconsin (although the Crossroads involvement in the last race was small).

Their work was not over on election night, however.

Post-2010 Election Activity

During a September floor debate on campaign finance reform, Sen. Clare McCaskill (D-Mo.) criticized Crossroads GPS and asked rhetorically: "How many people think these organizations are going to be around after November? Really? How naive are you?"[79]

American Crossroads and Crossroads GPS indeed stayed around, and the latter was especially busy at first. In order to convince the IRS that they deserve their 501(c)(4) status, such groups typically mount ad campaigns and other activities during the off-season. Even before the election, Crossroads GPS listed seven issues on which it would work during the next session of Congress.[80] The plan was light on specifics but it did indicate an intention to conduct policy advocacy. Soon after the 2010 election, Crossroads GPS circulated a polling memo about the tax legislation in the lame-duck session of Congress: "Supporters of extended tax cuts for all should drive the message that the best way to balance the budget is to cut spending, grow the economy, and create new jobs."[81]

It also made a $400,000 buy in the districts of a dozen House Democrats who had just narrowly won reelection.[82] "She's back—Nancy Pelosi's at it again, trying to raise taxes as our economy struggles," said a version running in Virginia's 11th District."[83] In February 2011, it launched ads about a GOP proposal to cut spending. In twelve Democratic House districts, the ads faulted the incumbent for opposing the measure and in ten Republican districts, the ads praised the incumbent for supporting it. Said Law, "One of our top priorities this year is to use educational spots to frame the issue debate for congressional action on reining in spending, blocking job-killing regulations and dismantling ObamaCare."[84] In March, Crossroads GPS ran a thirty-second television spot emphasizing President Obama's political debts to public-employee unions.[85]

In the same month, Crossroads GPS went after the administration over the issue of transparency. It sued the Department of Health and Human Services (HHS), saying that the department had violated the Freedom of Information Act by failing to supply information about waivers from the new health law.[86] It also launched Wikicountability, a website for "crowdsourcing" FOIA files from groups and individuals who have obtained public information from the Obama administration.[87] "It is incredibly ironic that Crossroads wants to talk about openness when they are highly secretive," said Melanie Sloan, the executive director of Citizens for Responsibility and Ethics in Washington.[88]

American Crossroads was also active, launching the Presidential Action Fund, to carry out survey and issue research, microtargeting, issue advocacy and get-out-the-vote efforts. Officials from Crossroads got a green light from their major donors from 2010. "They have told us they are sticking with us, and most of them have said they plan to come in at a significantly higher level," said Law, who added that there would be new donors as well.[89] More activity was to come. "You can't outspend the unions—but you can outcompete them with a faster and leaner organization that offers more bang for the buck," said Collegio.[90]

The story of these groups illustrates what Sen. Daniel Patrick Moynihan called the "Iron Law of Emulation," the idea that organizations in conflict come to resemble each other. The process had been at work for some time. Back in 1969, a Republican Senate staffer named Paul Weyrich witnessed a meeting of liberal activists who were coordinating legislative and political strategy. He later recalled: "All of a sudden, I was granted the opportunity to see the mechanics ... Wherever I went I said, we've got to do something about this. We've got to have our own organizations. We've got to have our own meeting, and you know, so on."[91]

During the 1970s and 1980s, Weyrich and other conservatives helped build a network of organizations to counter what they saw as an entrenched liberal Democratic establishment. By the first decade of the twenty-first century, liberals and Democrats had come to see this network as a threat. And like Weyrich in 1969, they decided to do something about it. Thus began groups such as the Democracy Alliance, which says it was "created to build progressive infrastructure that could help counter the well-funded and sophisticated conservative apparatus."[92] In turn, as we have seen, the Crossroads groups were part of a deliberate conservative effort to emulate what liberals and Democrats had done. And after GOP gains in the 2010, Democrats were asking the same question that Karl Rove had asked two years before: What does the other side have that we don't have? In response, they started forming their own super PACs.

The cycle went on.

Endnotes

1 American Crossroads, *2010 Performance Report*, Washington, DC, 2010; Crossroads Grassroots Policy Strategies, *2010–2011 Interim Performance Report*, Washington, DC, 2011.

2 Quoted in Tim Dickinson, "Rove Rides Again," *Rolling Stone*, May 12, 2010, www.rollingstone.com/politics/news/rove-rides-again-20100512.

3 *Citizens United v. Federal Election Commission*, 558 U.S. 205 (2010).

4 *Federal Election Commission v. Wisconsin Right to Life, Inc.*, 551 U.S. 449 (2007).

5 *SpeechNow.org v. Federal Election Commission*, 08-5223, (D.C. Cir. 2010).

6 Federal Election Commission, Advisory Opinion 2010–11, July 22, 2010, http://saos.nictusa.com/aodocs/AO%202010-11.pdf

7 Quoted in Joe Hagan, "Goddangit, Baby, We're Making Good Time," *New York*, February 27, 2011, http://nymag.com/news/politics/karl-rove-2011-3.

8 See, for instance, Jacob S. Hacker, and Paul Pierson, *Off Center: The Republican Revolution and American Democracy* (New Haven: Yale University Press, 2005).

9 Federal Election Commission, "FEC Summarizes Political Party Activity for January 1–June 30, 2009," August 19, 2009, www.fec.gov/press/press2009/20090819_6monthParty.shtml.

10 Philip A. Klinkner, *The Losing Parties: Out-Party National Committees, 1956–1993* (New Haven: Yale University Press, 1994).

11 Quoted in Dan Balz and Chris Cillizza, *The Washington Post*, "Many Republican Leaders Bypassing RNC Chief Steele Ahead of Midterms," July 20, 2010, www.washingtonpost.com/wp-dyn/content/article/2010/07/06/AR2010070605165.html

12 Matthew C. Nisbet, "Climate Shift: Clear Vision for the Next Decade of Public Debate," American University School of Communication, April 18, 2011, http://climateshiftproject.org/report/climate-shift-clear-vision-for-the-next-decade-of-public-debate.

13 Dickinson, "Rove Rides Again."

14 Karl Rove, "A Way Out of the Wilderness," *Newsweek*, November 14, 2008, www.newsweek.com/2008/11/14/a-way-out-of-the-wilderness.html

15 Ed Gillespie, *Winning Right: Campaign Politics and Conservative Policies* (New York: Simon & Schuster, Threshold Editions, 2006), 57–58.

16 Quoted in Mike Allen and Kenneth P. Vogel, "Karl Rove, Republican Party Plot Vast Network to Reclaim Power," *Politico*, May 6, 2010, www.politico.com/news/stories/0510/36841.html.

17 Quoted in Joseph Rago, "The Republican Answer to George Soros's Money," *The Wall Street Journal*, September 17, 2010, http://online.wsj.com/article/SB10001424052748703904304575497754131295506.html.

18 Michael Crowley, "The New GOP Money Stampede," *Time*, September 16, 2010, www.time.com/time/politics/article/0,8599,2019509,00.html.

19 American Crossroads, Form 8871 initial notice, filed with the Internal Revenue Service on March 29, 2010, http://forms.irs.gov/politicalOrgsSearch/search/Print.action?for mId=50983&formType=E71

20 Quoted in Brody Mullins, "Former GOP Officials Launch Group," *The Wall Street Journal Washington Wire*, March 31, 2010, http://blogs.wsj.com/washwire/2010/03/31/ former-gop-officials-launch-political-group/tab/article.

21 Dan Eggen, "Mining Interests Are Heavily Invested in Capitol Hill," *The Washington Post*, April 8, 2010, www.washingtonpost.com/wp-dyn/content/article/2010/04/07/ AR2010040704707.html

22 American Crossroads, Form 8872 report of contributions and expenditures (amended), April 28, 2010, http://forms.irs.gov/politicalOrgsSearch/search/Print.action?formId= 52035&formType=E72; Form 8872 report of contributions and expenditures, May 20, 2010, http://forms.irs.gov/politicalOrgsSearch/search/Print.action?formId=5259 2&formType=E72.

23 Quoted in Wayne Slater, "3 Dallas Executives Give $1 Million Each to Target Senate Majority Leader Harry Reid, Other Democrats," *Dallas Morning News*, July 30, 2010, www.dallasnews.com/news/politics/national-politics/20100730-3-Dallas-executives-give-1-2907.ece.

24 Hagan, "Goddangit."

25 David Magleby, "Dictum Without Data: The Myth of Issue Advocacy and Party Building," (Provo, UT: Center for the Study of Elections and Democracy, 2000), http://csed.byu.edu/Assets/Pew/Dictum.pdf.

26 Quoted in Michael Luo, "Money Talks Louder Than Ever in Midterms," *The New York Times*, October 8, 2010, www.nytimes.com/2010/10/08/us/politics/08donate.html.

27 American Crossroads, "NV-Paying Off," June 13, 2010, www.youtube.com/ watch?v=osn9ljIMQ7o.

28 Quoted in Jim Rutenberg and Jeff Zeleny, "Democrats Outrun by a 2-Year G.O.P. Comeback Plan," *The New York Times*, November 3, 2010, www.nytimes .com/2010/11/04/us/politics/04campaign.html.

29 Quoted in Kenneth P. Vogel, "New GOP 527 Far Short of $52M Goal," *Politico*, June 21, 2011, www.politico.com/news/stories/0610/38825.html.

30 Quoted in Chris Cillizza, "The Fix: Senior Democrats Form Outside Group Aimed at 2010 Elections," *The Washington Post*, June 11, 2010, http://voices.washingtonpost .com/thefix/morning-fix/1-2-3-9.html.

31 Quoted in Michael Beckel, "Karl Rove-Linked Conservative Group, American Crossroads, Adapts to New Campaign Finance Landscape," *OpenSecrets Blog*, August 19, 2010, www.opensecrets.org/news/2010/08/karl-rove-linked-conservative-group.html.

32 Alliance Resource Partners, Form 10-K, Securities and Exchange Commission, February 26, 2010, www.faqs.org/sec-filings/100226/ALLIANCE-RESOURCE-PARTNERS-LP_10-K/.

33 Jim Rutenberg, "A Billionaire Finances Ads Hitting Obama," *The New York Times*, August 23, 2008, www.nytimes.com/2008/08/23/us/politics/23ads.html.

34 Dan Eggen and T. W. Farnam, "Familiar Faces Funding Conservative Attack Ads," *The Washington Post*, October 23, 2010, www.washingtonpost.com/wp-dyn/content/ article/2010/10/22/AR2010102206603.html.

35 U.S. Internal Revenue Service, "Social Welfare Organizations," August 20, 2010, www
    .irs.gov/charities/nonprofits/article/0,,id=96178,00.html. As of early 2012, the IRS
    had not given formal approval to Crossroads GPS as a 501(c)(4).

36 Michael Luo and Stephanie Strom, "Donor Names Remain Secret as Rules Shift," *The
    New York Times*, September 21, 2010, www.nytimes.com/2010/09/21/us/
    politics/21money.html.

37 Quoted in Kenneth P. Vogel, "Secrecy Flip-Flop Fueled Crossroads," *Politico*, October
    25, 2010, www.politico.com/news/stories/1010/44104.html.

38 Quoted in Luo and Strom, "Donor Names Remain Secret as Rules Shift."

39 American Crossroads GPS concept paper, www.politico.com/static/PPM169_cross
    roadsgpsconceptpaper.html.

40 Dan Eggen and T. W. Farnam, "New 'Super PACs' Bringing Millions Into Campaigns,"
    The Washington Post, September 28, 2010, www.washingtonpost.com/wp-dyn/
    content/article/2010/09/27/AR2010092706500.html.

41 Quoted in Vogel, "Secrecy Flip-Flop Fueled Crossroads."

42 Factcheck.org, "Cash Attack 2010: Political Advertising in a Post–Citizens United
    World," December 13, 2010, http://factcheck.org/UploadedFiles/2011/01/rep_panel
    .pdf.

43 Crossroads GPS donor memorandum, www.politico.com/static/PPM170_101022_
    crossroadsdonormemo.html.

44 Danny Yadron, "The Number: $15.4 Million More for Crossroads GPS," *The Wall
    Street Journal*, December 3, 2010, http://blogs.wsj.com/washwire/2010/12/03/the-
    number-154-million-more-for-crossroads-gps.

45 Quoted in Jim Rutenberg, Don Van Natta Jr., and Mike McIntire, "Offering Donors
    Secrecy, and Going on Attack," *The New York Times*, October 11, 2010, www.nytimes
    .com/2010/10/12/us/politics/12donate.html.

46 Quoted in Sam Stein, "American Crossroads GPS, New Rove Group, Has Dems
    Questioning Obama's Political Operations." *The Huffington Post*, July 21, 2010, www
    .huffingtonpost.com/2010/07/21/american-crossroads-gps-n_n_654407.html.

47 Quoted in Rago, "The Republican Answer."

48 Allen and Vogel, "Karl Rove, Republican Party Plot Vast Network."

49 Fred Barnes, "Inside the Republican Money Machine," *The Wall Street Journal*,
    September 24, 2010, http://online.wsj.com/article/SB100014240527487041292045
    75505563870827420.html.

50 Jim Rutenberg, "Rove Returns, With Team, Planning G.O.P. Push," *The New York
    Times*, September 25, 2010, www.nytimes.com/2010/09/26/us/26rove.html.

51 Kenneth P. Vogel and Ben Smith, "Karl Rove's Karl Rove," *Politico*, October 18, 2010,
    www.politico.com/news/stories/1010/43731.html.

52 Institute of Politics, *Campaign for President: The Managers Look at 2004* (Lanham,
    Maryland: Rowman & Littlefield, 2006), 238.

53 Federal Election Commission, "Coordinated Communications and Independent
    Expenditures," February 2001, www.fec.gov/pages/brochures/indexp.shtml.

54 Quoted in Holly Bailey, "A Guide to the 'Shadow GOP': The Groups That May Define
    the 2010 and 2012 Elections," *The Upshot*, August 5, 2010, http://news.yahoo.com/s/
    yblog_upshot/20100805/el_yblog_upshot/a-citizens-guide-to-the-shadow-gop.

55   Quoted in Peter Overby and Andrea Seabrook, "'Independent' Groups Behind Ads Not So Independent," National Public Radio, October 27, 2010, www.npr.org/templates/story/story.php?storyId=130836771.

56   Nathan L. Gonzales, "Parties' Opposition Research Efforts Fuel Late Ads," *Rothenberg Political Report*, September 30, 2010, http://rothenbergpoliticalreport.com/news/article/parties-opposition-research-efforts-fuel-late-ads

57   "Carl Forti," *Campaigns and Elections*, July 19, 2010, www.campaignsandelections.com/publications/campaign-election/2010/july_2010/carl-forti.

58   Clyde Wilcox, quoted in Federal Election Commission, Findings of Fact, SpeechNow v. FEC, October 28, 2010, www.fec.gov/law/litigation/speechnow_fec_finding_facts.pdf.

59   John McArdle, "For Many '06 NRCC Aides, Revenge May Be Sweetest," *Roll Call*, October 5, 2010, www.rollcall.com/issues/56_36/-50543-1.html.

60   Quoted in Tom Hamburger and Kathleen Hennessey, "Conservatives Struggle to Unify for Voter Outreach," *Los Angeles Times*, October 26, 2010, http://articles.latimes.com/2010/oct/26/nation/la-na-conservatives-endgame-20101026.

61   Factcheck.org, "Cash Attack 2010: Political Advertising in a Post-Citizens United World," December 13, 2010, http://factcheck.org/UploadedFiles/2011/01/rep_panel.pdf.

62   Chris Cillizza, "The Fix: American Crossroads Announces 11 Senate Targets," *The Washington Post*, June 17, 2010, http://voices.washingtonpost.com/thefix/morning-fix/1-2-members-of-the.html.

63   Manu Raju, "Karl Rove Bets Big Against Harry Reid," *Politico*, September 15, 2010, www.politico.com/news/stories/0910/42180.html.

64   Right after the election, Gallup found that just 6 percent of Republicans had a favorable opinion of Reid, compared with 71 percent unfavorable. Jeffrey M. Jones, "Boehner's Image Improves, Reid's Does Not After Midterms," Gallup Poll, November 10, 2010, www.gallup.com/poll/144362/boehner-image-improves-reid-not-midterms.aspx.

65   The decapitation strategy goes beyond the ballot box. During the 1980s, House Republicans launched ethics attacks on House Speaker Jim Wright (D-Tex.) and majority whip Tony Coelho (D-Calif.), and both had to resign. After becoming House Speaker, Newt Gingrich faced similar attacks from Democrats. "Being in the legislative leadership in either chamber now means that you are a high value target to the opposition," wrote Stuart Rothenberg in 2005. "Take down the leader, and you can discredit his or her party, or at least create the sense that the opposition is in disarray." Stuart Rothenberg, "In Modern Politics, It's Open Season on Congressional Leaders," *Rothenberg Political Report*, October 14, 2005, http://rothenbergpoliticalreport.com/news/article/in-modern-politics-its-open-season-on-congressional-leaders.

66   American Crossroads, "Illinois 'Driver Error,'" September 21, 2010, www.youtube.com/watch?v=M-iBXHJ1L-8; Viveca Novak, "Crossroads Jam-Up," Factcheck.org, October 1, 2010, www.factcheck.org/2010/10/crossroads-jam-up/.

67   American Crossroads, "Kentucky Puzzle," October 21, 2010, www.youtube.com/watch?v=9VtAVcnP1Yc.

68 Karl Rove, *Courage and Consequence: My Life as a Conservative in the Fight* (New York: Simon & Schuster, 2010), 78.
69 Maeve Reston and Anthony York, "Karl Rove-Linked Group Launches New Hit Against Boxer," *Los Angeles Times*, August 25, 2010, http://latimesblogs.latimes.com/california-politics/2010/08/karl-rovelinked-group-launches-new-hit-against-boxer.html.
70 Crossroads GPS, "CA 'Worried,'" August 25, 2010, www.youtube.com/watch?v=wQd74O3PEM8
71 Jonathan Collegio, "Crossroads GPS Launches New Issue Ads in Pennsylvania, California and Kentucky," August 25, 2010, www.crossroadsgps.org/news/crossroads-gps-launches-new-issue-ads-pennsylvania-california-and-kentucky.
72 Jonathan Collegio, "American Crossroads Announces 2010 Get Out the Vote Action Plan," American Crossroads, August 27, 2010, www.americancrossroads.org/news/american-crossroads-announces-2010-get-out-vote-action-plan.
73 Jessica Yellin, "American Crossroads Hopes iPads Will Drive Your Vote," CNN, November 2, 2010, http://politicalticker.blogs.cnn.com/2010/11/01/american-cross roads-hopes-ipads-will-drive-your-vote/.
74 Quoted in Rutenberg and Zeleny, "Democrats Outrun."
75 Quoted in Kim Geiger, "Outside Groups Made the Difference for Some Republicans," *Los Angeles Times*, November 4, 2010, http://articles.latimes.com/2010/nov/04/nation/la-na-money-impact-20101104.
76 Quoted in Brody Mullins and Danny Yadron, "GOP Groups Launch Massive Ad Blitz," *Wall Street Journal*, October 13, 2010, http://online.wsj.com/article/SB10001 424052748704164004575548451695013866.html.
77 Sun Tzu, *The Art of War*, trans. Samuel B. Griffith (New York: Oxford University Press, 1971), 98.
78 Crossroads GPS, "Jim Costa Boondoggle," October 25, 2010, www.youtube.com/watch?v=FQGshcp3dSM.
79 *Congressional Record* (daily), September 22, 2010, S7325.
80 Jonathan Collegio, "Crossroads GPS Announces National '7 in '11' Issues Agenda," Crossroads GPS, August 17, 2010, www.crossroadsgps.org/news/crossroads-gps-announces-national-7-11-issues-agenda.
81 Glen Bolger, "Key Findings—National Survey on the 2001 Tax Cuts," Public Opinion Strategies (for Crossroads GPS), December 4, 2010, www.politico.com/static/PPM182_101206_crossroads_memo.html.
82 Alex Isenstadt, "Crossroads GPS Prepares Offensive," *Politico*, December 14, 2010, www.politico.com/news/stories/1210/46356.html.
83 Quoted in David Sherfinski, "Crossroads Ads Hit Connolly, Freshly Elected Dems," *Washington Examiner*, December 17, 2010, http://washingtonexaminer.com/blogs/capital-land/2010/12/crossroads-ads-hit-connolly-re-elected-dems.
84 Jonathan Collegio, "Crossroads GPS Launches New Issue Ads in 22 U.S. House Districts Nationwide," Crossroads GPS, February 23, 2011, http://crossroadsgps.org/news/crossroads-gps-launches-new-issue-ads-22-us-house-districts-nationwide.
85 Jonathan Martin, "Crossroads GPS Airs Anti-Union Ad," *Politico*, March 9, 2011, www.politico.com/news/stories/0311/50915.html.

86 Jonathan Collegio, "Crossroads GPS Sues Obama Administration Over Failure to Release Obamacare Waiver Documents," Crossroads GPS, March 23, 2011, www.crossroadsgps.org/news/crossroads-gps-sues-obama-administration-over-failure-release-obamacare-waiver-documents.

87 Wikicountability main page at wikicountability.org; Mike Allen, "Crossroads GPS Launches Collaborative FOIA Site," *Politico*, March 23, 2011, www.politico.com/news/stories/0311/51796.html.

88 Michael D. Shear, "Rove Group Introduces Web Site Seeking Disclosures," *The New York Times* "Caucus" blog, March 23, 2011, http://thecaucus.blogs.nytimes.com/2011/03/23/rove-group-demands-openness-wont-disclose-donors/.

89 Quoted in Brody Mullins, "2012 Election Spending Race Heats Up," *The Wall Street Journal*, March 1, 2001, http://online.wsj.com/article/SB100014240527487037495 04576172853080331590.html.

90 Quoted in Michael D. Shear, "Crossroads Sets $120 Million Goal to Defeat Obama," *The New York Times* "Caucus" blog, March 1, 2011, http://thecaucus.blogs.nytimes.com/2011/03/01/crossroads-sets-120-million-goal-to-defeat-obama

91 Brian Lamb interview with Paul Weyrich, "Q&A," C-SPAN, March 27, 2005, www.q-and-a.org/Transcript/?ProgramID=1016.

92 The Democracy Alliance, www.democracyalliance.org/.

CHAPTER 9

Nimble Giants

How National Interest Groups Harnessed Tea Party Enthusiasm

Jonathan Mummolo

With less than two months to go until the 2010 midterm elections, the streets of Capitol Hill were flooded with thousands of true believers. They came from all over the country, many on buses procured by local volunteers, often at considerable personal cost. They marched purposefully down Pennsylvania Avenue toward the U.S. Capitol—the perceived source of their grievances—armed with signs decrying everything from government intrusiveness, restrictive gun laws, abortion policies, and federal spending run amuck. And, though drawn from hundreds of vaguely affiliated and dispersed local groups, most of the protestors at the 9/12 Taxpayer March on Washington identified under one common banner: the Tea Party.

Looking at this impressive display of civic activism, a casual observer of the Tea Party movement might deem it a purely grassroots phenomenon. But, as became evident over the course of the midterm election cycle, these activists enjoyed an unusual advantage over previous nascent political movements: from practically the movement's inception, grassroots Tea Party activists had the backing of powerful national interest groups and elite political operatives. Many marchers that day had, no doubt, first heard of the movement on Fox News—a network that demonstrated an uncommon affinity for promoting the Tea Party, even before it had become a prevalent political news story. Many others likely learned of the Tea Party via the websites and e-mail blasts of several national groups such as FreedomWorks—which helped organize the march—Tea Party Express, and Americans for Prosperity, all of which were headed or founded by seasoned conservative power brokers.[1] Between them, these same large groups would raise and spend millions in advertising dollars during the campaign season, endorse dozens of candidates, and lend on-the-ground support—in the forms of training seminars, yard signs, door knockers, and targeted phone banking systems—to grassroots activists working to defeat incumbent House members in their home districts.[2] At least one national group was decades old, and run by committed ideologues who suddenly found their preexisting policy goals in lockstep with an emerging movement. In other cases, interest groups appeared to contort their missions to fit in with the Tea Party message of the moment.

Regardless of how they came to be affiliated with the movement, several of these large organizations were successful in assuming the Tea Party brand as their own. Indeed, the Tea Party saga of 2010 highlighted the savvy and flexibility of modern American interest groups, several of which quickly recognized an emerging source of political energy in the electorate, and steered their operations in its direction. While early empirical analyses suggest that candidates affiliated with these groups saw little to no boost in general election performance, national Tea Party organizations appear to have been instrumental in the primaries, using vast resources to effectively define, in many cases, *which* conservative candidates would be trumpeted as the movement's standard bearers. These groups also helped cement the Tea Party's agenda into a fixture of the national political debate. Unlike countless prior political movements, the Tea Party's message caught on with impressive speed during the 2010 election cycle, and has remained relevant since thanks, in large part, to the assistance of these nimble giants.

This chapter first chronicles the origins of the Tea Party movement. It then outlines how several prominent national interest groups came to be affiliated with the Tea Party, and attempted to influence the GOP primaries in 2010. It then discusses whether these groups were successful in propelling their chosen candidates to elected office, lending discussion to what empirical research has shown on this question thus far. The chapter concludes with a discussion of the movement's chances of survival.

How the Tea Was Brewed: The Formation of a Movement

In describing the Tea Party's origins, many point to CNBC reporter Rick Santelli's now-famous "rant" on the floor of the Chicago Mercantile Exchange on February 19, 2009.[3] Speaking to a news anchor about the Obama administration's proposed mortgage assistance plan, Santelli, to the audible cheers of financial sector employees around him, grew sardonic:

> How 'bout this, president and new administration: Why don't you put up a website to have people vote on the internet as a referendum to see if we really want to subsidize the losers' mortgages, or would we like to at least buy cars and buy houses in foreclosure and give them to people that might have a chance to actually prosper down the road, and reward people that can carry the water, instead of drink the water?…We're thinking of having a Chicago tea party in July. All you capitalists that want to show up to Lake Michigan, I'm gonna start organizing.[4]

Santelli did not found the Tea Party. As *New York Times* reporter Kate Zernike points out in her chronicle of the movement's origins, *Boiling Mad: Inside Tea Party America*, "The first Tea Party had already taken place three days earlier in Seattle," in the form of a small protest led by a twenty-nine-year-old math teacher.[5] But Santelli did succeed in articulating a pervasive frustration with big government among the electorate—especially among conservatives—and his message quickly went viral. As Zernike put it, his rant didn't spawn the movement, but Santelli gave a growing mood of discontent, "a name, and a bit of imagery."[6] This was no small contribution, because Santelli's moniker—uttered at a time when the GOP label was sullied[7]—evoked the defiant protests of America's founding fathers against a tyrannical empire. It was a powerful rhetorical call to arms that, to this day, allows many in the movement to view their political struggle as nothing short of righteous.

Following the rant, the race was on to co-opt the sentiment Santelli expressed. Unlike some previous nascent political movements, the Tea Party had a cast of elites ready and willing to assist in spreading the message. Among them, it seemed, were the anchors of Fox News. The network lent an unusually large megaphone to the promotion of the first national Tea Party "tax day" rallies in April 2009—a coordinated group of nationwide protests that has since become an annual event for Tea Partiers. A Media Matters report found that, "from April 6 to April 13 [2009], Fox News featured at least 20 segments on the 'tea party' protests scheduled to take place on April 15, and aired at least 73 in-show and commercial promotions for their April 15 coverage of the events."[8] Fox was instrumental in making sure the movement's seeds found fertile ground. Coverage of the Tea Party on Fox and CNN spiked at the time of the first April 15 tax day rallies, but unlike CNN, Fox sustained its coverage of the movement *before and after* the event. "This key outlet echoed by other conservative outlets, helped to create and sustain the Tea Party mobilization in the first place."[9]

The media spotlight, combined with the ease of reaching like-minded potential supporters through online social networking, allowed the movement's ranks to swell rapidly. By the spring of 2010, just over a year after the Santelli rant, a CBS News/*New York Times* poll estimated that 18 percent of American adults supported the Tea Party movement.[10] Tea Party bus tours, protests, and rallies would become commonplace throughout the remainder of the 2010 election cycle. *The New York Times* and *The Washington Post* assigned members of their national reporting staffs to be Tea Party beat reporters. By the end of 2010, hundreds of loosely affiliated local Tea Party groups sprouted up across the country.[11]

Disparate as it was, the movement managed to produce a distilled declaration of its principles, known as the "Contract From America." Houston attorney Ryan Hecker told the media that he assembled the document after a months-long "open-sourced" process that drew on the ideas that the movement's grassroots activists had submitted online.[12] The contract focused on fiscal conservatism, small government, and largely avoided social issues (though strong concern for such issues, including abortion, was widespread within the rank and file of the movement, polls showed).[13]

The Contract From America issued ten hard-line demands, including one that would require every bill proposed in Congress to identify the specific provision within the Constitution authorizing the proposal—a requirement that Republicans added to the House rules at the outset of the 112th Congress. Another demand supports a constitutional amendment requiring a balanced budget and a "two-thirds majority" to pass any tax hike. The document also calls for a simplified, single-rate tax system, a moratorium on earmarks, and a rejection of a cap and trade energy policy. It is difficult to say for sure how comprehensively the contract summarizes the goals of the entire fractured movement, but it became widely known among conservatives, and many candidates affiliated with the Tea Party went on to announce support for its provisions. In addition, political scientists later found that—controlling for other contributing factors—signatories of the Contract From America outperformed other candidates in the GOP primaries, on average, by 20 points.[14] In the midst of the primary season, the Tea Party would be dubbed an undeniable force in American Politics.

The Primaries: How Deep-Pocketed Backers Help Solidify the Tea Party Brand

After the Tea Party gained saliency between 2009 and 2010, there emerged a crop of upstart primary election candidates affiliated with the movement who pledged to fight for drastically smaller government and an adherence to the Constitution. Often (but not always) political novices, they were overwhelmingly Republicans. They were unafraid—if not eager—to challenge entrenched GOP incumbents, even in races where the defeat of an incumbent Republican meant the seat would become extremely vulnerable to Democrats in the general election. And they were aided, in large part, by a collection of deep-pocketed interest groups that had decided to throw all their weight behind promoting the Tea Party and its candidates. Key, high profile victories—particularly in Senate primaries in Nevada, Alaska, Utah, Kentucky, and Delaware—shocked veteran political observers. If the Santelli rant was instrumental in getting the Tea Party moniker into the national zeitgeist, the primaries were instrumental in forcing the mainstream news media to acknowledge the movement as something more than a right-wing gimmick.[15]

Few could have been as stunned by the speed and force with which the Tea Party affected Republican politics as former Utah senator Bob Bennett (R-Utah). A three-term senator, Bennett was seen in political Washington as a tested conservative—the kind of candidate who could cruise to victory in an anti-Democratic year like 2010. But after supporting George W. Bush's bank bailout, and working with Sen. Ron Wyden (D-Ore.) on a health care overhaul proposal, he became *persona non grata* among small-government libertarians.[16] One of Bennett's opponents, Mike Lee, a lawyer who had never held public office before,[17] secured the primary endorsement of Dick Armey. Armey was former GOP House majority leader, and the head of FreedomWorks, a decades-old interest group promoting fiscal conservatism that had successfully aligned itself with the Tea Party movement by this time.[18] By the end of the 2010 election cycle, FreedomWorks would assist Lee with 4,000 door hangers, 350 yard signs, and other get-out-the-vote assistance, according to data shared by the organization. In March, with the primary fast approaching, Tea Party Express—a political action committee (PAC) run out of Sacramento by longtime GOP political operatives—sent out an e-mail blast with the subject line: "Senator Bennett in Crosshairs Today—Tea Party Express Rally." The e-mail promoted an upcoming rally hosted by Tea Party Express in Salt Lake City, where Bennett's challengers would be given a "platform to speak to the crowd and provide voters an alternative to Bennett."[19] Lee went on to become a U.S. senator.

In late May, about ten days after Bennett's defeat, Rand Paul—an eye doctor who hailed himself as a political outsider despite the fact that his father is Texas Rep. Ron Paul (Tex. District 14)—defeated Trey Grayson, Kentucky secretary of state for the GOP Senate nomination in that state.[20] The well-credentialed Grayson seemed groomed for the office, and his defeat at the hands of Paul was hailed as yet another Tea Party victory over the GOP establishment.[21] Paul had also secured an early endorsement from FreedomWorks. In his primary election night victory speech, he summed up the message of his speedy ascent nicely for the next day's newspapers: "I have a message, a message from the tea party, a message that is loud and clear and does not mince words: We've come to take our government back."[22]

The movement was on a roll. The following month, the Tea Party winner was Sharron Angle of Nevada, where the primary winner would go on to face Democrat Harry Reid, the entrenched Senate majority leader and a symbol to conservatives of the big-government status quo. Early in the race, Angle, a former state legislator with a conservative voting record, was competing against a wide field of candidates, many who were vying for the support of the emerging local Tea Party faction. In the end, Angle, with the financial backing of Tea Party Express, ran away with it. Through their PAC, Tea Party Express spent "roughly $500,000 on ads late in the primary, mostly attacking one of her primary opponent's conservative credentials."[23] Other high-profile candidates, like Christine O'Donnell (Del.), Joe Miller (Alaska) and Marco Rubio (Fla.) also went on to upset the Republican establishment during the primaries.

From Party Guest to Party Host: How National Interest Groups Defined the Tea Party Candidates

If there was a common thread tying these primary campaigns together, it was this: each was afforded massive support—support that continued through the general election—by a collection of national political interest groups that had worked hard to affiliate themselves with the Tea Party movement. It is clear that the Tea Party was endowed with substantial grassroots support early on, but one thing the movement lacked in the days before the 2010 primary elections was a definitive list of *which* candidates truly represented its ideals. This information vacuum effectively allowed national interest groups to decide which candidates would be the movement's standard bearers by pouring vast resources into their preferred candidates' campaign coffers, thereby muting the efforts of other plausible "Tea Party candidates."

The branding of candidates was accomplished by traditional elite-level methods, such as independent expenditures, endorsements, and phone banking. But these groups also worked tirelessly to develop a pervasive ground game, training and guiding grassroots movement enthusiasts to campaign in targeted races for their preferred candidates. Compared to burgeoning movements in prior cycles, the Tea Party had several technological and organizational advantages while doing so. For one, the Tea Party was one of the first large political movements to develop in the United States after the use of digital social networks had become part of daily life. No longer did movement entrepreneurs—elites who encourage social movements—have to scour the countryside for potential new members, printing expensive newsletters, purchasing pricey advertising, and convincing other elites to take up the cause. Facebook, Twitter, and a host of sites like TeaPartyPatriots. org allowed Tea Party supporters to connect without having to leave their couches, and easily obtain information on candidates that espoused the movement's views. The costs of getting involved had never been lower.

Though myriad groups are currently identified with the Tea Party, three deserve special note for their ability to rapidly align their brands with the movement despite having predated it by many years: (1) FreedomWorks, (2) Tea Party Express, and (3) Americans for Prosperity. Chaired by Armey since 2003, Freedom-Works was founded in 1984 under the name Citizens for a Sound Economy, which advocated for small government and a flat tax.[24] The group was "underwritten by the Koch family," billionaires and frequent backers of right-wing organizations like the Cato Institute.[25] FreedomWorks had been advocating libertarian politics and Tea Party–esque demonstrations against big government for years before the movement coalesced in 2009.[26] The group actually floated the idea of a second Boston Tea Party in the early 2000s, to little notice, and in 2007, two of its executives wrote an op-ed, "proposing the Boston Tea Party as a model of grassroots pressure on an overbearing central government."[27]

When the first grassroots rumblings of the Tea Party movement were felt in 2009, FreedomWorks saw a natural alliance and a chance to grow, and the group pounced. Throughout the election cycle, the group held nationwide training seminars, teaching elderly political novices right-wing economic theory, strategies for bringing friends and neighbors into the fold, and techniques for designing effective rally signs.[28] The group also worked diligently to corral grassroots Tea Party activists into organized get-out-the-vote operations for candidates. These included massive "phone-from-home" programs that allowed activists to make targeted calls to voters in competitive areas across the country with ease. Shortly before the November election, FreedomWorks claimed 2,100 registered callers in their program nationwide.[29] They also built a widely circulated endorsement list, and poured get-out-the-vote resources into targeted House districts. Its coffers reflected this expanded reach. In the 2008 election cycle, it raised $898. In the 2010 cycle, that figure grew to $688,362.[30]

FreedomWorks was particularly methodical in its outreach at the grassroots level. Rather than sinking money into TV ads (which the organization was convinced came across to voters as inauthentic), FreedomWorks operatives worked hard to identify influential local leaders and community figures, bring them onboard, and have those trusted local voices make the case for the movement to other locals *for* them, according to Adam Brandon, vice president of communications for FreedomWorks.[31]

"We call them 'nodes,' or 'connectors,'" Brandon said of the local-level elites FreedomWorks worked to recruit.[32] "An active pillar in the community— your local dentist, a fireman....If the guy in charge of your local pee-wee football league in South Carolina is all excited about Tim Scott [a 2010 GOP House candidate there], that's going do a whole lot more than a TV ad."[33]

In exchange for grassroots support, FreedomWorks would sometimes offer sweeteners to local activists, even if doing so clashed with their strategic calculations. For example, when deciding which candidates to endorse, the organization first weighed a candidate's record on fiscal conservatism.[34] If they passed that initial review, the group then gauged whether a candidate actually stood a shot at winning before pouring resources into their district.[35] Often, however, local activists working hard to defeat an entrenched Democratic incumbent, like Rep. Dennis Kucinich (Ohio District 10), would demand that FreedomWorks endorse a GOP challenger with little chance of success.[36] In many cases, FreedomWorks obliged these activists.[37] As a result, by the general election, the group's initially modest endorsement list grew to include 113 House candidates, several of whom were likely not ideologically pure movement affiliates. But whether it made strategic sense or not, failure to endorse these candidates might have made it harder to ask grassroots activists to work on the races FreedomWorks *did* care about.[38]

The horse-trading did not end with endorsements because, as *Washington Post* Tea Party reporter Amy Gardner reported in an article on the FreedomWorks phone-from-home program, "one of the quirks of the tea party is that many supporters don't like being told what to do, and some have balked at abandoning local races just because a national organizer tells them that a candidate in another state has a better chance of winning."[39] Recognizing this independent spirit and suspicion of authority, FreedomWorks was adept at nudging grassroots supporters to do their bidding without offending their maverick sensibilities. Take the following conference call exchange, chronicled in *The Washington Post,* between Russ Walker, the national political director for FreedomWorks, and local Tea Party activists in Oregon. In it, Walker attempts to direct the energy of activists toward preferred out-of-state candidates, even though some were upset by the lack of support for Jim Huffman, an Oregon Republican and favorite among local movement activists who was trailing incumbent Sen. Jim Wyden (D) by a large margin:

> He [Russ Walker] … didn't ask them to stop working for Huffman…. Instead, Walker began the call by asking everyone how FreedomWorks can help them. Sounding a little like an auctioneer, he promised 1,500 Huffman yard signs here and 2,000 door hangers there.
>
> "Randi and Heather and then Jack: How many more do you need for southern Oregon?"
>
> "I could go for another 2,000," responded one.
>
> "Okay, and Jodi?" Walker asked. "How many did we say we were going to send you?"
>
> Only then did Walker move on to what he was really after: asking coordinators to sign up as many volunteers as possible to make calls to other states.[40]

Given the policies it had been advocating for decades, and its attitude toward big government, FreedomWorks was a natural ally for the Tea Party. By contrast, journalists' accounts suggest that another group, Tea Party Express, seems to have contorted its aims to align with the movement. Headed by chief strategist Sal Russo—a GOP insider who has worked for a slew of high-profile GOP politicians, and got his start working for Gov. Ronald Reagan—Tea Party Express became the financial powerhouse of the Tea Party.[41] A foundering PAC before 2009 called Our Country Deserves Better, the group proved adept at capitalizing on the Tea Party message as it began to gain steam.[42] *The New York Times* reported that immediately following the first tax day rallies in 2009, "Joe Wierzbicki, a senior associate at Mr. Russo's [political consulting] firm, Russo Marsh & Associates in Sacramento, sketched out a proposal to latch onto the nascent Tea Party movement, according to internal e-mails."[43] The *Times* wrote that Wierzbicki saw the movement as an opportunity to bolster the firm's struggling PAC:

"Here is the plan I've been cooking up in my head," Mr. Wierzbicki wrote in an e-mail to Mr. Russo. "About how we really make a big impact with the 2010 elections coming up, on the heels of the successful Tea Party push on April 15, and my desire to give a boost to our PAC and position us as a growing force/leading force."

The plan called for a two-week road trip with an "awesome looking" luxury tour bus that would make stops in dozens of cities represented by members of Congress deemed big spenders, and therefore worthy of ouster, including two Democratic senators, Harry Reid of Nevada, the majority leader, and Christopher J. Dodd of Connecticut, who decided to retire this year amid faltering poll numbers.[44]

The plan worked. Tea Party Express went on to host several national bus tours, carting grassroots enthusiasts to rallies with big-name right-wing headliners like former Alaska governor Sarah Palin. Unlike FreedomWorks, Tea Party Express was not averse to TV advertising, and the group rained money on high-profile races, like the Nevada GOP primary and general election. In the 2008 election cycle, the firm's PAC raised $1.3 million.[45] According to a February 2011 analysis by the Center for Responsive Politics, the group was dominant among Tea Party PACs in 2010, raising $7.6 million—96 percent of all money raised by PACs with the words *Tea Party* in their name in the election cycle.[46] Tea Party Express also spent $2.7 million on independent expenditures, "to back its preferred federal candidates."[47] In September 2010, *The New York Times* dubbed Tea Party Express "the single biggest independent supporter of Tea Party candidates, raising more than $5.2 million in donations since January 2009, according to federal records."[48] But the paper also pointed out that "at least $3 million of that total has since been paid to Mr. Russo's political consulting firm or to one controlled by his wife, according to federal records."[49]

Brian Seitchik, a Republican operative who said he has worked with Russo in the past, saw the influence of Tea Party Express firsthand while managing the campaign of Nevada Senate GOP primary candidate Danny Tarkanian. As that primary race got underway, Seitchik viewed the contest as essentially a two-way race that did not include Angle—a conservative candidate, he said, but one not ready for primetime in his view. "Angle did not run a grown-up campaign by any stretch of the imagination," Seitchik said. "I think the misconception was: Sharon Angle was too conservative to win in Nevada. I don't believe that. I think she was simply too kooky."[50]

Seitchik was referring to several early gaffes and political oddities that became strongly associated with Angle's campaign through the general election. Angle developed a reputation for dodging the questions of local and national reporters, gaining YouTube notoriety in the general election campaign for physically evading reporters after her own press conference.[51] She was also rumored to be a Scientologist, a rumor she repeatedly denied.[52] But after an endorsement from Tea Party Express, and an infusion of hundreds of thousands of dollars in TV ads late in the primary, Angle—who would ultimately lose the general election to Reid—cruised to victory in the primary by more than 10 points over the second place finisher, Sue Lowden. The fact that established GOP operatives headed the Tea Party Express was not well known at the time. To the public, and to some in the news media, the inclusion of the phrase *Tea Party* in the name of the group backing Angle was what stood out. Tea Party Express "gained traction largely because of its name—and because the hallmark of local tea party groups was *not* to endorse," the *Post*'s Amy Gardner said in an interview. "So it was able to step into a vacuum, and become the arbiter of who was *the* tea party candidate."[53]

But not everyone saw Tea Party Express as an authentic affiliate of the movement. Seitchik described the group as "a business run out of Sacramento," which simply used the Tea Party as a way to rebrand itself and grow its network. Angle's "entire campaign was outsourced to the Tea Party Express," he said. "Without them, I think she probably would have finished where she hovered in the polls for a long time, which was between 5 and 8%. … I think [in Angle] they saw an opportunity… an opportunity to raise their profile. They certainly did."[54]

Seitchik was not the only one to view the motives of the group with suspicion. "These are folks who have done what so many feared would be done: They tapped into the movement to raise money for their own interests," Mark Meckler, cofounder and national coordinator for Tea Party Patriots—a group that served as an online hub for local Tea Party groups across the country—said of Tea Party Express to the *Los Angeles Times*.[55] "We have millions of people, and they've got a bus with six or eight people and a fundraising machine."[56] Despite predating the Tea Party movement, Tea Party Express succeeded, like FreedomWorks, in carving out a piece of the movement's emerging identity for itself, and translating that updated brand into electoral power.

One other deep-pocketed group, Americans for Prosperity (AFP), also fits this description. An advocacy group that promotes free market principles, AFP was founded in 2004, when its backers broke away from Citizens for a Sound Economy (now FreedomWorks).[57] Cofounded by conservative magnate David Koch—who, along with his brother, Charles, has advocated for myriad conservative causes over the years—as a 501(c)(4) the group may not directly endorse candidates or promote partisan causes.[58] Nevertheless, AFP came under fire for the millions it spent during the 2010 cycle promoting a conservative agenda through ads and rallies.[59] According to a June 2010 *Washington Post* report, AFP "planned to spend more than $45 million targeting more than fifty House districts and half a dozen Senate races in key battleground states. AFP President Tim Phillips said the group does not offer direct endorsements but will hold rallies, organize door-to-door canvassing, and buy radio and television advertising aimed at 'educating voters about where candidates stand' on conservative issues."[60]

Throughout the cycle, AFP's website became an important gathering place for current and potential Tea Party supporters.[61] As *New Yorker* reporter Jane Meyer wrote in her examination of the Koch brothers' involvement with AFP,

> Americans for Prosperity has worked closely with the Tea Party since the movement's inception. In the weeks before the first Tax Day protests, in April, 2009, Americans for Prosperity hosted a Web site offering supporters "Tea Party Talking Points." The Arizona branch urged people to send tea bags to Obama; the Missouri branch urged members to sign up for "Taxpayer Tea Party Registration" and provided directions to nine protests. The group continues to stoke the rebellion. The North Carolina branch recently launched a "Tea Party Finder" Web site, advertised as "a hub for all the Tea Parties in North Carolina."[62]

As a Republican consultant and associate of the Koch brothers put it, "The Koch brothers gave the money that founded [the Tea Party]. It's like they put the seeds in the ground. Then the rainstorm comes, and the frogs come out of the mud—and they're our candidates!"[63]

Who Drank the Tea? How Tea Party Candidates Faired in the General Election

For all this effort, how many Tea Party candidates actually made it to Congress? The answers depend on whose definition of *Tea Party* one embraces. Figures 9.1 and 9.2 display various measures of how well House and Senate Tea Party candidates did in the general election. In the House, 72 out of 113 FreedomWorks-endorsed candidates were victorious, for a win ratio of 64 percent. In the general election, 85 out of 138 candidates endorsed by Tea Party Express won their races, for a win ratio of 62 percent. Sarah Palin—a national figure strongly associated with the Tea Party movement—endorsed 32 candidates, 19 of whom won (59 percent); in addition, *The New York Times* identified 129 Tea Party candidates, 42 of whom were victorious in November (33 percent). Also, 60 House members affiliated themselves with the movement by joining the House Tea Party Caucus in the 112th Congress. So, depending on which measure is used, the movement has secured anywhere between 19 and 85 seats in the House of Representatives. In the Senate, winners included the following: 10 out of 21 candidates endorsed by FreedomWorks (48 percent); 9 out of 17 candidates endorsed by Tea Party Express (53 percent); 6 out of 11 (55 percent) endorsed by Palin; and 5 out of 9 (56 percent) labeled Tea Party by *The New York Times*.

FIGURE 9.1   Tea Party Success in 2010 House Races

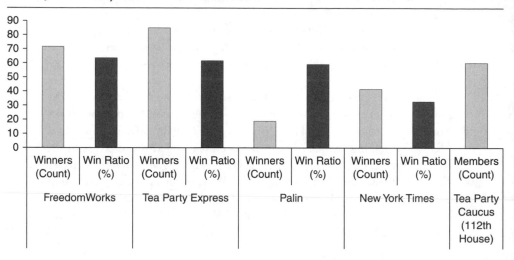

Source: The figures above were generated using data on endorsements from FreedomWorks, Tea Party Express and Sarah Palin, and a list of Tea Party candidates compiled by *The New York Times*. Freedom-Works endorsement data shared by organization. Tea Party Express data retrieved from the group's website. Palin endorsement data retrieved from *The Washington Post's* online "Palin Endorsements Tracker." *The New York Times* data retrieved from nyt.com.

Yet another way to measure how many Tea Party candidates made it to Congress is to construct an additive score based on the previous measures. For example, a House candidate endorsed by FreedomWorks, Tea Party Express, Sarah Palin, *and* labeled Tea Party by the *Times* would be a 4 on the scale—a hard-core movement affiliate; a candidate only endorsed by one group is less convincingly affiliated. Figure 9.3 shows that very few current members of the House were considered Tea Party candidates by multiple sources during 2010. Only two winning candidates—Paul Gosar (Ariz. District 1) and Dan Benishek (Mich. District 1)—scored a 4. Twenty winning candidates scored a 3, 39 scored a 2, 72 scored a 1 and 109 scored a 0. These stratified results are evidence that national interest groups, as well as the news media, were not in agreement as to which candidates represented Tea Party ideals. They also indicate that interest groups (*The New York Times* excepted) were likely competing—not cooperating—in seeking to define which candidates would wear the Tea Party brand.

Shortly after the election, political scientists began conducting more controlled tests of whether Tea Party candidate performance differed from that of other GOP candidates. One analysis found that traditional factors such as the incumbent's previous electoral performance, the normal party vote in the district, candidate

FIGURE 9.2   Tea Party Success in 2010 House Races

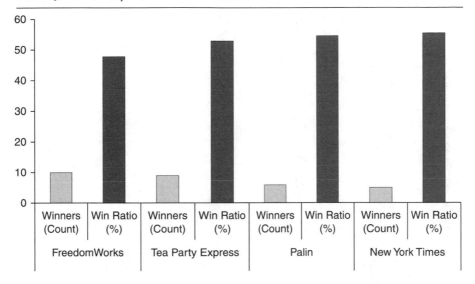

Source: The figures above were generated using data on endorsements from FreedomWorks, Tea Party Express and Sarah Palin, and a list of Tea Party candidates compiled by *The New York Times*. FreedomWorks endorsement data shared by organization. Tea Party Express data retrieved from the group's website. Palin endorsement data retrieved from *The Washington Post's* online "Palin Endorsements Tracker." *The New York Times* data retrieved from nyt.com.

spending, and challenger experience were primarily responsible for 2010 GOP victories, not Tea Party affiliation.[64] In comparing candidate performances to lagged 2008 performances in the same districts for candidates endorsed by Tea Party Express, or FreedomWorks, or both, "Tea Party endorsements of Republicans were most common in those districts that probably would have voted for Republicans anyway."[65] In the Senate, "Tea Party endorsees ran three percentage points *behind* non-endorsed Republicans running in similar states."[66] Furthermore, with the exception of FreedomWorks, being endorsed by a Tea Party organization or figurehead, like Sarah Palin, had no statistically significant impact on Republican vote share in the 2010 general election.[67] On average, being endorsed by FreedomWorks was associated with about a 2-percentage point boost for Republican candidates, with other standard controls in place.[68] An examination of the impact of endorsements in primary elections, however, shows much stronger result. On average, primary candidates endorsed by Tea Party Express and Sarah Palin got roughly 8 and 9 percentage points more of the vote, respectively. Those candidates who signed the Contract From America saw, on average, a staggering a 20-point boost in vote share.[69]

FIGURE 9.3   Degree of Tea Party Affiliation in the House of Representatives
(112th Congress)

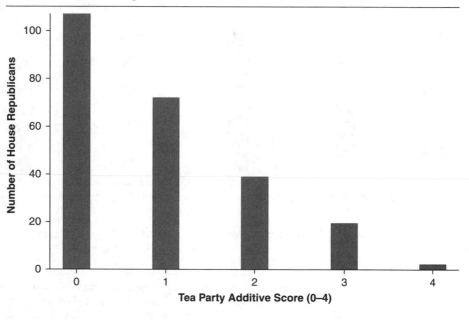

Source: Calculated by author. See text.

Most empirical studies of the Tea Party's electoral impact to date have used endorsement data to identify Tea Party candidates, but other plausible measures of whether a candidate is affiliated with the movement exist. In addition to being endorsed by groups like FreedomWorks, candidates can hail from a district where constituents have a high opinion of the Tea Party, or where many grassroots Tea Party activists live. Incumbent candidates also had the option, prior to the 2010 election, of joining the House Tea Party Caucus. One study used all four of these measures to test whether Tea Party affiliation was associated with better performance among GOP candidates.[70] Somewhat surprisingly, the most robust and consistent mode of movement affiliation to predict significantly better GOP performance in 2010 House races was the number of grassroots activists in a congressional district.[71] To a lesser degree, endorsement by FreedomWorks also was associated with statistically significantly better GOP performance, but no other national endorsements—including Tea Party Express and Sarah Palin—showed a significant effect.[72] (Constituent opinion of the Tea Party in a district and membership in the House Tea Party Caucus showed no robust impact on GOP performance.)

Taken together, anecdotal and empirical evidence thus far suggests that national Tea Party groups had their biggest electoral impact in the primaries, not the general election. But even if national groups were not directly altering general election results, the mere fact that endorsements by a group like Tea Party Express were associated with significant boosts in primary performance—controlling for other relevant factors—suggests that they may have been instrumental in choosing which *types* of Republicans appeared on ballots in November. If this is true—that is, if these endorsements were not merely correlated with boosts in primary performance, but actually *caused* them—then it can be said that in roughly a year's time between the Santelli rant and the first primaries, these nimble interest groups were able to align themselves with the Tea Party's energy, and effectively direct it toward their preferred candidates. That is truly an impressive display of interest group flexibility, and power.

How Strong Is the Tea? The Movement's Chances of Survival

Even by the more conservative estimates, there is now a sizeable segment of the legislative branch affiliated with the Tea Party movement. But will this presence persist, or go down as a political oddity that lasted only one or two election cycles? The long-term survival of the movement depends, in large part, on three factors: (1) the ability of elected officials affiliated with the movement to successfully shift the policy space to the right in order to accommodate their hard-line positions, (2) the willingness of elites to continue to back—and associate themselves—with the movement, and (3) the persistence of high levels of frustration with government among grassroots activists.

On the policy front, the Tea Party may have painted itself into a legislative corner. By taking such extreme policy positions during the campaign—endorsing the Contract From America, for example—and declaring "compromise" as a four-letter word, the movement has put forth a rigid policy agenda that has little chance of surviving a nuanced (some would say, convoluted) American legislative process. Very few hard-line stances actually make it through the meat grinder of the U.S. Congress in their original form. If Tea Party politicians want to stick to their guns, and not water down their policy stances to the outrage of their base, they will have to convince the rest of the Republican Party to move toward them on the policy spectrum. They will have to achieve the stated goal of groups like FreedomWorks: a "hostile takeover" of the Republican Party.[73] Whether the movement will be a "flash in the pan," or a persistent force in American politics, depends "almost entirely on whether [movement supporters] are able to first significantly influence the Republican Party. The ability to move the party toward their views on the issues, to get the party to stress their issues and to take control over at least some of the official party apparatus will all be necessary for the Tea Party to achieve anything of value in upcoming years."[74]

Efforts to do so have already resulted in a visible conflict between Tea Party–affiliated members and more mainstream GOP members of Congress since the

2010 election. Legislative battles over fiscal policy that have nearly halted the wheels of government, including whether to raise the debt ceiling in 2011, have left the GOP a fractured party, and it remains to be seen whether established Republicans will adopt the Tea Party's hard-line stances, or work to root Tea Party members out of the halls of government.

In addition, several candidates who bore the Tea Party label during the campaign appeared to actively distance themselves from it after assuming office, indicating that there is uncertainty among politicians about the long-term value of the brand. For example, though seventy-two and eighty-five House candidates endorsed by FreedomWorks and Tea Party Express, respectively, made it to the House of Representatives, the House Tea Party Caucus attracted only sixty members. At its unveiling in the 112th Congress, the caucus included fewer than a dozen freshmen—enough to raise the eyebrows of journalists on Capitol Hill.[75] In the Senate, an informal Tea Party caucus, which formed in January 2011, was snubbed by such campaign season Tea Party icons as Sen. Marco Rubio (R-Fla.) and Sen. Pat Toomey (R-Pa.).[76] In January 2011, Rubio questioned the need for the caucus, arguing that formalizing the movement might rob it of its grassroots flavor. "I think that the real power of the Tea Party," he said, "comes from its ability to drive the debate and the issues from the grassroots up, as opposed to from the politicians down."[77]

It is within the grassroots element that another threat to the movement's survival may be looming. According to a Pew report in March 2011, anger toward the federal government—the supposed fuel that powered the Tea Party engine—has dissipated since the election, especially among Tea Party supporters.[78] In September 2010, the report stated that 47 percent of those who agree with the Tea Party were "angry" toward the government. By the following March, that figure had fallen to 28 percent. Others suggest that the ranks of the movement may have already swelled to capacity:

> Poll trends suggest that the Tea Party may have little room left for growth. Despite all the media attention, one-third of Americans were still unfamiliar with the Tea Party in late 2010, and to the extent that people are familiar with the phenomenon, the Tea Party's popularity has stagnated or declined. If the Tea Party is nearing its capacity to appeal to more voters, the 2010 midterm elections may prove an electoral highwater mark.[79]

As with any burgeoning force in the competitive landscape of U.S. politics, there appear to be formidable obstacles to the Tea Party's long-term survival. Igniting an opposition movement for a single election cycle is one thing; sustaining enthusiasm and influence throughout multiple elections is another. But given its unforeseen and rapid ascent, and persistence thus far, there is no reason to predict the movement's demise at this time. The Tea Party can, at this moment, still claim a network of grassroots support across the country, the backing of deep-pocketed elites, a caucus in the House of Representatives bearing its name, a major news network sympathetic to its goals and an upcoming election featuring perhaps the movement's greatest foe—Barack Obama—to help stoke enthusiasm. And of course, the movement is also aligned with organized, politically experienced, well-financed interest groups. Many nascent political movements begin with a shout and end with a whimper. In part because of these savvy, flexible national groups, the movement—with all its various facets—is now recognized as a formidable political interest. If all these advantages remain in place, the Tea Party could have a significant impact on American politics for years to come.

Endnotes

1 Sandhya Somashekhar, "Tea Partiers Claim the Momentum," *The Washington Post*, September 13, 2010, p. A03.

2 Kate Zernike, *Boiling Mad: Inside Tea Party America*. (New York: Times Books, 2010).

3 Ibid., 13.

4 "Rick Santelli Rant—Chicago Tea Party— Join Now," YouTube video, November 29, 2010, www.youtube.com/watch?v= APAD7537RN0.

5 Zernike, *Boiling Mad: Inside Tea Party America*, 13–14.

6 Ibid., 20.

7 Vanessa Williamson, Theda Skocpol, and John Coggin. "The Tea Party and the Remaking of Republican Conservatism," *Perspectives on Politics* 9 (2011): 35.

8 "Hosting the Party: Fox Aired at Least 20 Segments, 73 Promos on "Tea Party" Protests—in Just 8 Days." *Media Matters for America* 15 (April 2009).

9 Vanessa Williamson, Theda Skocpol, and John Coggin, "The Tea Party and the Remaking of Republican Conservatism," 29.

10 Kate Zernike and Megan Thee-Brenan, "Poll Finds Tea Party Backers Wealthier and More Educated," *The New York Times*, April 14, 2010, www.nytimes.com/2010/04/15/us/politics/15poll.html?pagewanted=all.

11 Amy Gardner, "Gauging the Scope of the Tea Party Movement in America," *The Washington Post*, October 24, 2010, www.washingtonpost.com/wpdyn/content/article/2010/10/23/AR2010102304000.html.

12 Kate Zernike, "Seeking a Big Tent, Tea Party Avoids Divisive Social Issues," *The New York Times*, March 13, 2010, www.nytimes.com/2010/03/13/us/politics/13tea.html.

13 Ibid.

14 Christopher F. Karpowitz, J. Quin Monson, Kelly D. Patterson, and Jeremy C. Pope, "Tea Time in America? The Impact of the Tea Party Movement on the 2010 Midterm Elections," *PS: Political Science & Politics* 44 (2011): 303–309.

15 Zernike, *Boiling Mad: Inside Tea Party America*.

16 Ibid., 104.

17 "New Faces in Congress," *The New York Times*, November 4, 2010.

18 Alexander Bolton, "Armey Endorses Conservative Primary Challenger to Bennett," *The Hill*, February 18, 2010, http://thehill.com/homenews/campaign/81907-armey-to-endorse-gop-primary-challenger-to-sen-bennett.

19 Eric Lach, "Tea Party Express E-Mail Puts Sen. Bob Bennett In 'Crosshairs'," *Talking Points Memo*, March 30, 2010, http://tpmlivewire.talkingpointsmemo.com/2010/03/tea-party-express-putting-sen-bob-bennet-in-crosshairs-today.php.

20 In 2010, Paul's credentials as an eye doctor came under scrutiny, when news outlets reported that he was not certified with the American Board of Ophthalmology, the profession's leading group. Paul helped create a rival certification group more than a decade prior to 2010, and he derided the questions over his medical credentials as, "a personal assault on my ability to make a living."; "Rand Paul's Doctor Credentials Questioned For Lacking Top Board's Certification," *Associated Press*, June 14, 2010, as quoted by Fox News, www.foxnews.com/politics/2010/06/14/rand-pauls-doctor-credentials-questioned-lacking-boards-certification/; see also www.foxnews.com/politics/2010/06/14/rand-pauls-doctor-credentials-questioned-lacking-boards-certification/#ixzz1pgj5WV9a.

21 Zernike, *Boiling Mad: Inside Tea Party America*, 160.

22 Ibid., 177.

23 Paul Kane, "In Nevada Republican Primary, Former Front-Runner Sue Lowden Ponders Her Fall," *The Washington Post*, June 9, 2010, www.washingtonpost.com/wp-dyn/content/article/2010/06/09/AR2010060900105.html?wprss=rss_politics/congress.

24 Zernike, *Boiling Mad: Inside Tea Party America*, 35.

25 Ibid., 35.

26 Ibid, 33–34

27 Ibid., 34.

28 Ibid., 2–6

29 Amy Gardner, "Tea Party Activists Banking on Phone Calls to Turn Out Voters." *The Washington Post*, October 21, 2010.

30 Data from the Center for Responsive Politics, www.opensecrets.org.

31 Adam Brandon, telephone communication, April 5, 2011.

32 Ibid.

33 Ibid.

34 Ibid.

35 Ibid.

36 Ibid.

37 Ibid.

38 Ibid.

39 Gardner, "Tea Party Activists Banking on Phone Calls to Turn Out Voters."

40 Ibid.

41 Janie Lorber and Eric Lipton, "G.O.P. Insider Fuels Tea Party and Suspicion," *The New York Times*, September 18, 2010, www.nytimes.com/2010/09/19/us/politics/19russo.html?pagewanted=all.

42 Ibid.

43 Ibid.

44 Ibid.

45 Data retrieved from the Center For Responsive Politics, www.opensecrets.org.

46 Analysis available at the Center for Responsive Politics, www.opensecrets.org/news/2011/02/tea-party-activists-press-forward.html

47 Ibid.

48 Lorber and Lipton, "G.O.P. Insider Fuels Tea Party and Suspicion."

49 Ibid.

50 Brian Seitchik, telephone communication, February 15, 2011.

51 "Sharron Angle Runs From Reporters at Her Own Press Conference" [Video], *The Huffington Post*, July 22, 2010, www.huffingtonpost.com/2010/07/22/sharron-angle-runs-from-r_n_655515.html.

52 "Midterms 2010: Tea Party Primary Candidates: The GOP's Worst Nightmares," *The Guardian*, September 15, 2010, www.guardian.co.uk/world/2010/sep/15/tea-party-primary-candidates-gop.

53 Amy Gardner, e-mail communication, May 11, 2011.

54 Brian Seitchik, telephone communication, February 15, 2010.

55 Matea Gold, "Sal Russo, the Firepower Behind the 'Tea Party,'" *Los Angeles Times*, September 18, 2010, http://articles.latimes.com/2010/sep/18/nation/la-na-tea-party-ads-20100919.

56 Ibid.

57 Jane Mayer, "Covert Operations: The Billionaire Brothers Who Are Waging a War Against Obama," *The New Yorker*, August 30, 2010, http://www.newyorker.com/reporting/2010/08/30/100830fa_fact_mayer.

58 Robin Pogrebin, "Billionaire Pledges $100 Million to New York State Theater," *The New York Times*, July 10, 2008, http://query.nytimes.com/gst/fullpage.html?res=980C E2DE1038F933A25754C0A96E9C8B63&pagewanted=all.

59 Eric Lichtblau, "Group Is Accused on Tax Exemption," *The New York Times*, August 27, 2010.; Lichtblau wrote, "In August 2010, the Democratic Congressional Campaign Committee filed a complaint with the Internal Revenue Service charging that AFP violated federal law by running ads opposing Obama's stimulus plan and health care overhaul."

60 Dan Eggen "Interest Groups Prepared to Spend Record Amounts in 2010 Elections," *The Washington Post*, June 3, 2010, www.washingtonpost.com/wp-dyn/content/article/2010/06/02/AR2010060204451.html.

61 Mayer, "Covert Operations: The Billionaire Brothers Who Are Waging a War Against Obama."

62 Ibid.

63 Ibid.

64 Jon R. Bond, Richard Fleisher, and Nathan Ilderton, "Was the Tea Party Responsible for the Republican Victory in the 2010 House Elections?" (paper presented at 2011 Annual Meeting of American Political Science Association, Seattle, http://ssrn.com/abstract=1901627).

65 Stephen Ansolabehere and James M. Snyder Jr., "Weak Tea," *The Boston Review*, March, 2011, http://bostonreview.net/BR36.2/stephen_ansolabehere_james_snyder_jr_tea_party.php.

66 Ibid.

67 Christopher F. Karpowitz, J. Quin Monson, Kelly D. Patterson, and Jeremy C. Pope. "Tea Time in America? The Impact of the Tea Party Movement on the 2010 Midterm Elections," *PS: Political Science & Politics* 44 (2011): 303–309.

68 However, as Karpowitz et al. note, this is more likely the result of FreedomWorks strategically backing winners, rather than evidence of the group's endorsement causing a boost in vote share.

69 Karpowitz et al., "Tea Time in America? The Impact of the Tea Party Movement on the 2010 Midterm Elections."

70 Michael Bailey, Jonathan Mummolo, and Hans Noel, "Tea Party Influence: A Story of Activists and Elites," *American Politics Research*, forthcoming.

71 Data on the number of Tea Party activists per district were compiled using Devin Burghart and Leonard Zeskind, "Tea Party Nationalism: A Critical Examination of the Tea Party Movement and the Size, Scope, and Focus of Its National Factions," (paper presented at the Berkeley Tea Party Conference, Berkeley, CA, October 22, 2010, www.teapartynationalism.com/the-databri-report-data- and-visualizations/tea-party-membership-map).

72 Bailey, Mummolo, and Noel have doubts about whether the observed FreedomWorks effect was causal, however, because FreedomWorks spokesman Adam Brandon said the group considered whether candidates could win before endorsing them.

73 Kate Zernike, "Republicans Get a Partner, But Who Will Lead?" *The New York Times,* September 16, 2010, www.nytimes.com/2010/09/16/us/politics/16assess.html.

74 Martin Cohen, "The Future of the Tea Party: Scoring an Invitation to the Republican Party" (paper presented at Berkeley Tea Party Conference, Berkeley, CA, October 22, 2010).

75 Shane D'Aprile and Russell Berman, "House Tea Party Caucus Gains Fewer Than a Dozen House Freshmen," *The Hill*, February 28, 2011, http://thehill.com/blogs/ballot-box/house-races/146637-house-tea-party-caucus-gains-less-than-a-dozen-house-freshmen.

76 According to the United States Senate's official website, there is only one officially recognized caucus in the United States Senate, the Senate Caucus on International Narcotics Control established by law in 1985. All other caucus-like groups operate without official recognition from the chamber (see www.senate.gov/pagelayout/committees/d_three_sections_with_teasers/committees_home.htm).

77 "Senator Rubio Questions Need for the Senate Tea Party Caucus," *The Shark Tank,* January 24, 2011, http://shark-tank.net/2011/01/24/senator-rubio-questions-the-need-for-senate-tea-party-caucus-video/.

78 "Fewer Are Angry at Government, But Discontent Remains High." Pew Research Center, March 3, 2011, www.people-press.org/2011/03/03/fewer-are-angry-at-government-but-discontent-remains-high/.

79 Vanessa Williamson, Theda Skocpol, and John Coggin. "The Tea Party and the Remaking of Republican Conservatism," *Perspectives on Politics* 9 (2011): 36.

CHAPTER 10

School of Hard Knocks

Netroots Political Associations

David Karpf

For America's Internet-mediated, netroots political associations (introduced in Chapter 1), the 2010 election was characterized by modest innovation, strategic repositioning, and an ongoing struggle for power within the Democratic Party network. Without question, 2010 was a tough election year, presenting a dramatic shift in the congressional landscape that removed several progressive champions from office. The netroots had built their electoral strategies during the Democratic wave elections of 2006 and 2008, so 2010 marked a decisive transition point— from "offense" to "defense," so to speak. Noticeably, however, the electoral mobilization of the netroots was influenced less by the Tea Party or *Citizens United v. Federal Election Commission* than by the previous two years of Democratic legislative activity. Key leaders, disappointed in the policy accomplishments of the 111th Congress, treated the 2010 election cycle as a venue for increasing the strength of the House Progressive Caucus. They also worked to support vulnerable Senate incumbents, while mobilizing around a high-profile challenge to conservative Arkansas Democratic Sen. Blanche Lincoln. Though the election will be best remembered for the impact of the Tea Party and *Citizens United*–derived super PACs, it also marked a key transition in the ongoing institutionalization of new progressive groups within the Democratic network.

Netroots is a portmanteau, a combination of *Internet* and *grassroots*. The term refers to a cluster of outspokenly partisan, Internet-mediated advocacy groups and political blogs within the American left.[1] All of these organizations have been formed within the past dozen years, with the majority cropping up in response to the Bush administration.[2] The largest of these groups—MoveOn.org and the progressive blog DailyKos—have become household names. MoveOn is the proverbial "800 pound gorilla" in progressive issue campaigning, with 5 million Internet-based members who contributed an estimated $90 million and nearly 1 million volunteer hours during the 2008 election season.[3] DailyKos is the largest progressive community blog, with an active membership that donates several million dollars per election cycle as well.[4] Registered as both a limited liability company (LLC) and a political action committee (PAC), sites like DailyKos expand the boundaries of interest group activity beyond the traditional set of nonprofits and electoral committees. Other netroots groups, such as the Progressive Change Campaign Committee (PCCC), Democracy for America (DFA) and the progressive blog FireDogLake, all engage in legislative and electoral mobilization around a wide array of issues. Netroots organizations tend to have minimal office space, small core staffs, and massive Internet-based member lists. They are predominantly issue generalists, mobilizing their constituency around whatever topic dominates the current political agenda.[5]

The term, netroots, refers exclusively to liberal/progressive organizations.[6] Their right-wing equivalents have traditionally adopted the term *rightroots,* though in the 2010 election they were largely subsumed under the mantle of the Tea Party movement. Though conservatives have developed an advantage on the newest social media platforms such as Twitter and Facebook,[7] they have failed to build equivalents to the Internet-mediated, membership-driven nonprofits that populate the progressive netroots. The top conservative blogs feature substantially less traffic and community engagement than their progressive equivalents, and several well-financed attempts to build "a conservative MoveOn.org" have collapsed in disarray.[8] Given the different institutional setting that netroots and rightroots/Tea Party organizations find themselves in—including the Tea Party's active interaction with and promotion by Fox News Channel and longstanding conservative elites like Dick Armey, Michele Bachmann, and Sarah Palin—this chapter does not attempt to lump the two networks together. Rather, the chapter uses the activity of Internet-mediated Tea Party organizations as a point of comparison for evaluating the tactical and strategic choices the political netroots make. The focus here is on a new set of interest groups, as opposed to the use of technology in elections more generally.

Netroots organizations pride themselves on combining technological and political expertise to innovate new tactics. This includes MoveOn's "Bush in 30 Seconds" user-generated campaign commercial in 2004, DailyKos's active engagement with George Allen's "macaca moment" video in 2006, and the Superdelegate Transparency Project in 2008.[9] The year 2010 was no exception to this trend, as the PCCC and DFA debuted their Call Out the Vote initiative, which supported a distributed volunteer apparatus that made over 1,000,000 get-out-the-vote (GOTV) calls in the final days of the 2010 election. These groups also experimented with new microsites, meant to emphasize the mistakes of a political opponent and capitalize on short-run media attention. Facing increased conservative partisan enthusiasm, a depressed Democratic base, and an attendant shift in media attention from the left to the right, the netroots engaged in only modest technological innovations.

Moreover, because of their low overhead costs and ideological opposition to many corporate sectors, *Citizens United* opened up no new opportunities for the political netroots. They could not capitalize on the new availability of corporate dollars, and their greatest strengths, such as small-dollar bundling through donation portals like ActBlue.com, remained unaffected by the ruling. Netroots organizations made campaign finance reform an issue priority during the 2010 legislative season, but it does not appear as though the availability of unlimited corporate spending influenced their electoral mobilization decisions (presumably because there was no effective vehicle for the issue during the specific time frame in question).

The strategic priorities and overall effectiveness of the netroots in the 2010 election were shaped less by cross-party competition with Republican interest groups than by intraparty competition with centrist Democratic interests. Of particular note was the PCCC/DFA Open Seat Project, which augmented the primary campaigns of viable progressive candidates in open-seat races. Likewise, the political netroots coalesced around Arkansas Lt. Gov. Bill Halter's primary challenge of Sen. Blanche Lincoln (D-Ark.), providing a high-profile challenge in spring of 2010. Lincoln, the most conservative member of the Democratic Senate majority, had angered these groups through her opposition to the "public option" in the Affordable Care Act, and thus earned a concentrated primary challenge, much like Joe Lieberman (D-Conn.) had in the 2006 Connecticut Senate primary. Heavily trailing potential Republican opponents in early polls, the political netroots joined allies in the labor movement in viewing the primary challenge as a "free shot," of sorts—an opportunity to mount a challenge to an intraparty opponent incumbent without endangering an additional Senate seat. It was the Democratic legislative agenda, and the strategic position of Obama's field organization, Organizing for America (housed within the Democratic National Committee), that most affected the electoral choices of the political netroots in the 2010 election.

Through a detailed look at the Lincoln-Halter primary campaign, as well as the PCCC/DFA Open Seat Project, this chapter examines the strategic rationale and tactical repertoire employed by this new segment of the interest group universe. The chapter also highlights the general election activities of netroots organizations, including their general shift from electing "more Democrats" to electing "better Democrats," and the comparable activities of rightroots/Tea Party groups. It concludes by discussing some of the medium-term effects that the election cycle has had on the Democratic Party coalition, and the increasing overlaps between legislative or issue-based mobilization and electoral mobilization.

Operating at the Intersection of Technology and Politics: The Netroots Generation

There are three attributes that make the political netroots distinct from the "interest group society" more generally:[10] (1) Whereas most interest groups, stemming from the interest group explosion of the 1970s, are devoted to a single issue area, netroots political associations tend to be issue generalists. (2) Whereas most membership-based interest groups define membership through annual dues payments, netroots organizations consider all e-mail supporters to be members. (3) Whereas traditional interest groups use those dues payments (and other revenue streams) to support a large lobbying program based in DC, netroots groups have minimal staffing and infrastructure. These three attributes are tied to one another, and actively influence the strategies the netroots employ in electoral politics.

Rather than representing a single issue area, groups like DFA, PCCC, MoveOn, and DailyKos are progressive generalists. Over the course of 2010, these groups sought to mobilize their membership on issues including health care, environment, women's rights, gay rights, and financial reform. The topic of their mobilization appeals is tightly linked to the day's political headlines. As a general rule, the issues covered by *The Rachel Maddow Show* and *Countdown with Keith Olbermann* (a pair of hour-long news commentary programs on *MSNBC* known for their liberal perspective) are the issues covered in a MoveOn political appeal.[11] This practice of *headline chasing* allows the organizations to direct member attention toward whichever topic is at the top of the political agenda, optimizing their ability to remain relevant to a fast-moving media cycle.

Internet-mediated issue generalists constantly test action alerts and message frames, sending them out to segments of their member list and measuring open rates and response rates of messages. They refer to this as a *culture of analytics,* and treat the resulting data as a proxy for public opinion amongst their membership base. At times, headline chasing leads them to augment the work of traditional single-issue interest groups, such as when the Senate held hearings on the military's "don't ask, don't tell" policy. At other times, it leads them to act as the only groups mobilizing citizen activity in an issue area, such as Keith Olbermann's brief suspension from *MSNBC* for making political donations. One clear benefit of this strategy is that it maximizes membership activation by focusing on the topics that are already primed for citizen response. Another is that there are many short-term topics of political controversy that are of interest to citizens, but do not fit within the purview of any public-interest advocacy groups. Rather than falling between the cracks, so to speak, these issue topics now receive mobilization attention from netroots associations. The drawback of this strategy is that it is of limited use in shaping the policy agenda. Whereas single-issue advocacy groups cultivate expertise, develop longstanding relationships with government decision makers, and spend years advancing policy proposals in the hopes of a window of opportunity for passage, netroots groups jump from topic to topic, mobilizing their large member lists around the issue of the day.[12]

The multi-issue, headline-chasing approach is particularly well suited to the netroots redefinition of organizational membership. This has been described as a shift from "issue based" membership to "activity based" membership.[13] Beginning in the 1970s with the propagation of direct mail nonprofit fundraising programs, interest groups long have sought to define themselves around a single-issue niche. This allows for identification and cultivation of citizens with particularly strong preferences on that issue, who can then form a stable donor or member base. List cultivation is particularly important because each piece of mail-based membership communication carries a marginal cost.[14] The marginal cost of e-mail-based communications approximates zero, so netroots groups seek instead to build much wider lists. Headline chasing allows them to expand their reach to a larger set of motivated progressives.[15]

Traditional interest groups use e-mail as well, but engage in less headline chasing than netroots groups. This is at least in part because of the path-dependent impact of organizational routines and staff structure. Netroots groups rely on small, nimble core staffs that can easily move from one issue to another. An organization with 30 staff can launch a new campaign much more easily than an organization with 300 staff. It is not that these organizations lack hierarchy altogether (MoveOn is hardly an anarchy), but rather that reduced scale leads to different hierarchies. These organizations instead rely on *phantom staff*—short-term contract employees, brought in to work for a limited-duration campaign—to enhance their effectiveness in election cycles.[16] Whereas institutional isomorphism has led single-issue interest groups to adopt similar staff structures and organizational routines,[17] netroots groups have largely been developed in response to the perceived shortcomings of the single-issue interest group model, along with the perceived opportunities provided by online communication.

Online traffic tends to approximate a power law distribution, leading to heavy concentrations of activity among a small set of hub sites.[18] A similar pattern is present among the netroots. Though the lowered costs of association building allow for a wide expansion of small (and usually short-term) organizations, the value derived from large member lists enables a concentration of activity among a small set of issue generalists. As such, in studying the political netroots, it is useful to distinguish between the large "hubs," with substantial member lists, name recognition, and organizational capacity, and the vast array of smaller niche groups. The netroots are not synonymous with all online organizing. They are, rather, a specific cluster of large organizations with shared best practices, organizational routines, and broad strategic stances. It is for this reason that the current chapter focuses solely upon DailyKos, MoveOn, DFA, and the PCCC. These groups constitute the largest hubs of electoral activity.

The practice of headline chasing leads to a different series of strategic priorities for netroots interest group leaders. Whereas environmental organizations, for instance, attempt to evaluate candidates on the basis of their environmental records, regardless of party status, the netroots are explicitly a Democratic constituency.

Groups like DailyKos have been harshly and publicly critical of left-leaning nonpartisan groups like the Sierra Club when those organizations have endorsed friendly Republicans in contested Senate races.[19] Rather than advancing a single-issue priority, the netroots instead are actively engaged in an intraparty rivalry within the Democratic network. They seek to displace centrist Democratic ideas and actors with ideas and actors stemming from the party's House Progressive Caucus. In so doing, they develop *organizational hybridity*—blending the strategic repertoires of traditional interest groups, social movement organizations, and political parties.[20]

Three specific results of this organizational hybridity are particularly relevant to the 2010 election. First, due to their constant headline chasing, netroots organizations use elections as an opportunity to pursue legislative politics by other means. Democratic incumbents who act as champions during the legislative session are rewarded. Democratic incumbents who frequently attract progressive ire are punished. This strategy presents itself in the Lincoln–Halter primary challenge. Second, the focus on intraparty competition leads the netroots to be especially active in Democratic primaries. No Democratic constituency (with the possible exception of labor) places such a high priority on recruiting and supporting strong primary candidates. And third, the hybrid repertoires and expertise in online political mobilization leads the groups to actively experiment with new technologies in electoral campaigns. In so doing, they play a role traditionally reserved for party organizations, further blending the distinctions between left-leaning interest groups and the broader party network. Each of these trends is discussed subsequently.

The Lincoln–Halter Primary Challenge

On February 22, 2010, MoveOn sent out an e-mail to its member list titled "An awful conservative Democrat." The opening sentences of the action alert made the organization's concerns clear:

> If the final health care reform bill doesn't include a public option, it'll be because of conservative Senate Democrats like Blanche Lincoln. After taking more than $700,000 from Big Insurance and HMO interests, she was one of just a handful of senators who vowed to filibuster health care reform until the public option was removed—and just Friday she denounced it again. But now we've got a huge opportunity to replace her, *and to send a powerful message to Washington that obstructing progressive legislation has heavy political costs.*[21]

The message, which included supporting quotes from Arkansas-based MoveOn members, linked to a petition urging Arkansas Lt. Gov. Bill Halter to challenge her in the Democratic primary. The resulting primary election became the central focus of netroots political associations over the following three months. The rhetorical linkage of the public option and the primary challenge is instructive: the netroots actively engaged in Democratic primary elections in order to further their legislative goals. Primaries served as another venue for pursuing their broad policy agenda—legislative politics by other means.

The technique of launching one of these *draft candidate petitions* is a common netroots tactic. It was used in the 2004 election to draft Wesley Clark into the presidential race, and used in 2006 to encourage James Webb to run for the Senate in Virginia. Candidate draft petitions are sent out in advance of the candidate entering the race (sometimes in quiet collaboration with the candidate, sometimes not). Using Facebook groups, Twitter accounts, web pages and e-mail, such petitions build a list of potential activists and donors, attract early media attention, and send signals that can discourage other challengers from entering the race. They send a credible signal that there is activist and donor support for the candidate. In Halter's case, progressive opposition to Blanche Lincoln had been brewing for months, and the petition served an additional purpose of acting as a pressure tactic around the Affordable Care Act. Netroots organizations that were still fighting hard for the inclusion of the public option were attempting to weaken Lincoln's opposition to the progressive policy option by threatening a well-funded primary challenge.

Bill Halter announced his primary challenge to Senator Lincoln one week after MoveOn's e-petition. Over the course of the following three months, the Arkansas Democratic Senate primary became a central campaign focus for netroots interest groups. MoveOn sent out eighteen action alerts to their national membership—fully one-third of the action alerts sent between March 1 and June 8 were devoted to the Halter–Lincoln race.[22] Nearly all of these messages included a donation link, and MoveOn members donated nearly $3 million to Halter's campaign. The Progressive Change Campaign Committee sent out fourteen messages—39 percent of their action alerts in that time frame—and generated over $250,000 in donations to the candidate's field campaign. The PCCC also lent out two staff members, Michael Snook and Keaunu Gregory, to direct the candidate's field program. Democracy for America sent out seventeen messages—34 percent of their action alerts—and collaborated with the PCCC on their fundraising and field mobilization efforts. DailyKos posted 120 front-page articles devoted to the Arkansas Senate race in that three-month time span as well, with links to an ActBlue fundraising page that contributed over $125,000 to the candidate.[23]

The level of attention paid to this race is particularly noteworthy given the other issues competing for attention at that time. Health care reform was a topic of intense debate in the Senate until its passage on March 21, occupying much of these organizations' available bandwidth. The Deepwater Horizon oil spill began on April 20 and continued unabated through mid-July. The Pennsylvania Democratic Senate primary was scheduled for the same day as the Arkansas primary. It also received the attention of these organizations, with Rep. Joe Sestak

(Pa. District 7) challenging and ultimately defeating incumbent Sen. Arlen Specter (D-Pa.), who had switched parties in 2009 to avoid a right-wing primary challenge. The Pennsylvania Senate primary received less attention than the Arkansas race though, with three messages from DFA, zero from PCCC, and zero from MoveOn. Sestak's challenge to Specter had attracted previous attention from the netroots; the two of them took part in a lunchtime debate at the 2009 Netroots Nation annual convention, and their race attracted thirty-four front-page articles on DailyKos between March 1 and the May 18 Pennsylvania Democratic primary. Those front-page articles lacked a donation link, however, as DailyKos was offering poll coverage and race analysis, rather than mobilizing its online reader-base to support the more liberal candidate. The Arkansas Senate primary was the biggest priority for the netroots during primary season—a natural outgrowth of their long-running fight over the public option.

Labor unions—including the AFL-CIO, Service Employees International Union (SEIU), and American Federation of State, County and Municipal Employees (AFSCME)—made the Arkansas Senate primary a priority as well, investing several million dollars in the outcome of the race.[24] A key distinction between the political netroots and organized labor, however, lies in where they devoted these resources. Labor organizations set up their own independent campaign operations. Netroots organizations, by contrast, contributed resources directly to the Halter campaign. Their capacity for bundling small online donations led to direct campaign donations. Embedded field staff integrated traditional get-out-the-vote activities with a distributed call-out-the-vote program (detailed in a subsequent section), in which PCCC, DFA, DailyKos, and MoveOn members could obtain lists of Democratic voters and make election day reminder calls from home. This is one reason why *Citizens United* had such a limited direct impact on netroots organizations. The existing strengths of their strategic repertoire—bundling small donations and coordinating online volunteer efforts—could already be integrated into close coordination with candidate campaigns. Changing the boundaries for independent corporate expenditure thus offered them few new opportunities.

Halter's challenge to Lincoln proved effective enough to prompt a runoff election. On May 18, Senator Lincoln received 45 percent of the vote, with Lt. Gov. Halter receiving 43 percent and a third candidate receiving the remaining votes. Arkansas primaries require a majority vote, so this necessitated a runoff election on June 8, which Lincoln then won by a 52 to 48 percent margin. In the aftermath of that election, an unnamed administration official offered harsh words for labor and netroots groups, calling Politico.com reporter Ben Smith and telling him, "Organized labor just flushed $10 million of their members' money down the toilet in a pointless exercise. If even half that total had been well-targeted and applied in key House races across this country, that could have made a real difference in November."[25] AFL-CIO spokesman Eddie Vale offered a pointed response that "labor isn't an arm of the Democratic Party."[26] Both MoveOn and PCCC offered a similar perspective in follow-up e-mails to their membership, quoting Greg Sargent of *The Washington Post*. Sargent's reaction to the White House quote was as follows, "Make no mistake: Progressive activists and labor mounted a challenge that was barely months in the making, and rallying behind Bill Halter, came within a hair of unseating a longtime incumbent who had the backing of the entire Democratic establishment.... No matter what you read about this, the Halter challenge was a show of force by the left. Period."[27]

The strategic choice of whether or not to engage in primary challenges tells us much about an interest group's broader position within the party network. Netroots interest groups self-define as "progressive," but this should not be confused with third-party support. Leaders such as Markos Moulitsas display an outright hostility to Green Party supporters whom he considers unrealistic. Senior staff in MoveOn, PCCC, and DFA are former labor organizers and Democratic Party operatives. The netroots view themselves as part of the progressive wing of the Democratic Party coalition, and they seek to advance policy goals by pressuring the party leadership. Where they depart from other left-leaning interest groups is in their calculus of the value of a strong primary challenge. Lacking a substantial lobbying presence on Capitol Hill, the netroots display little concern for endangering relationships with congressional staffers. They view themselves as complementing "inside" lobbying strategies with aggressive "outside" mobilization efforts. This is particularly in keeping with their lack of long-term DC infrastructure. Headline chasing is designed for a rapidly moving media agenda, but does a poor job of influencing the issues that rise on the public's agenda. Heavy involvement in Democratic primaries helps these groups to exert an influence over the broader state of the party platform.

Blanche Lincoln was a particularly attractive target for two reasons. First was her voting record. With a sixty-seat Democratic Senate majority for most of the 111th Congress, Lincoln occupied an important veto point. Without Lincoln's support, Democratic legislation could not overcome a Republican filibuster. The netroots felt she had used this power to extract too many policy concessions, both regarding health care reform and other pieces of the progressive agenda. Like Connecticut senator Joe Lieberman in 2006, the netroots attempted to send a signal to centrist Democratic legislators through a robust challenge to Lincoln.

The second reason was Lincoln's early polling numbers. Election forecasters had concluded early on that the Arkansas Senate seat was a near-certain Republican pickup. Lincoln was deeply unpopular in her state, trailing likely Republican challenger John Boozman by a 56 to 33 percent margin in a February 2010 survey by Public Policy Polling ("off-the-charts bad" poll numbers, to quote the well-respected election-blogger Nate Silver).[28] Early polls also showed Halter losing to Boozman, but by smaller margins and with lower name recognition, leading netroots organizations to argue that he had a better chance of defending the seat than his incumbent opponent. Indeed, Markos Moulitsas highlighted early poll results indicating that Halter, though still favored to lose a general election race, fared better than Lincoln in matchups with Boozman and other Republican candidates.[29]

In general, these netroots organizations viewed the primary challenge to Lincoln to be a "free shot," of sorts. If she had been conservative-but-popular in her state, there would have been a strong rationale against challenging her, the reasoning being that a senator caucusing with the Democrats will side with liberal interests more often than a member of the highly disciplined Republican Party. Lincoln's poor standing in her home state left netroots interest groups with no such concern. By their reasoning, she was bound to lose her seat either in the primary or in the general election. They believed Halter to be at least a marginally stronger candidate, but just as important, they believed that a stiff primary challenge would send a message to competing segments of the party network. The risks and opportunity costs were minimal, because they were not putting an additional Senate seat in danger. As an added benefit, some in the netroots argued that a primary challenge from the left would push Lincoln to take more progressive policy stances during the course of the primary campaign, so as to mute progressive critiques. Netroots observers credited the strong stance she took on derivatives reform in the Wall Street reform bill to this primary challenge.[30]

In formulating their challenge to Senator Lincoln, netroots groups were modifying a well-trodden strategy developed by the conservative Club for Growth in 2000, and further pursued by rightroots/Tea Party groups in 2010. Through aggressive primary challenges, conservative interest groups have demonstrated a credible threat to those centrist officials who depart from Republican orthodoxy. As the following section demonstrates, that strategy was on full display in 2010.

Conservative Parallels

The netroots perspective on primary challenge is based upon observation of conservative successes within the Republican Party network. Since 2000, the conservative Club for Growth has invested heavily in primary challenges of centrist Republicans. Though rarely producing outright victories, these challenges have helped to attach a significant cost in the decision calculus of centrist Republicans on legislative issues. The Club for Growth (and, in 2010, the Tea Party movement) has supported conservative challengers across the country, regardless of incumbency or the partisan district composition. Witnessing the strong Republican Party unity around orthodox conservative policy positions, the netroots have reasoned that robust primary challenges could likewise serve as an effective tool within the Democratic Party network.[31]

Rightroots organizations, operating under the Tea Party metabrand in 2010, continued this tradition of aggressive primary challenges. Beginning in Utah, where the Republican Party selects their Senate nominee through a convention, incumbent senator Bob Bennett was unseated by two challengers, Mike Lee and Tim Bridgewater. The Utah primary convention presented some extreme circumstances—less than 3,500 Republican partisans took part in the balloting, giving a strong voice to the most active and motivated party activists. It nonetheless served as an encouraging signal to conservative activists and donors, as well as media watchdogs. For the next several months, Tea Party challengers emerged in several states to challenge centrist incumbents and leadership-supported candidates. In Kentucky, Tea Party–supported Rand Paul defeated Trey Grayson, despite Grayson's support from Mitch McConnell (R-Ky.), who was both the senior senator from Kentucky and the Republican Senate minority leader. In Nevada, state assembly member Sharron Angle defeated party leadership-backed Sue Lowden. In Colorado, Ken Buck defeated former lieutenant governor Jane Norton. In Florida, state senator Marco Rubio bested sitting Republican governor Charlie Crist. In Alaska, Tea Party–backed Joe Miller beat sitting senator Lisa Murkowski. Perhaps most famously, Delaware Tea Party candidate Christine O'Donnell pulled off a surprise upset of centrist representative Mike Castle (R-At Large). Castle's loss in the primary converted the race from an almost-certain Republican pickup to a likely Democratic hold, leading Karl Rove (former Bush administration strategist and current head of the American Crossroads super PAC) to publicly lash out at the Tea Party strategy on Fox News.

Because of the diffuse structure of the Tea Party movement, rightroots activity around these races varied dramatically (See Chapter 9). The Tea Party is more of an overarching metabrand than it is a cohesive network of organizations. With nonprofits, PACs, super PACs, independent-expenditure committees, and even for-profit businesses declaring themselves as members of the Tea Party, almost any segment of the conservative activist base can stake an equal claim to the Tea Party mantle. The segments that were most active in the election were locally based conservative groups, nationally based advocacy organizations such as FreedomWorks and Americans for Prosperity, and large-donor super PACs. The combination of these diffuse elements provided Tea Party candidates with motivated volunteers and a steady stream of donations. Rather than coming from a small set of visible organizations, however, these resources came through an opaque network of organizations, with some organizations providing volunteers and others providing funding or campaign consultants.

Tea Party groups were at their strongest in local primaries, where low turnout (relative to the general election) favored a motivated activist base. This was not, however, an Internet-driven activity. Conservative bloggers and online activists primarily focused on message dissemination rather than political mobilization.[32] They took to Twitter's microblogging platform in droves, using the surface to drive links to web pages and longer blog posts. They also actively embraced Facebook, supporting candidate "fan" pages and creating supporter groups.[33] It is unclear what impact, if any, Twitter and Facebook activity had on election outcomes, however. To date, no researcher has been able to demonstrate an impact of these—the newest of new media platforms—on fundraising, volunteer levels, turnout, or other traditional metrics of campaign success. In the areas where the Tea Party was most influential in the 2010 election, it was expanding upon the tried-and-true strategies the Club for Growth developed over the previous decade (See chapter 8 on emulation). Organizations operating under the Tea Party banner—some of them rightroots, others more traditional—presented credible challengers to virtually every centrist Republican candidate.

The Open Seat Project

The netroots concern over costing centrist Democrats is a critical difference between their primary strategy and the strategies the conservative Tea Party and Club for Growth have employed. These conservative groups seek to offer primary challenges everywhere, regardless of partisan district makeup. The result has indeed been increased party unity, but it has come from three sources: (1) election of more conservative public officials, (2) greater adherence to conservative orthodoxy among existing elected officials, and (3) the replacement of centrist Republican-elected officials with Democratic opponents. This third source, most obvious through the near-complete disappearance of northeast Republican senators and representatives, is a loss for the party. The netroots have sought to develop a more nuanced primary strategy, challenging select incumbents opportunistically, rather than challenging all centrist incumbents regardless of partisan district makeup. Beyond the Arkansas Senate Democratic primary, this also is evidenced through the Open Seat Project, a second major netroots undertaking during the 2010 primary season.

In keeping with the netroots emphasis on intraparty competition, these Internet-mediated organizations adopted a limited approach for increasing the power of the Democratic Party's Progressive Caucus through the 2010 election cycle. This included two prongs: support for longstanding champions such as Alan Grayson (Fla. District 8), Raul Grijalva (Ariz. District 7), Jared Polis (Colo. District 2) and Chellie Pingree (Maine District 1), and support for progressive candidates in open-seat primary races. The support for progressive champions, at least during the early months, was relatively straightforward. After Polis, Pingree, and Grayson coauthored a sign-on letter in the House, calling for the public option to be passed through reconciliation,[34] the PCCC and DFA held an online fundraiser for them, raising over $100,000 in small donations.[35] The open-seat strategy was more interesting and innovative. Lacking the financial resources of free-spending conservative super PACs such as American Crossroads, and cognizant of the Democrats' endangered majority status, the netroots chose to focus on a very limited set of primary challenges. Rather than supporting left-wing challengers to members of the centrist Blue Dog Coalition, PCCC and DFA invested resources on recruiting and supporting viable progressive candidates in open-seat races.

The PCCC named this the Open Seat Project, and placed organizers with a handful of progressive candidates across the country. DFA called it the "Primaries Matter Pledge."[36] The rationale in both cases involved maximizing the value of activist enthusiasm and field mobilization in areas that would not endanger the Democratic majority. Both groups chose to focus on reliably Democratic electoral districts that had been vacated due to incumbents retiring or running for a different office. In Rhode Island's 1st congressional district, for instance, incumbent Patrick Kennedy chose not to run for reelection. A strongly Democratic district, with a Cook Partisan Voting Index score of D+13, both groups chose to endorse state representative David Segal, an outspoken progressive and former member of the Green Party. PCCC's Greg Ross, deputy political director, moved to Providence for several months in order to help set up the candidate's field operation.[37]

Through early expert campaign support and e-mail alerts to their national list, netroots interest groups attempt to give an organizational advantage to progressive political candidates. They devote their distributed get-out-the-vote calling programs and national fundraising efforts to help boost turnout in targeted Democratic primaries. In so doing, these groups attempt to strengthen the Democratic Progressive Caucus without endangering congressional majorities or directly targeting Blue Dog Democrats. Rather than investing heavily in challenges to incumbent centrists, as the Club for Growth and Tea Party groups do, netroots groups sought to maximize their influence in those Democrat-leaning districts where a retirement creates an open primary. In so doing, they are again engaging in an intraparty rivalry, seeking to selectively apply resources in locations where competing segments of the party apparatus exercise a high degree of gate-keeping control. Some of these candidates, like Segal, failed to win their primary, while others, like Ann Marie Kuster (N.H. District 2) defeated their centrist opponents.

The focus on open-seat primary races was at least partially influenced by the shadow cast by Organizing For America (OFA), the quasi-netroots offshoot of the Obama presidential campaign. With a list of 13 million supporters, OFA is larger than any independent advocacy group. Housed within the Democratic National Committee, OFA had engaged in citizen mobilization around health care, Wall Street reform, and a variety of other topics supporting the President's agenda. OFA operates using many of the same tactics as netroots organizations—e-mail mobilization messages, distributed calling tools, online fundraising, and so forth—but has a dramatically different strategic repertoire. Given its role within the Democratic Party, OFA consistently supported incumbents in contested Democratic primaries. In Arkansas, where Obama pledged support for Blanche Lincoln, OFA provided field support for the centrist incumbent. In open-seat races, by contrast, OFA remained neutral.

The sheer size of OFA's list demanded strategic repositioning by the political netroots. OFA's member list and association with President Obama and the formal party apparatus meant that it would be a central contender for online volunteer hours and donations in the general election. If online activists were going to engage in political mobilization through groups other than OFA, it would have to be in areas where OFA was not engaging—areas like open-seat races, where the national party apparatus was remaining neutral.

General Election: Incumbent Defense and Modest Technological Innovations

Moving into the general election, netroots groups sought to engage their online membership in selecting priority candidates. Through online vote processes pioneered in the 2004 and 2006 election cycles,[38] the groups sought primarily to determine which Democratic incumbents most excited their grassroots membership base. The technique was particularly important in 2010 due to the general deflation of left-wing volunteer enthusiasm. Democracy for America sought to nationalize a limited set of races, inviting their membership to vote in a "Grassroots All-Star" competition, which winnowed a pool of Democratic candidates down to a single race where they would focus heavy attention. The design of the competition, in which ten candidates were selected, then narrowed to five, then concluding with one, encouraged local activists to get involved with the DFA network, building its member rolls in the process. They eventually selected Beth Krom, the former mayor of Irvine, California. Krom would later lose her election challenge to Republican incumbent John Campbell.

MoveOn similarly invited its member list to nominate "progressive heroes," and eventually selected four priority campaigns: senators Barbara Boxer (Calif.), and Russ Feingold (Wis.), and representatives Alan Grayson (Fla. District 8) and Tom Perriello (Va. District 5). It bears noting that each of these campaigns focused on supporting incumbents who had stood up for netroots priorities in the past. Facing the prevailing anti-incumbent winds and recognizing that netroots small donors would be heavily outspent by conservative super PACs, the netroots made the strategic decision not to compete everywhere. Leaving the lion's share of Democratic races to the party apparatus, including the Democratic Congressional Campaign Committee (DCCC), Democratic Senatorial Campaign Committee (DSCC), and Organizing for America, the netroots instead focused on protecting their champions. Both DailyKos and PCCC also focused attention on defending Rep. Raul Grijalva, the Arizona-based chair of the Congressional Progressive Caucus, against a tough Republican challenger. MoveOn volunteers were encouraged to support local candidates in close races, but their nationwide fundraising and mobilization efforts were reserved for these key champions.

DailyKos, in its hybrid role as advocacy group and quasi-news organization, was the only major netroots organization to respond actively to the activities of the Tea Party. Tea Party Senate candidates Sharron Angle (Nev.), Christine O'Donnell (Del.), Ken Buck (Colo.), Rand Paul (Ky.) and Joe Miller (Alaska) all defeated establishment-backed candidates in their Republican primaries, creating a number of additional competitive Senate races. Though DailyKos does not employ any full-time reporters (unlike other progressive political blogs like Talking Points Memo and Huffington Post), its front-page authors do frequently comment on the news. As Angle, O'Donnell, Paul, and others made news headlines, Markos Moulitsas and his colleagues sought to frame the Tea Party movement as an extreme, John Birch–style arm of the Republican Party coalition. These framing efforts had strong equivalents at top right-wing blogs like RedState.com and HotAir.com. DailyKos's mobilization efforts, however, lacked a right-wing equivalent. And these remained devoted to a much smaller set of priority candidates. DailyKos did choose to add three Senate Democrats to their endorsement list—Chris Coons (Del.), Scott McAdams (Alaska), and Jack Conway (Ky.), but they did not choose to compete with the Tea Party in every district.[39]

DailyKos also frequently promoted links to Democratic Party microsites designed to capitalize on the Republican candidate gaffes, fueling additional media coverage around issues deemed beneficial to the Democratic Party. A *microsite* is an independent website launched around a single-issue topic, not directly tied to an organization's broader web offerings. As one example, when Republican Nevada Senate candidate Sue Lowden made a gaffe in discussing health care, suggesting that Nevadans could revert to a bartering system in which patients paid their doctor with a chicken, the DSCC quickly launched a microsite, chickensforcheckups.com, which let people choose medical procedures and then calculated the number of "chickens" that would be required as payment.[40] Lowden, the leading Republican candidate at the time, was roundly mocked for this claim, and the microsite helped emphasize this mistake, providing fodder for additional media coverage and late night talk-show commentary.

Netroots interest groups deployed several technological tools in the 2010 election, but as a whole they were modest innovations in comparison to previous election cycles. MoveOn.org, for instance, created a viral GOTV video one week before the election. Titled "Back from the Future," the Terminator-themed four-minute video starred actress Olivia Wilde as a post-apocalyptic time traveler, warning the recipient that their decision not to vote on election day enables a Republican takeover of the House, with outlandishly disastrous consequences. Through integration with Facebook, the video was able to incorporate pictures and location names personalized to each individual recipient.[41] MoveOn members forwarded the video to their personal networks through Facebook, and it was viewed over 500,000 times. MoveOn had used a similar video in the 2008 election, but the 2010 video appears to boast a higher degree of personalized Facebook integration.

Likewise, Progressive Change Campaign Committee and Democracy for America partnered to launch CallOutTheVote.com, a microsite designed to support distributed GOTV calls (see Figure 10.1). The site lets volunteers download a list of likely candidate supporters in a given district, along with a call script and their polling place. Motivated volunteers across state lines can thus augment field operations in priority races without leaving home, augmenting a central electoral practice historically reserved for party organizations. Distributed GOTV in 2010 was not a new campaign technique—it has been used at least since the 2004 election—but the scale and the sophistication of the operation set records. PCCC and DFA volunteers made over 1 million GOTV phone calls in the final days of the 2010 election.

These modest innovations did little if anything to change the overall tide of the 2010 election, of course. Of the four candidates prioritized by MoveOn, only Barbara Boxer avoided defeat. Ann Kuster, the Open Seat Project candidate in New Hampshire's 2nd district, lost a close race, as did Sen. Russ Feingold and several others. Raul Grijalva was reelected, but he was one of many candidates who, months earlier, netroots groups had not expected would face such tough challenges. Between

FIGURE 10.1   Screenshot of CallOutTheVote.com

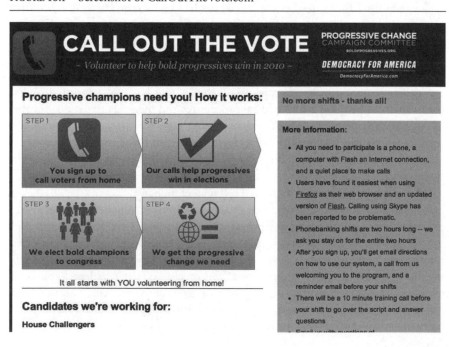

the poor state of the economy, anti-incumbent sentiment, the flood of corporate contributions post–*Citizens United* and the emergence of the Tea Party, the political netroots were not a central part of the general 2010 election narrative. Rather, their activities help indicate trends in the ongoing professionalization of online campaign techniques and Internet-mediated advocacy group political involvement.

Conclusion

On Wednesday, November 3, PCCC cofounder Stephanie Taylor woke up early, logged into her e-mail account, and set her Google-chat status to a simple message: "Back to Work." Her organization had worked ceaselessly since early March on election-related activities—focusing at first on the Open Seat Project and the Arkansas Senate primary, then turning attention to the general election. The 1 million GOTV calls produced through CallOutTheVote.com had been a monumental organizational success, but the results had doubtless been dispiriting. All of the major netroots groups sent out membership-wide messages, summarizing the disappointing results, summarizing levels of volunteer activity and membership fundraising, and pressing a hopeful long-term vision for progressive policies. Within days, then, they got back to work, focusing on the next set of political issues that demanded membership attention. Election seasons provide a venue for advancing netroots issue priorities: building power within the party network, positioning their organizations to advance liberal policy proposals, and sharpening their expertise in technology and politics. When election season ends, they switch to the next set of opportunities.

Intraparty rivalry is a key feature of the 2010 election cycle. In the days that followed, netroots groups were quick to point out that centrist Blue Dog Democrats had fared at least as poorly as progressive candidates. Within weeks, they had refocused member attention on the latest set of political headlines—the debate over extension of the Bush tax cuts, repeal of "don't ask, don't tell" policy, and other lame duck session priorities. For a set of organizations that engage in headline chasing, this should perhaps be unsurprising. Netroots groups focus on electoral mobilization when elections are the focus of our national attention. When the election ends, they pivot to the next set of legislative issues. Rather than focusing on countering the Tea Party movement, the netroots focus on supporting their congressional champions and challenging their biggest opponents within the party network. Likewise, Tea Party organizations experienced their greatest successes in challenging centrist Republican candidates. The wave of newly elected Republican officials was even more deeply partisan than the membership of the 111th Congress (2009–10).

The long-term effectiveness of this strategy will bear further scholarly attention. One incidental impact of *Citizens United* seems to be a relative devaluation of netroots key resources. Whereas small-dollar online bundling can still provide millions in direct support to the right candidates, the utility of those donations decreases as outside interests are free to spend unlimited quantities. Given their generally anti-corporate positioning, *Citizens United* has opened up no new avenues for the netroots, while diminishing the relative value of their fundraising capacity. Netroots groups continue to make campaign finance reform an issue priority, but the near-term landscape for legislative reform appears bleak.

More generally, while high-profile challenges to centrist Democrats like Blanche Lincoln and primary campaign support for viable progressive candidates can help strengthen the Congressional Progressive Caucus, it is unclear whether these efforts will achieve results similar to the conservative Club for Growth. It was not the rightroots elements of the Tea Party metabrand that drove success in Republican primaries, but the extended Club for Growth–style groups, along with the locally based activist organizations. Progressive Democrats have sought to emulate the strategies of conservative interest groups in increasing party unity through primary challenges, but they have modified the strategy to avoid losing contested seats in centrist territory. Against a host of other variables governing party competition, it is too early to tell what impact, if any, this endorsement strategy will have on the vote calculus of elected officials.

Netroots electoral strategies were forged in the 2006 and 2008 elections—two wave elections that favored the Democratic Party, and 2010 featured strategic repositioning among these groups. Facing a motivated Tea Party, well-funded opposition, and generally anti-incumbent public opinion, the netroots sought to support key congressional champions. Particularly in light of OFA's activity, which boasted similar technological sophistication and a massive member list, netroots groups did not seek to support Democrats everywhere. Rather, they focused attention on those races where their motivated online-supporter base would be most energized, and used that activist attention to bolster their long-term power within the party network while seeking to affect the outcome of a few close priority races. Looking ahead to 2012, we should expect the netroots to continue promoting their congressional champions, pursuing a selective primary strategy and using electoral periods as a venue for furthering their priority legislative goals.

Endnotes

1 Matthew Kerbel, *Netroots: Online Progressives and the Transformation of American Politics* (Boulder, CO: Paradigm Publishers, 2009).
2 David Karpf, "Online Political Mobilization from the Advocacy Group's Perspective: Looking Beyond Clicktivism," *Policy & Internet* 2, no. 4 (2010): Article 2.
3 MoveOn Staff, "People Powered Politics 2008: MoveOn Post-Election Report." (December 2008), http://s3.moveon.org/pdfs/moveon_postelectionreport_ah14.pdf.
4 David Karpf, "Macaca Moments Reconsidered: Electoral Panopticon or Netroots Mobilization?" *Journal of Information Technology and Politics* 7, no. 2, (2010): 143–62.
5 David Karpf, *The MoveOn Effect: Unexpected Transformation of American Political Advocacy* (New York: Oxford University Press, 2012).

6   The two terms are used interchangeably. Most netroots leaders have adopted the term *progressive*, due to negative public connotations associated with the term *liberal*. Others, in particular the leadership of LivingLiberally.org, have sought to reclaim the term liberal.

7   Rasmus Kleis Nielsen and Cristian Vaccari, "Twitter in the Midterms," Blog post, http://rasmuskleisnielsen.net/2010/11/15/twitter-in-the-midterms/ (November 15, 2010.)

8   Karpf, *The MoveOn Effect: Unexpected Transformation of American Political Advocacy.*

9   Karpf, "Macaca Moments Reconsidered."

10 Jeffrey Berry, *The Interest Group Society* (New York: Little, Brown, 1984). Also see Jeffrey Berry, *The New Liberalism* (Washington, DC: Brookings Institution Press, 1999).

11 Karpf "Online Political Mobilization from the Advocacy Group's Perspective."

12 See John Kingdon, *Agendas, Alternatives, and Public Policies* (New York: Longman, 1984) for a discussion of policy windows, or "windows of opportunity." Not all netroots organizations are issue generalists. The lowered operating costs of the organizational model gives rise to a set of niche specialists as well—groups like the Courage Campaign, Change Congress, and 1Sky.org. As a rule, these niche organizations are much smaller than their generalist brethren, and few of them engage in electoral mobilization.

13 Bruce Bimber, *Information and American Democracy* (Cambridge, UK: Cambridge University Press, 2003).

14 For a discussion of nonprofit fundraising practices, see Kim Klein, *Fundraising for Social Change,* 3rd ed. (Berkeley, CA: Chardon Press, 1994).

15 The scale of these organizations is still small in comparison to the total U.S. population— MoveOn is the largest group, with over 5 million members (less than 2 percent of the U.S. population). Demographically, there is no indication that netroots organizations are doing any better at mobilizing underrepresented segments of the U.S. population than their single-issue equivalents. See Kay Lehman Schlozman, Sidney Verba and Henry Brady, "Weapon of the Strong? Participatory Inequality and the Internet," *Perspectives on Politics* 8, no. 2 (2010): 487–509.

16 Karpf, *The MoveOn Effect.*

17 Paul Dimaggio and W. Powell, "The Iron Cage Revisited: Institutional Isomorphism and Collective Rationality in Organizational Fields," *American Sociological Review* 48 (1983): 147–160.

18 Matthew Hindman, *The Myth of Digital Democracy*, (Princeton, NJ: Princeton University Press, 2008).

19 The 2006 endorsement of Lincoln Chafee (R-R.I.) was one such example. See Markos Moulitsas, "RI-Sen: Morons at the Sierra Club," *DailyKos.com*, April 20, 2006, www.dailykos.com/story/2006/04/20/203557/-RI-Sen:-Morons-at-the-Sierra-Club?via=search.

20 Andrew Chadwick, "Digital Network Repertoires and Organizational Hybridity," *Political Communication* 24, no. 3 (2007): 283–301.

21 Adam Ruben, e-mail message to MoveOn distribution list, February 22, 2010 (emphasis added).

22 Based on data compiled through the Membership Communications Project, see Karpf "Online Political Mobilization from the Advocacy Group's Perspective," for details.

23   Entry "Orange to Blue 2010," https://secure.actblue.com/entity/fundraisers/23963.

24   Ben Smith, "White House Official: 'Organized labor just flushed $10 million down the toilet.'" *Politico.com,* June 8, 2010, www.politico.com/blogs/bensmith/0610/White_House_official_Organized_labor_just_flushed_10_million_of_their_members_money_down_the_toilet_.html.

25   Ibid.

26   Ibid.

27   Greg Sargent, "Election Night Open Thread," *WashingtonPost.com,* June 8, 2010, http://voices.washingtonpost.com/plum-line/2010/06/election_night_open_thread_1.html

28   Nate Silver, "Lincoln Logs a Challenger as Halter Tries to Halt Her—But Are Democrats Spinning Their Wheels?" fivethirtyeight.com, March 1, 2010, www.fivethirtyeight.com/2010/03/lincoln-logs-challenger-as-halter-tries.html.

29   Markos Moulitsas, "AR-Sen: Halter Gains on Lincoln, Strongest vs GOP," DailyKos.com, March 25, 2010, www.dailykos.com/story/2010/03/25/850719/-AR-Sen:-Halter-gains-on-Lincoln,-strongest-vs-GOP?via=search.

30   Joan McCarter, "AR-Sen and Wall Street Reform: The Value of a Good Primary Challenge," DailyKos.com, May 13, 2010, www.dailykos.com/story/2010/05/13/866174/-AR-Sen-and-Wall-Street-reform:-The-value-of-a-good-primary-challenge?via=search.

31   See https://secure.actblue.com/page/olbd for a discussion of this "Better Democrats" philosophy.

32   Karpf, *The MoveOn Effect,* ch. 6.

33   Nielsen and Vaccari, "Twitter in the Midterms."

34   Reconciliation bills cannot be filibustered in the Senate, thus requiring fifty-one votes rather than sixty votes for passage, changing the relevant veto point.

35   Adam Green, "Thanks...," e-mail to Progressive Change Campaign Committee distribution list, February 10, 2010.

36   Jim Dean, "Better Democrats," e-mail to Democracy for America distribution list, March 19, 2010.

37   Full disclosure: The author served as supporter housing for part of Ross's visit, and also volunteered briefly with Segal's campaign while a Rhode Island resident.

38   MoveOn held its first "MoveOn primary" in the 2004 Presidential campaign, attracting heavy media attention through its full-membership vote on whether or not to endorse a presidential candidate prior to the Iowa Caucuses. Democracy for America premiered an online endorsement system through its DFALink system in 2006.

39   ActBlue, https://secure.actblue.com/page/orangetoblue2010.

40   Huffington Post staff, "Chickens for Checkups? Democrats New Website Mocks Sue Lowden for Barter-for-Healthcare Proposal," HuffingtonPost.com, April 21, 2010, www.huffingtonpost.com/2010/04/21/chickens-for-checkups-dem_n_546762.html

41   See The Daily Beast, www.thedailybeast.com/video/item/olivia-wildes-moveon-back-from-the-future-campaign-ad-.

CHAPTER 11

Interest Groups Unleashed

Beyond the 2010 Election Cycle

Paul S. Herrnson, Christopher J. Deering, Clyde Wilcox

> *You, the Colbert Nation, could have a voice in the form of my voice shouted through a megaphone made of cash.*
> —Stephen Colbert, 2011[1]

So said the comedian Stephen Colbert to his audience on *The Colbert Report* as part of his long running political satire poking fun at the implications of recent free speech rulings by the U.S. Supreme Court. The on-show shtick was not enough, of course; Colbert also announced his intention to form a new independent expenditure-only committee, a super PAC, called Americans for a Better Tomorrow, Tomorrow (ABTT). And he did just that in much ballyhooed visits to the FEC, first to file and then to seek rulings on the legal parameters governing its operation. Because ABTT must reveal the identities of its contributors, Colbert next organized a 501(c)(4) group, the Colbert Super PAC SHH, which may spend independently as much as Colbert can raise and is *not* required to report the identity of its donors.[2]

In keeping with the theme of Colbert's gambit, interest groups were indeed unleashed prior to the 2010 national elections. A series of Supreme Court decisions, culminating with the January 21, 2010 landmark case *Citizens United v. Federal Election Commission*, has left corporations, labor unions, and citizen groups effectively unfettered in the use of funds from their own treasuries to mount independent media campaigns in direct support for or opposition to candidates for federal office.[3] And, as we have seen in the preceding chapters, many did just that. In addition, the *Citizens* decision and a follow-up appeals court decision in *SpeechNow.org v. FEC*, created a major new organizational form, the so-called super PAC, that may accept unlimited contributions from individuals, companies, and other groups, and spend this money in independent expenditures directly advocating the election or defeat of federal candidates.[4] But perhaps the major impact of these rulings, combined with the decisions of other federal courts and the FEC, was to further empower the full range of interest group organizations—527s, 501(c)s, and PACs—that compete in the electoral process.

As the chapters in this volume make clear, this did not mean that all groups responded to the *Citizens* decision in the same way. Groups in some sectors, defense and health care for example, largely chose to "stay the course" through the 2010 election cycle. That is, they did not form new super PACs, 527s, or 501(c)s, and they did not engage in large-scale independent expenditures or electioneering communications. Instead, these groups mostly rewarded incumbents, balanced their contributions across both political parties, and pursued what is generally called an *access strategy*—that is, a strategy that ensures easy access to policymakers rather than one that seeks to change the balance of political forces (see Chapter 3 and Chapter 4 for details).

By contrast, others—American Crossroads, the Club for Growth, and the National Education Association, for example—did quickly establish super PACs as a means to make their voices heard more loudly than in previous elections. In fact, in total, the eighty-four super PACs organized for the 2010 election cycle reported spending more than $65 million. American Crossroads was by far the loudest of those voices with over $21 million in expenditures (see Chapter 8), while Club for Growth doled out nearly $5 million, and the NEA Advocacy Fund just over $4 million. Although, to be sure, super PACs have received the most attention, they are far from the whole story. As reported in Chapter 8, Crossroads GPS, the 501(c)(4) counterpart to Crossroads, spent more than $16 million in the 2010 cycle. And the U.S. Chamber of Commerce, to date, remains a 501(c)(6). This has enabled this deep–pocketed group to shell out $33 million in electioneering communications without revealing who contributed the money or which candidates it supported or opposed (again, see Chapter 2).

So with each year the electoral advocacy landscape becomes more diverse and legally more Byzantine, as detailed in Chapter 1. It remains an open question whether more groups will shift their election strategies to exploit the new regulatory environment, if new regulations will result from further court rulings or new legislation, or if some combination of these possibilities will take place. But it is quite clear that interest groups employ an increasingly wide variety of organizational forms to pursue their electoral goals. This confusing array is attended by a variety of different restrictions and disclosure requirements, offering interest groups myriad choices in how to structure their involvement.

The case studies in the preceding chapters are not, however, just about changing legal circumstances. Changing technology also allowed interest groups to use the Internet in new and creative ways, developing microsites for particular candidates, and using social networking and other new forms of communication.

Internet advertising, for example, came into its own in 2010, as a new generation of interest group activists began to consider how to move beyond the dwindling circulations, market shares, and scattershot readership or viewership of old media.

Finally, the growing Republican tsunami gave many groups incentives to either protect Democratic incumbents or to invest heavily in GOP challengers and open-seat candidates, particularly ideological groups and others that are closely associated with one party. In the final weeks of the campaign groups reacted quickly to changing fortunes of individual candidates, cutting loose those unlikely to win in order to concentrate their activities on those who were still viable. In the end the 2010 elections continued a trend of wave elections that began in 1994, when the Republicans gained fifty-four House seats, and then continued in 2006 and 2008 with a combined Democratic pickup of fifty-two seats. The Republican gain of sixty-three House seats and six Senate seats ushered in another period of divided government—the norm since the 1968 elections.

Regulations and Resources

The case studies in this volume help us better understand whether and how groups change their strategies in response to relaxed regulations in an election with strong partisan winds. Since passage of the comprehensive amendments to the Federal Election Campaign Act (FECA) in 1974, there have been three distinct regulatory regimes governing the way that interest groups are active in federal elections (again, see Chapter 1).

From 1976 through the late 1980s interest group activity was mostly confined to PACs. It took several elections for the PAC system to mature, but by 1984 there were more than 4,000 PACs registered with the FEC. By channeling interest group activity through PACs, the FECA advantaged groups with large numbers of individual members over those with a few wealthy patrons. The maximum individual contribution to a PAC was $5,000, and an organization's treasury funds could be used to offset only the expenses of administering the PAC. Moreover, PAC contributions to candidates and parties were capped, so that large PACs were encouraged to spread around their contributions because they could not concentrate solely on a few key races. The PAC regime was compatible with the needs of many small corporations and trade associations, however, which wanted to support a few key policymakers but did not want to invest large sums in elections.

Throughout the 1990s and into the new century, the rapid growth in soft money, relatively unregulated contributions to party organizations, created an additional path for groups to support parties. Soft money contributions were not capped, and could come from interest group treasuries, including funds contributed from the general operating funds of businesses, labor unions, trade associations, and other groups. Labor unions gave substantial soft money to national and state Democratic parties, and corporations and often their top officers made sizable contributions, sometimes to both political parties. Wealthy members of various other groups also made soft money contributions to parties. Although in practice party leaders did honor to some degree the requests of donors to spend money in particular races, soft money was an imprecise tool to target key races. The PAC and soft money regime was especially suited to interest groups that sought access to policymakers of both parties. But it also bolstered the role of the parties.[5]

During the last decade, a series of court decisions have enabled groups to spend treasury money and large contributions from patrons on issue advocacy and electioneering ads. Party soft money has been banned, but contributions of unlimited size can flow to an array of organizational forms, each of which has somewhat different restrictions on spending, and somewhat different disclosure requirements. Groups operate in a regulatory landscape that is ever changing, so groups may shift their organizational structure even in the middle of the campaign. As discussed in Chapter 8, for example, American Crossroads changed one of its organizations from a 527 to a super PAC during the course of the 2010 campaigns. Where the PAC regime gave an advantage to groups with large numbers of members, the current electioneering regime allows a group to form to channel money from a single donor. Moreover, the electioneering regime allows groups to concentrate their efforts in a few key races.

Taking Stock of Interest Group Behavior in 2010

Stay the course or break new ground? Exploit new technology or stick with traditional modes of communication? Keep to the shadows or accept the glare of public scrutiny? As noted, the chapters in this volume make it quite clear that the strategies that groups adopted in the 2010 campaigns vary a great deal. The chapters also begin to offer some hints about what the ensuing election cycles will look like and where the campaign finance regime stands today. With that in mind we conclude with the following lessons.

1. Follow the money—if you can. One consistent theme across the chapters in this volume is the decreasing transparency of the campaign finance system. Scholars can still trace some of the money spent in elections, but in 2010 large sums were spent outside of the disclosure system. As reported in Chapter 5, in 2010, 501(c) groups that do not report their donors accounted for more than half of the electioneering spending. And as we learned in Chapter 2, only the totals that the U.S. Chamber of Commerce says it spent are explicit—some $50 million.

Estimates of the amount spent on television are a bit more transparent with data from the Wesleyan Media Project, but the totals some groups spent on mail, phone, and door-to-door campaigning can only be guessed. As new groups spring up and spend large sums in elections, it is increasingly difficult to determine whom they represent, and what their interests are.

Consider, once again, the somewhat mysterious attack ad that Concerned Taxpayers of America launched against Rep. Peter Defazio (D-Ore.), or the $1.6 million campaign by Americans for Job Security on an Alaskan referendum, another $6 million during the 2010 primary season, and $4 million during the general election. Or consider the short life of a corporation named W Spann LLC that was headquartered in Delaware. The corporation's statement of incorporation did not include any description of the company's business interests. But the corporation donated $1 million to Restore Our Future, a super PAC associated with Mitt Romney's presidential campaign. The company was formed in March 2011, made the $1 million contribution in April, thereby complying with the requirement that PACs report all donors, and disbanded in July. The corporation, unlike the PAC, was *not* required to report the sources of the money that it donated to the super PAC. And, only after fairly intense press scrutiny that caused embarrassment to the Romney campaign did the donor come forward.[6] W Spann was not alone in contributing to the coffers of Restore Our Future, and thereby to the Romney campaign. FEC records show that the PAC reported $12 million in receipts, but no expenditures, through the first half of 2011—including $1 million from hedge fund manager John Paulson, $500,000 from Bob Perry of Perry Homes, and a combined $1 million from hoteliers J. W. and Richard Marriott.

2. If it ain't broke, don't change it. Many interest groups reacted to the opportunity to run electioneering ads with a yawn. Small- to medium-sized corporations and trade associations, small labor unions, and smaller membership groups appeared content to contribute money to a few key legislators as an aid to their lobbying efforts. In some cases, groups support either party, and merely want to maintain good relations with key policymakers. Chapter 4, for example, reports that defense industry PACs continued to operate primarily through their PACs, and through true issue advertising to elites about particular weapon systems. Furthermore, the discussion in Chapter 3 suggests that health-related groups also did not respond to the new opportunities, although in the case of PhRMA it is difficult to be certain.

This is partially explained by the nature of the benefits that these groups realize through the policy process. For defense companies interested in pork barrel contracts, partisan politics operates somewhat at the margins. Yes, Republicans are more sympathetic to the interests of the defense industry, and to the health care industry's long-term aversion to government control for that matter. But it makes relatively little sense to put all their proverbial eggs in one partisan basket. Access is consequential regardless of which party controls a majority of seats in the House and in the Senate. Thus, it occasions no surprise that of the relative handful of companies that appear in the top fifty PACs, only two—UPS, which favors Republicans and

Time Warner, which favors Democrats—have partisan leanings, and then not heavily so.

But it also is a numbers game. Despite the huge amounts of money being poured into campaign activity in the United States there still are limits, it would seem, to the number of donors and the amount of money they are willing to spend to influence elections. As of April 2012, interest group spending approached $100 million on the 2012 elections, including over $80 million in spending by super PACs.[7] Of course, at least two of these groups—Colbert's PAC and 501(c)(4)— were created in jest and one has to wonder how seriously to take certain others—Americans Citizens of Modest Means and Committee for the Reelection of the President (CREEP), for example. At the very least, some, Draft Christie for President, for example, become moot practically before they are brought into being, while others like the American Dental Association's super PAC spend relatively little and for a highly focused purpose. In this case, their $169,000 in independent spending was invested in a single, successful, House race, won by Rep. Paul Gasor (R-Ariz.), who is a dentist.[8] This suggests that most interest group federal election activity is more likely to continue to take the form of the relatively inconspicuous, but fully legal and transparent, PAC that the Federal Election Campaign Act formalized.

3. More money means more polarization. For groups whose policy agendas depend on which party controls Congress, the new deregulation led to more spending. Chapter 6 illustrates how organized labor used the new rules to increase their activity, and also their relative importance compared with other Democratic leaning groups. Similarly, Chapter 2 showed the U.S. Chamber of Commerce's increased activity, and Chapter 7 highlighted the League of Conservation Voters' heightened involvement.

Not only were these groups more active, they were more partisan as well. A number of groups continued their nominal bipartisanship by giving to sure winners in the other party, while mustering significant resources to marginal candidates of the preferred party. Increasingly, many interest groups are becoming part of the party network, sharing resources, information, and coordinating strategy. For example, Chapter 8 notes the close coordination between American Crossroads and various Republican committees. Only two of the eighty-four super PACs created during the 2010 election cycle did not have a liberal or conservative valence —the National Association of Realtors Congressional Fund and the American Dental Association. Likewise, only four of the top twenty-five interest groups listed among OpenSecrets's Heavy Hitters, are partisan fence sitters. The top twenty-five is dominated by unions that are pro-Democratic, but groups representing several economic sectors—auto dealers, bankers, beer wholesalers, and home builders—veer toward the Republicans, though not dramatically so.[9]

4. Expect an ever-shifting cast. The last decade has witnessed the creation and subsequent demise of a number of interest groups. In the 2004 election, liberal groups and activists used funds from a few key patrons to form Americans Coming Together, the Media Fund, and other groups. These organizations might be seen as formalized coalitions, where the contributing groups can prevent each other from shirking commitments, and where hired staff can coordinate these joint efforts. Chapter 7 shows how LCV and other environmental groups joined with unions and other liberal organizations to form Vote Vets Action Fund, which spent more than $2 million in independent expenditures for Democrats and against Republicans.

Other new organizations appear to be conduits for single individuals or small groups of donors. The infamous Swift Boat Veterans for Truth was funded largely by a small group that included Texas billionaire Harold Simmons. In the 2004 elections, a group called Let Freedom Ring distributed videos touting George Bush's faith in churches in battleground states to be played the Sunday before the election. The group had one principle donor, one paid employee, and one unpaid intern. In the 2010 campaigns, a few large donors funded American Crossroads (again see Chapter 8) and the Koch brothers reportedly funded Americans for Prosperity.

But some new groups resemble social movements. Chapter 9 describes the rise of local Tea Party organizations, and the efforts by large national organizations to harness the energy of these local groups. Whether the Tea Party endures remains to be seen, for in many ways it was a social movement that was heavily subsidized by large donors and free coverage from Fox News. In some ways, Tea Party activism in 2010 resembled the "Year of the Angry White Male" of 1994, but with rapidly flowing cash and information through the Internet. Finally, Chapter 10 traces the slowly coalescing network of activists on the left, the netroots, many of whom blog and use Twitter to communicate their views. Scholars are increasingly viewing interest groups as networks of activists, and this chapter reminds us of the power of an electronically organized community to channel resources to candidates.

Wither the Party?

Although the primary goal of the Federal Election Campaign Act was to provide for more stringent disclosure requirements for campaign contributions and to establish federally-funded presidential elections, subsequent amendments in 1976 and 1979 also had the aim of strengthening the role of the political parties. At the time, it was the broad perception that candidate-centered campaigns—for both the presidency and Congress—had caused the party system to wither. So, with lower limits on individual contributions and higher limits on parties, the hope was that parties would regain some of their lost influence in the nominating and governing phases of American politics. It would be an overstatement to say that this goal was fully achieved, or that it is a primary cause of increased party discipline over the last three decades, but parties, leadership PACs, and party-allied groups certainly have helped to shape the electoral landscape in the recent past.[10]

Now, however, the recent court and FEC rulings cast some doubt upon whether that will remain the case. Can parties match the fundraising and spending prowess of purely private, albeit ideologically driven, super PACs? As important, will the parties be able to work in concert with or will they be forced to compete with these new organizational forms? Heretofore, the "big six" party committees—the RNC, DNC, and the four House and Senate campaign committees—have masterminded party strategies. But now, super PACs and 501(c)s have caused concern in some quarters about the emergence of a shadow party system and that has some operatives worried.[11] Rep. Tom Cole (R-Okla.), former executive director of the National Congressional Republican Committee and former chief of staff of the RNC, was blunt about his concerns: "There's no question that with the way we structure these super PACs, it will enormously diminish the role the committees play. There's a recognition that we don't have the clout we once had."[12]

Not that the parties are giving up. Operatives associated with Republican Speaker John Boehner and Majority Leader Eric Cantor have established super PACs designed specifically to maintain Republican control of the House. These are in addition to their leadership PACs, Cantor's Every Republican is Crucial (ERIC) and Boehner's Freedom Project, that ranked first and second for the top money spots among such PACs for the 2010 cycle and continue to hold those positions. Former leadership aides run the two super PACs, the Congressional Leadership Fund (Boehner) and the YG Action Fund (Cantor), but these have yet to make a big splash in the 2012 cycle.[13] And there are other efforts on the super PAC and 501(c)(4) front as well, as party operatives on both sides of the aisle scramble to adapt to the new organizational forms. Democrats, for example, have established Majority PAC and a linked 501(c)(4), Patriot Majority, too, as one Democratic campaigner put it, "[S]et up a super PAC structure that mirrors the party committee structure, and that's something that most of these donors understand. It works for people."[14]

Parties and Interests in 2012 and Beyond

Major changes in the regulations governing campaign finance, such as those addressed herein, make it challenging, perhaps even foolhardy, to speculate about the future. As the parties' responses to the advent of super PACs demonstrates, campaign finance laws are continually being probed by the nation's foremost political and legal talent—a pool of talent that, like money, flows to where it is most useful. Moreover, the recentness of the unraveling of regulations governing interest group participation in federal elections means that many groups have not yet determined their best course of action within the new legal environment. Given a chance to adjust, interest group efforts in future congressional and presidential elections might well differ from those shown here for the 2010 cycle. And, consequentially, organized interests are just now being unleashed in a presidential election.

Still, as Chapter 1 suggests, some reasonable speculation is possible. First, business and labor groups that embraced directly financed independent expenditures or issue advocacy ads during the 2010 election cycle likely will do so in future federal elections. Second, with more lead time to prepare (i.e., raise money), their expenditures most certainly will increase. Third, because organization tends to beget counter-organization, some groups that stayed the course in the 2010 election cycle will not necessarily do so in 2012 and beyond. Future elections probably will involve more fundraising and spending by interest group entities that raise large sums from corporations, unions, and other groups and do not provide full and timely disclosure of their campaign activities. Fourth, because most members of Congress are risk averse when it comes to reelection, even those with arguably safe seats, new forms of interest group spending likely will cause them to ramp up their fundraising efforts even further—partly just for fear of the unknown.

Should these predictions prove correct, they likely will lead to a number of undesirable outcomes. Election costs will increase more than they might have otherwise. Policymaking and district work time will shift even more to time spent on fundraising. Challengers will, of course, be further disadvantaged in the lopsided race to raise the money needed to contest an election, further aggravating the scare-off effects already firmly in place that deter potential candidates. And, to the extent that groups that are ideologically driven, which generally are the best able to raise funds, possess the most expensive megaphones, elections may become even more polarized. Finally, there is no reason to think that recent decisions by the Supreme Court and the FEC that have relaxed statutory and regulatory restraints on campaign activities have come to an end. This means, of course, that interest groups have not yet been fully unleashed.

Endnotes

1 Colbert quoted in Dan Eggen, "Waiting for the Punch Line: TV's Colbert Plays His PAC for Comedy, But Some See Little to Laugh About," *The Washington Post,* June 30, 2011, A3.

2 See www.colbettsuperpac.com. According to the Center for Responsive Politics, Colbert's super PAC raised almost $1.1 million and spent roughly $300,000 as of March 19, 2012 (opensecrets.org). Colbert's 501(c)(4) is called *Colbert Super PAC SHH.* See Dan Eggen, "Seriously, Folks, Colbert Gets His Super PAC." *The Washington Post,* July 1, 2011, A4; and Justin Sink, "Colbert Creates Shell Corporation to Lampoon Karl Rove's Groups," *The Hill,* September 30, 2011.

3 *Citizens United v. FEC,* 558 U.S. 08-205 (2010).
4 *SpeechNow.org v. FEC,* U.S. Court of Appeals for the D.C. Circuit, No. 08-5223 (2010).
5 Paul S. Herrnson, "Political Parties, Party-Connected Committees, and Party Allies in Elections," *Journal of Politics,* 71 (2009): 1207–1224.
6 Dan Eggen, "Romney: Controversy Should End Now That PAC Donor Has Identified Himself," *The Washington Post,* August 8, 2011.
7 Center for Responsive Politics, www.opensecrets.org/outsidespending/index.php?cycle=2012&view=Y&chart=N#viewpt.
8 According to Gosar's campaign website, he was the Arizona ADA's "dentist of the year" in 2001 and served as president of the Northern Arizona Dental Society and the Arizona ADA. The national ADA's "regular" PAC also was active, spending $2.4 million in the 2010 cycle with contributions to Democratic House candidates higher than to Republicans, while the reverse was true for the Senate races they supported.
9 From 60 to 69 percent of the money donated by these groups goes to Republican candidates.
10 Herrnson, "Political Parties, Party-Connected Committees, and Party Allies in Elections."
11 See Kenneth P. Vogel and Alex Isenstadt, "Super PACs Giving Party Committees a Run for Their Money," *Politico,* October 28, 2011; Dan Eggen, "New Breed of 'Super PACs,' Other Independent Groups Could Define 2012 Campaign," *The Washington Post,* July 4, 2011; and Shira Toeplitz, "House GOP Leaders to Headline November Super PAC Event," *Roll Call,* October 13, 2011.
12 Quoted in Vogel and Isenstadt, "Super PACs Giving Party Committees a Run for Their Money."
13 YG (Young Guns) Action Fund did raise the ire of some *within* the Republican Party when it backed Rep. Adam Kinzinger against Rep. Don Manzullo, a member-on-member Illinois primary induced by redistricting. Cantor caught flak for endorsing Kinzinger and, as a result, being linked to $52,000 in radio advertising by YG Action Fund on Kinzinger's behalf. Intervening in such intraparty contests is considered a violation of Ronald Reagan's Eleventh Commandment—"Thou shalt not speak ill of any fellow Republican."
14 Quoted in Vogel and Isenstadt, "Super PACs Giving Party Committees a Run for Their Money."

Appendix: *Citizens United v. Federal Election Commission (2010)*

OPINION FOR THE COURT, JUSTICE ANTHONY M. KENNEDY

DISSENTING OPINION, JUSTICE JOHN PAUL STEVENS

On January 21, 2010, the Supreme Court handed down its much anticipated decision in *Citizens United v. Federal Election Commission.* In this case the court faced the issue of whether a partisan documentary ("Hillary the Movie") financed by corporate money was protected "political speech" or whether it could be regulated as "campaign speech" (via the Bipartisan Campaign Reform Act of 2002). In this sweeping and highly controversial decision, the court struck down the provisions of the law prohibiting corporations, unions, and other groups from spending general treasury funds to advocate expressly the election or defeat of a federal candidate. Corporations and trade unions would still be prohibited from directly contributing to federal candidates but they would be free to spend as much as they wished as independent participants in the electoral process. And in 2010 many did just that.

As with many consequential Court decisions of recent years, this one was split 5-4. Justice Anthony Kennedy's opinion for the Court (ie, the majority) was supported by the conservative members of the court—Chief Justice Roberts and Justices Scalia, Thomas, and Alito. Justice Kennedy argues, in effect, that a previous decision by the Court in *Austin v. Michigan Chamber of Commerce* (1990) should be overruled and that corporations' freedom of speech, even in elections, cannot be limited. Justice Stevens's dissenting opinion represented the liberal wing of the Court—as he was joined by Justices Ginsberg, Breyer, and Sotomayor. Justice Stevens argues, in effect, that overruling *Austin* is an unwarranted and hasty violation of the principal of *stare decisis* and that regulation of corporate (or union) speech is a reasonable government protection against the potential for corruption and imbalance that it poses to the electoral process.

Extended excerpts of these two main opinions are presented below. Both opinions are quite long in the original. To make them more readable the "syllabus," the internal legal citations in both opinions, the footnotes to Justice Stevens's opinion, and a couple of narrow additional dissents have been removed. In addition, certain sections of each decision [indicated by notes within brackets] and other less essential portions have been edited out of the text (and indicated by ellipses). The two opinions follow.

No. 08–205 __ (2010)

CITIZENS UNITED, APPELLANT v. FEDERAL
ELECTION COMMISSION

ON APPEAL FROM THE UNITED STATES DISTRICT
COURT FOR THE DISTRICT OF COLUMBIA

[January 21, 2010]

JUSTICE KENNEDY delivered the opinion of the Court.

Federal law prohibits corporations and unions from using their general treasury funds to make independent expenditures for speech defined as an "electioneering communication" or for speech expressly advocating the election or defeat of a candidate. Limits on electioneering communications were upheld in *McConnell v. Federal Election Comm'n* (2003). The holding of *McConnell* rested to a large extent on an earlier case, *Austin v. Michigan Chamber of Commerce* (1990). *Austin* had held that political speech may be banned based on the speaker's corporate identity.

In this case we are asked to reconsider *Austin* and, in effect, *McConnell*. It has been noted that "*Austin* was a significant departure from ancient First Amendment principles." We agree with that conclusion and hold that stare decisis does not compel the continued acceptance of *Austin*. The Government may regulate corporate political speech through disclaimer and disclosure requirements, but it may not suppress that speech altogether. We turn to the case now before us.

I

A

Citizens United is a nonprofit corporation. It brought this action in the United States District Court for the District of Columbia. A three-judge court later convened to hear the cause. The resulting judgment gives rise to this appeal.

Citizens United has an annual budget of about $12 million. Most of its funds are from donations by individuals; but, in addition, it accepts a small portion of its funds from for-profit corporations.

In January 2008, Citizens United released a film entitled *Hillary*: The Movie. We refer to the film as *Hillary*. It is a 90-minute documentary about then-Senator *Hillary* Clinton, who was a candidate in the Democratic Party's 2008 Presidential primary elections. *Hillary* mentions Senator Clinton by name and depicts interviews with political commentators and other persons, most of them quite critical of Senator Clinton. *Hillary* was released in theaters and on DVD, but Citizens United wanted to increase distribution by making it available through video on-demand.

Video-on-demand allows digital cable subscribers to select programming from various menus, including movies, television shows, sports, news, and music. The viewer can watch the program at any time and can elect to rewind or pause the program. In December 2007, a cable company offered, for a payment of $1.2 million, to make *Hillary* available on a video-on-demand channel called "Elections '08." Some video-on-demand services require viewers to pay a small fee to view a selected program, but here the proposal was to make *Hillary* available to viewers free of charge.

To implement the proposal, Citizens United was prepared to pay for the video-on-demand; and to promote the film, it produced two 10-second ads and one 30-second ad for *Hillary*. Each ad includes a short (and, in our view, pejorative) statement about Senator Clinton, followed by the name of the movie and the movie's Website address. Citizens United desired to promote the video-on-demand offering by running advertisements on broadcast and cable television.

B

Before the Bipartisan Campaign Reform Act of 2002 (BCRA), federal law prohibited—and still does prohibit— corporations and unions from using general treasury funds to make direct contributions to candidates or independent expenditures that expressly advocate the election or defeat of a candidate, through any form of media, in connection with certain qualified federal elections. BCRA §203 amended §441b to prohibit any "electioneering communication" as well. An electioneering communication is defined as "any broadcast, cable, or satellite communication" that "refers to a clearly identified candidate for Federal office" and is made within 30 days of a primary or 60 days of a general election. The Federal Election Commission's (FEC) regulations further define an electioneering communication as a communication that is "publicly distributed." "In the case of a candidate for nomination for President . . . publicly distributed means" that the communication "[c]an be received by 50,000 or more persons in a State where a primary election . . . is being held within 30 days." §100.29(b)(3)(ii). Corporations and unions are barred from using their general treasury funds for express advocacy or electioneering communications. They may establish, however, a "separate segregated fund" (known as a political action committee, or PAC) for these purposes. The moneys received by the segregated fund are limited to donations from stockholders and employees of the corporation or, in the case of unions, members of the union.

C

Citizens United wanted to make *Hillary* available through video-on-demand within 30 days of the 2008 primary elections. It feared, however, that both the film and the ads would be covered by §441b's ban on corporate funded independent expenditures, thus subjecting the corporation to civil and criminal penalties under §437g. In December 2007, Citizens United sought declaratory and injunctive relief against the FEC. It argued that (1) §441b is unconstitutional as applied to *Hillary*; and (2) BCRA's disclaimer and disclosure requirements, BCRA §§201 and 311, are unconstitutional as applied to *Hillary* and to the three ads for the movie.

The District Court denied Citizens United's motion for a preliminary injunction and then granted the FEC's motion for summary judgment. The court held that §441b was facially constitutional under McConnell, and that §441b was constitutional as applied to *Hillary* because it was "susceptible of no other interpretation than to inform the electorate that Senator Clinton is unfit for office, that the United States would be a dangerous place in a President *Hillary* Clinton world, and that viewers should vote against her." The court also rejected Citizens United's challenge to BCRA's disclaimer and disclosure requirements. It noted that "the Supreme Court has written approvingly of disclosure provisions triggered by political speech even though the speech itself was constitutionally protected under the First Amendment."

We noted probable jurisdiction. The case was reargued in this Court after the Court asked the parties to file supplemental briefs addressing whether we should overrule either or both *Austin* and the part of McConnell which addresses the facial validity of 2 U. S. C. §441b.

II

Before considering whether *Austin* should be overruled, we first address whether Citizens United's claim that §441b cannot be applied to *Hillary* may be resolved on other, narrower grounds....

[A detailed rebuttal of these narrower grounds follows.]

.... As the foregoing analysis confirms, the Court cannot resolve this case on a narrower ground without chilling political speech, speech that is central to the meaning and purpose of the First Amendment. It is not judicial restraint to accept an unsound, narrow argument just so the Court can avoid another argument with broader implications. Indeed, a court would be remiss in performing its duties were it to accept an unsound principle merely to avoid the necessity of making a broader ruling. Here, the lack of a valid basis for an alternative ruling requires full consideration of the continuing effect of the speech suppression upheld in *Austin*.

III

The First Amendment provides that "Congress shall make no law . . . abridging the freedom of speech." Laws enacted to control or suppress speech may operate at different points in the speech process. The following are just a few examples of restrictions that have been attempted at different stages of the speech process—all laws found to be invalid: restrictions requiring a permit at the outset, imposing a burden by impounding proceeds on receipts or royalties, seeking to exact a cost after the speech occurs, and subjecting the speaker to criminal penalties.

The law before us is an outright ban, backed by criminal sanctions. Section 441b makes it a felony for all corporations—including nonprofit advocacy corporations—either to expressly advocate the election or defeat of candidates or to broadcast electioneering communications within 30 days of a primary election and 60 days of a general election. Thus, the following acts would all be felonies under §441b: The Sierra Club runs an ad, within the crucial phase of 60 days before the general election, that exhorts the public to disapprove of a Congressman who favors logging in national forests; the National Rifle Association publishes a book urging the public to vote for the challenger because the incumbent U. S. Senator supports a handgun ban; and the American Civil Liberties Union creates a Web site telling the public to vote for a Presidential candidate in light of that candidate's defense of free speech. These prohibitions are classic examples of censorship.

Section 441b is a ban on corporate speech notwithstanding the fact that a PAC created by a corporation can still speak. A PAC is a separate association from the corporation. So the PAC exemption from §441b's expenditure ban, §441b(b)(2), does not allow corporations to speak. Even if a PAC could somehow allow a corporation to speak—and it does not—the option to form PACs does not alleviate the First Amendment problems with §441b. PACs are burdensome alternatives; they are expensive to administer and subject to extensive regulations. For example, every PAC must appoint a treasurer, forward donations to the treasurer promptly, keep detailed records of the identities of the persons making donations, preserve receipts for three years, and file an organization statement and report changes to this information within 10 days.

And that is just the beginning. PACs must file detailed monthly reports with the FEC, which are due at different times depending on the type of election that is about to occur.... PACs have to comply with these regulations just to speak. This might explain why fewer than 2,000 of the millions of corporations in this country have PACs. PACs, furthermore, must exist before they can speak. Given the onerous restrictions, a corporation may not be able to establish a PAC in time to make its views known regarding candidates and issues in a current campaign.

Section 441b's prohibition on corporate independent expenditures is thus a ban on speech. As a "restriction on the amount of money a person or group can spend on political communication during a campaign," that statute "necessarily reduces the quantity of expression by restricting the number of issues discussed, the depth of their exploration, and the size of the audience reached." Were the Court to uphold these restrictions, the Government could repress speech by silencing certain voices at any of the various points in the speech process. If §441b applied to individuals, no one would believe that it is merely a time, place, or manner restriction on speech. Its purpose and effect are to silence entities whose voices the Government deems to be suspect.

Speech is an essential mechanism of democracy, for it is the means to hold officials accountable to the people. The right of citizens to inquire, to hear, to speak, and to use information to reach consensus is a precondition to enlightened self-government and a necessary means to protect it. The First Amendment " 'has its fullest and most urgent application' to speech uttered during a campaign for political office."

For these reasons, political speech must prevail against laws that would suppress it, whether by design or inadvertence. Laws that burden political speech are "subject to strict scrutiny," which requires the Government to prove that the restriction "furthers a compelling interest and is narrowly tailored to achieve that interest." While it might be maintained that political speech simply cannot be banned or restricted as a categorical matter, the quoted language from [*Wisconsin Right to Life*] provides a sufficient framework for protecting the relevant First Amendment interests in this case. We shall employ it here.

Premised on mistrust of governmental power, the First Amendment stands against attempts to disfavor certain subjects or viewpoints. Prohibited, too, are restrictions distinguishing among different speakers, allowing speech by some but not others. As instruments to censor, these categories are interrelated: Speech restrictions based on the identity of the speaker are all too often simply a means to control content.

Quite apart from the purpose or effect of regulating content, moreover, the Government may commit a constitutional wrong when by law it identifies certain preferred speakers. By taking the right to speak from some and giving it to others, the Government deprives the disadvantaged person or class of the right to use speech to strive to establish worth, standing, and respect for the speaker's voice. The Government may not by these means deprive the public of the right and privilege to determine for itself what speech and speakers are worthy of consideration. The First Amendment protects speech and speaker, and the ideas that flow from each.

The Court has upheld a narrow class of speech restrictions that operate to the disadvantage of certain persons, but these rulings were based on an interest in allowing governmental entities to perform their functions.

The corporate independent expenditures at issue in this case, however, would not interfere with governmental functions, so these cases are inapposite. These precedents stand only for the proposition that there are certain governmental functions that cannot operate without some restrictions on particular kinds of speech. By contrast, it is inherent in the nature of the political process that voters must be free to obtain information from diverse sources in order to determine how to cast their votes. At least before *Austin*, the Court had not allowed the exclusion of a class of speakers from the general public dialogue.

We find no basis for the proposition that, in the context of political speech, the Government may impose restrictions on certain disfavored speakers. Both history and logic lead us to this conclusion.

A

1

The Court has recognized that First Amendment protection extends to corporations.... .... This protection has been extended by explicit holdings to the context of political speech. Under the rationale of these precedents, political speech does not lose First Amendment protection "simply because its source is a corporation." The Court has thus rejected the argument that political speech of corporations or other associations should be treated differently under the First Amendment simply because such associations are not "natural persons."

At least since the latter part of the 19th century, the laws of some States and of the United States imposed a ban on corporate direct contributions to candidates. Yet not until 1947 did Congress first prohibit independent expenditures by corporations and labor unions in §304 of the Labor Management Relations Act 1947. In passing this Act Congress overrode the veto of President Truman, who warned that the expenditure ban was a "dangerous intrusion on free speech."

For almost three decades thereafter, the Court did not reach the question whether restrictions on corporate and union expenditures are constitutional. The question was in the background of *United States v. CIO* (1948). There, a labor union endorsed a congressional candidate in its weekly periodical. The Court stated that "the gravest doubt would arise in our minds as to [the federal expenditure prohibition's] constitutionality" if it were construed to suppress that writing."...

In *United States v. Automobile Workers* (1957) the Court again encountered the independent expenditure ban, which had been recodified at 18 U. S. C. §610 (1952 ed.). After holding only that a union television broadcast that endorsed candidates was covered by the statute, the Court "[r]efus[ed] to anticipate constitutional questions" and remanded for the trial to proceed....

Later, in *Pipefitters v. United States* (1972), the Court reversed a conviction for expenditure of union funds for political speech—again without reaching the constitutional question. The Court would not resolve that question for another four years.

2

In *Buckley* the Court addressed various challenges to the Federal Election Campaign Act of 1971 (FECA) as amended in 1974. These amendments created 18 U. S. C. §608(e), an independent expenditure ban separate from §610 that applied to individuals as well as corporations and labor unions.

Before addressing the constitutionality of §608(e)'s independent expenditure ban, *Buckley* first upheld §608(b), FECA's limits on direct contributions to candidates. The *Buckley* Court recognized a "sufficiently important" governmental interest in "the prevention of corruption and the appearance of corruption." This followed from the Court's concern that large contributions could be given "to secure a political quid pro quo." Ibid.

The *Buckley* Court explained that the potential for quid pro quo corruption distinguished direct contributions to candidates from independent expenditures. The Court emphasized that "the independent expenditure ceiling . . . fails to serve any substantial governmental interest in stemming the reality or appearance of corruption in the electoral process," because "[t]he absence of prearrangement and coordination . . . alleviates the danger that expenditures will be given as a quid pro quo for improper commitments from the candidate". *Buckley* invalidated §608(e)'s restrictions on independent expenditures, with only one Justice dissenting.

Buckley did not consider §610's separate ban on corporate and union independent expenditures, the prohibition that had also been in the background in *CIO, Automobile Workers,* and *Pipefitters.* Had §610 been challenged in the wake of *Buckley*, however, it could not have been squared with the reasoning and analysis of that precedent. The expenditure ban invalidated in *Buckley*, §608(e), applied to corporations and unions; and some of the prevailing plaintiffs in *Buckley* were corporations. The *Buckley* Court did not invoke the First Amendment's overbreadth doctrine to suggest that §608(e)'s expenditure ban would have been constitutional if it had applied only to corporations and not to individuals. *Buckley* cited with approval the Automobile Workers dissent, which argued that §610 was unconstitutional.

Notwithstanding this precedent, Congress recodified §610's corporate and union expenditure ban at 2 U. S. C. §441b four months after *Buckley* was decided. Section 441b is the independent expenditure restriction challenged here.

Less than two years after *Buckley*, [*First National Bank of Boston v.*] *Bellotti* (1978) reaffirmed the First Amendment principle that the Government cannot restrict political speech based on the speaker's corporate identity. *Bellotti* could not have been clearer when it struck down a state-law prohibition on corporate independent expenditures related to referenda issues....

It is important to note that the reasoning and holding of *Bellotti* did not rest on the existence of a viewpoint-discriminatory statute. It rested on the principle that the Government lacks the power to ban corporations from speaking.

Bellotti did not address the constitutionality of the State's ban on corporate independent expenditures to support candidates. In our view, however, that restriction would have been unconstitutional under *Bellotti*'s central principle: that the First Amendment does not allow political speech restrictions based on a speaker's corporate identity.

3

Thus the law stood until *Austin*. *Austin* "uph[eld] a direct restriction on the independent expenditure of funds for political speech for the first time in [this Court's] history." There, the Michigan Chamber of Commerce sought to use general treasury funds to run a newspaper ad supporting a specific candidate. Michigan law, however, prohibited corporate independent expenditures that supported or opposed any candidate for state office. A violation of the law was punishable as a felony. The Court sustained the speech prohibition.

To bypass *Buckley* and *Bellotti*, the *Austin* Court identified a new governmental interest in limiting political speech: an antidistortion interest. *Austin* found a compelling governmental interest in preventing "the corrosive and distorting effects of immense aggregations of wealth that are accumulated with the help of the corporate form and that have little or no correlation to the public's support for the corporation's political ideas."

B

The Court is thus confronted with conflicting lines of precedent: a pre-*Austin* line that forbids restrictions on political speech based on the speaker's corporate identity and a post-*Austin* line that permits them. No case before *Austin* had held that Congress could prohibit independent expenditures for political speech based on the speaker's corporate identity. Before *Austin* Congress had enacted legislation for this purpose, and the Government urged the same proposition before this Court. In neither of these cases did the Court adopt the proposition.

In its defense of the corporate-speech restrictions in §441b, the Government notes the antidistortion rationale on which *Austin* and its progeny rest in part, yet it all but abandons reliance upon it. It argues instead that two other compelling interests support *Austin*'s holding that corporate expenditure restrictions are constitutional: an anticorruption interest and a shareholder-protection interest. We consider the three points in turn.

1

As for *Austin*'s antidistortion rationale, the Government does little to defend it. And with good reason, for the rationale cannot support §441b.

If the First Amendment has any force, it prohibits Congress from fining or jailing citizens, or associations of citizens, for simply engaging in political speech. If the antidistortion rationale were to be accepted, however, it would permit Government to ban political speech simply because the speaker is an association that has taken on the corporate form. The Government contends that *Austin* permits it to ban corporate expenditures for almost all forms of communication stemming from a corporation. If *Austin* were correct, the Government could prohibit a corporation from expressing political views in media beyond those presented here, such as by printing books.

Political speech is "indispensable to decisionmaking in a democracy, and this is no less true because the speech comes from a corporation rather than an individual." This protection for speech is inconsistent with *Austin*'s antidistortion rationale. *Austin* sought to defend the antidistortion rationale as a means to prevent corporations from obtaining "'an unfair advantage in the political marketplace'" by using "'resources amassed in the economic marketplace.'" But *Buckley* rejected the premise that the Government has an interest "in equalizing the relative ability of individuals and groups to influence the outcome of elections." *Buckley* was specific in stating that "the skyrocketing cost of political campaigns" could not sustain the governmental prohibition. The First Amendment's protections do not depend on the speaker's "financial ability to engage in public discussion."

The Court reaffirmed these conclusions when it invalidated the BCRA provision that increased the cap on contributions to one candidate if the opponent made certain expenditures from personal funds. The rule that political speech cannot be limited based on a speaker's wealth is a necessary consequence of the premise that the First Amendment generally prohibits the suppression of political speech based on the speaker's identity.

Either as support for its antidistortion rationale or as a further argument, the *Austin* majority undertook to distinguish wealthy individuals from corporations on the ground that "[s]tate law grants corporations special advantages—such as limited liability, perpetual life, and favorable treatment of the accumulation and distribution of assets." This does not suffice, however, to allow laws prohibiting speech. "It is rudimentary that the State cannot exact as the price of those special advantages the forfeiture of First Amendment rights."

It is irrelevant for purposes of the First Amendment that corporate funds may "have little or no correlation to the public's support for the corporation's political ideas." All speakers, including individuals and the media, use money amassed from the economic marketplace to fund their speech. The First Amendment protects the resulting speech, even if it was enabled by economic transactions with persons or entities who disagree with the speaker's ideas.

Austin's antidistortion rationale would produce the dangerous, and unacceptable, consequence that Congress could ban political speech of media corporations. Media corporations are now exempt from §441b's ban on corporate expenditures. Yet media corporations accumulate wealth with the help of the corporate form, the largest media corporations have "immense aggregations of wealth," and the views expressed by media corporations often "have little or no correlation to the public's support" for those views. Thus, under the Government's reasoning, wealthy media corporations could have their voices diminished to put them on par with other media entities. There is no precedent for permitting this under the First Amendment.

The media exemption discloses further difficulties with the law now under consideration. There is no precedent supporting laws that attempt to distinguish between corporations which are deemed to be exempt as media corporations and those which are not. With the advent of the Internet and the decline of print and broadcast media, moreover, the line between the media and others who wish to comment on political and social issues becomes far more blurred.

The law's exception for media corporations is, on its own terms, all but an admission of the invalidity of the antidistortion rationale. And the exemption results in a further, separate reason for finding this law invalid: Again by its own terms, the law exempts some corporations but covers others, even though both have the need or the motive to communicate their views. The exemption applies to media corporations owned or controlled by corporations that have diverse and substantial investments and participate in endeavors other than news. So even assuming the most doubtful proposition that a news organization has a right to speak when others do not, the exemption would allow a conglomerate that owns both a media business and an unrelated business to influence or control the media in order to advance its overall business interest. At the same time, some other corporation, with an identical business interest but no media outlet in its ownership structure, would be forbidden to speak or inform the public about the same issue. This differential treatment cannot be squared with the First Amendment.

There is simply no support for the view that the First Amendment, as originally understood, would permit the suppression of political speech by media corporations. The Framers may not have anticipated modern business and media corporations. Yet television networks and major newspapers owned by media corporations have become the most important means of mass communication in modern times. The First Amendment was certainly not understood to condone the suppression of political speech in society's most salient media. It was understood as a response to the repression of speech and the press that had existed in England and the heavy taxes on the press that were imposed in the colonies. The great debates between the Federalists and the Anti-Federalists over our founding document were published and expressed in the most important means of mass communication of that era— newspapers owned by individuals. At the founding, speech was open, comprehensive, and vital to society's definition of itself; there were no limits on the sources of speech and knowledge. The Framers may have been unaware of certain types of speakers or forms of communication, but that does not mean that those speakers and media are entitled to less First Amendment protection than those types of speakers and media that provided the means of communicating political ideas when the Bill of Rights was adopted.

Austin interferes with the "open marketplace" of ideas protected by the First Amendment. It permits the Government to ban the political speech of millions of associations of citizens. Most of these are small corporations without large amounts of wealth. See Supp. This fact belies the Government's argument that the statute is justified on the ground that it prevents the "distorting effects of immense aggregations of wealth." It is not even aimed at amassed wealth.

The censorship we now confront is vast in its reach. The Government has "muffle[d] the voices that best represent the most significant segments of the economy." And "the electorate [has been] deprived of information, knowledge and opinion vital to its function." By suppressing the speech of manifold corporations, both for-profit and nonprofit, the Government prevents their voices and viewpoints from reaching the public and advising voters on which persons or entities are hostile to their interests. Factions will necessarily form in our Republic, but the remedy of "destroying the liberty" of some factions is "worse than the disease." Factions should be checked by permitting them all to speak and by entrusting the people to judge what is true and what is false.

The purpose and effect of this law is to prevent corporations, including small and nonprofit corporations, from presenting both facts and opinions to the public. This makes *Austin*'s antidistortion rationale all the more an aberration. Corporate executives and employees counsel Members of Congress and Presidential administrations on many issues, as a matter of routine and often in private. An amici brief filed on behalf of Montana and 25 other States notes that lobbying and corporate communications with elected officials occur on a regular basis. When that phenomenon is coupled with §441b, the result is that smaller or nonprofit corporations cannot raise a voice to object when other corporations, including those with vast wealth, are cooperating with the Government. That cooperation may sometimes be voluntary, or it may be at the demand of a Government official who uses his or her authority, influence, and power to threaten corporations to support the Government's policies. Those kinds of interactions are often unknown and unseen. The speech that §441b forbids, though, is public, and all can judge its content and purpose. References to massive corporate treasuries should not mask the real operation of this law. Rhetoric ought not obscure reality.

Even if §441b's expenditure ban were constitutional, wealthy corporations could still lobby elected officials, although smaller corporations may not have the resources to do so. And wealthy individuals and unincorporated associations can spend unlimited amounts on independent expenditures. Yet certain disfavored associations of citizens—those that have taken on the corporate form—are penalized for engaging in the same political speech.

When Government seeks to use its full power, including the criminal law, to command where a person may get his or her information or what distrusted source he or she may not hear, it uses censorship to control thought. This is unlawful. The First Amendment confirms the freedom to think for ourselves.

2

What we have said also shows the invalidity of other arguments made by the Government. For the most part relinquishing the antidistortion rationale, the Government falls back on the argument that corporate political speech can be banned in order to prevent corruption or its appearance. In *Buckley*, the Court found this interest "sufficiently important" to allow limits on contributions but did not extend that reasoning to expenditure limits. When *Buckley* examined an expenditure ban, it found "that the governmental interest in preventing corruption and the appearance of corruption [was] inadequate to justify [the ban] on independent expenditures."

With regard to large direct contributions, *Buckley* reasoned that they could be given "to secure a political quid pro quo," and that "the scope of such pernicious practices can never be reliably ascertained." The practices *Buckley* noted would be covered by bribery laws if a quid pro quo arrangement were proved. The Court, in consequence, has noted that restrictions on direct contributions are preventative, because few if any contributions to candidates will involve quid pro quo arrangements. The *Buckley* Court, nevertheless, sustained limits on direct contributions in order to ensure against the reality or appearance of corruption. That case did not extend this rationale to independent expenditures, and the Court does not do so here.

Limits on independent expenditures, such as §441b, have a chilling effect extending well beyond the Government's interest in preventing quid pro quo corruption. The anticorruption interest is not sufficient to displace the speech here in question. Indeed, 26 States do not restrict independent expenditures by forprofit corporations. The Government does not claim that these expenditures have corrupted the political process in those States....

When *Buckley* identified a sufficiently important governmental interest in preventing corruption or the appearance of corruption, that interest was limited to quid pro quo corruption. The fact that speakers may have influence over or access to elected officials does not mean that these officials are corrupt....The appearance of influence or access, furthermore, will not cause the electorate to lose faith in our democracy. By definition, an independent expenditure is political speech presented to the electorate that is not coordinated with a candidate. The fact that a corporation, or any other speaker, is willing to spend money to try to persuade voters presupposes that the people have the ultimate influence over elected officials. This is inconsistent with any suggestion that the electorate will refuse "'to take part in democratic governance'" because of additional political speech made by a corporation or any other speaker

The McConnell record was "over 100,000 pages" long, yet it "does not have any direct examples of votes being exchanged for . . . expenditures" This confirms *Buckley*'s reasoning that independent expenditures do not lead to, or create the appearance of, quid pro quo corruption. In fact, there is only scant evidence that independent expenditures even ingratiate. Ingratiation and access, in any event, are not corruption. The BCRA record establishes that certain donations to political parties, called "soft money," were made to gain access to elected officials. This case, however, is about independent expenditures, not soft money. When Congress finds that a problem exists, we must give that finding due deference; but Congress may not choose an unconstitutional remedy. If elected officials succumb to improper influences from independent expenditures; if they surrender their best judgment; and if they put expediency before principle, then surely there is cause for concern. We must give weight to attempts by Congress to seek to dispel either the appearance or the reality of these influences. The remedies enacted by law, however, must comply with the First

Amendment; and, it is our law and our tradition that more speech, not less, is the governing rule. An outright ban on corporate political speech during the critical preelection period is not a permissible remedy. Here Congress has created categorical bans on speech that are asymmetrical to preventing quid pro quo corruption.

3

The Government contends further that corporate independent expenditures can be limited because of its interest in protecting dissenting shareholders from being compelled to fund corporate political speech. This asserted interest, like *Austin*'s antidistortion rationale, would allow the Government to ban the political speech even of media corporations. Assume, for example, that a shareholder of a corporation that owns a newspaper disagrees with the political views the newspaper expresses. Under the Government's view, that potential disagreement could give the Government the authority to restrict the media corporation's political speech. The First Amendment does not allow that power. There is, furthermore, little evidence of abuse that cannot be corrected by shareholders "through the procedures of corporate democracy."

Those reasons are sufficient to reject this shareholder protection interest; and, moreover, the statute is both underinclusive and overinclusive. As to the first, if Congress had been seeking to protect dissenting shareholders, it would not have banned corporate speech in only certain media within 30 or 60 days before an election. A dissenting shareholder's interests would be implicated by speech in any media at any time. As to the second, the statute is overinclusive because it covers all corporations, including nonprofit corporations and for-profit corporations with only single shareholders. As to other corporations, the remedy is not to restrict speech but to consider and explore other regulatory mechanisms. The regulatory mechanism here, based on speech, contravenes the First Amendment.

4

We need not reach the question whether the Government has a compelling interest in preventing foreign individuals or associations from influencing our Nation's political process. Section 441b is not limited to corporations or associations that were created in foreign countries or funded predominately by foreign shareholders. Section 441b therefore would be overbroad even if we assumed, arguendo, that the Government has a compelling interest in limiting foreign influence over our political process.

C

Our precedent is to be respected unless the most convincing of reasons demonstrates that adherence to it puts us on a course that is sure error. "Beyond workability, the relevant factors in deciding whether to adhere to the principle of stare decisis include the antiquity of the precedent, the reliance interests at stake, and of course whether the decision was well reasoned." We have also examined whether "experience has pointed up the precedent's shortcomings."

These considerations counsel in favor of rejecting *Austin*, which itself contravened this Court's earlier precedents in *Buckley* and *Bellotti*....

For the reasons above, it must be concluded that *Austin* was not well reasoned. The Government defends *Austin*, relying almost entirely on "the quid pro quo interest, the corruption interest or the shareholder interest," and not *Austin*'s expressed antidistortion rationale. When neither party defends the reasoning of a precedent, the principle of adhering to that precedent through stare decisis is diminished. *Austin* abandoned First Amendment principles, furthermore, by relying on language in some of our precedents that traces back to the *Automobile Workers* Court's flawed historical account of campaign finance laws.

Austin is undermined by experience since its announcement. Political speech is so ingrained in our culture that speakers find ways to circumvent campaign finance laws.

Our Nation's speech dynamic is changing, and informative voices should not have to circumvent onerous restrictions to exercise their First Amendment rights. Speakers have become adept at presenting citizens with sound bites, talking points, and scripted messages that dominate the 24-hour news cycle. Corporations, like individuals, do not have monolithic views. On certain topics corporations may possess valuable expertise, leaving them the best equipped to point out errors or fallacies in speech of all sorts, including the speech of candidates and elected officials.

Rapid changes in technology—and the creative dynamic inherent in the concept of free expression—counsel against upholding a law that restricts political speech in certain media or by certain speakers. Today, 30-second television ads may be the most effective way to convey a political message. Soon, however, it may be that Internet sources, such as blogs and social networking Web sites, will provide citizens with significant information about political candidates and issues. Yet, §441b would seem to ban a blog post expressly advocating the election or defeat of a candidate if that blog were created with corporate funds. The First Amendment does not permit Congress to make these categorical distinctions based on the corporate identity of the speaker and the content of the political speech.

No serious reliance interests are at stake. As the Court stated in *Payne v. Tennessee* (1991), reliance interests are important considerations in property and contract cases, where parties may have acted in conformance with existing legal rules in order to conduct transactions. Here, though, parties have been prevented from acting—corporations have been banned from making independent expenditures. Legislatures may have enacted bans on corporate expenditures believing that those bans were constitutional. This is not a compelling interest for stare decisis. If it were, legislative acts could prevent us from overruling our own precedents, thereby interfering with our duty "to say what the law is."

Due consideration leads to this conclusion: *Austin* should be and now is overruled. We return to the principle established in *Buckley* and *Bellotti* that the Government may not suppress political speech on the basis of the speaker's corporate identity. No sufficient governmental interest justifies limits on the political speech of nonprofit or for-profit corporations.

D

Austin is overruled, so it provides no basis for allowing the Government to limit corporate independent expenditures. As the Government appears to concede, overruling *Austin* "effectively invalidate[s] not only BCRA Section 203, but also 2 U. S. C. 441b's prohibition on the use of corporate treasury funds for express advocacy." 12. Section 441b's restrictions on corporate independent expenditures are therefore invalid and cannot be applied to *Hillary*.

Given our conclusion we are further required to overrule the part of McConnell that upheld BCRA §203's extension of §441b's restrictions on corporate independent expenditures. The McConnell Court relied on the antidistortion interest recognized in *Austin* to uphold a greater restriction on speech than the restriction upheld in *Austin* and we have found this interest unconvincing and insufficient. This part of McConnell is now overruled.

IV

A

Citizens United next challenges BCRA's disclaimer and disclosure provisions as applied to *Hillary* and the three advertisements for the movie. Under BCRA §311, televised electioneering communications funded by anyone other than a candidate must include a disclaimer that "'_____ is responsible for the content of this advertising.'" The required statement must be made in a "clearly spoken manner," and displayed on the screen in a "clearly readable manner" for at least four seconds. Ibid. It must state that the communication "is not authorized by any candidate or candidate's committee"; it must also display the name and address (or Web site address) of the person or group that funded the advertisement. §441d(a)(3). Under BCRA §201, any person who spends more than $10,000 on electioneering communications within a calendar year must file a disclosure statement with the FEC. That statement must identify the person making the expenditure, the amount of the expenditure, the election to which the communication was directed, and the names of certain contributors.

Disclaimer and disclosure requirements may burden the ability to speak, but they "impose no ceiling on campaign related activities," *Buckley*, and "do not prevent anyone from speaking." The Court has subjected these requirements to "exacting scrutiny," which requires a "substantial relation" between the disclosure requirement and a "sufficiently important" governmental interest.

In *Buckley*, the Court explained that disclosure could be justified based on a governmental interest in "provid[ing] the electorate with information" about the sources of election-related spending. The McConnell Court applied this interest in rejecting facial challenges to BCRA §§201 and 311. There was evidence in the record that independent groups were running election-related advertisements "'while hiding behind dubious and misleading names.'" The Court therefore upheld BCRA §§201 and 311 on the ground that they would help citizens "'make informed choices in the political marketplace.'"

Although both provisions were facially upheld, the Court acknowledged that as-applied challenges would be available if a group could show a "'reasonable probability'" that disclosure of its contributors' names "'will subject them to threats, harassment, or reprisals from either Government officials or private parties.'" For the reasons stated below, we find the statute valid as applied to the ads for the movie and to the movie itself.

B

Citizens United sought to broadcast one 30-second and two 10-second ads to promote *Hillary*. Under FEC regulations, a communication that "[p]roposes a commercial transaction" was not subject to 2 U. S. C. §441b's restrictions on corporate or union funding of electioneering communications. The regulations, however, do not exempt those communications from the disclaimer and disclosure requirements in BCRA §§201 and 311.

Citizens United argues that the disclaimer requirements in §311 are unconstitutional as applied to its ads. It contends that the governmental interest in providing information to the electorate does not justify requiring disclaimers for any commercial advertisements, including the ones at issue here. We disagree. The ads fall within BCRA's definition of an "electioneering communication": They referred to then-Senator Clinton by name shortly before a primary and contained pejorative references to her candidacy. The disclaimers required by §311 "provid[e] the electorate with information," and "insure that the voters are fully informed" about the person or group who is speaking. At the very least, the disclaimers avoid confusion by making clear that the ads are not funded by a candidate or political party.

Citizens United argues that §311 is underinclusive because it requires disclaimers for broadcast advertisements but not for print or Internet advertising. It asserts that §311 decreases both the quantity and effectiveness of the group's speech by forcing it to devote four seconds of each advertisement to the spoken disclaimer. We rejected these arguments in McConnell, supra, at 230–231. And we now adhere to that decision as it pertains to the disclosure provisions.

As a final point, Citizens United claims that, in any event, the disclosure requirements in §201 must be confined to speech that is the functional equivalent of express advocacy. The principal opinion in *Wisconsin Right to Life* limited 2 U. S. C. §441b's restrictions on independent expenditures to express advocacy and its functional equivalent. Citizens United seeks to import a similar distinction into BCRA's disclosure requirements. We reject this contention.

The Court has explained that disclosure is a less restrictive alternative to more comprehensive regulations of speech. In *Buckley*, the Court upheld a disclosure requirement for independent expenditures even though it invalidated a provision that imposed a ceiling on those expenditures. In McConnell, three Justices who would have found §441b to be unconstitutional nonetheless voted to uphold BCRA's disclosure and disclaimer requirements. And the Court has upheld registration and disclosure requirements on lobbyists, even though Congress has no power to ban lobbying itself. For these reasons, we reject Citizens United's contention that the disclosure requirements must be limited to speech that is the functional equivalent of express advocacy.

Citizens United also disputes that an informational interest justifies the application of §201 to its ads, which only attempt to persuade viewers to see the film. Even if it disclosed the funding sources for the ads, Citizens United says, the information would not help viewers make informed choices in the political marketplace. This is similar to the argument rejected above with respect to disclaimers. Even if the ads only pertain to a commercial transaction, the public has an interest in knowing who is speaking about a candidate shortly before an election. Because the informational interest alone is sufficient to justify application of §201 to these ads, it is not necessary to consider the Government's other asserted interests.

Last, Citizens United argues that disclosure requirements can chill donations to an organization by exposing donors to retaliation. Some amici point to recent events in which donors to certain causes were blacklisted, threatened, or otherwise targeted for retaliation. In McConnell, the Court recognized that §201 would be unconstitutional as applied to an organization if there were a reasonable probability that the group's members would face threats, harassment, or reprisals if their names were disclosed. The examples cited by amici are cause for concern. Citizens United, however, has offered no evidence that its members may face similar threats or reprisals. To the contrary, Citizens United has been disclosing its donors for years and has identified no instance of harassment or retaliation.

Shareholder objections raised through the procedures of corporate democracy can be more effective today because modern technology makes disclosures rapid and informative. A campaign finance system that pairs corporate independent expenditures with effective disclosure has not existed before today. It must be noted, furthermore, that many of Congress' findings in passing BCRA were premised on a system without adequate disclosure. With the advent of the Internet, prompt disclosure of expenditures can provide shareholders and citizens with the information needed to hold corporations and elected officials accountable for their positions and supporters. Shareholders can determine whether their corporation's political speech advances the corporation's interest in making profits, and citizens can see whether elected officials are "'in the pocket' of so-called moneyed interests." The First Amendment protects political speech; and disclosure permits citizens and shareholders to react to the speech of corporate entities in a proper way. This transparency enables the electorate to make informed decisions and give proper weight to different speakers and messages.

C

For the same reasons we uphold the application of BCRA §§201 and 311 to the ads, we affirm their application to *Hillary*. We find no constitutional impediment to the application of BCRA's disclaimer and disclosure requirements to a movie broadcast via video-on-demand. And there has been no showing that, as applied in this case, these requirements would impose a chill on speech or expression.

V

When word concerning the plot of the movie *Mr. Smith Goes to Washington* reached the circles of Government, some officials sought, by persuasion, to discourage its distribution. Under *Austin*, though, officials could have done more than discourage its distribution—they could have banned the film. After all, it, like *Hillary*, was speech funded by a corporation that was critical of Members of Congress. *Mr. Smith Goes to Washington* may be fiction and caricature; but fiction and caricature can be a powerful force.

Modern day movies, television comedies, or skits on Youtube.com might portray public officials or public policies in unflattering ways. Yet if a covered transmission during the blackout period creates the background for candidate endorsement or opposition, a felony occurs solely because a corporation, other than an exempt media corporation, has made the "purchase, payment, distribution, loan, advance, deposit, or gift of money or anything of value" in order to engage in political speech. Speech would be suppressed in the realm where its necessity is most evident: in the public dialogue preceding a real election. Governments are often hostile to speech, but under our law and our tradition it seems stranger than fiction for our Government to make this political speech a crime. Yet this is the statute's purpose and design. Some members of the public might consider *Hillary* to be insightful and instructive; some might find it to be neither high art nor a fair discussion on how to set the Nation's course; still others simply might suspend judgment on these points but decide to think more about issues and candidates. Those choices and assessments, however, are not for the Government to make. "The First Amendment underwrites the freedom to experiment and to create in the realm of thought and speech. Citizens must be free to use new forms, and new forums, for the expression of ideas. The civic discourse belongs to the people, and the Government may not prescribe the means used to conduct it."

The judgment of the District Court is reversed with respect to the constitutionality of 2 U. S. C. §441b's restrictions on corporate independent expenditures. The judgment is affirmed with respect to BCRA's disclaimer and disclosure requirements. The case is remanded for further proceedings consistent with this opinion.

It is so ordered.

Opinion of Stevens, J.

SUPREME COURT OF THE UNITED STATES
CITIZENS UNITED, APPELLANT *v.* FEDERAL
ELECTION COMMISSION

APPEAL FROM THE UNITED STATES DISTRICT COURT FOR THE DISTRICT OF
COLUMBIA

[January 21, 2010]

Justice Stevens, with whom Justice Ginsburg, Justice Breyer, and Justice Sotomayor join, concurring in part and dissenting in part.

The real issue in this case concerns how, not if, the appellant may finance its electioneering. Citizens United is a wealthy nonprofit corporation that runs a political action committee (PAC) with millions of dollars in assets. Under the Bipartisan Campaign Reform Act of 2002 (BCRA), it could have used those assets to televise and promote *Hillary: The Movie* wherever and whenever it wanted to. It also could have spent unrestricted sums to broadcast *Hillary* at any time other than the 30 days before the last primary election. Neither Citizens United's nor any other corporation's speech has been "banned." All that the parties dispute is whether Citizens United had a right to use the funds in its general treasury to pay for broadcasts during the 30-day period. The notion that the First Amendment dictates an affirmative answer to that question is, in my judgment, profoundly misguided. Even more misguided is the notion that the Court must rewrite the law relating to campaign expenditures by *for-profit* corporations and unions to decide this case.

The basic premise underlying the Court's ruling is its iteration, and constant reiteration, of the proposition that the First Amendment bars regulatory distinctions based on a speaker's identity, including its "identity" as a corporation. While that glittering generality has rhetorical appeal, it is not a correct statement of the law. Nor does it tell us when a corporation may engage in electioneering that some of its shareholders oppose. It does not even resolve the specific question whether Citizens United may be required to finance some of its messages with the money in its PAC. The conceit that corporations must be treated identically to natural persons in the political sphere is not only inaccurate but also inadequate to justify the Court's disposition of this case.

In the context of election to public office, the distinction between corporate and human speakers is significant. Although they make enormous contributions to our society, corporations are not actually members of it. They cannot vote or run for office. Because they may be managed and controlled by nonresidents, their interests may conflict in fundamental respects with the interests of eligible voters. The financial resources, legal structure, and instrumental orientation of corporations raise legitimate concerns about their role in the electoral process. Our lawmakers have a compelling constitutional basis, if not also a democratic duty, to take measures designed to guard against the potentially deleterious effects of corporate spending in local and national races.

The majority's approach to corporate electioneering marks a dramatic break from our past. Congress has placed special limitations on campaign spending by corporations ever since the passage of the Tillman Act in 1907. We have unanimously concluded that this "reflects a permissible assessment of the dangers posed by those entities to the electoral process," *FEC* v. *National Right to Work Comm.* (1982) *(NRWC)*, and have accepted the "legislative judgment that the special characteristics of the corporate structure require particularly careful regulation." The Court today rejects a century of history when it treats the distinction between corporate and individual campaign spending as an invidious novelty born of *Austin* v. *Michigan Chamber of Commerce* (1990). Relying largely on individual dissenting opinions, the majority blazes through our precedents, overruling or disavowing a body of case law including *FEC* v. *Wisconsin Right to Life* (2007), *McConnell* v. *FEC* (2003), *FEC* v. *Beaumont* (2003), *FEC* v. *Massachusetts Citizens for Life, Inc.* (1986), *FEC v. National Right to Work Committee* (1982), and *California Medical Assn.* v. *FEC* (1981).

In his landmark concurrence in *Ashwander* v. *TVA* (1936) Justice Brandeis stressed the importance of adhering to rules the Court has "developed ... for its own governance" when deciding constitutional questions. Because departures from those rules always enhance the risk of error, I shall review the background of this case in some detail before explaining why the Court's analysis rests on a faulty understanding of *Austin* and *McConnell* and of our campaign finance jurisprudence more generally. I regret the length of what follows, but the importance and novelty of the Court's opinion require a full response. Although I concur in the Court's decision to sustain BCRA's disclosure provisions and join Part IV of its opinion, I emphatically dissent from its principal holding.

I

The Court's ruling threatens to undermine the integrity of elected institutions across the Nation. The path it has taken to reach its outcome will, I fear, do damage to this institution. Before turning to the question whether to overrule *Austin* and part of *McConnell*, it is important to explain why the Court should not be deciding that question....

[Justice Stevens here reviews why the scope of the case, as-applied challenges, facial challenges and other narrower challenges could and should have been the basis for a decision.]

This brief tour of alternative grounds on which the case could have been decided is not meant to show that any of these grounds is ideal, though each is perfectly "valid." It is meant to show that there were principled, narrower paths that a Court that was serious about judicial restraint could have taken. There was also the straightforward path: applying *Austin* and *McConnell*, just as the District Court did in holding that the funding of Citizens United's film can be regulated under them. The only thing preventing the majority from affirming the District Court, or adopting a narrower ground that would retain *Austin*, is its disdain for *Austin*.

II

The final principle of judicial process that the majority violates is the most transparent: *stare decisis.* I am not an absolutist when it comes to *stare decisis,* in the campaign finance area or in any other. No one is. But if this principle is to do any meaningful work in supporting the rule of law, it must at least demand a significant justification, beyond the preferences of five Justices, for overturning settled doctrine. "[A] decision to overrule should rest on some special reason over and above the belief that a prior case was wrongly decided." No such justification exists in this case, and to the contrary there are powerful prudential reasons to keep faith with our precedents. [17]

The Court's central argument for why *stare decisis* ought to be trumped is that it does not like *Austin*. The opinion "was not well reasoned," our colleagues assert, and it conflicts with First Amendment principles. This, of course, is the Court's merits argument, the many defects in which we will soon consider. I am perfectly willing to concede that if one of our precedents were dead wrong in its reasoning or irreconcilable with the rest of our doctrine, there would be a compelling basis for revisiting it. But neither is true of *Austin*, as I explain at length in Parts III and IV, and restating a merits argument with additional vigor does not give it extra weight in the *stare decisis* calculus....

In the end, the Court's rejection of *Austin* and *McConnell* comes down to nothing more than its disagreement with their results. Virtually every one of its arguments was made and rejected in those cases, and the majority opinion is essentially an amalgamation of resuscitated dissents. The only relevant thing that has changed since *Austin* and *McConnell* is the composition of this Court. Today's ruling thus strikes at the vitals of *stare decisis*, "the means by which we ensure that the law will not merely change erratically, but will develop in a principled and intelligible fashion" that "permits society to presume that bedrock principles are founded in the law rather than in the proclivities of individuals." *Vasquez* v. *Hillery* (1986).

III

The novelty of the Court's procedural dereliction and its approach to *stare decisis* is matched by the novelty of its ruling on the merits. The ruling rests on several premises. First, the Court claims that *Austin* and *McConnell* have "banned" corporate speech. Second, it claims that the First Amendment precludes regulatory distinctions based on speaker identity, including the speaker's identity as a corporation. Third, it claims that *Austin* and *McConnell* were radical outliers in our First Amendment tradition and our campaign finance jurisprudence. Each of these claims is wrong.

The So-Called "Ban"

Pervading the Court's analysis is the ominous image of a "categorical ba[n]" on corporate speech. Indeed, the majority invokes the specter of a "ban" on nearly every page of its opinion. *Ante*, at 1, 4, 7, 10, 11, 12, 13, 16, 20, 21, 22, 23, 26, 27, 28, 29, 30, 31, 33, 35, 38, 40, 42, 45, 46, 47, 49, 54, 56. This characterization is highly misleading, and needs to be corrected.

In fact it already has been. Our cases have repeatedly pointed out that, "[c]ontrary to the [majority's] critical assumptions," the statutes upheld in *Austin* and *McConnell* do "not impose an *absolute* ban on all forms of corporate political spending." For starters, both statutes provide exemptions for PACs, separate segregated funds established by a corporation for political purposes. "The ability to form and administer separate segregated funds," we observed in *McConnell*, "has provided corporations and unions with a constitutionally sufficient opportunity to engage in express advocacy. That has been this Court's unanimous view."....

....At the time Citizens United brought this lawsuit, the only types of speech that could be regulated under §203 were: (1) broadcast, cable, or satellite communications; (2) capable of reaching at least 50,000 persons in the relevant electorate; (3) made within 30 days of a primary or 60 days of a general federal election; (4) by a labor union or a non-*MCFL*, nonmedia corporation; (5) paid for with general treasury funds; and (6) "susceptible of no reasonable interpretation other than as an appeal to vote for or against a specific candidate." The category of communications meeting all of these criteria is not trivial, but the notion that corporate political speech has been "suppress[ed] ... altogether," that corporations have been "exclu[ded] ... from the general public dialogue," or that a work of fiction such as *Mr. Smith Goes to Washington* might be covered is nonsense. Even the plaintiffs in *McConnell,* who had every incentive to depict BCRA as negatively as possible, declined to argue that §203's prohibition on certain uses of general treasury funds amounts to a complete ban.

In many ways, then, §203 functions as a source restriction or a time, place, and manner restriction. It applies in a viewpoint-neutral fashion to a narrow subset of advocacy messages about clearly identified candidates for federal office, made during discrete time periods through discrete channels. In the case at hand, all Citizens United needed to do to broadcast *Hillary* right before the primary was to abjure business contributions or use the funds in its PAC, which by its own account is "one of the most active conservative PACs in America."

So let us be clear: Neither *Austin* nor *McConnell* held or implied that corporations may be silenced; the FEC is not a "censor"; and in the years since these cases were decided, corporations have continued to play a major role in the national dialogue. Laws such as §203 target a class of communications that is especially likely to corrupt the political process, that is at least one degree removed from the views of individual citizens, and that may not even reflect the views of those who pay for it. Such laws burden political speech, and that is always a serious matter, demanding careful scrutiny. But the majority's incessant talk of a "ban" aims at a straw man.

Identity-Based Distinctions

The second pillar of the Court's opinion is its assertion that "the Government cannot restrict political speech based on the speaker's ... identity." The case on which it relies for this proposition is *First Nat. Bank of Boston* v. *Bellotti* (1978). As I shall explain, the holding in that case was far narrower than the Court implies. Like its paeans to unfettered discourse, the Court's denunciation of identity-based distinctions may have rhetorical appeal but it obscures reality.

"Our jurisprudence over the past 216 years has rejected an absolutist interpretation" of the First Amendment. The First Amendment provides that "Congress shall make no law... abridging the freedom of speech, or of the press." Apart perhaps from measures designed to protect the press, that text might seem to permit no distinctions of any kind. Yet in a variety of contexts, we have held that speech can be regulated differentially on account of the speaker's identity, when identity is understood in categorical or institutional terms. The Government routinely places special restrictions on the speech rights of students, prisoners, members of the Armed Forces, foreigners, and its own employees. When such restrictions are justified by a legitimate governmental interest, they do not necessarily raise constitutional problems.[46] In contrast to the blanket rule that the majority espouses, our cases recognize that the Government's interests may be more or less compelling with respect to different classes of speakers....

.... If taken seriously, our colleagues' assumption that the identity of a speaker has *no* relevance to the Government's ability to regulate political speech would lead to some remarkable conclusions. Such an assumption would have accorded the propaganda broadcasts to our troops by "Tokyo Rose" during World War II the same protection as speech by Allied commanders. More pertinently, it would appear to afford the same protection to multinational corporations controlled by foreigners as to individual Americans: To do otherwise, after all, could " 'enhance the relative voice' " of some (*i.e.,* humans) over others (*i.e.,* nonhumans). Under the majority's view, I suppose it may be a First Amendment problem that corporations are not permitted to vote, given that voting is, among other things, a form of speech.

In short, the Court dramatically overstates its critique of identity-based distinctions, without ever explaining why corporate identity demands the same treatment as individual identity. Only the most wooden approach to the First Amendment could justify the unprecedented line it seeks to draw.

Our First Amendment Tradition

A third fulcrum of the Court's opinion is the idea that *Austin* and *McConnell* are radical outliers, "aberration[s]," in our First Amendment tradition. The Court has it exactly backwards. It is today's holding that is the radical departure from what had been settled First Amendment law. To see why, it is useful to take a long view....

[Justice Stevens here presents a lengthy dissertation on original understandings of the First Amendment, legislative and judicial interpretations of the Amendment, and the Court's decisions in *Buckley v. Valeo* and *First National Bank of Boston v. Belotti*

.... In sum, over the course of the past century Congress has demonstrated a recurrent need to regulate corporate participation in candidate elections to " '[p]reserv[e] the integrity of the electoral process, preven[t] corruption, ... sustai[n] the active, alert responsibility of the individual citizen,' " protect the expressive interests of shareholders, and " '[p]reserv[e] ... the individual citizen's confidence in government.' " These understandings provided the combined impetus behind the Tillman Act in 1907. Continuously for over 100 years, this line of "[c]ampaign finance reform has been a series of reactions to documented threats to electoral integrity obvious to any voter, posed by large sums of money from corporate or union treasuries." Time and again, we have recognized these realities in approving measures that Congress and the States have taken. None of the cases the majority cites is to the contrary. The only thing new about *Austin* was the dissent, with its stunning failure to appreciate the legitimacy of interests recognized in the name of democratic integrity since the days of the Progressives.

IV

Having explained why this is not an appropriate case in which to revisit *Austin* and *McConnell* and why these decisions sit perfectly well with "First Amendment principles," I come at last to the interests that are at stake. The majority recognizes that *Austin* and *McConnell* may be defended on anticorruption, antidistortion, and shareholder protection rationales. It badly errs both in explaining the nature of these rationales, which overlap and complement each other, and in applying them to the case at hand.

The Anticorruption Interest

Undergirding the majority's approach to the merits is the claim that the only "sufficiently important governmental interest in preventing corruption or the appearance of corruption" is one that is "limited to *quid pro quo* corruption." This is the same "crabbed view of corruption" that was espoused by Justice Kennedy in *McConnell* and squarely rejected by the Court in that case. While it is true that we have not always spoken about corruption in a clear or consistent voice, the approach taken by the majority cannot be right, in my judgment. It disregards our constitutional history and the fundamental demands of a democratic society.

On numerous occasions we have recognized Congress' legitimate interest in preventing the money that is spent on elections from exerting an " 'undue influence on an officeholder's judgment' " and from creating " 'the appearance of such influence,' " beyond the sphere of *quid pro quo* relationships. Corruption can take many forms. Bribery may be the paradigm case. But the difference between selling a vote and selling access is a matter of degree, not kind. And selling access is not qualitatively different from giving special preference to those who spent money on one's behalf. Corruption operates along a spectrum, and the majority's apparent belief that *quid pro quo* arrangements can be neatly demarcated from other improper influences does not accord with the theory or reality of politics. It certainly does not accord with the record Congress developed in passing BCRA, a record that stands as a remarkable testament to the energy and ingenuity with which corporations, unions, lobbyists, and politicians may go about scratching each other's backs—and which amply supported Congress' determination to target a limited set of especially destructive practices....

.... Our "undue influence" cases have allowed the American people to cast a wider net through legislative experiments designed to ensure, to some minimal extent, "that officeholders will decide issues ... on the merits or the desires of their constituencies," and not "according to the wishes of those who have made large financial contributions"—or expenditures—"valued by the officeholder." When private interests are seen to exert outsized control over officeholders solely on account of the money spent on (or withheld from) their campaigns, the result can depart so thoroughly "from what is pure or correct", that it amounts to a "subversion ... of the electoral process>' At stake in the legislative efforts to address this threat is therefore not only the legitimacy and quality of Government but also the public's faith therein, not only "the capacity of this democracy to represent its constituents [but also] the confidence of its citizens in their capacity to govern themselves."

The cluster of interrelated interests threatened by such undue influence and its appearance has been well captured under the rubric of "democratic integrity." This value has underlined a century of state and federal efforts to regulate the role of corporations in the electoral process.

Unlike the majority's myopic focus on *quid pro quo* scenarios and the free-floating " First Amendment principles" on which it rests so much weight, this broader understanding of corruption has deep roots in the Nation's history. "During debates on the earliest [campaign finance] reform acts, the terms 'corruption' and 'undue influence' were used nearly interchangeably. Long before *Buckley*, we appreciated that "[t]o say that Congress is without power to pass appropriate legislation to safeguard ... an election from the improper use of money to influence the result is to deny to the nation in a vital particular the power of self protection." And whereas we have no evidence to support the notion that the Framers would have wanted corporations to have the same rights as natural persons in the electoral context, we have ample evidence to suggest that they would have been appalled by the evidence of corruption that Congress unearthed in developing BCRA and that the Court today discounts to irrelevance. It is fair to say that "[t]he Framers were obsessed with corruption," which they understood to encompass the dependency of public officeholders on private interests. They discussed corruption "more often in the Constitutional Convention than factions, violence, or instability." When they brought our constitutional order into being, the Framers had their minds trained on a threat to republican self-government that this Court has lost sight of.

Quid Pro Quo Corruption

There is no need to take my side in the debate over the scope of the anticorruption interest to see that the Court's merits holding is wrong. Even under the majority's "crabbed view of corruption," the Government should not lose this case.

"The importance of the governmental interest in preventing [corruption through the creation of political debts] has never been doubted." Even in the cases that have construed the anticorruption interest most narrowly, we have never suggested that such *quid pro quo* debts must take the form of outright vote buying or bribes, which have long been distinct crimes. Rather, they encompass the myriad ways in which outside parties may induce an officeholder to confer a legislative benefit in direct response to, or anticipation of, some outlay of money the parties have made or will make on behalf of the officeholder....It has likewise never been doubted that "[o]f almost equal concern as the danger of actual *quid pro quo* arrangements is the impact of the appearance of corruption." Congress may "legitimately conclude that the avoidance of the appearance of improper influence is also critical ... if confidence in the system of representative Government is not to be eroded to a disastrous extent." A democracy cannot function effectively when its constituent members believe laws are being bought and sold.

In theory, our colleagues accept this much. As applied to BCRA §203, however, they conclude "[t]he anticorruption interest is not sufficient to displace the speech here in question."

Although the Court suggests that *Buckley* compels its conclusion, *Buckley* cannot sustain this reading. It is true that, in evaluating FECA's ceiling on independent expenditures by all persons, the *Buckley* Court found the governmental interest in preventing corruption "inadequate." But *Buckley* did not evaluate corporate expenditures specifically, nor did it rule out the possibility that a future Court might find otherwise. The opinion reasoned that an expenditure limitation covering only express advocacy (*i.e.*, magic words) would likely be ineffectual, a problem that Congress tackled in BCRA, and it concluded that "the independent advocacy restricted by [FECA §608(e)(1)] *does not presently appear* to pose dangers of real or apparent corruption comparable to those identified with large campaign contributions." *Buckley* expressly contemplated that an anticorruption rationale might justify restrictions on independent expenditures at a later date, "because it may be that, in some circumstances, 'large independent expenditures pose the same dangers of actual or apparent *quid pro quo* arrangements as do large contributions.'" Certainly *Buckley* did not foreclose this possibility with respect to electioneering communications made with corporate general treasury funds, an issue the Court had no occasion to consider.

The *Austin* Court did not rest its holding on *quid pro quo* corruption, as it found the broader corruption implicated by the antidistortion and shareholder protection rationales a sufficient basis for Michigan's restriction on corporate electioneering. Concurring in that opinion, I took the position that "the danger of either the fact, or the appearance, of *quid pro quo* relationships [also] provides an adequate justification for state regulation" of these independent expenditures. I did not see this position as inconsistent with *Buckley* 's analysis of individual expenditures. Corporations, as a class, tend to be more attuned to the complexities of the legislative process and more directly affected by tax and appropriations measures that receive little public scrutiny; they also have vastly more money with which to try to buy access and votes. Business corporations must engage the political process in instrumental terms if they are to maximize shareholder value. The unparalleled resources, professional lobbyists, and single-minded focus they bring to this effort, I believed, make *quid pro quo* corruption and its appearance inherently more likely when they (or their conduits or trade groups) spend unrestricted sums on elections.

It is with regret rather than satisfaction that I can now say that time has borne out my concerns. The legislative and judicial proceedings relating to BCRA generated a substantial body of evidence suggesting that, as corporations grew more and more adept at crafting "issue ads" to help or harm a particular candidate, these nominally independent expenditures began to corrupt the political process in a very direct sense. The sponsors of these ads were routinely granted special access after the campaign was over; "candidates and officials knew who their friends were". Many corporate independent expenditures, it seemed, had become essentially interchangeable with direct contributions in their capacity to generate *quid pro quo* arrangements. In an age in which money and television ads are the coin of the campaign realm, it is hardly surprising that corporations deployed these ads to curry favor with, and to gain influence over, public officials.

The majority appears to think it decisive that the BCRA record does not contain "direct examples of votes being exchanged for ... expenditures." It would have been quite remarkable if Congress had created a record detailing such behavior by its own Members. Proving that a specific vote was exchanged for a specific expenditure has always been next to impossible: Elected officials have diverse motivations, and no one will acknowledge that he sold a vote. Yet, even if "[i]ngratiation and access ... are not corruption" themselves, they are necessary prerequisites to it; they can create both the opportunity for, and the appearance of, *quid pro quo* arrangements. The influx of unlimited corporate money into the electoral realm also creates new opportunities for the mirror image of *quid pro quo* deals: threats, both explicit and implicit. Starting today, corporations with large war chests to deploy on electioneering may find democratically elected bodies becoming much more attuned to their interests. The majority both misreads the facts and draws the wrong conclusions when it suggests that the BCRA record provides "only scant evidence that independent expenditures ... ingratiate," and that, "in any event," none of it matters....

.... The majority's rejection of the *Buckley* anticorruption rationale on the ground that independent corporate expenditures "do not give rise to [*quid pro quo*] corruption or the appearance of corruption," is thus unfair as well as unreasonable. Congress and outside experts have generated significant evidence corroborating this rationale, and the only reason we do not have any of the relevant materials before us is that the Government had no reason to develop a record at trial for a facial challenge the plaintiff had abandoned. The Court cannot both *sua sponte* choose to relitigate *McConnell* on appeal and then complain that the Government has failed to substantiate its case. If our colleagues were really serious about the interest in preventing *quid pro quo* corruption, they would remand to the District Court with instructions to commence evidentiary proceedings.

The insight that even technically independent expenditures can be corrupting in much the same way as direct contributions is bolstered by our decision last year in *Caperton* v. *A. T. Massey Coal Co.* (2009). In that case, Don Blankenship, the chief executive officer of a corporation with a lawsuit pending before the West Virginia high court, spent large sums on behalf of a particular candidate, Brent Benjamin, running for a seat on that court. "In addition to contributing the $1,000 statutory maximum to Benjamin's campaign committee, Blankenship donated almost $2.5 million to 'And For The Sake Of The Kids,' " a §527 corporation that ran ads targeting Benjamin's opponent. "This was not all. Blankenship spent, in addition, just over $500,000 on independent expenditures ... ' "to support ... Brent Benjamin." ' " Applying its common sense, this Court accepted petitioners' argument that Blankenship's "pivotal role in getting Justice Benjamin elected created a constitutionally intolerable probability of actual bias" when Benjamin later declined to recuse himself from the appeal by Blankenship's corporation. "Though n[o] ... bribe or criminal influence" was involved, we recognized that "Justice Benjamin would nevertheless feel a debt of gratitude to Blankenship for his extraordinary efforts to get him elected." "The difficulties of inquiring into actual bias," we further noted, "simply underscore the need for objective rules"—rules which will perforce turn on the appearance of bias rather than its actual existence.

In *Caperton,* then, we accepted the premise that, at least in some circumstances, independent expenditures on candidate elections will raise an intolerable specter of *quid pro quo* corruption. Indeed, this premise struck the Court as so intuitive that it repeatedly referred to Blankenship's spending on behalf of Benjamin—spending that consisted of 99.97% independent expenditures ($3 million) and 0.03% direct contributions ($1,000)—as a "contribution."....The reason the Court so thoroughly conflated expenditures and contributions, one assumes, is that it realized that some expenditures may be functionally equivalent to contributions in the way they influence the outcome of a race, the way they are interpreted by the candidates and the public, and the way they taint the decisions that the officeholder thereafter takes.

Caperton is illuminating in several additional respects. It underscores the old insight that, on account of the extreme difficulty of proving corruption, "prophylactic measures, reaching some [campaign spending] not corrupt in purpose or effect, [may be] nonetheless required to guard against corruption." It underscores that "certain restrictions on corporate electoral involvement" may likewise be needed to "hedge against circumvention of valid contribution limits." It underscores that for-profit corporations associated with electioneering communications will often prefer to use nonprofit conduits with "misleading names," such as And For The Sake Of The Kids, "to conceal their identity" as the sponsor of those communications, thereby frustrating the utility of disclosure laws.

And it underscores that the consequences of today's holding will not be limited to the legislative or executive context. The majority of the States select their judges through popular elections. At a time when concerns about the conduct of judicial elections have reached a fever pitch, the Court today unleashes the floodgates of corporate and union general treasury spending in these races. Perhaps *"Caperton* motions" will catch some of the worst abuses. This will be small comfort to those States that, after today, may no longer have the ability to place modest limits on corporate electioneering even if they believe such limits to be critical to maintaining the integrity of their judicial systems.

Deference and Incumbent Self-Protection

Rather than show any deference to a coordinate branch of Government, the majority thus rejects the anticorruption rationale without serious analysis. [67] Today's opinion provides no clear rationale for being so dismissive of Congress, but the prior individual opinions on which it relies have offered one: the incentives of the legislators who passed BCRA. Section 203, our colleagues have suggested, may be little more than "an incumbency protection plan," a disreputable attempt at legislative self-dealing rather than an earnest effort to facilitate First Amendment values and safeguard the legitimacy of our political system. This possibility, the Court apparently believes, licenses it to run roughshod over Congress' handiwork.

In my view, we should instead start by acknowledging that "Congress surely has both wisdom and experience in these matters that is far superior to ours." Many of our campaign finance precedents explicitly and forcefully affirm the propriety of such presumptive deference. Moreover, "[j]udicial deference is particularly warranted where, as here, we deal with a congressional judgment that has remained essentially unchanged throughout a century of careful legislative adjustment." In America, incumbent legislators pass the laws that govern campaign finance, just like all other laws. To apply a level of scrutiny that effectively bars them from regulating electioneering whenever there is the faintest whiff of self-interest, is to deprive them of the ability to regulate electioneering.

This is not to say that deference would be appropriate if there were a solid basis for believing that a legislative action was motivated by the desire to protect incumbents or that it will degrade the competitiveness of the electoral process. Along with our duty to balance competing constitutional concerns, we have a vital role to play in ensuring that elections remain at least minimally open, fair, and competitive. But it is the height of recklessness to dismiss Congress' years of bipartisan deliberation and its reasoned judgment on this basis, without first confirming that the statute in question was intended to be, or will function as, a restraint on electoral competition. "Absent record evidence of invidious discrimination against challengers as a class, a court should generally be hesitant to invalidate legislation which on its face imposes evenhanded restrictions."

We have no record evidence from which to conclude that BCRA §203, or any of the dozens of state laws that the Court today calls into question, reflects or fosters such invidious discrimination. Our colleagues have opined that " '*any* restriction upon a type of campaign speech that is equally available to challengers and incumbents tends to favor incumbents.'" This kind of airy speculation could easily be turned on its head. The electioneering prohibited by §203 might well tend to favor incumbents, because incumbents have pre-existing relationships with corporations and unions, and groups that wish to procure legislative benefits may tend to support the candidate who, as a sitting officeholder, is already in a position to dispense benefits and is statistically likely to retain office. If a corporation's goal is to induce officeholders to do its bidding, the corporation would do well to cultivate stable, long-term relationships of dependency.

So we do not have a solid theoretical basis for condemning §203 as a front for incumbent self-protection, and it seems equally if not more plausible that restrictions on corporate electioneering will be self-denying. Nor do we have a good empirical case for skepticism, as the Court's failure to cite any empirical research attests. Nor does the legislative history give reason for concern. Congress devoted years of careful study to the issues underlying BCRA; "[f]ew legislative proposals in recent years have received as much sustained public commentary or news coverage"; "[p]olitical scientists and academic experts ... with no self-interest in incumbent protectio[n] were central figures in pressing the case for BCRA"; and the legislation commanded bipartisan support from the outset. Finally, it is important to remember just how incumbent-friendly congressional races were prior to BCRA's passage. As the Solicitor General aptly remarked at the time, "the evidence supports overwhelmingly that incumbents were able to get re-elected under the old system just fine." "It would be hard to develop a scheme that could be better for incumbents."

In this case, then, "there is no convincing evidence that th[e] important interests favoring expenditure limits are fronts for incumbency protection." "In the meantime, a legislative judgment that 'enough is enough' should command the greatest possible deference from judges interpreting a constitutional provision that, at best, has an indirect relationship to activity that affects the quantity ... of repetitive speech in the marketplace of ideas." The majority cavalierly ignores Congress' factual findings and its constitutional judgment: It acknowledges the validity of the interest in preventing corruption, but it effectively discounts the value of that interest to zero. This is quite different from conscientious policing for impermissibly anticompetitive motive or effect in a sensitive First Amendment context. It is the denial of Congress' authority to regulate corporate spending on elections.

Austin and Corporate Expenditures

Just as the majority gives short shrift to the general societal interests at stake in campaign finance regulation, it also overlooks the distinctive considerations raised by the regulation of *corporate* expenditures. The majority fails to appreciate that *Austin* 's antidistortion rationale is itself an anticorruption rationale tied to the special concerns raised by corporations. Understood properly, "antidistortion" is simply a variant on the classic governmental interest in protecting against improper influences on officeholders that debilitate the democratic process. It is manifestly not just an " 'equalizing' " ideal in disguise.

1.   Antidistortion

The fact that corporations are different from human beings might seem to need no elaboration, except that the majority opinion almost completely elides it. *Austin* set forth some of the basic differences. Unlike natural persons, corporations have "limited liability" for their owners and managers, "perpetual life," separation of ownership and control, "and favorable treatment of the accumulation and distribution of assets ... that enhance their ability to attract capital and to deploy their resources in ways that maximize the return on their shareholders' investments." Unlike voters in U. S. elections, corporations may be foreign controlled.[70] Unlike other interest groups, business corporations have been "effectively delegated responsibility for ensuring society's economic welfare"; they inescapably structure the life of every citizen. " '[T]he resources in the treasury of a business corporation,' " furthermore, " 'are not an indication of popular support for the corporation's political ideas.' " " 'They reflect instead the economically motivated decisions of investors and customers. The availability of these resources may make a corporation a formidable political presence, even though the power of the corporation may be no reflection of the power of its ideas.' "

It might also be added that corporations have no consciences, no beliefs, no feelings, no thoughts, no desires. Corporations help structure and facilitate the activities of human beings, to be sure, and their "personhood" often serves as a useful legal fiction. But they are not themselves members of "We the People" by whom and for whom our Constitution was established.

These basic points help explain why corporate electioneering is not only more likely to impair compelling governmental interests, but also why restrictions on that electioneering are less likely to encroach upon First Amendment freedoms. One fundamental concern of the First Amendment is to "protec[t] the individual's interest in self-expression." Freedom of speech helps "make men free to develop their faculties," it respects their "dignity and choice," and it facilitates the value of "individual self-realization." Corporate speech, however, is derivative speech, speech by proxy. A regulation such as BCRA §203 may affect the way in which individuals disseminate certain messages through the corporate form, but it does not prevent anyone from speaking in his or her own voice. "Within the realm of [campaign spending] generally," corporate spending is "furthest from the core of political expression." ....

..... Recognizing the weakness of a speaker-based critique of *Austin*, the Court places primary emphasis not on the corporation's right to electioneer, but rather on the listener's interest in hearing what every possible speaker may have to say. The Court's central argument is that laws such as §203 have " 'deprived [the electorate] of information, knowledge and opinion vital to its function,' " and this, in turn, "interferes with the 'open marketplace' of ideas protected by the First Amendment."

There are many flaws in this argument. If the overriding concern depends on the interests of the audience, surely the public's perception of the value of corporate speech should be given important weight. That perception today is the same as it was a century ago when Theodore Roosevelt delivered the speeches to Congress that, in time, led to the limited prohibition on corporate campaign expenditures that is overruled today. The distinctive threat to democratic integrity posed by corporate domination of politics was recognized at "the inception of the republic" and "has been a persistent theme in American political life" ever since. It is only certain Members of this Court, not the listeners themselves, who have agitated for more corporate electioneering.

Austin recognized that there are substantial reasons why a legislature might conclude that unregulated general treasury expenditures will give corporations "unfai[r] influence" in the electoral process, and distort public debate in ways that undermine rather than advance the interests of listeners. The legal structure of corporations allows them to amass and deploy financial resources on a scale few natural persons can match. The structure of a business corporation, furthermore, draws a line between the corporation's economic interests and the political preferences of the individuals associated with the corporation; the corporation must engage the electoral process with the aim "to enhance the profitability of the company, no matter how persuasive the arguments for a broader or conflicting set of priorities." In a state election such as the one at issue in *Austin,* the interests of nonresident corporations may be fundamentally adverse to the interests of local voters. Consequently, when corporations grab up the prime broadcasting slots on the eve of an election, they can flood the market with advocacy that bears "little or no correlation" to the ideas of natural persons or to any broader notion of the public good. The opinions of real people may be marginalized. "The expenditure restrictions of [2 U. S. C.] §441b are thus meant to ensure that competition among actors in the political arena is truly competition among ideas."

In addition to this immediate drowning out of noncorporate voices, there may be deleterious effects that follow soon thereafter. Corporate "domination" of electioneering, can generate the impression that corporations dominate our democracy. When citizens turn on their televisions and radios before an election and hear only corporate electioneering, they may lose faith in their capacity, as citizens, to influence public policy. A Government captured by corporate interests, they may come to believe, will be neither responsive to their needs nor willing to give their views a fair hearing. The predictable result is cynicism and disenchantment: an increased perception that large spenders " 'call the tune' " and a reduced " 'willingness of voters to take part in democratic governance.' " To the extent that corporations are allowed to exert undue influence in electoral races, the speech of the eventual winners of those races may also be chilled. Politicians who fear that a certain corporation can make or break their reelection chances may be cowed into silence about that corporation. On a variety of levels, unregulated corporate electioneering might diminish the ability of citizens to "hold officials accountable to the people," and disserve the goal of a public debate that is "uninhibited, robust, and wide-open." At the least, I stress again, a legislature is entitled to credit these concerns and to take tailored measures in response.

The majority's unwillingness to distinguish between corporations and humans similarly blinds it to the possibility that corporations' "war chests" and their special "advantages" in the legal realm, may translate into special advantages in the market for legislation. When large numbers of citizens have a common stake in a measure that is under consideration, it may be very difficult for them to coordinate resources on behalf of their position. The corporate form, by contrast, "provides a simple way to channel rents to only those who have paid their dues, as it were. If you do not own stock, you do not benefit from the larger dividends or appreciation in the stock price caused by the passage of private interest legislation."

Corporations, that is, are uniquely equipped to seek laws that favor their owners, not simply because they have a lot of money but because of their legal and organizational structure. Remove all restrictions on their electioneering, and the door may be opened to a type of rent seeking that is "far more destructive" than what noncorporations are capable of. It is for reasons such as these that our campaign finance jurisprudence has long appreciated that "the 'differing structures and purposes' of different entities 'may require different forms of regulation in order to protect the integrity of the electoral process.' "

The Court's facile depiction of corporate electioneering assumes away all of these complexities. Our colleagues ridicule the idea of regulating expenditures based on "nothing more" than a fear that corporations have a special "ability to persuade," as if corporations were our society's ablest debaters and viewpoint-neutral laws such as §203 were created to suppress their best arguments. In their haste to knock down yet another straw man, our colleagues simply ignore the fundamental concerns of the *Austin* Court and the legislatures that have passed laws like §203: to safeguard the integrity, competitiveness, and democratic responsiveness of the electoral process. All of the majority's theoretical arguments turn on a proposition with undeniable surface appeal but little grounding in evidence or experience, "that there is no such thing as too much speech." If individuals in our society had infinite free time to listen to and contemplate every last bit of speech uttered by anyone, anywhere; and if broadcast advertisements had no special ability to influence elections apart from the merits of their arguments (to the extent they make any); and if legislators always operated with nothing less than perfect virtue; then I suppose the majority's premise would be sound. In the real world, we have seen, corporate domination of the airwaves prior to an election may decrease the average listener's exposure to relevant viewpoints, and it may diminish citizens' willingness and capacity to participate in the democratic process.

None of this is to suggest that corporations can or should be denied an opportunity to participate in election campaigns or in any other public forum (much less that a work of art such as *Mr. Smith Goes to Washington* may be banned), or to deny that some corporate speech may contribute significantly to public debate. What it shows, however, is that *Austin* 's "concern about corporate domination of the political process," reflects more than a concern to protect governmental interests outside of the First Amendment. It also reflects a concern to *facilitate* First Amendment values by preserving some breathing room around the electoral "marketplace" of ideas, the marketplace in which the actual people of this Nation determine how they will govern themselves. The majority seems oblivious to the simple truth that laws such as §203 do not merely pit the anticorruption interest against the First Amendment, but also pit competing First Amendment values against each other. There are, to be sure, serious concerns with any effort to balance the First Amendment rights of speakers against the First Amendment rights of listeners. But when the speakers in question are not real people and when the appeal to " First Amendment principles" depends almost entirely on the listeners' perspective, it becomes necessary to consider how listeners will actually be affected.

In critiquing *Austin* 's antidistortion rationale and campaign finance regulation more generally, our colleagues place tremendous weight on the example of media corporations. Yet it is not at all clear that *Austin* would permit §203 to be applied to them. The press plays a unique role not only in the text, history, and structure of the First Amendment but also in facilitating public discourse; as the *Austin* Court explained, "media corporations differ significantly from other corporations in that their resources are devoted to the collection of information and its dissemination to the public." Our colleagues have raised some interesting and difficult questions about Congress' authority to regulate electioneering by the press, and about how to define what constitutes the press. *But that is not the case before us.* Section

203 does not apply to media corporations, and even if it did, Citizens United is not a media corporation. There would be absolutely no reason to consider the issue of media corporations if the majority did not, first, transform Citizens United's as-applied challenge into a facial challenge and, second, invent the theory that legislatures must eschew all "identity"-based distinctions and treat a local nonprofit news outlet exactly the same as General Motors. This calls to mind George Berkeley's description of philosophers: "[W]e have first raised a dust and then complain we cannot see." It would be perfectly understandable if our colleagues feared that a campaign finance regulation such as §203 may be counterproductive or self-interested, and therefore attended carefully to the choices the Legislature has made. But the majority does not bother to consider such practical matters, or even to consult a record; it simply stipulates that "enlightened self-government" can arise only in the absence of regulation. In light of the distinctive features of corporations identified in *Austin,* there is no valid basis for this assumption. The marketplace of ideas is not actually a place where items—or laws—are meant to be bought and sold, and when we move from the realm of economics to the realm of corporate electioneering, there may be no "reason to think the market ordering is intrinsically good at all."

The Court's blinkered and aphoristic approach to the First Amendment may well promote corporate power at the cost of the individual and collective self-expression the Amendment was meant to serve. It will undoubtedly cripple the ability of ordinary citizens, Congress, and the States to adopt even limited measures to protect against corporate domination of the electoral process. Americans may be forgiven if they do not feel the Court has advanced the cause of self-government today.

2.   Shareholder Protection

There is yet another way in which laws such as §203 can serve First Amendment values. Interwoven with *Austin* 's concern to protect the integrity of the electoral process is a concern to protect the rights of shareholders from a kind of coerced speech: electioneering expenditures that do not "reflec[t] [their] support." When corporations use general treasury funds to praise or attack a particular candidate for office, it is the shareholders, as the residual claimants, who are effectively footing the bill. Those shareholders who disagree with the corporation's electoral message may find their financial investments being used to undermine their political convictions.

The PAC mechanism, by contrast, helps assure that those who pay for an electioneering communication actually support its content and that managers do not use general treasuries to advance personal agendas. It " 'allows corporate political participation without the temptation to use corporate funds for political influence, quite possibly at odds with the sentiments of some shareholders or members.' " A rule that privileges the use of PACs thus does more than facilitate the political speech of like-minded shareholders; it also curbs the rent seeking behavior of executives and respects the views of dissenters. *Austin* 's acceptance of restrictions on general treasury spending "simply allows people who have invested in the business corporation for purely economic reasons"—the vast majority of investors, one assumes—"to avoid being taken advantage of, without sacrificing their economic objectives."

The concern to protect dissenting shareholders and union members has a long history in campaign finance reform. It provided a central motivation for the Tillman Act in 1907 and subsequent legislation, and it has been endorsed in a long line of our cases. Indeed, we have unanimously recognized the governmental interest in "protect[ing] the individuals who have paid money into a corporation or union for purposes other than the support of candidates from having that money used to support political candidates to whom they may be opposed."

The Court dismisses this interest on the ground that abuses of shareholder money can be corrected "through the procedures of corporate democracy," and, it seems, through Internet-based disclosures. I fail to understand how this addresses the concerns of dissenting union members, who will also be affected by today's ruling, and I fail to understand why the Court is so confident in these mechanisms. By "corporate democracy," presumably the Court means the rights of shareholders to vote and to bring derivative suits for breach of fiduciary duty. In practice, however, many corporate lawyers will tell you that "these rights are so limited as to be almost nonexistent," given the internal authority wielded by boards and managers and the expansive protections afforded by the business judgment rule. Modern technology may help make it easier to track corporate activity, including electoral advocacy, but it is utopian to believe that it solves the problem. Most American households that own stock do so through intermediaries such as mutual funds and pension plans, which makes it more difficult both to monitor and to alter particular holdings. Studies show that a majority of individual investors make no trades at all during a given year. Moreover, if the corporation in question operates a PAC, an investor who sees the company's ads may not know whether they are being funded through the PAC or through the general treasury.

If and when shareholders learn that a corporation has been spending general treasury money on objectionable electioneering, they can divest. Even assuming that they reliably learn as much, however, this solution is only partial. The injury to the shareholders' expressive rights has already occurred; they might have preferred to keep that corporation's stock in their portfolio for any number of economic reasons; and they may incur a capital gains tax or other penalty from selling their shares, changing their pension plan, or the like. The shareholder protection rationale has been criticized as underinclusive, in that corporations also spend money on lobbying and charitable contributions in ways that any particular shareholder might disapprove. But those expenditures do not implicate the selection of public officials, an area in which "the interests of unwilling ... corporate shareholders [in not being] forced to subsidize that speech" "are at their zenith." And in any event, the question is whether shareholder protection provides a basis for regulating expenditures in the weeks before an election, not whether additional types of corporate communications might similarly be conditioned on voluntariness.

Recognizing the limits of the shareholder protection rationale, the *Austin* Court did not hold it out as an adequate and independent ground for sustaining the statute in question. Rather, the Court applied it to reinforce the antidistortion rationale, in two main ways. First, the problem of dissenting shareholders shows that even if electioneering expenditures can advance the political views of some members of a corporation, they will often compromise the views of others. Second, it provides an additional reason, beyond the distinctive legal attributes of the corporate form, for doubting that these "expenditures reflect actual public support for the political ideas espoused." The shareholder protection rationale, in other words, bolsters the conclusion that restrictions on corporate electioneering can serve both speakers' and listeners' interests, as well as the anticorruption interest. And it supplies yet another reason why corporate expenditures merit less protection than individual expenditures.

V

Today's decision is backwards in many senses. It elevates the majority's agenda over the litigants' submissions, facial attacks over as-applied claims, broad constitutional theories over narrow statutory grounds, individual dissenting opinions over precedential holdings, assertion over tradition, absolutism over empiricism, rhetoric over reality. Our colleagues have arrived at the conclusion that *Austin* must be overruled and that §203 is facially unconstitutional only after mischaracterizing both the reach and rationale of those authorities, and after bypassing or ignoring rules of judicial restraint used to cabin the Court's lawmaking power. Their conclusion that the societal interest in avoiding corruption and the appearance of corruption does not provide an adequate justification for regulating corporate expenditures on candidate elections relies on an incorrect description of that interest, along with a failure to acknowledge the relevance of established facts and the considered judgments of state and federal legislatures over many decades.

In a democratic society, the longstanding consensus on the need to limit corporate campaign spending should outweigh the wooden application of judge-made rules. The majority's rejection of this principle "elevate[s] corporations to a level of deference which has not been seen at least since the days when substantive due process was regularly used to invalidate regulatory legislation thought to unfairly impinge upon established economic interests." At bottom, the Court's opinion is thus a rejection of the common sense of the American people, who have recognized a need to prevent corporations from undermining self-government since the founding, and who have fought against the distinctive corrupting potential of corporate electioneering since the days of Theodore Roosevelt. It is a strange time to repudiate that common sense. While American democracy is imperfect, few outside the majority of this Court would have thought its flaws included a dearth of corporate money in politics.

I would affirm the judgment of the District Court.

Index

$SAGE research**methods**

The essential online tool for researchers from the world's leading methods publisher

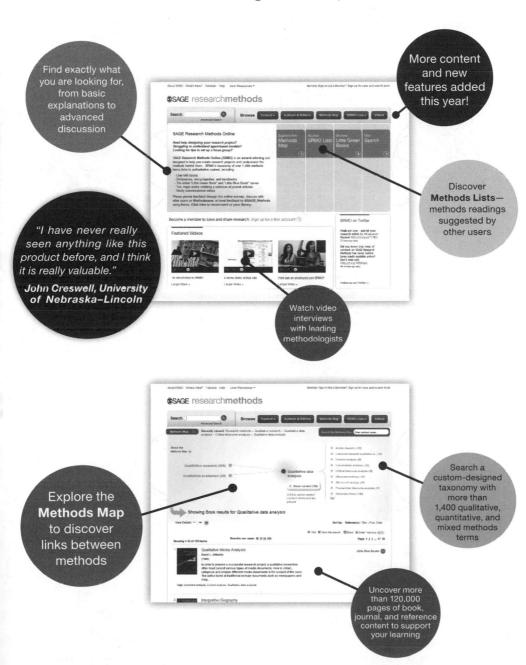

Find exactly what you are looking for, from basic explanations to advanced discussion

More content and new features added this year!

Discover **Methods Lists**—methods readings suggested by other users

"I have never really seen anything like this product before, and I think it is really valuable."

John Creswell, University of Nebraska–Lincoln

Watch video interviews with leading methodologists

Explore the **Methods Map** to discover links between methods

Search a custom-designed taxonomy with more than 1,400 qualitative, quantitative, and mixed methods terms

Uncover more than 120,000 pages of book, journal, and reference content to support your learning

Find out more at
www.sageresearchmethods.com